Inclusion

Schools for All Students

J. David Smith, Dean
School of Education and Human Services
Longwood College

Wadsworth Publishing Company

I(T)P® An International Thomson Publishing Company

Belmont, CA • Albany, NY • Bonn • Boston • Cincinnati • Detroit • Johannesburg • London
Madrid • Melbourne • Mexico City • New York • Paris • Singapore • Tokyo • Toronto • Washington

Education Editor: Joan Gill
Marketing Manager: Jay Hu
Editorial Assistant: Valerie Morrison
Project Editor: Jennie Redwitz
Print Buyer: Barbara Britton
Permissions Editor: Peggy Meehan
Designer: Cuttriss & Hambleton
Photo Editor: Sarah Evertson

Copy Editor: Adrienne Armstrong
Illustrator: Nadine Sokol
Cover Design: Cuttriss & Hambleton
Cover Images: Boy in wheelchair: D. Ryan/Superstock; all other images © 1977 Photo Disc., Inc.
Production: Matrix Productions
Compositor: Thompson Type
Printer: R.R. Donnelley, Crawfordsville

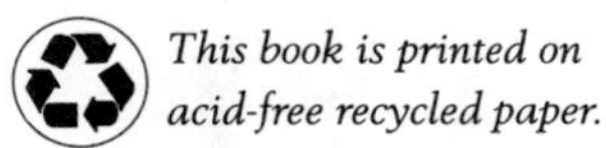

Printed in the United States of America
1 2 3 4 5 6 7 8 9 10—04 03 02 01 00 99 98

For more information, contact Wadsworth Publishing Company, 10 Davis Drive, Belmont, CA 94002, or electronically at http://www.thomson.com/wadsworth.html

International Thomson Publishing Europe
Berkshire House 168–173
High Holborn
London, WC1V7AA, England

Thomas Nelson Australia
102 Dodds Street
South Melbourne 3205
Victoria, Australia

Nelson Canada
1120 Birchmount Road
Scarborough, Ontario
Canada M1K5G4

International Thomson Publishing GmbH
Königswinterer Strasse 418
53227 Bonn, Germany

International Thomson Editores
Campos Eliseos 385, Piso 7
Col. Polanco
11560 México D.F. México

International Thomson Publishing Asia
221 Henderson Road
#05-10 Henderson Building
Singapore 0315

International Thomson Publishing Japan
Hirakawacho Kyowa Building, 3F
2-2-1 Hirakawacho
Chiyoda-ku, Tokyo 102, Japan

International Thomson Publishing
Southern Africa
Building 18, Constantia Park
240 Old Pretoria Road
Halfway House, 1685 South Africa

Library of Congress Cataloging-in-Publication Data
Smith, J. David
Inclusion : schools for all students / J. David Smith.
p. cm.
Includes bibliographical references and index.
ISBN 0-534-33922-0 (alk. paper)
1. Inclusive education—United States—Case studies. 2. Classroom management—United States—Case studies. 3. Handicapped children—Education—United States—Case studies. 4. Special education—United States—Case studies. I. Title.
LC1201.S55 1998
371.9\046\0973—dc21 97-16313

Dedication

This book is dedicated to my father, Walter H. Smith, Jr. and to his sister, my aunt, Catherine Virginia Gregory. It is also dedicated to the memory of his brothers, my uncles, Albert Lee Smith and William Francis Smith.

Thank you,

John David

Contents

Chapter 2

Chapter 7

Chapter 8

Chapter 9

Chapter 10

Creating Classrooms That Welcome The Families of Students with Disabilities 251

Preface

I recently saw the movie *Mr. Holland's Opus*. This story of a dedicated music teacher reminded me of one of my own teachers. He was not a music teacher, but he taught me about music. More importantly, and like Mr. Holland did for his students, he taught me a passion for learning.

When I registered for my senior year in college, I had room in my course schedule for several electives. Probably typical of a college senior, I was torn between taking courses that might be stimulating and challenging, the ones that would be "good for me," and taking courses that might allow for a more leisurely senior year. From the first category, I elected to take a course entitled "The Philosophy of Science." It indeed proved to be stimulating and challenging! I learned a great deal about Galileo, Locke, Bacon, and physics majors—the class was full of the latter. As a psychology major, I hadn't come close to a slide rule in years. Now I was surrounded by them several times each week. It was hard work learning the new language and concepts that the course required, but I am still influenced today by many of the ideas I acquired in that course.

Ironically, however, I continue to be influenced even more by values that came to me as a result of taking a class that I intended to be one of my "leisure" selections. The course was called "Music Appreciation." When I registered for the course, I did so with confidence that what I had heard about it would be accurate. I expected to go to class, listen to recordings, listen to the professor's comments about the recordings, and do little else for the "A" I was sure to earn.

The course did involve a lot of listening. We heard recordings of the works of the great masters. We were encouraged to hear the difference between movements in a symphony, and we explored the cultural roots of various musical forms. It was a pleasant course, and I did, indeed, learn a new appreciation for music. I also learned to appreciate the instructor's patience with me as a musical illiterate. The greatest impact of the course, however, was to come from a source outside of the Music Appreciation classroom.

One of the psychology professors whom I had for several courses was actually a professor emeritus. He had been retired from full-time teaching for several years; I am sure that he was more than eighty years old. He taught one course each semester. Mr. Blake always corrected students if they referred to him as Dr. Blake. He explained to them that he had been in a doctoral program at Johns Hopkins many years before. He had to leave, however, before he finished his dissertation. It was obvious that he regretted not completing his doctorate, but he also made it clear that he respected the degree so much that he did not want it to be mistakenly assigned to him. Mr. Blake loved the history of psychology and knew many obscure facts about the great people and great ideas in the field. He delighted in sharing these stories with his students. He was an inspiring teacher who loved his discipline.

He also loved cigars. He seemed to have one in the corner of his mouth constantly. He bought imperfect cigars from a local tobacco factory and repaired them with tape. The cigars had a heavy aroma as he smoked them in class. When the fire reached the tape, however, it created an acrid fume that was almost unbearable. Mr. Blake sometimes noticed the smell himself and would extinguish the foul cigar butt. Almost immediately he would fire up a fresh stogie.

One morning as I was passing Mr. Blake's office, I heard music coming from his radio. I recognized it. His door was ajar, and I knocked. I commented on the music, saying that I noticed he was listening to the third movement of Beethoven's Fifth Symphony. He glowed with enthusiasm as he told me about the orchestra and conductor who were performing. He was so enthusiastic about my interest in classical music that I could hardly get a word into the conversation. By the time I could have told him that I recognized the music only because it had been the topic of my most recent class session, it was too late. Mr. Blake was convinced he had found a young person who truly appreciated the nuances of the classics.

The next day as I passed Mr. Blake's office, he called to me. I think he had been waiting for me. On his desk was a stack of record albums, all classical. Some of the giants were there, Brahms, Mozart, and Beethoven. He announced to me with happiness in his voice that he wanted to lend them to me. He knew, he said, that I would appreciate them. He talked in some detail about each album. I could not find the courage to tell him that I didn't even have a record player in my room. After a half hour, I left his office with the stack of records, took them to my dormitory and wondered if there would be any way to tell him that I hadn't listened to them. I knew, of course, that someone would let me use their stereo to listen to the albums, but I also knew that I would not get around to it.

I never told Mr. Blake that I didn't play the records. Although he insisted that I keep them for as long as I wanted, I returned the records to him the next week. When I took them to his office, he had another stack waiting for me. This time he wanted to share the work of Schubert. He once again gave me a brief introduction to each album and told me of the particular things to listen for. I left his office with mixed feelings. I felt dishonest. On the other hand, I was happy that he was enjoying telling me about the music and musicians that he loved.

Every week or so for the rest of my senior year, I visited Mr. Blake's office, returned a stack of albums, and listened to his stories and instructions about the music he had ready for me. Fortunately, Mr. Blake never asked directly if I listened to the records. I always read the album jackets. I sometimes asked my Music Appreciation professor about a composer or performer so that I could talk a bit more knowledgeably with Mr. Blake, but I never listened to the music he shared with me. I did, however, hear the enthusiasm in his voice when he spoke of music and musicians. I learned about his love for an art that was not his profession but was his passion. I was moved by his joy in sharing with a younger person the things that he valued so much. I wish I could tell him that now, so many years later, I truly do listen to "his" music.

When I think of Mr. Blake, I realize that the most important lessons he taught me were about the gratification of intellectual exchange and the excitement of passing on something that is of great value to you. In their book, *Habits of the Heart*, Robert Bellah and his colleagues observe that educators are under increasing pressure to produce pragmatic results in their students. Political and economic voices call for more technologically skilled and career-oriented graduates. This is an important part of what education is rightly expected to do in our culture. There are other voices in our society, however, that believe that schools should also be committed to the teaching of values and traditions that will enable students to become responsible, sensitive, and creative citizens in a free society. Bellah and his colleagues believe that traditions are preserved because there are still teachers who love teaching and who, therefore, cannot help but transmit their intellectual and cultural values.

Inclusion: Creating Inclusive Schools for All Students is a book about loving, creative, and competent teachers, and the classrooms that they can create that will be inclusive and welcoming environments for all students. It is about diversity in the abilities and needs of students. It is also about the common human needs and aspirations of all people.

The values expressed in this book could be symbolized by two images. The first is flying squirrels. The significance of flying squirrels to me will be made more evident later in the story of my childhood friend, Tiny, and the lessons that he taught me about these creatures. I choose to use flying squirrels as a symbol for the importance of inclusive schools, however, because they are wonderful creatures that simply do things differently than their brethren. They sometimes fly instead of climbing and leaping. They are different, but they are interesting, beautiful, and precious in their differences. They deserve a place in the forest. The same is true of the students discussed in this book whose differences are known as disabilities. They too are different but valuable. They deserve a place in a world that values them.

The second image is of "better angels." I borrowed this symbol from Abraham Lincoln's first inaugural address. He closed his address to a Union that was torn and filled with anger with an appeal to "the better angels of our nature." He hoped the better angels in us would lead us to peace and solidarity.

I believe that the creation of more inclusive classrooms for all students depends on teachers calling upon the "better angels" of their character and commitment as educators. The information and guidelines for creating inclusive classrooms that are offered in this book can become effective only if applied to classrooms by teachers who have truly found these "better angels" in themselves.

Acknowledgments

The first word of thanks for help with this book goes, as always, to Joyce Smith. She and our wonderful children, Link, Allison, and Sallie, make my life as a husband and father a deeply felt joy. They have given me the support and encouragement that have made my life as a teacher and scholar possible.

I owe a sincere debt of gratitude to Dr. Keith Barron. His constant help and good advice were essential to the completion of this work. He is an excellent scholar, a loyal friend, and a fine human being.

Janet Hawkins helped me meet my other professional duties and responsibilities throughout the time I worked on this book. Her organization and insight are much appreciated.

My final acknowledgments are to Vicki Knight and Joan Gill, wonderful editors and people. Thank you, Vicki and Joan, for the care and belief that you both put into this book.

I am grateful to the reviewers: Dr. Sharon Blocker, Colorado State University; Dr. Nancy Brawner-Jones, Portland State University; Dr. Carol Burdett, University of Vermont; Dr. Bruno J. D'Alonzo, New Mexico State University, Main; Dr. Lou Denti, San Jose State University; Dr. Debi Gartland, Towson State University; Dr. John Maag, University of Nebraska, Lincoln; Dr. Susan Meyers, San Jose State University; Prof. Maurice Miller, Indiana State University; Dr. Gayle L. Nash, Eastern Michigan University; Dr. Thomas B. Pierce, University of Nevada, Las Vegas; Kay Price, Western Washington University; Prof. Susan Severson, Moorhead State University; Dr. Judy Skyllingstad, Sinclair College; Dr. Colleen Shea Stump, San Francisco State University; Dr. Deborah L. Voltz, University of Wisconsin, Milwaukee; Dr. Jerry J. Wellik, St. Cloud State University.

J. David Smith

Note: Earlier versions of some of the stories that open the chapters of this book were published in the author's books *The Other Voices: Profiles of Women in the History of Special Education*, *The Eugenic Assault on America: Scenes in Red, White, and Black*, and *Pieces of Purgatory: Mental Retardation In and Out of Institutions*.

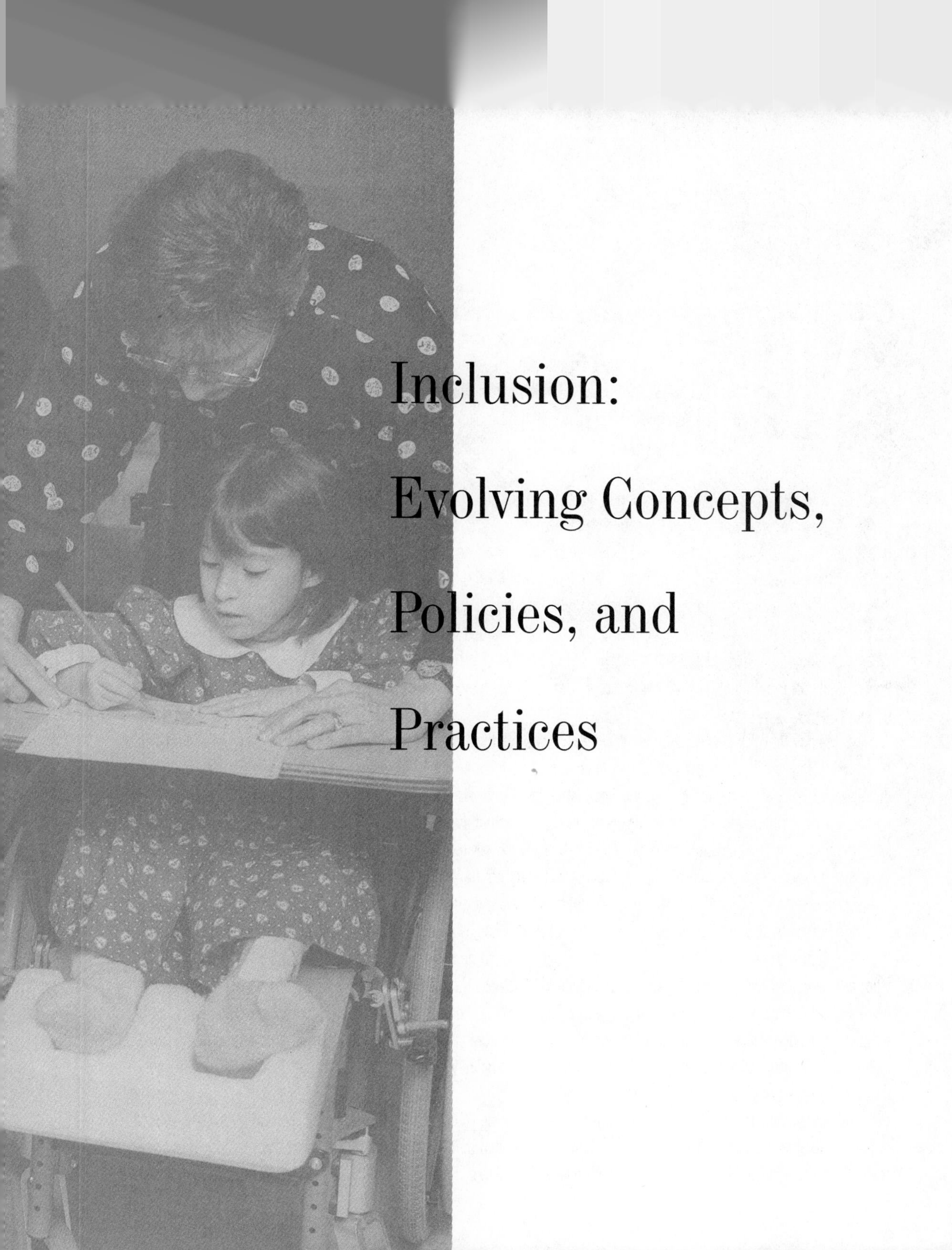

Inclusion: Evolving Concepts, Policies, and Practices

Inclusion, Exclusion, and Other Matters of the Heart: The Story of Nan

My years in elementary school in Roanoke, Virginia, were markedly absent of children who were really different in any significant way from our next-door-neighbor norms. There were no children of African-American heritage, no children who spoke a different native tongue, and no children with disabilities. School in the world of my community was for those children who met some unarticulated but well-understood standard of normality.

There were, of course, the Wilk children, who came to school, even in the frost of fall, without shoes; that they came from a poor family was self-evident. Everyone knew their ragged clothes and body odor made them different. They got low grades and were not invited to birthday parties. Even with their blond hair and agile bodies, they were eyed with pity and humor for the low step on the elementary school hierarchy that they occupied. I remember Daniel, the oldest of the many Wilks in our school. He was my classmate for several years. Daniel was good at kickball, even with his bare, calloused feet; but I cringed when his turn came to read in Mrs. Weaver's third-grade class. Yet I also giggled with the others at his mistakes and hesitations. Eventually, Daniel learned to laugh at himself: not a participatory, good-humored laugh, as I now understand, but a laugh of defense, of self-protection.

One day, the Wilk children came to school with patches of shaved scalp and purple medicine glistening on their heads. Ringworm. Somehow, we all knew that this was just more evidence that the Wilks were dirty, defective, and different.

One day the Wilk kids were gone. Mrs. Ramble, the fourth-grade teacher who was known for expressing her opinions candidly, explained that "Those Wilk children have moved back to the sticks, where they belong." She explained to us that the Wilk children did not belong in school in the first place: "School is for children who can learn; you can't teach trash."

My only other experience with "diversity" in those elementary school years was a little girl I will call Nan. She was what might have been called an "honorary member" of my classes for several years. Nan did not come to our classroom except on special occasions. She came to the Christmas party on the last day of school before the holiday break and received her cookies and candy canes. At the Valentine's Day party, she came to collect the brown paper bag full of the cards we had all been instructed to bring her. At school assemblies, Nan was rolled in after the lights were lowered.

Nan had no arms, and her legs were short—one more so than the other. She looked much like those children who, a few years later, came to be known as thalidomide babies. The reason for her condition was never a question in my mind at the time and, I suppose, is not important now. In fact, I don't think I wondered much about the reason for her disability or anything else about her in my narrow grasp of the human condition at the time. All that I remember is thinking of her as the curious "crippled girl" who came to school on holidays. I don't think I ever got close to her—I'm sure that I never spoke with her.

A few years passed; my family moved from the city to the country; and I found myself focused on the importance of being a teenager. Shortly after my sixteenth birthday, I decided that I was a man. Recognizing my maturity, and after several confrontations with my parents over their failure to realize it, I made a resolution. I had to find a way to get away from home during the forthcoming summer vacation from school. I made several bold, but reasonable (I thought), propositions to my parents. I would travel with a couple of older guys who were graduating and were going to be selling magazines in North Carolina and South Carolina. No? Well, I could spend the summer picking fruit with the crews that went from orchard to orchard in the region. I would never really be that far from home. No! Misery.

Finally, my big break came. One day, while listening to the best rock and roll station in the "Star City of the South," I heard an announcement that would change my life. Just how much, I didn't realize at the time. A summer camp was looking for "junior counselors." No experience was necessary, and you only had to be sixteen years old to apply. I wrote down the number, called, and asked that an application be sent to me.

Two weeks later, I hardly noticed that it was to Camp Easter Seal that I was sending my employment application. I suppose that I had some vague notion that it was "crippled kids" who attended the camp. The important thing, however, was that this was my chance to get away from home for the summer. It worked. In early June I was on the road to adventure with the opportunity to be the independent adult I was convinced I could be.

The first few days at Camp Easter Seal were glorious. There were lots of other "adults" like me there, both male and female. There were even some college women. The summer held great promise.

On the second day of orientation for new counselors, we went to various activity areas to see what the children would be doing, and how we were to assist. After visiting the pool for a lecture from the lifeguard, we toured the nature study cabin, learned the joys of relay racing from the director of athletics, and learned the camp song from the music coordinator. Our final stop was arts and crafts.

We were met at the door by the very enthusiastic director of the program. She was bright, beautiful, and imbued with the spirit of popsicle-stick baskets and mosaic tile ashtrays. She was one of the college women. I was immediately dedicated to doing all that I could to promote the arts that summer.

I was so occupied that I did not notice the young woman sitting on the table at the back of the room until the director introduced her as the assistant director of arts and crafts. She had no arms, her legs were very short, and she was mixing tempera paint with a tongue depressor that she held between her toes. Her smile was radiant. Nan had been coming to the camp since she was ten. After six years as a camper, she had been hired as a staff member. I immediately recognized her, but embarrassment held me back from mentioning to her that we had met before. In a real sense, of course, we had not. It was weeks later that I finally told her that we had been "classmates" at Morningside Elementary.

Through the summer, I came to know Nan as a talented and captivating person. She had learned to use her feet for most of the things that "normal" people use hands to do—and more. She typed, played an electric piano, and was learning guitar. The counselors and the children were drawn to her. She was a great talker, a sensitive listener, and a marvelous laugher. We talked of politics and religion and philosophy as we knew them at that time in our adolescent lives. As we explored the large and general issues of life, we also became comfortable in sharing the personal fears and hopes that we each harbored. We were remarkably the same. By the end of the summer, Nan was no longer the little "crippled girl" who had come to school to pick up her Christmas candy and valentines. She had become a person to me, and somehow her disabilities had faded from my perception of her. My understanding of people and my vision of life were transformed.

Nan was an important part of the change that took place in me that summer, but there were other factors. I came to the camp as an exercise in what I perceived to be "manhood." Through my work that summer with children with mental retardation, physical disabilities, and speech impairments, I learned lessons in humility, compassion, and care—I did, in fact, take my first true steps toward adulthood. Work for me up to that time had meant delivering newspapers, mowing lawns, and carrying golf clubs. I learned that work could mean doing something that was critical to the growth of another human being. Things were never quite the same for me again.

At the end of the summer, I returned to my family and another year of high school. It was difficult to explain to my friends—in fact it was impossible—what my summer had been about.

For the next two years, the focus of much of my attention was Camp Easter Seal. Oh, I had my share of high school revelries, perhaps more than my share. I even managed to devote enough time to my studies to graduate. My memory of that period, however, is that the most important thing for me was being at Camp Easter Seal or thinking of being there.

Each summer, a core group of "regulars" returned to the camp staff. Nan and I were "regulars." We grew in the responsibilities we assumed and in our closeness with each other. Nan was central to the camp. She provided us with inspiration through her optimism and courage. Most important to me, she was a reliable friend. It was easy, and common, to forget that Nan was "missing" anything. In fact, she was not—she had more of most of the truly important human qualities than I. I readily acknowledged that Nan had much to teach others about being human.

One day toward the end of my third summer at the camp, Nan asked me if we could talk after lunch while the campers were having rest time. We met under a large shade tree outside the dining hall. Nan had been having difficulty making a decision and working out arrangements for going to college in the fall. She had finally decided on the same school where I would be going and wanted to talk with me about it. I told her how happy I was with her decision. It would really be nice seeing her at college. She knew, however, that there were going to be problems. Some of the buildings had long flights of steps at the entrances. She was also sure that some of her classes would be in second-floor rooms. Getting around in her wheelchair would not be easy. I was quick to reassure her that things would work out with no major difficulties. I was certain we could arrange classes so that I could help her with any barriers that might exist. Things were going to be fine . . . and being at college with Nan would be a little like being at camp. How neat!

Things did work amazingly well the first week of college. As it turned out, another friend and longtime neighbor of Nan's was also there. Through minimal adjustments, our schedules allowed all of us to get to classes on time and with no trouble. One of us would meet Nan at the steps outside a classroom building, carry her up, go back for her wheelchair, and repeat the procedure at inside stairs if necessary. Nan waited outside her classrooms for the trip down the stairs after the bell. Often the way was crowded with other students, but most were courteous and made sure we had ample room.

Going to college was a great social adventure for me, perhaps more so in my mind initially than an academic event. I had purchased my clothing carefully. I wanted to "look college." I had visions of the new girls I would meet, the guys I would be hanging around with, and the parties I would be invited to. I was ready to be, not necessarily a Big Man on Campus, but a solidly "cool guy."

Sometimes, as I was carrying Nan or her wheelchair to a class, however, I felt people were staring. It bothered me. I now understand how I could have been troubled by those stares. My difficulty in comprehending their meaning at that time, however, was to have a profound influence on the course of my life.

Camp Easter Seal had been a special place. I am sure that I was not aware while I was there of the many ways it was different from the "real world." The camp was an isolated culture unto itself. Disabilities had a way of disappearing from our perception of people there. As I have said, Nan became, in that environment, a person who was interesting and fun to be with. The fact that she lacked arms, that she did manual things with her feet, became unimportant. But I had known Nan only in that separated, caring, understanding place.

Courtesy of the Author

Suddenly I found myself challenged in a very fundamental and disturbing way. Now that I can look back on it, I suppose that during my three summers at Camp Easter Seal I felt that I had overcome the prejudices and misunderstandings of "handicapism." I think I was convinced that I had become a genuine advocate for people with disabilities.

What I now had to admit was that I was embarrassed being seen carrying Nan up and down the steps between classes. I knew that other people at the college didn't understand. Their stares convinced me that I was becoming associated with her disability. They didn't understand about Nan; they wouldn't understand our relationship; I would be stigmatized. What would happen to my college social life?

I detested myself. How shallow I must be. What I had thought was conviction was only convenience. It had been so easy to talk and act as an advocate for people with disabilities in the seclusion and safety, and segregation, of the camp. Now with the slightest test of my beliefs, I was selling out, at least emotionally.

Just as I was about convinced that my social life was headed for the rocks, there was a glimmer of hope. I was invited to the party of the fall season. It was what we termed a "cabin party"—music and dancing in a rustic and romantic venue. The invitation came from a socially prominent source: All the really "neat" people would be there. Wonderful! What an opportunity to meet the key people on campus. Maybe I would even have a chance to make them understand why I was regularly seen carrying an armless girl.

I arrived at the Friday night event fashionably late and in my best madras shirt. As I entered the large, open room, I looked around for familiar faces. Seeing none, I headed for the refreshments. Filling a milk shake cup with a beverage, I glanced to the corners, again in hopes of finding someone I knew. Most people, however, were standing with their backs to me at the far end of the room. I walked in that direction. When I got close enough, I tried to subtly peek over a shoulder to see what the center of attention was. It was Nan! She was sipping her drink through a straw and telling jokes.

That night, through Nan, I met many people. They were all impressed that I knew her so well. That night, also, Nan unknowingly taught me a lesson that has lasted: Beliefs and commitments, genuine beliefs and commitments, must be public and primary. Nan's lesson has been a connecting thread to the discrete events of my personal life and of my career.

At the end of the year, I transferred to another college. Over the next couple of years, I saw Nan very infrequently. Eventually we lost touch with each other altogether. For some years, I had news of her life through mutual friends. She finished college, did graduate work in counseling, and took a position providing rehabilitation services to disabled veterans. I can't think of anyone who could have been a more compassionate and insightful counselor for veterans, particularly those who returned from Vietnam with wounds to body and mind.

A delightful story that was passed along to me about Nan was that a group of prisoners at the state penitentiary heard about her life and work and wanted to do something special for her. It seems that one of them found out that the one thing she most wanted, but had been unable to do, was to drive. Her independence was limited in that sense. Apparently, these men organized a fund-raising campaign, had a van modified for her, and arranged for special driving instruction. With total foot control and a hydraulic lift for getting into the van, she was set free on the highways. The story goes that her only difficulties have been speeding tickets on the interstate highways.

I have often talked of Nan to my students. As I relate her story and others from my personal experience, I have been reminded of the reality of exclusion and the promise of inclusion in the lives of people with disabilities. This, in turn, has led me to reflect on and examine the central role of integration, of an ethic of inclusiveness in the field of education. Children with disabilities deserve to be valued and fully included in the lives of our schools. Adults with disabilities need to be seen not as people who are "missing" something, who are incomplete or defective, but as people whose presence we welcome. I also recognize that although legislation and litigation can grant rights and provide programs, true inclusion is a matter of the heart. It will happen when our society has a change of heart about people with disabilities. I think the change has begun, and I am gratified to see it occurring. I am also thankful for Nan, the transformation she brought to my life, and the change of heart she gave me.

Nan and I found each other again during the Thanksgiving holiday in 1993. I had corresponded with her two years earlier after visiting Camp Easter Seal and inquiring about her there. I had also sent her a copy of the story that I had shared with so many of my students. I was relieved that she liked it!

Nan's real name, which she gave me permission to use, is Norma Milam Garrett. She has been married since 1981 to a wonderful man who obviously loves her dearly. She helped in the raising of his two children from a previous marriage. Norma is now a grandmother. She continues to be a radiant and positive person. I continue to feel fortunate to know her.

Mainstreaming, the Least Restrictive Environment, the Regular Education Initiative, and Inclusion: The History of a Concept

PEOPLE WITH DISABILITIES AND INVISIBILITY

When the writer Ralph Ellison died in 1994, a great deal of attention was focused on his only novel, *Invisible Man*. The novel, which was first published in 1952, is not, as the title might suggest, a science fiction adventure. It is, rather, a story through which a young black man relates the events surrounding his experience of social and personal isolation. In the opening sentence of the novel, Ellison's character declares, "I am an invisible man. No, I am not a spook like those who haunted Edgar Allen Poe; nor am I one of your Hollywood-movie ectoplasms. I am a man of substance, of flesh and bone, fiber and liquids—and I might even be said to possess a mind. I am invisible, understand, simply because people refuse to see me." Ellison has his character go on to explain that this is an invisibility created when people lose their humanity because others view them with a perception that has come to be dominated by prejudice, bias, and false assumptions. "That invisibility to which I refer occurs because of a peculiar disposition of the eyes of those with whom I come in contact. A matter of the construction of their **inner** eyes . . . , you often doubt if you really exist. You wonder whether you aren't simply a phantom in other people's minds" (Ellison, 1952, p. 3).

Ellison's powerful words help his readers understand in a new way that race is much more than a set of physical characteristics or a shared social history that a group of people have in common. He shows that the result of racial differences has often been the construction of a social perception about a minority group by a more powerful majority group. The result of this construction of meaning around a physical or cultural difference has often been racism and oppression.

CONSTRUCTING THE MEANING OF DISABILITY

There has also been a long history of the construction of meaning around people with disabilities. In fact, it has been recognized for some time that there is a conceptual difference between the terms *disability* and *handicap*. A disability is an actual physical, mental, or emotional condition. A person who is blind or deaf, for example, has a disability; that person is unable to either see or hear. A handicap,

N. R. Rowan/Stock Boston

however, is the limitation that is imposed on the individual by the disability. This limitation may often result more from attitudes and suppositions than objective necessities. The woman who is deaf, for example, may have more difficulty in living and working in a community because of the prejudices of other people than because of her inability to hear.

In speaking of the social construction of the meaning of the term *mental retardation*, James Trent in his book *Inventing the Feeble Mind* describes this disability as "a construction whose changing meaning is shaped both by individuals who initiate and administer policies, programs and practices, and by the social context to which these individuals are responding" (Trent, 1994, p. 2). Trent argues that the construction of the meaning of disabilities is sometimes done in the name of science, sometimes in the name of caring for people with disabilities, and sometimes in the name of social or economic necessity. Each of these reasons for defining people and their differences, however, has often been for the purpose of controlling a group of people perceived to be a threat or an inconvenience to society. The construction of the meaning of disabilities has, from this perspective, been motivated more by a search for control than by a concern for the best interests of people with these disabilities.

HELEN KELLER: A WONDERFUL EXCEPTION

There are, of course, exceptions to these constructions of meaning about persons with disabilities. These exceptions have most often occurred in relation to individuals with disabilities who have achieved prominence through extraordinary accomplishments. Helen Keller is a wonderful example of a person with severe disabilities but magnificent achievements who was, therefore, able to eclipse the prevailing attitudes about people with blindness and deafness. Her life and her relationship with her teacher, Annie Sullivan Macy, are inspiring and worthy of study. Her experiences as a person with multiple disabilities also constitute a rare story. Joseph Lash observes in his biography of Helen that her disabilities may have, in fact, been vehicles for the achievement of her insight and influence. He quotes one of her contemporaries as having speculated on what Helen might have accomplished if she had not been blind and deaf and then adding that perhaps these were the differences that created her "high intelligence and purity of soul." Helen agreed, saying, "I have made my limitations tools of learning and true joy" (Lash, 1980, p. 766).

MARTHA'S VINEYARD: "THEY WERE JUST LIKE EVERYONE ELSE"

There are also rare examples of whole communities that have constructed the meaning of disabilities in ways that do not create handicaps for the people who experience them. A fascinating example is provided in Nora Ellen Groce's book, *Everyone Here Spoke Sign Language*. Groce describes a community on Martha's Vineyard, an island off the coast of Massachusetts, that from the time of its European settlement had inordinate numbers of people who were deaf. This apparently resulted from a genetic characteristic of several families who originally settled the island, intermarriage within these families, and the relatively low level of contact with people on the mainland who might have introduced competing genetic traits to Martha's Vineyard.

According to Groce, the social climate of Martha's Vineyard could be characterized as follows during the eighteenth and nineteenth centuries:

> On the Vineyard . . . the hearing people were bilingual in English and the Island sign language. This adaptation had more than linguistic significance, for it eliminated the wall that separates most deaf people from the rest of society. How well can deaf people integrate themselves into the community if no communication barriers exist and if everyone is familiar and comfortable with deafness? The evidence from the Island indicates that they are extremely successful at this (Groce, 1985, p. 4).

Since most people on Martha's Vineyard (both those who were deaf and those who could hear) spoke sign language, being deaf was not even thought of as a disability. A few miles away on the Massachusetts mainland, deafness was thought to be a major handicap with serious social implications. On the island, deafness was seen as a difference that required only a sensitivity to the communication needs of people who could not hear. An older resident with hearing recalled that when people came together in the small communities of Martha's Vineyard, they would

> sit around and wait for the mail to come in and just talk. And the deaf would be there, everyone would be there. And they would be part of the crowd, and they were accepted. They were fishermen and farmers and everything else. And they wanted to find out the news just as much as the rest of us. And oftentimes people would tell stories and make signs at the same time so everyone could follow. . . . Of course, sometimes, if there were more deaf than hearing there, everyone would speak sign language—just to be polite, you know (Groce, 1985, p. 60).

During the eighteenth and nineteenth centuries, about 80 percent of the people with deafness on Martha's Vineyard married. This was about the same marriage rate as for all people on the island. In the rest of the United States, at the time, only 45 percent of people with deafness married. On the island only 35 percent of the residents with deafness married other people with deafness. This was markedly different than the national figure at that time. During that period, 79 percent of people in the United States with deafness married other people who could not hear. The people of Martha's Vineyard with deafness were just as likely to have children, and to have large families, as their neighbors with hearing.

Residents of this island community who had deafness worked at the same variety of jobs and had the same likelihood for economic success as their hearing relatives and neighbors. On the mainland, a disproportionate number of people with deafness were limited in their vocational options and earned substantially less than hearing workers. This pattern of economic, vocational, social, and personal limitations for people who cannot hear continues today, but Martha's Vineyard is no longer an island of exception in this regard.

Nora Ellen Groce ends *Everyone Here Spoke Sign Language* by reflecting on a comment made by an elderly islander she interviewed:

> The stories these elderly Islanders shared with me, of the deaf heritage of the Vineyard, merit careful consideration. The most striking fact about these deaf men and women is that they were *not* handicapped, because no one perceived their deafness as handicaps. As one woman said to me, "You

HARVEY FINKLE/IMPACT VISUALS

know, we didn't think anything special about them. They were just like anyone else. When you think about it, the Island was an awfully nice place to live." Indeed it was (Groce, 1985, p. 110).

A HISTORY OF EXCLUSION

The Martha's Vineyard experience was, of course, an exception. People with disabilities in most parts of the United States, as in most parts of the world, have been excluded from many of the usual privileges and benefits of the society in which they lived. This has been as true of schools as of any other social institution. Although the rhetoric of public education has often emphasized equality of opportunity, the practice of education well into the twentieth century belied this rhetoric.

Institutionalized inequalities in American schools are most evident in the ways that children of racial minorities have been legally excluded from equitable learning opportunities under the rationale that they could be provided "separate but equal" schools. Less known is the history of exclusion of children with disabilities through legal and administrative practices. In 1893 the expulsion of a child from the Cambridge Public Schools because the child was "weak in mind" was upheld by the Massachusetts Supreme Court (*Watson* v. *City of Cambridge,* 1893). The extent to which school decisions leading to the exclusion of children with disabilities were based on factors other than a child's academic ability is illustrated by the wording of another state supreme court decision. In 1919 the Supreme Court of Wisconsin heard the case of a child with cerebral palsy who had the academic ability and physical capacity to be in school, but who drooled, had impaired speech, and had frequent facial muscle contractions. The court ruled that the child could be denied continuation in public school because he "produces a depressing and nauseating effect upon the teachers and school children" (*Beattie* v. *State Board of Education, City of Antigo,* 1919).

During the first half of the twentieth century, exclusion of children with disabilities was common and legal in every state. A striking example of the justification given for segregated education for children with disabilities is the statement of the Superintendent of the Baltimore Public Schools in 1908. James Van Sickle said:

> If it were not for the fact that the presence of mentally defective children in a school room interfered with the proper training of the capable children, their [separate] education would appeal less powerfully. . . . But the presence in a class of one or two mentally or morally defective children so absorbs the energies of the teacher and makes so imperative a claim upon her attention that she cannot under these circumstances properly instruct the number commonly enrolled in a class. School authorities must therefore, greatly reduce this

number, employ many more teachers, and build many more school rooms to accommodate a given number of pupils, or else they must withdraw into small classes these unfortunates who impede the regular progress of normal children. The plan of segregation is now fairly well established in large cities, and superintendents and teachers are working on the problem of classification, so that they may make the best of this imperfect material (Van Sickle, 1908, pp. 102–103).

BROWN V. BOARD OF EDUCATION: A TURNING POINT

The beginning point for the dismantling of the philosophy of "separate but equal" in education was, of course, the landmark decision in 1954 by the Supreme Court of the United States. In the case known as *Brown* v. *Board of Education*, this concept and policy were found to be unconstitutional. As Chief Justice Earl Warren noted in the decision of the Court:

> In these days, it is doubtful that any child may reasonably be expected to succeed in life if he is denied the opportunity of an education. Such an opportunity, where the State has undertaken to provide it, is a right which must be made available to all on equal terms. . . . We conclude that in the field of public education the doctrine of "separate but equal" has no place. Separate educational facilities are inherently unequal (*Brown* v. *Board of Education*, 1954, p. 493).

It is interesting to note that John W. Davis, the attorney for South Carolina in *Brown* v. *Board of Education*, opened his argument to the Supreme Court by saying: "May it please the Court, I think if the appellants' construction of the Fourteenth Amendment should prevail here, there is no doubt in my mind that it would catch the Indian within its grasp just as much as the Negro. If it should prevail, I am unable to see why a state would have any further right to segregate its pupils on the ground of sex or on the ground of age or on the ground of mental capacity" (Davis, 1952, p. 1). Davis was correct, of course, in his projections of the implications of *Brown* v. *Board of Education*. The decision did lead the way to issues of equality for other racial groups, to gender issues in education, and to the idea that all children, regardless of disability, have the right to equal educational opportunities.

Brown v. *Board of Education* was a profound statement of the right to integrated schooling for all children. Its impact, however, was not as immediate as some hoped nor was it as broad in application as John Davis had argued it would be. It would take years before the principles articulated in the case would be applied to the rights of children with disabilities. Nonetheless, through recognizing that educating African-American children separately, even in supposedly "equal" circumstances, was unfair and stigmatizing, the groundwork was provided for the inclusion of children with disabilities in integrated classrooms.

The idea that children with disabilities have a right to an education, and that they should be educated in integrated settings, somewhat haltingly followed the school integration implementation efforts that were put into motion following *Brown* v. *Board of Education*. Although there were increasing allocations in the 1960s of federal funds for training special education teachers and supporting special classes, these were incentive programs that school districts could choose to participate in, or not. The question of a *right* to an education for children with disabilities was not addressed for nearly two decades after the decision in *Brown* v. *Board of Education.*

THE PARC CASE

It was on the very premise that John W. Davis articulated in *Brown* v. *Board of Education* that the Pennsylvania Association for Retarded Children brought its case before the United States District Court for the Eastern District of Pennsylvania in January 1971. The case was brought to the court by parents of children with mental retardation. This class action suit sought a remedy to the exclusion being experienced by children with mental retardation from the public education that was provided to other children in the state.

This Pennsylvania case, which was to become a turning point in special education, was *Pennsylvania Association for Retarded Children (PARC)* v. *Pennsylvania.* In 1971 the district court that heard the case ruled that children could not be denied education on the basis of their disabilities without due process of law. Most important for the development of integrated schooling for children with special needs, however, was the provision in its decree that presumed that "placement in a regular school class is preferable to placement in a special public school class" (*Pennsylvania Association for Retarded Children* v. *Commonwealth of Pennsylvania,* 1971).

MILLS V. BOARD OF EDUCATION

The PARC decision was followed in 1972 by another case that addressed the educational rights of children with disabilities on the basis of equal protection and due process as provided by the Fourteenth Amendment of the U.S. Constitution. In this case, *Mills* v. *Board of Education,* the court mandated that the diagnosis and educational placement of children with disabilities should include the right to a hearing concerning the process of diagnosis and placement, the right to appeal a placement decision, access to records, and written notification to parents at all stages of the process. In the *Mills* decision, the court also addressed the issue of what was to become know as *mainstreaming.* It voiced "a presumption that among the alternative programs of education, placement in a regular public school class with appropriate ancillary services is preferable to placement in a special school class" (*Mills* v. *Board of Education,* 1972).

GROWING PUBLIC AWARENESS OF DISABILITY ISSUES: THE REHABILITATION ACT OF 1973

The rulings in *PARC* and *Mills,* a number of similar cases being heard in other states, and a growing public awareness of the educational needs of children with disabilities contributed to an increased level of activity in Congress around the issue of special education in the early 1970s. Congressional hearings in 1973 and 1974 illuminated a number of problems with special education as it existed at that time. The hearings provided evidence, for example, that there were striking inconsistencies among the states in the quality of educational programs provided for children with disabilities and in the funds allocated to these efforts. It also became apparent in the process of the hearings that millions of children were not receiving appropriate educational programs or were not being served at all (Rothstein, 1990).

With the passage of the Rehabilitation Act of 1973, Congress demonstrated its growing awareness of the needs of people with disabilities, including children in schools. Section 504 of that act prohibits discrimination against individuals with disabilities in government employment and federally supported housing, and it insists on access to public programs and facilities that come under federal regulations. Section 504, while not providing funding for special education, did make it illegal for educational programs receiving federal funding to discriminate against students on the basis of disabilities. It also encouraged the inclusion of students with disabilities in regular education programs and settings. Section 504 stated: "A recipient [of funds] shall place a handicapped person in the regular educational environment operated by the recipient unless it is demonstrated by the recipient that the education of the person in the regular environment with the use of supplementary aids and services cannot be achieved satisfactorily" (*Section 504*, 1973).

Under Section 504 an individual qualifies for services if she or he has a physical or mental disability, has a record or history of a disability, or is regarded by others as having a disability that substantially limits one or more major life activities. One of the major life activities listed in Section 504 is learning. Section 504 is still used in some cases to ensure educational services for students with specific disabilities (for example, attention-deficit/hyperactivity disorder) that are not covered by other educational legislation (Reid and Katsiyannis, 1995).

PUBLIC LAW 94-142

In 1975 the interest and commitment in Congress to special education had evolved to the point that legislation was passed that provided the basic foundation for the education of students with disabilities that exists today. That legislation, entitled the Education of All Handicapped Children Act of 1975 (PL 94-142), mandated that appropriate educational services be provided to all students with disabilities. It provided funding for the implementation of these services. It also mandated the manner in which these services should be planned and provided, and it included safeguards for students and their families (see Box 1.1).

The statement in the law that most directly addressed the issue of integrated education for students with disabilities is one that provides for what has come to be known as the *least restrictive environment*: "Each public agency shall insure that special classes, separate schooling, or other removal of handicapped children from the regular educational environment occurs only when the nature or severity of the handicap is such that education in regular classes with the use of supplementary

BOX 1.1

PL 94-142: The Major Features

- A free, appropriate, public education must be provided for all students with disabilities regardless of the nature or severity of their disabilities.
- Students with disabilities must be educated with nondisabled children to the maximum extent appropriate.
- An Individualized Educational Program (IEP) must be developed and implemented for each student found eligible for special education.
- Parents of students with disabilities are to be given an active role in the process of making any educational decisions about their children.
- States meeting the requirements of PL 94-142 must receive federal funds to help offset the additional costs associated with special education services.

aids and services cannot be achieved satisfactorily" (*Public Law 94-142*, 1975).

AMENDMENTS TO THE LAW

In 1986 PL 94-142 was amended by PL 99-457. This legislation included a mandate that the states provide free appropriate education to preschool children ages three to five with disabilities. It also provided funding incentives to encourage the development of early intervention programs for infants and toddlers with disabilities, and those at risk of developing disabilities (see Box 1.2).

THE INDIVIDUALS WITH DISABILITIES EDUCATION ACT

PL 94-142 was further amended in 1990 with the passage of PL 101-476. Among other modifications, this amendment changed the name of the existing law to the Individuals with Disabilities Education Act or, as it is now commonly called, IDEA (see Box 1.3).

BOX 1.2

PL 99-457: Extending Services to Infants, Toddlers, and Preschool Children with Disabilities

- Beginning with the 1990–91 school year, each state was required to serve all preschoolers with disabilities (three to five years of age).
- The law encourages the provision of services to infants and toddlers with disabilities (ages birth through two years) by providing federal funding to states that identify and serve all children in this age category.
- Requires an IFSP (Individualized Family Service Plan) for every child served. It therefore extends the concept of the IEP (Individualized Educational Program) to provide support for the child *and* family.

The IDEA includes language that is very explicit in its call for including children with disabilities in regular school programs. It states that schools must have a continuum of placements available in order to appropriately meet the needs of these students. It emphasizes, however, that unless a child's individualized education program specifies some other necessary arrangement, the student must be educated in the school he or she would attend if he or she did not have a disability. The IDEA reiterates the requirement that children with disabilities and those without disabilities be educated together to the maximum extent appropriate. The law also underscores the requirement that states ensure that special classes, separate schooling, or other forms of segregation of students with disabilities occur only when the education of these students with the use of supplementary aids and services cannot be achieved satisfactorily in regular classrooms (*Individuals with Disabilities Education Act*, 1990).

THE AMERICANS WITH DISABILITIES ACT

In 1990 Congress also passed into law PL 101-336, the Americans with Disabilities Act (ADA). The ADA expands those rights of individuals with disabilities that were first guaranteed by Section 504 of the Rehabilitation Act of 1973. It essentially requires schools to make all reasonable accommodations to become accessible to students with disabilities, and it extends the provisions requiring fairness in employment to employers not receiving federal funds. It also addresses transportation and public accommodations. The provisions of the ADA are summarized in Box 1.4.

MAINSTREAMING

Although the word *mainstreaming* has been in common use among educators for decades, the term itself was not used in any of the legislation or court cases that have been discussed in this chapter. In this regard, it is ironic that PL 94-142 has often been referred to by administrators and the general public as "the mainstreaming law." Mainstreaming, as both a concept and a term, has been used widely but defined very imprecisely. Like other educational terms, it has been used by professionals, parents, and politicians as if there were a common understanding of what was being communicated. In fact, that has often not been the case. Rather, the term has meant different things to different individuals and groups.

One early attempt to offer a model of mainstreaming outlined three elements that should characterize it: a continuum of types of services for students with disabilities, a reduction in the number of children "pulled out" of regular classes, and the increased provision of special services within regular classrooms rather than outside of those classrooms (Berry, 1972).

BOX 1.3

PL 101-476: Education of the Handicapped Act Amendments of 1990

- Changed the title of the Act to the Individuals with Disabilities Education Act (IDEA).
- Autism and traumatic brain injury were added as two new categories of disability.
- Schools are now required to provide transition services, which promote movement from school to postschool activities, for students with disabilities.
- Each student's IEP must contain a statement of transition services by no later than age 16.
- Rehabilitation counseling and social work services were added as "related services" that students may be eligible for under the law.

BOX 1.4

Americans with Disabilities Act, 1990: Major Provisions

- Employers with 15 or more employees may not refuse to hire or promote a person because of a disability.
- New vehicles bought by public transit authorities must be accessible to people with disabilities.
- Under ADA it is illegal to exclude people with disabilities from public accommodations (for example, hotels, restaurants, grocery stores, parks).

Source: Council for Exceptional Children. "Americans with Disabilities Act, 1990: Major Provisions." *Exceptional Children*, Supp. to Vol. 57, No. 2, October/November 1990.

SPECIAL CLASSES: THE CRITICS

The impetus for mainstreaming as it was defined by Berry, and as it was interpreted elsewhere under the term *least restrictive environment*, can perhaps be seen most clearly in Lloyd Dunn's 1968 article entitled "Special Education for the Mildly Retarded: Is Much of It Justifiable?" In the article, Dunn called for special educators to consider carefully the efficacy research then available indicating that children with disabilities made greater academic progress in regular classrooms than in special classes. He urged special educators to resist "being pressured into a continuing and expanding program (special classes) that we know now to be undesirable for many of the children we are dedicated to serve" (Dunn, 1968, p. 5). He also argued that the labeling of children for placement in special classes led to a stigma that was very destructive to their self-concepts. Dunn asserted that "removing a

SHAFFER PHOTOGRAPHY

child from the regular grades for special education probably contributes significantly to his feelings of inferiority and problems of acceptance" (Dunn, 1968, p. 9).

Following the publication of Dunn's article, there were others who called for the activating of Dunn's concerns in educational policy and practice. A "zero reject model" was advocated that suggested that no child with mental retardation should be "rejected" from a regular class and placed in a special class (Lilly, 1970). The Council for Exceptional Children Policies Commission adopted a policy that specified that all students with disabilities "should spend only as much time outside of regular classroom settings as is necessary to control learning variables" (Council for Exceptional Children Policies Commission, 1973, p. 494).

THE REGULAR EDUCATION INITIATIVE

Even though it was variously defined and understood, the concept of mainstreaming grew in importance and in its acceptance among professionals and the public during the 1970s and 1980s. However, the actual practice of mainstreaming was not, according to some critics, as common as the rhetoric that endorsed it. In 1986 a new call for the integration of children with disabilities into regular education programs was issued from the Assistant Secretary for Special Education and Rehabilitative Services of the U.S. Department of Education. Secretary Madeline Will proposed what she called the Regular Education Initiative (REI). The REI proposed the restructuring of American education into a single system for the delivery of services to all children. Will argued that by merging special and regular education, a "shared responsibility" would be created that would serve children without the stigma of diagnostic labels or segregated classrooms (Will, 1986).

Will's proposal for the REI generated a great deal of controversy and concern in the special education profession. In 1987, for example, a group of leaders in the field met to assess the implications of the proposal. They praised the intent of Secretary Will's call for restructuring but cautioned that it "is important to acknowledge that special education cannot seek institutional solutions to individual problems without changing the nature of the institution . . . school organization is what fundamentally must change" (Heller and Schilit, 1987). This idea, that special education can change in fundamental ways only if the institution of the public school changes, is to be found repeatedly in the literature on special education reform that has been written in recent years (McLaughlin and Warren, 1992).

REI: PROPONENTS AND CRITICS

The critics of the REI have voiced strong concern over the implications of the proposal.

Kauffman, for example, expressed fears that the special services needed by children with disabilities might be diluted or eliminated if the REI became a reality. He also argued that most regular classroom teachers do not have the training and/or inclination to work with many of the students who are served by special education. In language reflective of his strong beliefs on this issue, Kauffman stated, "The belief systems represented by the REI are a peculiar case in which both conservative ideology (for example, focus on excellence, federal disengagement) and liberal rhetoric (for example, nonlabeling, integration) are combined to support the diminution or dissolution of a support system for handicapped students" (Kauffman, 1989, p. 273).

Supporters of the REI asserted that the response to Lloyd Dunn's challenge in 1968 to the efficacy of special classes had not been genuine or widespread. They questioned the essential validity of what had been tried and accomplished during the 1970s and 1980s in the name of mainstreaming. REI proponents maintained that only through a merger of special education into the regular education structure could all children be given the educational services they need without the stigma that had become associated with special education (Robinson, 1990).

REI: A GROOM WITHOUT A BRIDE

The interest in a merger of special and regular education as it was advocated by REI supporters proved, however, to be a one-dimensional interest. REI advocates were almost exclusively special educators. Ironically, regular education showed very little interest in the Regular Education Initiative. This lack of interest in a merger of structures and efforts between regular and special education inspired an early critic to write: "We have thrown a wedding and neglected to invite the bride. If this is an invitation to holy matrimony, it was clearly written by the groom (special education), for the groom, and the groom's family. In fact, the bride (general education) wasn't even asked. She was selected" (Lieberman, 1985, p. 513).

Fuchs and Fuchs analyzed the reasons that the REI garnered little interest on the part of regular educators. They concluded that this lack of interest may have been because those who were concerned with the reform of schooling in the United States saw special education as a separate concern, and because the interest of general educators during this time was more focused on excellence than on equity. Whatever roles various factors may have played, REI rhetoric and activity, according to Fuchs and Fuchs, "tended to parallel rather than converge with general education's renewal efforts" (Fuchs and Fuchs, 1994, p. 295).

INCLUSION: DIFFERING MEANINGS

The most recent descriptor for the effort to create greater integration of children with disabilities into school programs is the term *inclusion.* For many educators, the term is viewed as a more positive description of efforts to include children with disabilities in genuine and comprehensive ways in the total life of schools. Whereas mainstreaming might have meant the same thing for many people, it could also be taken as having as its primary focus the physical presence of a child with disabilities in a regular classroom. Mainstreaming in this form could be only the appearance of integration. The Regular Education Initiative was seen by some people, even some of its supporters, as meaning the dismantling of special education.

Inclusion, however, can mean that the goal of education for children with disabilities is the genuine involvement of each child in the total life of the school. Inclusion can mean welcoming children with disabilities into the curriculum, environment, social interaction, and self-concept of the school.

Inclusion, of course, can (and already does) mean different things to different people. Some people interpret it to be just a new way of talking about mainstreaming. For others it may be seen as the REI with a new label. Some have even used the term *inclusion* as a banner for calling for "full inclusion" or "uncompromising inclusion," meaning the abolishment of special education (Fuchs and Fuchs, 1994).

The premise that this book is based on, however, and the one that will be developed throughout its chapters, is that the most effective and needed services that special education can provide must be preserved. At the same time, the education of children with disabilities must be viewed by all educators as a shared responsibility and privilege. Most importantly, every child must have a place and be made welcome in a regular classroom. Inclusion, as it will be approached in this book, will mean the commitment to include students with disabilities in every possible facet of their schools. Instead of using the term *full inclusion,* which has taken on a negative and uncompromising connotation for many people, the philosophical framework used here will be that of *optimal inclusion.* That is, this text is intended to encourage educators to strive to find the most satisfactory type and level of inclusion for each individual student. A primary goal, in fact, will be to help the reader become a professional educator who sees the student first in every circumstance and the disability as only one characteristic of that individual. In recent years there has been an emphasis in special education on "person first" language. At first glance it may seem a trivial matter whether a child is called a "child who is blind" rather than a "blind child," or a "child with mental retardation" rather than a "retarded child," but the change in attitude that this kind of difference in language reflects may be crucial for students. When disabilities are seen as secondary to the overall humanity of the student, our thinking may change to reflect a greater openness to the person and a greater optimism in regard to the amelioration of the disability.

Before developing these themes further, it is important to understand some of the recent data that have been collected concerning special education services. This information and the trends it indicates are important for an understanding of how the education of children with disabilities may be evolving and what reforms continue to be needed.

Inclusion: Trends and Controversy

THE TREND TOWARD REGULAR CLASS PLACEMENT

Although mandates for the integration of students with special needs have existed for many years, the actual placement of these students in general education classrooms has lagged behind the mandates. McLeskey and Pacchiano (1994), for example, found that over an eleven-year period, from the late 1970s through the late 1980s, the proportion of students with learning disabilities served in separate classes *increased* by 4.4 percent.

More recent figures, however, indicate that this trend is changing. As shown in Figure 1.1, during the 1992–93 school year, 93.6 percent of students with disabilities, ages 6–21, received educational and related services in regular school buildings. This includes students in regular classes, resource rooms, and separate class placements in regular schools. More specifically, Figure 1.1 also shows that 39.87 percent were served in regular classes, 31.7 percent in resource rooms, and 23.57 percent in separate classes. Of the remaining students with disabilities, 4.9 percent were served in separate schools. Far fewer students, 1.5 percent, were served in residential and homebound/hospital settings.

Table 1.1 presents the percentage of students served in different types of educational placements in 1990–91, 1991–92, and 1992–93. Between 1990–91 and 1992–93, the percentage of students served in regular classes increased from 32.8 percent to 39.8 percent. The percentage of resource

TABLE 1.1

Percentage of Students Ages 6–21 Served in Six Educational Environments: School Years 1990–91, 1991–92, and 1992–93

Educational Environment	1990–91	1991–92	1992–93
Regular class	32.8	34.9	39.8
Resource room	36.5	36.3	31.7
Separate class	25.1	23.5	23.5
Separate school	4.2	3.9	3.7
Residential facility	0.8	0.9	0.8
Homebound/hospital	0.6	0.5	0.5
Total	100.0	100.0	100.0

Source: Office of Special Education Programs. *Fifteenth, Sixteenth, and Seventeenth Annual Report to Congress on the Implementation of the Individuals with Disabilities Education Act.* Washington, DC: U.S. Department of Education, 1993–1995.

FIGURE 1.1

Percentage of All Students with Disabilities Ages 6–21 Served in Six Educational Placements: School Year 1992–93

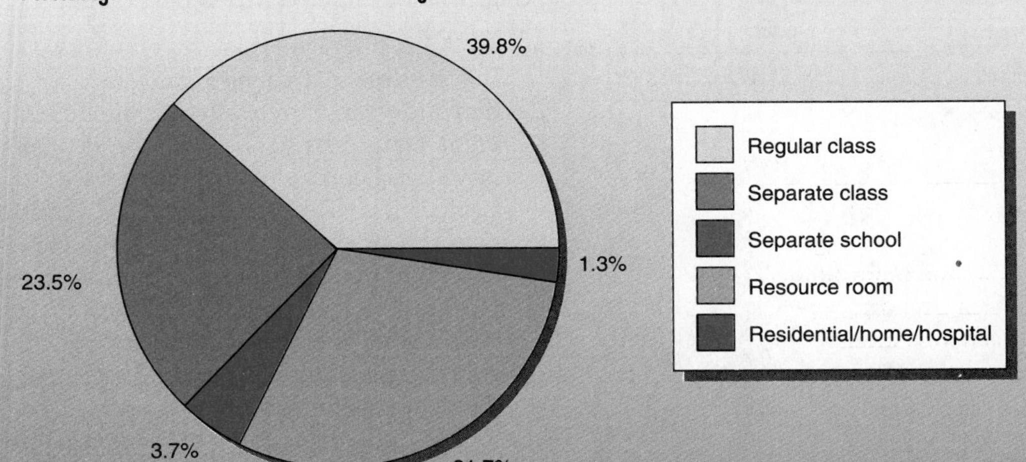

Source: Office of Special Education Programs. *Seventeenth Annual Report to Congress on the Implementation of the Individuals with Disabilities Education Act.* Washington, DC: U.S. Department of Education, 1995, p. 14.

room placements decreased from 36.5 percent to 31.7 percent. There were small decreases in the percentage of students served in separate classes and separate schools. The percentage of residential facility and homebound/hospital placements remained essentially unchanged.

These placement figures suggest that greater numbers of students were placed in more inclusive settings in the 1992–93 school year compared with previous years. This pattern is consistent with another study of integration trends (Sawyer, McLaughlin, and Winglee, 1992), which found that for all disabilities combined, regular class placement increased by 6.1 percent from 1985–86 to 1989–90.

TABLE 1.2

Percentage of Students with Disabilities Ages 6–11, 12–17, and 18–21 Served in Different Educational Environments: School Year 1992–93

	Age Group		
Educational Environment	**6–11**	**12–17**	**18–21**
Regular class	49.8	30.2	23.5
Resource room	26.4	37.7	32.7
Separate class	20.5	26.3	29.2
Separate school	2.6	4.0	10.7
Residential facility	0.4	1.1	2.6
Homebound/hospital	0.3	0.7	1.3
Total	100.0	100.0	100.0

Source: Office of Special Education Programs. *Seventeenth Annual Report to Congress on the Implementation of the Individuals with Disabilities Education Act.* Washington, DC: U.S. Department of Education, 1995.

INCLUSION AND STUDENT AGE

Table 1.2 shows that in 1992–93 49.8 percent of children ages 6 through 11 with disabilities were served in regular classes, compared with 30.2 percent of children ages 12 through 17 with disabilities and 23.5 percent of those ages 18 through 21. Elementary school children were also the least likely to receive services in resource rooms. The same age pattern is evident in regard to separate special class placements and placements in separate schools, residential facilities, and in homebound/hospital programs. In general, then, elementary age students were served in the least restrictive, most inclusive settings. The older the students, the greater the likelihood of more restrictive, less inclusive placements. This difference in placement patterns according to age has been evident for a number of years. The *Fifteenth Annual Report to Congress on the Implementation of the Individuals with Disabilities Education Act* includes a discussion of why elementary age students are served in the most inclusive settings when compared with older students. The report says:

> It is possible that younger students with disabilities are more easily accommodated in integrated settings because the elementary school curriculum may pose fewer significant challenges to these children than does the junior high and high school curriculum for older students with disabilities. However, as these children become older, school personnel may decide that less integrated settings are more appropriate for the delivery of more intensive specialized services. Students age 18–21 may be more likely to be served in less integrated settings because the actual population of these students may represent students with more

severe disabilities who have not completed school within the usual time frame. Students with more severe disabilities are typically served in less integrated settings. In addition, some 18 through 21-year-olds with disabilities may be enrolled in specialized vocational education and transition programs which are likely to be conducted in separate classes and separate schools (Office of Special Education Programs, 1993, pp. 18–19).

INCLUSION AND DISABILITY: CATEGORY AND SEVERITY

Considerable variance in the placement of students in more inclusive educational environments is also evident when different categories of disabilities are compared. Table 1.3

TABLE 1.3

Percentage of Students Ages 6–21 Served in Different Educational Environments by Disability: School Year 1992–93

	Educational Environment					
Disability	Regular Class	Resource Room	Separate Class	Separate School	Residential Facility	Homebound/ Hospital
Specific learning disability	34.8	43.9	20.1	0.8	0.2	0.2
Speech or language impairments	81.8	10.7	6.0	1.4	0.1	0.1
Mental retardation	7.1	26.8	56.8	7.9	0.9	0.5
Serious emotional disturbance	19.6	26.7	35.2	13.7	3.5	1.3
Hearing impairments	29.5	19.7	28.1	8.3	14.0	0.4
Multiple disabilities	7.6	19.1	44.6	23.6	3.4	1.8
Orthopedic impairments	35.1	20.0	34.1	6.7	0.6	3.5
Other health impairments	40.0	27.4	20.6	2.5	0.5	9.1
Visual impairments	45.5	21.1	18.0	5.6	9.4	0.5
Traumatic brain injury	16.4	19.8	28.4	28.4	4.4	2.6
Deaf-blindness	12.3	9.7	31.4	21.2	24.6	1.0
Autism	9.0	9.6	50.0	27.6	3.2	0.6
All disabilities	39.8	31.7	23.5	3.7	0.8	0.5

Note: Percentages may not total 100 percent because of rounding.
Source: Office of Special Education Programs. *Seventeenth Annual Report to Congress on the Implementation of the Individuals with Disabilities Education Act.* Washington, DC: U.S. Department of Education, 1995, p. 17.

TABLE 1.4

Percentage of Students Classified by Race and Category of Disability

Disability	Black	White	Hispanic
Mental retardation	26	11	18
Learning disabilities	43	51	66
Emotional disabilities	8	8	4
Speech impairments	23	30	23

Source: "Separate and Unequal." *U.S. News & World Report,* December 13, 1993, p. 54.

shows that students with less severe disabilities are more likely to be served in regular classes and resource rooms. Those with more severe disabilities are more likely to be served in separate classes, separate schools, or even more restrictive environments. Certain categories of students seem to be particularly likely to be placed in separate classes, however, regardless of the level of disability. This clearly appears to be the case for students with mental retardation. This fact also has implications for minority students receiving special education services. An investigative report published in *U.S. News & World Report* in 1993 summarized data from the Office of Civil Rights, which indicated that because federal guidelines for classification are vague, great disparities exist among the states in the percentage of black special education students who are categorized as having mental retardation.

The percentages ranged from 47 percent of the African-American students receiving special education in Alabama being labeled as retarded to a low of 3 percent in Alaska (*U.S. News & World Report,* 1993, p. 55). The magazine also reported on the overall percentage of African-American, white, and Hispanic students classified as having mental retardation, learning disabilities, and speech impairments (see Table 1.4). It is obvious from these figures that African-American students are at a highly increased risk for being classified in a manner that leads to a more restrictive, less inclusive placement.

TABLE 1.5

Percentage of Students with Disabilities Ages 3–21 Served in Regular Classes in Selected States: School Year 1992–93

States with High Percentages		States with Low Percentages	
Vermont	84.7%	Arizona	6.7%
North Dakota	73.5	West Virginia	6.8
Oregon	64.6	Iowa	20.1
Massachusetts	63.9	Texas	25.2

Source: Office of Special Education Programs. *Seventeenth Annual Report to Congress on the Implementation of the Individuals with Disabilities Education Act.* Washington, DC: U.S. Department of Education, 1995, p. A-40.

INCLUSION: OTHER VARIABLES

Patterns of placement also vary in other regards from state to state. These differences are apparently the result of actual variations in the populations of states, real differences in the needs of students served in different parts of the United States, the interpretations of federal guidelines by states, and other factors. Even though these variations may have legitimate sources, it is clear that the likelihood of a child with a disability being placed in a more inclusive educational setting depends not only on the child's disability and needs, but on other personal characteristics and the influence of demographic good or ill fortune. (See Table 1.5 for an example of the variation in regular class placement in selected states.)

The Continuing Need for the Continuum: Options in Placement and Services

DEBATES OVER THE NUANCES AND fine points of difference between mainstreaming, the Regular Education Initiative, inclusion, full inclusion, and whatever the next term or concept may be are surely not reflective of the grassroots concerns of parents, teachers, and school leaders who are earnestly trying to do their best for children with disabilities. Coupled with the other vagaries and demands that are placed on parents and educators in our increasingly complex society, the confusion that exists over the rights and responsibilities of the various constituencies in the education arena must seem overwhelming. The shrill voices that have enunciated sometimes one polarity and sometimes another of thought on this issue have done little to provide helpful suggestions for administrators, teachers, and parents in their attempts to chart the most effective and fair course of action in providing an appropriate education for students with disabilities.

The most sound basis for providing an inclusive education for students with disabilities in public schools must ultimately consist of the legislative foundation that created services for these students, and the interpretation that courts have given to questions about this foundation.

The legislative foundation for inclusion has been discussed previously in this chapter in the examination of PL 94-142, IDEA, and Section 504 of the Rehabilitation Act of 1973. From this examination it is clear that these statutes stress two things: the policy of the least restrictive environment *and* the requirement that a continuum of services must be available so that an appropriate education may be provided to every child who has the need for special education. The court decisions about this foundation are a fitting topic for the close of this introductory chapter on inclusion.

Although the cases and decisions of the courts concerning inclusion have varied, the principles derived from this litigation have been clear and compelling. Yell (1995) has shown that school districts must make every good-faith effort to maintain students with disabilities in general class placements with whatever appropriate aids and services might be needed to support a student in that environment. School districts that have not done so have consistently been found by courts to be in violation of the law. On the other hand, it is apparent from judicial review and decisions that some children may be so disruptive to general classrooms that these settings are not in their best interests or those of their nondisabled peers. The following suggestions to educators and others interested in the inclusion of children with disabilities in the total school environment are based on Yell's study (1995) of court decisions concerning the issue of the least restrictive environments for the education of students with disabilities:

- Determination of the LRE (least restrictive environment) must be based on the individual needs of the child.
- Good-faith efforts must be made to keep students in integrated settings. The beginning assumption should always be that a student belongs in a general classroom. Exceptions may be made to this assumption based on individual needs.
- A complete continuum of alternative placements and services must be available.

- In making LRE/inclusion decisions, the needs of the student's peers should be considered.
- When students are placed appropriately in more restrictive settings, they must still be integrated into general classes and other school activities to the maximum extent feasible and beneficial to the student.
- The LRE/inclusion decision-making process must be thoroughly documented.

If children, parents, teachers, and schools are to thrive in an environment of greater fairness and sensitivity to individuals and with a renewed sense of mission, it is necessary that an atmosphere of increased trust and cooperation be created. All of the people involved in the challenge of preparing students with disabilities for life in a more open society must be in communication with one another. To this end, education for these students must be truly an individually designed effort that takes into account both the need for inclusion, and the need for special services and the supportive environments that some students may require for educational success. As Webber (1994) has observed, all educators must adopt a sense of "ownership" for all students, including those who have disabilities. At the same time, however, it is critical that the protection and assurances of individual educational programs, parental involvement safeguards, the availability of specially trained teachers and therapists, and the provision of related developmental and therapeutic services be preserved.

The achievement of an individualized and appropriate educational program for any student is a dynamic process. Decisions regarding the most effective blend of special services and inclusive practices must be continually reviewed and changed in the best interests of the student.

Case Studies and Questions to Consider

A Note on Case Studies

At the end of each chapter of this book, case studies are provided. The children, families, and schools described in these studies do not always refer to the particular content of the chapter they follow. They are intended only as a way for readers to consider the issues and information presented in this book in a manner that focuses on the real needs and circumstances that young people, parents, and teachers encounter each day.

The case studies are brief by design. They intentionally leave a wide berth for filling in details about the lives of the students and families described, and the resources available in their schools. It is hoped that the case studies will serve as a stimulus for class discussions and/or exercises in the application of some of the principles discussed in the text.

The cases presented in this book are based on the experiences of the author. Each, however, is a composite. The people and life situations described here, then, are real but do not profile any particular child, family, or school.

STUDENT: BRIAN LITTLE

SCHOOL: HOPEFUL ELEMENTARY

CURRENT PLACEMENT: REGULAR CLASS/RESOURCE ROOM

AGE: 11 YEARS, 3 MONTHS

Family Structure and Home Environment

Brian lives with his mother and father, Brenda and Charlie Little. Mr. Little is a thirty-nine-year-old painting contractor. Ms. Little, who is thirty-seven, works as a machine operator. Brian also lives with his sister, Pamela, who is sixteen years old. The Little family lives in a pleasant older neighborhood.

Almost a year ago, Mr. Little fell from a house while painting and suffered a very serious fracture of his leg. As a result, he was unable to work for six months. During this time, it became necessary for the family to move in with Brian's grandmother. They recently moved back into a rented house of their own shortly after Mr. Little was able to return to work.

Ms. Little reports that Brian has been in good health. His only childhood health problems have been allergies. These are under control with the regular injections he receives.

Parental Perception of the Student's School Program

Ms. Little feels that Brian's greatest area of difficulty and need continues to be in reading. She says that his trouble with reading is specific to the materials and expectations at school. She remarked that when Brian goes to the public library, he checks out books with enthusiasm and loves reading them at home. She noted, however, that the difference is that at the library, Brian is able to choose the type of book he wants to read. She said that he selects books he can read without great difficulty, books that are really at his level.

Ms. Little feels that Brian has benefited greatly from receiving special education services. Three years ago he was found to be eligible for learning disability services. He has been receiving resource room help since that time. She says that although Brian still experiences difficulties with mastering his schoolwork, she believes that the special help he has been given for the last three years has made a significant difference in his academic performance. She feels that Brian has a continuing need for learning disability services. Brian, however, has recently commented that he is embarrassed when he leaves class to go to the resource room. He doesn't feel that he needs this kind of help any longer. He is going to middle school next year, and he wants to discontinue resource room help entirely when he does.

In general, Ms. Little believes, Brian's development is within the normal limits for a boy his age. She describes both his attitude and behavior at home as being positive. She does not believe that he shows any major deficits in his personal and interpersonal skills.

Additional Comments

Ms. Little's primary goal for her son is that he grows up to be a happy adult who has a chance of achieving whatever aims he chooses for himself. She would like to see him learn to be able to focus and sustain his concentration more effectively. Ms. Little is most pleased by Brian's sensitivity. She describes him as being a good boy. She said that he is "real softhearted."

Both Brian's classroom teacher and his resource teacher are pleased with his work at school. They noticed a slump in his attitude and performance while his father was injured and unable to work, but they have seen real improvement since the family moved back into their own house. They both also agree that it is appropriate to begin decreasing the amount of time that Brian spends in the resource room. Neither is sure, however, that he should stop completely the special services that have been so helpful to him.

Questions

1. How would you advise Mr. and Ms. Little in dealing with the issue of Brian's concerns about receiving special help?
2. How can Brian's interest in library books be used to improve his reading program at school?
3. What kind of planning should begin for Brian's transition to middle school? What options could Brian and his parents consider with the school personnel at his new school?

STUDENT: SAMIKA ANGEL

SCHOOL: LINKING ELEMENTARY

CURRENT PLACEMENT: SPECIAL EDUCATION CLASS

AGE: 10 YEARS

Family Structure and Home Environment

Samika lives with her mother, Brenda Angel. Ms. Angel is thirty years old and is employed as a nursing assistant at Community Hospital. Ms. Angel is separated from Samika's father, Marshall Angel. Mr. Angel is twenty-nine-years old and is self-employed as a mechanic. According to Ms. Angel, Samika sees her father daily, and he is a loving and supportive parent. She remarked that Samika was initially upset by her parents' separation, but has since adjusted well to the change in their lives. Ms. Angel and Samika live in a terrace-level apartment in a house owned by a retired couple. Their home is pleasant and well managed. Samika lives in a positive and encouraging environment.

Parental Perception of the Student's School Program

Samika has a history of complex health problems, which have complicated her life. Samika's physical health has been an important variable in her academic performance. She has a liver disease that has resulted essentially in a constant spilling over of bile into her bloodstream. The consequence of this is continual skin irritation and itching. The itching has, according to her mother, caused Samika to be quite distracted and to have a short attention span. There are numerous other physical by-products of the liver disease, such as skin eruptions and complexion problems, that cause physiological and social consequences for Samika. In addition, she has had problems with bronchitis and asthma.

Ms. Angel feels that Samika has definitely benefited from receiving special services. Although Ms. Angel believes that Samika still has significant learning disabilities, she is convinced that the learning disability services that her daughter has been provided in a self-contained learning disabilities class have promoted the development of her academic skills. She feels that it is important that Samika continue to receive help, but wonders if Samika will be ready for a regular class next year. Ms. Angel feels that her daughter's social and emotional development fall within normal limits for a girl her age. She does not feel that there are any other particular difficulties in this area of Samika's life. On the contrary, Ms. Angel feels that, given her physical problems, Samika has done remarkably well in her emotional and social development.

Additional Comments

Ms. Angel hopes to see her daughter get a good education. Her goal is that Samika be able to choose and be happy in a career of her own. The only thing she would change in Samika's life would be her health. Given her health problems, however, Ms. Angel thinks that Samika is doing wonderfully in most areas of her life. She is very proud of her.

Samika's teacher feels that Samika has made very good academic progress in her class. In fact, she thinks that Samika's only learning disability is the distractibility she experiences when she has a crisis with her health problem. Otherwise, Samika's teacher feels that Samika's placement in a self-contained learning disabilities class is inappropriate. She does acknowledge that Samika's image of herself is very poor and that she desperately needs positive social experiences through which to gain self-confidence.

Questions

1. What can be done to increase the inclusiveness of Samika's school experiences?
2. What additional services might be provided that would help Samika make the transition to a regular class placement?
3. How could other children and teachers in Samika's school be included in the process of helping her prepare for a regular class?

References

Beattie v. State Board of Education, City of Antigo, 169 Wisc. 231, 172 N.W. 153, 1919.

Berry, K. *Models for Mainstreaming.* San Rafael, CA: Dimension, 1972.

Brown v. Board of Education of Topeka, 347 U.S. 483, 74 Sup. Ct. 686, 1954.

Council for Exceptional Children. "Americans with Disabilities Act, 1990: Major Provisions." *Exceptional Children*, Supp. to Vol. 57, 1990: 2.

Council for Exceptional Children Policies Commission. "Proposed CEC Policy Statement on the Organization and Administration of Special Education," *39*, 1973: 493–497.

Davis, J. W. "Argument on Behalf of the Appellees *Briggs v. Elliot* in *Brown v. Board of Education of Topeka*," 1952. In L. Friedman, *Argument: The Oral Argument Before the Supreme Court in* Brown v. Board of Education of Topeka. New York: Chelsea House, 1969: 1–25.

Dunn, L. M. "Special Education for the Mildly Retarded: Is Much of It Justifiable?" *Exceptional Children, 34*, 1968: 5–22.

Ellison, R. *Invisible Man.* New York: Random House, 1952.

Fuchs, D., and L. Fuchs. "Inclusive Schools Movement and the Radicalization of Special Education Reform." *Exceptional Children, 60*(4), 1994: 294–309.

Groce, N. E. *Everyone Here Spoke Sign Language: Hereditary Deafness on Martha's Vineyard.* Cambridge, MA: Harvard University Press, 1985.

Heller, H. W., and J. Schilit. "The Regular Education Initiative: A Concerned Response." *Focus on Exceptional Children, 20*(3), 1987: 1–7.

Individuals with Disabilities Education Act (PL 101-476), 20 U.S.C. Ch. 33, Sec. 1400–1485, 1990.

Kauffman, J. M. "The Regular Education Initiative as Reagan-Bush Education Policy: A Trickle-Down Theory of Education of the Hard-to-Teach." *Journal of Special Education, 23*, 1989: 256–278.

Lash, J. P. *Helen and Teacher: The Story of Helen Keller and Anne Sullivan Macy.* New York: Delacorte Press, 1980.

Lieberman, L. M. "Special Education and Regular Education: A Merger Made in Heaven?" *Exceptional Children, 51*(6), 1985: 513–516.

Lilly, M. S. "Special Education: A Tempest in a Tempest." *Exceptional Children, 37*, 1970: 43–48.

McLaughlin, M., and S. Warren. *Issues and Options in Restructuring Schools and Special Education Programs.* College Park, MD: Center for Policy Options in Special Education, University of Maryland, 1992.

McLesky, J., and D. Pacchiano. "Mainstreaming Students with Learning Disabilities: Are We Making Progress?" *Exceptional Children, 60*, 1994: 508–517.

Mills v. Board of Education, 348 F. Supp. 866 (D.D.C., 1972).

Office of Special Education Programs. *Fifteenth Annual Report to Congress on the Implementation of the Individuals with Disabilities Education Act.* Washington, DC: U.S. Department of Education, 1993.

———. *Sixteenth Annual Report to Congress on the Implementation of the Individuals with Disabilities Education Act.* Washington, DC: U.S. Department of Education, 1994.

———. *Seventeenth Annual Report to Congress on the Implementation of the Individuals with Disabilities Education Act.* Washington, DC: U.S. Department of Education, 1995.

Pennsylvania Association for Retarded Citizens v. Commonwealth of Pennsylvania, 334 F. Supp. 1257 (E.D. Pa., 1971).

Public Law 94-142, The Education of All Handicapped Children Act of 1975, 34 C.F.R. 300.550 (b)(2), 1975.

Reid, R., and A. Katsiyannis. "Attention-Deficit/Hyperactivity Disorder and Section 504." *Remedial and Special Education, 16*, 1995: 44–52.

Robinson, V. "Regular Education Initiative: Debate on the Current State and Future Promise of a New Approach to Educating Children with Disabilities." *Counterpoint,* Fall 1990: 5.

Rothstein, L. *Special Education Law.* White Plains, NY: Longman, 1990.

Sarason, S. B., and J. Doris. *Educational Handicap, Public Policy, and Social History: A Broadened Perspective on Mental Retardation.* New York: Free Press, 1979.

Sawyer, R. J., M. J. McLaughlin, and M. Winglee. *Is Integration of Students with Disabilities Happening? An Analysis of National Trends Over Time.* Rockville, MD: Westat, 1992.

Section 504, Vocational Rehabilitation Act of 1973, 34 C.F.R. 104.34 (a), 1973.

Trent, J. W. *Inventing the Feeble Mind: A History of Mental Retardation in the United States.* Berkeley, CA: University of California Press, 1994.

U.S. News & World Report. "Separate and Unequal." December 13, 1993: 46–50, 54–57, 60.

Van Sickle, J. H. "Provision for Exceptional Children in the Public Schools." *Psychological Clinic, 2,* 1908: 102–111.

Watson v. City of Cambridge, 157, Mass. 561, 32 N.E. 864, 1893.

Webber, J. "Caring for Students with Emotional and Behavioral Disorders Amidst School Reform." In L. M. Bullock and R. A. Gamble, *Monograph on Inclusion: Ensuring Appropriate Services to Children and Youth with Emotional/Behavioral Disorders.* Reston, VA: Council for Exceptional Children, 1994: 1–6.

Will, M. C. "Educating Children with Learning Problems: A Shared Responsibility." *Exceptional Children, 52,* 1986: 411–415.

Yell, M. L. "Least Restrictive Environment, Inclusion, and Students with Disabilities: A Legal Analysis." *Journal of Special Education, 28,* 1995: 389–404.

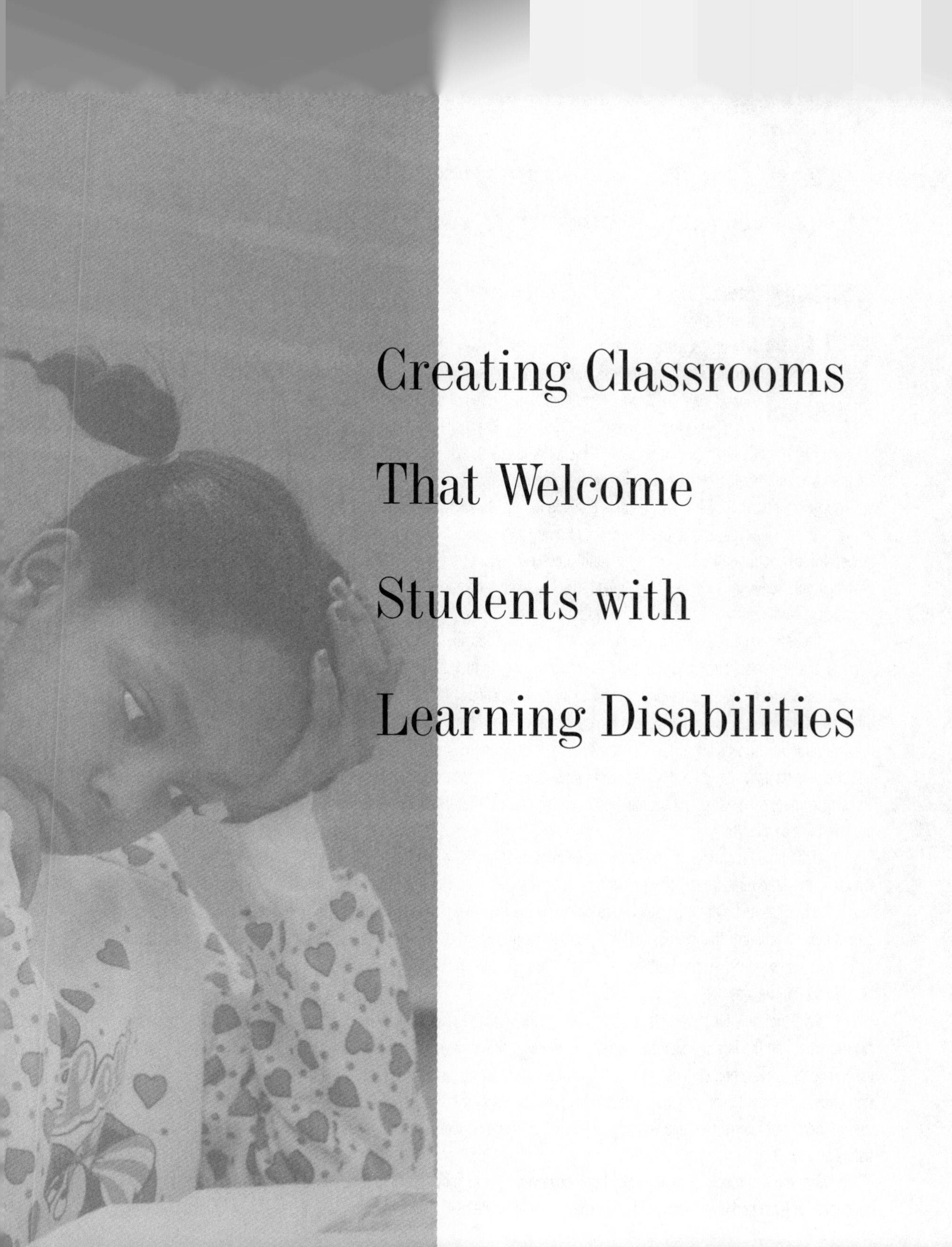

Creating Classrooms That Welcome Students with Learning Disabilities

Lessons Learned and Flying Squirrels: Reflections on Schools, Disabilities, and Values

I often ponder, as do many people in the field of special education, what is really meant today by the term *learning disabled.* How valid are the concepts that underlie the term, and how well-served by schools are children when we describe them as having learning disabilities? In the midst of these ponderings, I sometimes remember a boy from my childhood. He was a large boy, and almost everyone thought he was not very bright. He helped me learn lessons, however, that have been deeply meaningful to me in my life. These were lessons about fish and squirrels, schools and values.

I first met the boy when I was in the seventh grade at a small rural school. My family had moved during the summer from our home in the city to a house in the country. In the city, I had gone to school with the same children each year through the sixth grade. I was frightened during my first few days at the new school. Most of the "country" students in my class seemed older and larger. I was still at an awkward, in-between point in my development. Puberty had not yet arrived for me. Some of the boys in my seventh-grade class were shaving. The girls also showed clear signs of adolescent development. Suddenly, I felt like I was going to school with grown men and women. It was all very intimidating. I longed to be back with the other "children" in my old school in the city.

The boy I remember during my musings on learning disabilities was one of the tallest of the "men" in my class. He was big and his looks were imposing, but he was very quiet. In fact, he was shy, and he was also the brunt of many jokes. He was rarely able to answer when called on with questions from the teacher. This inability was mocked by the other students. He was often unable to finish seatwork or chalkboard problems, and this became fodder for constant teasing. Although he was larger than most of the other boys, he took their kidding, and even their ridicule, without retaliation. He was an easy target for the harshest of jokes about his appearance. He was large, but everyone called him Tiny. This was a spoof on his size, but his real name was so unusual that it was also used as a source of ridicule. And so he preferred to be called Tiny.

At the time, I considered Tiny just as strange as the others thought him to be. Although there was nobody of great wealth in this little rural school, Tiny's clothing clearly showed signs of being handed down for several more recyclings than most. The lunches he brought to school were obviously made with whatever had been left from the previous day's supper. Sometimes he brought stale biscuits and cold, cooked vegetables. This was quite different from the standard fare of peanut butter and jelly sandwiches and fruit that most of us brought from home. Tiny was always clean and neat, but it was obvious to all that he was poor.

It was not only his poverty that made him appear strange to the other seventh graders. He was a loner. He usually rode to school on the bus in a seat by himself. He rarely spoke to anyone, and often gave only one-word responses when asked questions. Tiny had younger sisters. If he were seen walking with anyone at school, it would be with them. The only sign of assertiveness I ever saw in him was in his protectiveness of his sisters. I do not recall anything specific about his care of them, but I know that people understood that although he would not respond to their attacks, he would not let his sisters be hurt.

After the first couple of months of school, however, I got to know Tiny in a different light. We became friends. It happened, at least partially, because I had become a loner at the new school myself. I was the only new student in the seventh grade and, as I have said, I had not yet hit that spurt of growth that would propel me into adolescence. I lacked confidence in myself, and I was still too childlike to fit in very well with most of my new classmates.

After school each day, I spent time alone. One afternoon I explored a cornfield that was brown and dry with the remains of an earlier harvest. I had overheard some of the other kids say that somewhere beyond the field was a pond. I discovered the pond that sunny November day, but, more important, I found a friend. As I climbed over the fence that surrounded the pond, I saw Tiny. He was fishing. He saw me climbing awkwardly over the barbed wire and nodded. We were both embarrassed at having stumbled upon each other, but there was no way to avoid a conversation. I'm not sure who spoke first, but I think it must have been me. Although I had become a loner in my new environment, Tiny was definitely the more private person.

That afternoon I learned how to fish for what Tiny called sunfish. In telling me about them, he talked more than I had ever heard from him. He told me with enthusiasm, for example, that some people called sunfish either panfish or crappies. Whether they were crappies, panfish, or sunfish, the pond was full of them! It was so full that there was ferocious competition among them for food. We fished using balls of sandwich bread on hooks with four prongs. We sometimes caught two fish on the same line. They seemed to literally leap for the bait as soon as it hit the water. When we ran out of bread, Tiny showed me how to pull the hook through the water and snag the hungry fish with the bare metal. He had a zinc bucket of water in which we placed the fish to keep them alive. Periodically, he would check the bucket, pick out the smaller fish that had not been injured too badly by the hooks, and return them to the pond. After all of our fishing was done, Tiny strung the ones that he wanted to take home with him on a long piece of twine. He also strung my share for me. Tiny led me on a shortcut through the cornfield, over the railroad tracks that bordered it, and up a path that led to the back of his house. His house was very modest. Its wood frame was covered with shingled siding. He invited me into the kitchen, which was off the back porch. His sisters were busy helping their mother with supper. They were surprised and embarrassed to have me suddenly appear in their home. Tiny's mother, however, was delighted to see us and soon made everyone feel comfortable. She had a bright smile and gentle manner. I liked her immediately. She was glad to have the fish and quickly had the girls at work cleaning them for frying.

We talked for a little while about school, the pond, and the fish. I left shortly, and as I walked the short distance to my own home I felt a sense of well-being that I had come to know Tiny. I had a friend, and I looked forward to seeing him again.

Although we barely spoke at school, I spent lots of afternoons fishing with Tiny. One day in January we went sliding on the frozen pond. We also played ice hockey with dead oak branches and a flat rock. Although most of the pond was frozen thick, I broke through near the bank. Both of my legs went into the icy water up to my knees. Tiny helped me get out, and he built a fire to warm my feet and to dry my shoes and socks. He always seemed to know how to take care of things like that. Tiny was wise and mature beyond his years in many ways. It was apparent that he liked helping people when he got the chance.

The next fall we both went to the eighth grade at the high school. We had continued our friendship during the summer. We even worked together to earn spending money. I was accustomed to making money by mowing lawns, delivering newspapers, and working at a golf course. Tiny involved me in *real* work that summer. We loaded pulp wood—long pine logs—onto a railroad flatcar. This was the most exhausting, dirtiest, and most discouraging work that I had ever tried. It rivals any demanding physical work I have done since. The more wood we loaded onto the flatcar, the bigger the stack of logs on the siding seemed to grow. Several times a day a truck would arrive from the cutting site on a nearby mountain with even more wood! The logs were thrown from the truck in a haphazard fashion that looked a lot easier than the lifting we were doing to get them up and in place on the flatcar. I actually came close to crying at times. I was tired, scratched and bleeding from the pine bark, and wishing that I could somehow escape the commitment to finish the job. In reality, Tiny did more than his share of the work. I took frequent and long breaks. He never complained but kept working while I rested. Yet he shared with me equally the money we were paid when the job was over. The whole experience was a great motivational lesson to me. It convinced me of the wisdom of staying in school and "getting an education."

Things did not go well for Tiny during our first year at high school. We had no classes together, but I knew that he was not doing well. Socially, he continued to be a loner, and at the high school he was teased by an even larger number of students. Still, he never retaliated. He suffered in silence the insults about his size, his shyness, and his poor school performance. I don't remember ever coming to his defense. I'm sure I lacked the maturity and insight to do so.

Our friendship after school and on weekends continued. I enjoyed his company, and he always seemed happy to see me. We went fishing, took hikes, and once made a dam in the creek that ran at the foot of the hill below his house. In the water we put some of the smaller fish that we caught from the pond. We shared good times, but we never talked about school.

After our first year in high school, I saw even less of Tiny. When we started classes the next September, he was classified again as an eighth grader and his schedule was completely different from mine. The next year he did not return to school. It turned out that he had failed earlier elementary grades and that he was, after all, a couple of years older than me. He was, in fact, old enough to drop out of high school.

The next time I talked with Tiny, he gave me a very short answer to my question about school. "I'm just a slow learner, that's what they said. I can't make it in school anymore, and I have to find something else to do now." He told me this as we were exploring in the woods just beyond the pond, the same place where, a year earlier, he had shown me how to harvest mistletoe. His technique was based on his excellent aim with a .22 caliber rifle. He lay on his back and shot the mistletoe out of the oak branches where it grew in the large and damp tree joints. He explained to me that his mother sent him to the woods every year around that time to shoot mistletoe. She decorated the bunches with ribbons and sold them to neighbors for Christmas trimmings. Tiny was a good crack shot. He showed me that it took exact aim to knock out only part of the plant; if the whole plant were blown out of the tree, there would be no new growth for next year.

This time we were walking in the woods behind the pond to see something special that he had found. Under a big oak he pulled back a rustling cover of dry leaves to reveal a cardboard box. Inside the box were shredded rags swaddling a baby squirrel. It was special, he explained—it was a flying squirrel. Earlier in the day, he had discovered it helpless and trembling under the tree. After saving the baby, he found the mother's nest in a hollow spot in a tree. Tiny knew that flying squirrels forage for food at night. He planned to return the baby to the nest that night while the mother was away. He told me I could help him with the rescue.

That evening I held a flashlight as Tiny scaled the tree. He carried the baby squirrel in a cloth bag he had tied to one of his belt loops. He gently put the baby in the nest and climbed down the tree. As far as I know, the reunification was a success. On our walk back to his house, I asked Tiny how he knew so much about flying squirrels. He explained that he had learned it all from what he called his "books." When I asked what books he was talking about, he told me that he had an old set of encyclopedias that he read at night. It was a set that his mother had found for him. I have no idea what the circumstances were of her acquiring them, but he showed them to me with great pride. They were dated volumes, old and mildewed, but they were readable and he stored them carefully in a crate under his bed.

I was amazed! The boy who had dropped out of school and thought he was slow was a researcher. When I asked about this seeming contradiction, Tiny told me that he could read fine when he had enough time and when he wasn't going to be taking a test. He liked to read and he loved to learn. He just couldn't do it the way it was done in school.

Education was defined narrowly during my years in school. Learning was to be done the standard way or not at all. During the years that I knew Tiny, I had no comprehension of individual learning needs or what would come to be known as learning disabilities. I do know, however, that I must have sensed that something was terribly wrong when a rescuer of flying squirrels and expert on their habits and habitat thought that he was too slow, too different, to be in school.

The rescue of the baby flying squirrel was the last adventure that Tiny and I shared. Events took us in increasingly different directions, and I do not recall another conversation with him. I am sure that we must have seen each other after that, but I cannot recall it.

When I first thought of writing down my memories of Tiny, I began to wonder if I had simply forgotten that he eventually came back to school. I pulled out old yearbooks and checked for his face in all the classes for each of my high school years. He was missing. I also searched my memory for any recall of him during those years. I could remember nothing.

On a recent trip to my hometown, I asked some old friends about Tiny. I found that I had not experienced the memory lapses I had feared. Tiny never returned to school. For a while he found odd jobs that allowed him to help his mother and sisters. Finally, he found a way to help them even more. He joined the army. My friends say that Tiny's family benefited greatly from the money he was able to send home.

Another disturbing revelation came from my inquiries. Like many other boys of my generation who left school, and who joined or were drafted into the military, Tiny died in Vietnam. Without the options of educational deferments or the other opportunities that might have been available to him if he had more education, Tiny was sent into the worst heat of the conflict. I know nothing of the circumstances of his death, but I have imagined that he died in a jungle. In my imaginings I have hoped that he had a chance to see and be close to jungle animals before he was killed. Maybe he rescued a few. Maybe if he had returned from the jungle he would have looked them up in his "books."

If Tiny had lived in a time and in a place that measured ability and courage in ways different from the schools of our youth, he might have been seen as a bright and brave young man with great potential for learning. Instead, he died serving a system that viewed him in life, and taught him to view himself, as slow and as a dropout. I am grateful that I had the opportunity to know him as something more. I trust that our society and our schools have become and are becoming even more open, inclusive, and compassionate. I hope that there would be a place for Tiny's talents in our schools today. I trust that he would have been truly helped by the opportunities that would be available to him now. I hope that he would have been helped, rather than further handicapped, by being recognized as having a learning disability. I hope that he would have had the opportunity to help other people the way that he helped me.

Flying squirrels live in the hollows of trees. They hunt for food at night. They usually have babies twice each year. They glide from the highest branches, swoop low, and then soar higher again. Thanks for the lessons, Tiny.

Leonard Lee Rue III/Animals Animals

Learning Disabilities: The Creation of a Category

EDUCATION AND THE CONCEPT OF COMPETENCE

Before the twentieth century, literacy was not a major social issue in the United States. Most human relationships were based on direct personal exchanges. The information required for personal independence and competence was conveyed primarily by oral conversation. The ability to read and write was the exception rather than the rule.

The transformation of the culture and economy of the United States that had occurred by the turn of the century, however, brought with it a growing standard of competence based on literacy. The change from a primarily rural, agrarian society to a largely urban, industrial society obviously created a revolution in how people earned their livings. Less obviously, perhaps, it revolutionized how people communicated and otherwise related to one another. It also revolutionized the standards by which people were viewed as competent or incompetent. The concept that adult competence is the basic ability to provide for oneself and one's dependents by overcoming the trials of nature came to a close.

During this same period, the meaning of education changed. The idea that education should be universal, that all children (with the exceptions noted in the first chapter) should go to school, had become part of the American character. With the development of standard curricula and texts, it was also assumed that children in schools throughout the country would acquire the same body of knowledge and levels of skill, and at the same rate. This was particularly true of basic literacy and computational skills. By the middle of the twentieth century, illiteracy had come to be viewed as a mark of incompetence, and children who did not progress well in school were viewed as being defective.

EXPLAINING "INCOMPETENCE"

The "defectiveness" of children who did not appear to have disabilities, but who did not learn as well or as rapidly as expected by their school and society, tended to be explained in one of three ways. The first assumption offered by schools to explain the lack of expected progress from a student was that of mild mental retardation. By the 1960s the use of IQ tests to explain a child's school failure had become common. The term *slow learner* was often applied to a child who was not doing well in school. If the confirmation of a low IQ score was obtained, it was often seen as explanation enough of a child's lack of progress. Only later was the fact questioned that disproportionate numbers of poor and minority children were categorized in this fashion.

A second explanation offered for the lack of school progress of a child who did not have an obvious disability was that of emotional disturbance. The child might be explained to teachers or parents as having an "emotional block" to learning. Many of the characteristics that today are attributed to children described as being hyperactive or having attention problems were viewed during this time as symptoms of an emotional instability. That instability was, in turn, seen as the root cause of the problem that the child was having in learning.

The third explanation that might have been provided to schools and families with children who were not making "satisfactory progress" in school was that these children were not motivated, that they were "lazy." Parents and teachers were encouraged to "crack down" on the child who was "not working hard enough."

THE PARENT SEEKING HELP

Imagine yourself as the parent of a child having difficulty in school in 1957. Further imagine yourself to be that parent under two different circumstances.

In the first circumstance, you are a parent who did not have the opportunity to progress very far in school yourself. You are struggling to do everything you can for your child, but you have limited economic resources, and you stay busy trying to earn a living for your family. You are intimidated by people of authority, like teachers, principals, and psychologists, and do not feel that you can question the decisions or opinions of authority figures. You are told that the reason your child is not learning is because he is mildly retarded. You are told that there is a special class where your child can be placed even though some of the children in that class function at a level much lower than that of your child. This is the only option offered to you. It is either this or let your child continue to fail. You take the option and allow your child to be placed in the special class although you do not believe that your child is retarded. You have seen your child excel at other things, and people in your neighborhood talk about how bright he is in carpentry work and sports.

Imagine that you might find yourself resigned to a similar option if you were told that your child had an emotional problem. In this case, however, you might also be told that you and/or your child need therapy to correct the problems that have led to his emotional disorder. You accept the special class placement, the prescription for therapy, and the guilt of being a bad parent.

In the third scenario, you are told that your child is doing poorly in school because he is lazy. You are told that you must discipline him more strongly and insist that he finish all of his homework. You are told that it is your responsibility to see that he studies harder for tests. You agree to try even though you have already spent many long nights working with your son on homework and studying for examinations. You have seen his frustration and tears after working so hard and still not finding the right answers or understanding what he is supposed to do. You pledge, however, to make him work even harder.

PARENTS AND THE MYSTERY CHILDREN

Now imagine that you are the parent of the same child but under different circumstances. You have a college education and a good job. You respect authority but are not intimidated by it. You have been around schools all of your life, and you feel comfortable asking questions of teachers and other school personnel. You have plans for your child's future that include at least high school graduation. The options offered to you to explain your child's school difficulties are completely unacceptable. You know that your child is not retarded. In certain areas, you think he is very bright. You know that your child is not emotionally disturbed, and you resent the suggestion that there is something wrong with the way you have raised him. You know he is not lazy. You have been up late too many nights with him struggling and crying over homework assignments to accept such a charge against him. The school, however, is offering you no acceptable option concerning your child's learning problem; you must look elsewhere for help. You have a "mystery child," and you must search for a solution.

For decades, parents with resources like this turned to professionals in many different fields for possible solutions to their mystery children. Because the schools offered them no acceptable answers to the causes of their children's problems or techniques for helping those children, parents looked to physicians, psychologists, speech therapists, and others for help.

PIONEERS AND EARLY EFFORTS

There are many important figures in the history of learning disabilities. There are too many, in fact, to mention in a brief historical review. A description of the efforts of a few of these people, however, may help provide a sense of how the field arrived at its official "birth" in the 1960s. This is important in developing a sense of how a number of divergent ideas converged to create the concept of learning disabilities.

DYSLEXIA

In 1925 Samuel Torrey Orton, a professor of medicine at the University of Iowa, worked with a patient he called M.P., who was sixteen years old and who had never learned to read. The boy had normal intelligence and visual acuity. It was through his study of M.P., and subsequently others with similar reading problems, that Orton first described reversals of words like *was* and *saw,* rotations of letters like *b* and *d,* and other confusions in visual perception. Orton had earlier studied the relationship between the symptoms of language impairment in adults and the location and extent of brain damage discovered in these patients during autopsy. Orton hypothesized that children showing reading problems similar to those he had observed in brain-injured adults were impaired by "mixed dominance" in the brain that resulted in symptoms similar to those of brain injury. Orton coined the term *strephosymbolia,* literally meaning twisted symbols, to describe the condition. He also developed exercises that he argued could help students overcome the reading problems associated with the condition. In describing the origin of this term, Orton explained:

> The writer, in 1926, in the course of an intensive study of several cases of this disorder noted a striking tendency to distorted order in the recall of letters shown in the attempts of these children to read a word or to spell it and offered the term strephosymbolia—meaning "twisted symbols" (Orton, 1937, p. 71).

Orton's work was carried forward with a great deal of enthusiasm under the banner of dyslexia, a term and concept still used by some people today.

BRAIN INJURY

In the 1930s Alfred Strauss and Heinz Werner did pioneering work with individuals with mental retardation who showed characteristics very similar to those that had been attributed to persons with traumatic brain injury. These characteristics included perceptual problems and hyperactivity. These difficulties, of course, interfered with learning. Strauss and Werner also noted that these individuals tended to have retardation caused by exogenous (external) factors. In other words, their observations confirmed that problems in learning caused by external brain injury were very different from those resulting from genetic (endogenous) forms of mental retardation.

In the 1940s Strauss and Laura Lehtinen, his colleague at the Cove Schools for Brain-Injured Children, published a book that outlined a program for brain-injured students. Although the book provided many suggestions for procedures and materials for educating these children, particular emphasis was placed on the need for small classes and the necessity for reducing extraneous sensory stimulation and distractions. Strauss and Lehtinen stressed that since the brain damage itself could not be treated, the first step in teaching the child with brain damage was to control the environment in which that child was to learn. Second, it was important to teach the child to exert his or her own control over the learning environment (Strauss and Lehtinen, 1947). Many of the techniques that Strauss and Lehtinen developed are still used today, and many of their observations on brain injury were central to the evolution of the learning disabilities field.

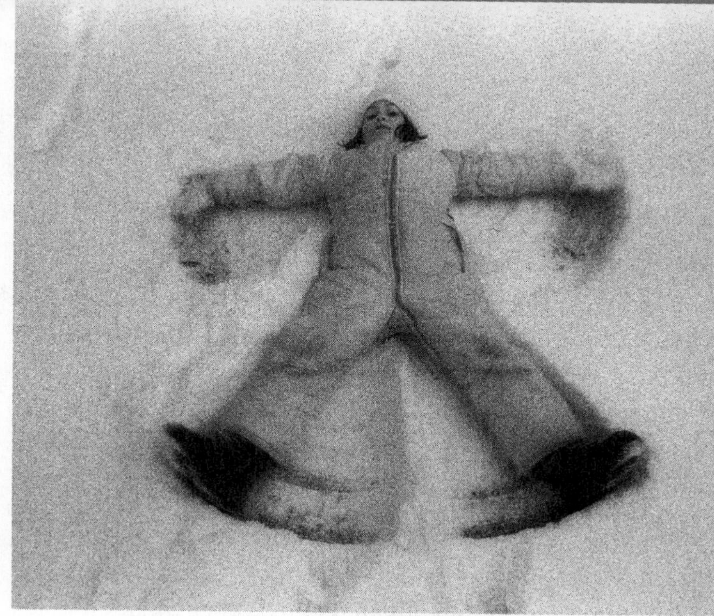

JOHN GRIFFIN/THE IMAGE WORKS

PERCEPTUAL-MOTOR DISABILITIES

Newell Kephart, who worked with Strauss and coauthored a book with him in 1955 on brain injury, focused his attention more on what he observed to be the perceptual problems of the "mystery children." Kephart believed that higher-level cognitive development (development that allows for the acquisition of academic skills like reading) depends upon earlier perceptual and motor functions. He argued that the earlier stages of perceptual-motor development (which include basic large body movements, increased control of fine movements, systematic exploratory activities, meaning derived from the various senses, and sensory integration) are prerequisites to the development of the complex concept formation required for academic learning. Kephart's remediation was based on the idea that children must be taken back to the stages of perceptual-motor development that they did not successfully complete. Then they must be given experiences to prepare them for competent school performance. The activities that he suggested included balance and posture training, body image and body differentiation activities, perceptual-motor exercises (for example, drawing a circle on the chalkboard with each hand simultaneously), ocular training (for example, following the movement of a light with each eye), and activities promoting the perception and use of shapes. Kephart detailed his theory and interventions most completely in *The Slow Learner in the Classroom* (1971).

HYPERACTIVITY

William Cruickshank also followed in the tradition of Heinz Werner and Alfred Strauss. One of his major contributions to special education, and to what would become known as the learning disabilities field, was the publication in 1961 of *A Teaching Method for Brain-Injured and Hyperactive Children.* In that book he outlined what he described as three elements of a positive environment in which hyperactive children could achieve optimal learning. These elements were:

1. A reduction in environmental stimuli, particularly stimuli that are not essential to the child's learning and achievement.

2. Reduced space for learning. The area should be small and unstimulating, with the material to be learned being the point of focus.
3. Optimization of the stimulus value of the material to be learned. Color, size, and other means of contrast should be used to draw the child's attention to the material to be learned.

The instructional principles that Cruickshank suggested were similar to and/or built on the work of Kephart, Strauss, Orton, and others who were part of what might be called the "brain-injury" tradition. This tradition contributed much to the creation of the field of learning disabilities. Another tradition that made a contribution to this emerging field focused on what were perceived to be the language disabilities of children who were not functioning well in school. Although some professionals assumed that disabilities in reading, writing, and speaking were the result of neurological impairments, their research and interventions were concentrated on the basic processes of language. This is particularly evident in the work of Samuel Kirk.

SAMUEL KIRK AND THE SYNTHESIS

Samuel Kirk worked for many years with students with mental retardation. Eventually, however, he became more interested in young people who functioned at a level that could be accurately described as retarded in some basic academic skills but whom he felt were not actually mentally retarded. This concern led him to the study of language development and the role of various language abilities in learning.

Kirk and some of his colleagues at the University of Illinois became convinced that many of the "mystery children" were having difficulties in learning because of differences in what they came to call *psycholinguistic abilities.* It was from their work that some concepts still much in evidence today, such as the *auditory learner* and the *visual learner,* had their beginnings. Kirk also led the team that developed the Illinois Test of Psycholinguistic Abilities (ITPA), which became the most widely used instrument for the assessment of language learning styles.

By the early 1960s, the concept of language-processing disabilities had become important in the field of special education, and in the thinking about children who did not fit into the existing categories of students with special needs. Samuel Kirk had also become recognized as an important figure in the field. It is not surprising, therefore, that he should be invited to speak at the event that has come to be known as the "official beginning of the learning disabilities movement."

In 1963, Kirk was invited to address a meeting of parents who were concerned about the children who were variously known as brain-injured, perceptually handicapped, hyperactive, and dyslexic. There were more than forty different terms being used to describe those children by that time. This fact had in itself become a concern. With so many terms and concepts being used to explain the difficulties these children were experiencing, it was not possible to effectively advocate for a public understanding of these students, or to lobby for provision of the services that they needed. There continued to be, therefore, much confusion surrounding the nature and needs of these children. The confusion that existed was aptly described by William Cruickshank:

> Why parents should be confused becomes quite apparent when one examines even this incomplete list of professional terms.

> If the child happens to live in the state of Michigan, some educators refer to him as a "perceptually disabled child." If the child is a resident of California, his education may be provided if he is classified as an "educationally handicapped" or "neurologically handicapped" child. In Bucks County, Pennsylvania, he will be placed in a class for children with "language disorders." If he moves from California to New York State, he may change from an "educationally handicapped child" to a "brain-injured child." . . . If by chance his parents move to Russia, he will be classified as one with "temporarily retarded psychological development" (Cruickshank, 1977, p. 4).

When Samuel Kirk spoke to the parents who were having their first meeting under the title of the Conference on Exploration into the Problems of the Perceptually Handicapped Child, he said that he had been using the term *learning disabilities* to describe children with disorders in the development of language, speech, reading, and other communication skills. The term *learning disabilities* apparently struck an immediate chord of approval with those parents. During the conference, they created the Association for Children with Learning Disabilities (ACLD). The ACLD, in the years that followed, became a powerful advocacy group. The term *learning disabilities* was disseminated rapidly. Within two decades it became the most widely used designation for children experiencing difficulties in school.

Samuel Kirk had provided the needed term. The various concepts that had been developed to explain the challenges and frustrations of generations of students and their families were synthesized into two words: learning disabilities. These two words would change the character of American education.

The Classroom Needs of Students with Learning Disabilities

In order to comprehend the classroom needs of students with learning disabilities, it is necessary to understand the fundamental ways in which these disabilities have been defined. Concurrent with the adoption of the term *learning disabilities* came a continuing effort to develop a definition that would encompass the complex needs and characteristics of students with these disabilities. At the same time, efforts have been made to clearly distinguish between learning disabilities and other types of disabilities. Achieving these two goals has been difficult and continues to be a pursuit of leaders in the field.

THE FEDERAL DEFINITION OF LEARNING DISABILITIES

The definition of learning disabilities that is endorsed by the federal government and that is, therefore, used for most purposes by states and school districts is the following:

> "Specific learning disability" means a disorder in one or more of the basic psychological processes involved in understanding or in using language, spoken or written, which may manifest itself in an imperfect ability to listen, think, speak, read, write, spell, or to do mathematical calculations. The term includes such conditions as perceptual handicaps, brain injury, minimal brain dysfunction, dyslexia, and developmental aphasia. The term does not include children who have learning problems which are primarily the result of visual, hearing, or motor handicaps, of mental retardation,

> of emotional disturbance, or of environmental, cultural, or economic disadvantage (*Federal Register,* 1977, p. 65083).

Having a single term to describe the children who had been mysterious for so long was a great advantage in beginning to better serve these children. Samuel Kirk made a great contribution to education by providing the term and the concept it implied. Similarly, having an official definition of the term has helped reduce the confusion and misunderstanding that has often interfered with serving these children well. The federal definition has not, however, enjoyed unquestioned acceptance. The National Joint Committee on Learning Disabilities (NJCLD), a group composed of representatives of several professional organizations, issued an alternative definition:

> Learning disabilities is a generic term that refers to a heterogeneous group of disorders manifested by significant difficulties in the acquisition and use of listening, speaking, reading, writing, reasoning, or mathematical abilities. These disorders are intrinsic to the individual, and presumed to be due to central nervous system dysfunction, and may appear across the life span. Problems in self-regulatory behaviors, social perception and social interaction may exist with learning disabilities but do not themselves constitute a learning disability. Although learning disabilities may occur concomitantly with other handicapping conditions (for example, sensory impairment, mental retardation, serious emotional disturbance) or with extrinsic influences (such as cultural differences, insufficient or inappropriate instruction), they are not the result of those conditions or influences (National Joint Committee on Learning Disabilities, 1989, p. 1).

As the NJCLD definition was being formulated, it was supported by its authors as being an improvement over the federal definition for several reasons:

1. It is not limited to children. It defines learning disabilities as a lifespan concern.
2. It does not use the term *basic psychological processes,* which has been considered vague and confusing by many critics.
3. It assumes that spelling is included as a writing skill rather than as a separate ability.
4. It does not use older terms that have been sources of confusion and controversy such as dyslexia, minimal brain dysfunction, and perceptual handicap.
5. It clearly states that learning disabilities may exist concomitantly with other disabling conditions. It thereby "softens" the exclusionary nature of the federal definition (Hammill, Leigh, McNutt, and Larsen, 1981, p. 339).

Having a rational and reasonable definition of learning disabilities is, of course, important. It facilitates communication, it is central to the delivery of educational services, and funding for remedial and preventative programs is usually associated with an accepted definition. It is important to remember, however, that the label *learning disabilities* is a broad and encompassing term that covers many kinds of learning problems. Although a definition can be important in classifying children and programs, and in securing resources, it may not be so helpful in the process of actually teaching a child. Effective teaching of students with learning disabilities, like all good teaching, is based on an understanding of individual needs. Teaching a child with learning disabilities calls for astute observation on the part of the teacher of that student's patterns of strength and weakness. Successful teaching of a child with learning disabilities is essentially informed and personalized instruction. Some general strategies for informed and personalized teaching are offered later in this chapter. First, however, it is critical to have a sense of the "who" and "what" of learning disabilities. Who are these students, and what kind of specific problems do they encounter in school?

STUDENTS WITH LEARNING DISABILITIES: WHO ARE THEY?

There have been many different estimates of and opinions on the number of children with learning disabilities. At one extreme of this continuum is the opinion of some critics that learning disabilities as a category is a fabrication that camouflages "slow learning" or poor teaching. Some of these critics, in fact, believe that there are no students with "real" learning disabilities. At the other end of the range of opinions is the view that everyone has some form of learning disability and that, therefore, the category includes practically everyone.

The numbers most widely accepted for the incidence and prevalence of learning disabilities are those reported by the U.S. Department of Education. Almost two and a half million children and young people in the United States with learning disabilities (ages 6–21) were served in school programs during 1993–94. There was a 3.3 percent increase in the number served from 1992–93 to 1993–94. In 1976–77 learning disabilities accounted for 23.8 percent of all disabilities among students. In 1993–94 learning disabilities accounted for 51.1 percent of the disabilities reported by the U.S. Department of Education (Office of Special Education Programs, 1995). Although the causes of this increase have been vigorously debated, this dramatic increase has been attributed primarily to two factors. According to Hallahan, one factor that has led to this increase is that the field of learning disabilities is relatively new. Each year educators and parents become more adept at recognizing students with learning disabilities. Therefore, each year more students have been identified and served. Secondly, Hallahan describes social changes such as increased poverty, substance abuse among pregnant women, and decreasing social services as causes of increases in the prevalence of learning disabilities. Hallahan argues that "of all the disability categories, learning disabilities is one of the most sensitive barometers of the biomedical status of children and the psychological climate in which they live" (Hallahan, 1992, p. 524).

The growth of the category of learning disabilities is also dramatically evident in the number of teachers employed to work with these students. Table 2.1 illustrates that during the 1992–93 school year there were more than twice as many learning disabilities teachers than teachers of any of the other larger categories of disabilities. Because many of these teachers are currently being asked to serve as consultants in general classrooms, rather than to teach students in segregated settings, these numbers are an important part of the effort to create more inclusive schools.

As is presented in Table 2.2, most students with learning disabilities are being taught primarily in regular classrooms (with no more than 20 percent of their time in special education services) or in resource rooms (these students are in regular classes as well but spend between 21 and 60 percent of their school day in special services). Only 20.1 percent of students with learning disabilities are placed in separate classes where

TABLE 2.1

Special Education Teachers Employed and Students with Learning Disabilities, Speech Impairments, Mental Retardation, and Emotional Disturbance, Ages 6–21: School Year 1992–93

Disability	Teachers	Students
Learning disabilities	98,125	2,366,494
Speech impairments	41,208	998,049
Mental retardation	43,106	532,365
Emotional disturbance	29,684	401,659

Source: Office of Special Education Programs. *Seventeenth Annual Report to Congress on the Implementation of the Individuals with Disabilities Education Act.* Washington, DC: U.S. Department of Education, 1995, pp. 11, 29.

they spend more than 60 percent of the school day. Very few students with learning disabilities are placed in more restrictive and separate settings.

It is clear from these figures that most teachers are certain to have in their classes students with learning disabilities. This is true both because of the increasing numbers of these children and the greater likelihood of their being placed in general classes for at least a substantial portion of their school days. It is important, therefore, that teachers know about the personal and learning characteristics of these students.

Cone et al. (1985), in a major demographic study of students with learning disabilities, found that of 1,839 students enrolled in learning disabilities programs in Iowa, boys outnumbered girls significantly (three to one). Most (75 percent) of these students' learning disabilities were first diagnosed while in elementary school. These researchers also found that more of the students identified with learning disabilities had problems in reading and spelling than in math. They reported that the students in their study tended to fall further behind as they progressed to higher grades in school. Finally, they found that the average IQ for their sample of students was 95.

The composite picture derived from Cone et al., then, is of learning disabilities as a difficulty that is encountered inordinately by

TABLE 2.2

Percentage of Students with Learning Disabilities, Speech Impairments, Mental Retardation, and Emotional Disturbance Ages 6–21 Served in Different Educational Environments: School Year 1992–93

	Educational Environment					
Disability	Regular Class	Resource Room	Separate Class	Separate School	Residential Facility	Homebound/ Hospital
Specific learning disability	34.8	43.9	20.1	0.8	0.2	0.2
Speech or language impairments	81.8	10.7	6.0	1.4	0.1	0.1
Mental retardation	7.1	26.8	56.8	7.9	0.9	0.5
Serious emotional disturbance	19.6	26.7	35.2	13.7	3.5	1.3

Source: Office of Special Education Programs. *Seventeenth Annual Report to Congress on the Implementation of the Individuals with Disabilities Education Act.* Washington, DC: U.S. Department of Education, 1995, p. 17.

males and that is noticed most frequently as children are expected to acquire the basic skills of literacy in the elementary grades. It may also indicate that greater emphasis is placed on reading skills than on math skills and that the result is that more disabilities are noted in this skill area. The results also indicate that although the average IQ for the students in the study falls within the normal range, performance by these students on IQ tests consistently decreased as grade level increased. This decrease appeared to be the function of increasing difficulties in verbal performance in higher grades. Similarly, the research demonstrated that students do not "grow out" of their learning difficulties. On the contrary, the academic achievement of the students in this study tended to progressively decrease as their grade level increased.

Data from the Office of Special Education Programs confirms that learning disabilities have serious consequences for students at the secondary level. Although more current data is not yet available, Table 2.3 shows that only slightly more than 50 percent of students with learning disabilities graduated with diplomas in 1990–91. Nearly 11 percent were awarded certificates of completion. Almost 38 percent of high school students with learning disabilities either drop out of school, reach the maximum age for school attendance and are therefore excluded from attendance, or are of unknown status.

TABLE 2.3

Basis of School Exit for Students with Learning Disabilities: School Year 1990–91

Exit Basis	Number	Percent
Diploma	63,590	51.7
Certificate	13,291	10.8
Maximum Age	845	0.7
Drop Out	27,276	22.1
Status Unknown	18,059	14.7
Total	123,061	100.0

Source: Office of Special Education Programs. *Fifteenth Annual Report to Congress on the Implementation of the Individuals with Disabilities Education Act.* Washington, DC: U.S. Department of Education, 1993, p. 18.

WHAT PROBLEMS DO STUDENTS WITH LEARNING DISABILITIES ENCOUNTER IN SCHOOL?

In recent years research on learning disabilities has focused on several areas that provide pieces of the puzzle of learning disabilities. These findings will likely prove to be much more important in our understanding of the mystery children than any attempt to develop a general definition of learning disabilities. It is the particular configuration of these learner characteristics in a student that may allow us to understand each learner as an individual. It is on this basis that development of an educational program that best meets her or his personal needs as a student is possible. The learner characteristics that seem to show the most promise for increasing our understanding of learning disabilities are: 1) language problems, 2) attention and activity problems, 3) memory problems, 4) cognitive problems, and 5) social and emotional problems.

Language Problems

A study of elementary school students found that over 90 percent of 242 students who had been classified as learning disabled had mild to moderate language problems (Gibbs and Cooper, 1989). Vogel noted earlier (1975) that often children who do not read well in school have underlying language problems. It has been reported, in fact, that children labeled as learning disabled have often been labeled earlier as being *language disordered.* Terrell believes that when children with language disorders reach school, their language problems are obscured by the emphasis there on reading and the acquisition of other academic skills. He believes that the same problems that have interfered earlier with language development in these children now become evident in their poor school performance (Terrell, 1990). Language problems often involve difficulties in understanding others, speaking clearly, finding the right words for expressing an idea or need, and a general lack of the ability to organize language for effective communication. Children with language problems may be thought of by their peers, and by adults, as being "backward" or as using "baby talk."

Attention and Activity Problems

Developmental psychologists have long noted that the ability of children to focus their attention increases with age. Very young children cannot be expected to focus for very long on any object, event, or person. They are easily distracted by any new stimulus. Indeed, the nature of early childhood is not that children lack the ability to "pay attention." It is that they "pay attention" to everything. Every sound, sight, or other sensation pulls the child to it. Research by Zukier and Hagen (1978) indicated that as they develop, children are more able to ignore less salient information and concentrate on tasks to be learned. In this sense, successful learning is dependent on being able to "ignore" information that is not essential to the task at hand.

Kindergarten children are usually still learning to "ignore" information. Effective teachers must be sensitive to this characteristic of young children. Some children continue to be unfocused with their attention and come to be thought of as having attention problems. They may be described as having a short attention span, as being easily distracted, or as having attention deficits.

Hyperactivity is often associated with attention problems. The term itself addresses the physical movements that may accompany an attention problem. Hyperactivity is the running, squirming, talkative, out-of-the-seat behavior that is so disturbing to teachers, parents, and other children. Attention disorders and hyperactivity are treated under a single category, attention-deficit/hyperactivity disorder (ADHD) by the American Psychiatric Association in its *Diagnostic and Statistical Manual of Mental Disorders* (American Psychiatric Association, 1987). The manual does not distinguish between the two because of the lack of evidence that hyperactivity and attention deficits are different categories of behavior. Box 2.1 presents the criteria that the American Psychiatric Association lists for diagnosing attention-deficit/hyperactivity disorder.

Certainly not all students with learning disabilities will have problems with attention and/or hyperactivity. There have been varying estimates concerning the prevalence of attention problems in children with learning disabilities. Silver (1990), for example, reports that up to 20 percent of children with learning disabilities also manifest the characteristics of attention-deficit/hyperactivity disorder. Epstein and his colleagues (1985), on the other hand, found that most students in the learning disabilities category have attention problems. Controversy concerning this question is likely to continue.

Memory Problems

It has been reported by researchers that children with learning disabilities often have difficulties in remembering facts, instructions, and rules. In their research on this question, Swanson et al. (1990) found that with tests of memory they could differentiate between learning disabled and non–learning disabled students. Deficits in the memory functions of students with learning disabilities have been attributed to the absence of effective memory strategies.

Most children, when given a list of terms, names, or numbers to memorize, will repeat the list to themselves over and over. Students will also group or "chunk" items that somehow fit together so that they can remember them more effectively. They may also use other devices such as memorizing the first letter of each word in a list. These are devices that most teachers have used themselves and that they observe, and even encourage, in their students. For reasons that are not well understood, children with learning disabilities often do not spontaneously devise these strategies on their own (Torgensen, 1989). They must, instead, be directly taught to use them.

Cognitive Problems

Related to memory difficulties is the overall ability to use cognitive strategies for problem solving. The term *cognition* is used to describe the process of analyzing problems, and the planning and organizing necessary for the solution of those problems. Children with learning disabilities often exhibit behavior in classrooms that appears to indicate a lack of analysis, planning, and organization. Their schoolwork may show evidence of being rushed and completed in a very disorganized fashion. Some of these students appear to be completely unaware of the importance of planning and organization in the tasks that they are given to complete in school.

Awareness of the strategies and skills necessary for successful task completion has been referred to as *metacognition.* Some researchers feel that an absence of this awareness is a central feature of many learning disabilities. They argue that the "lack of spontaneous access to these abilities and functions, as well as their ability to coordinate them" is fundamental to the problems of many children with learning disabilities (Reid and Hresko, 1981, p. 81). The teaching of metacognitive skills to students who do not spontaneously develop them is an area that has generated much in-

BOX 2.1

DSM-III-R Criteria: Attention-Deficit/Hyperactivity Disorder

A. A period of six months or more during which at least eight of the following symptoms are present:
   1. Has difficulty remaining seated.
   2. Often fidgets with hands or feet or squirms in seat.
   3. Has difficulty playing quietly.
   4. Often talks excessively.
   5. Often shifts from one uncompleted activity to another.
   6. Has difficulty sustaining attention to tasks and play activities.
   7. Has difficulty following through on instructions from others (not due to oppositional behavior or failure of comprehension).
   8. Is easily distracted by extraneous stimuli.
   9. Often interrupts or intrudes on others (e.g., butts into games).
   10. Often blurts out answers to questions before they have been completed.
   11. Has difficulty waiting on turns in games or group situations.
   12. Often engages in physically dangerous activities without considering possible consequences (not for the purpose of thrill seeking) (e.g., runs into street without looking).
   13. Often loses things necessary for tasks or activities at school or at home.
   14. Often does not seem to listen to what is being said to him or her.

B. Onset before the age of seven years.

C. Does not meet the criteria for pervasive developmental disorder.

Source: American Psychiatric Association. *Diagnostic and Statistical Manual of Mental Disorders,* rev. 3d ed., Washington, DC: American Psychiatric Association, 1987.

terest and enthusiasm in the field of learning disabilities.

Social and Emotional Problems

Students with learning disabilities are at an increased risk for social and emotional problems (Pearl, 1992). Licht (1987) found that repeated experiences of failure tend to create a context in which children develop beliefs about themselves that set the stage for maladaptive behaviors.

It is clear that social and emotional problems may result from some of the other problem areas that have been mentioned. An example could be a child who has attention problems. Silver reports that many children with learning disabilities develop family and community problems that may actually reflect the attention difficulties they experience. He describes studies that show that large numbers of adolescents and young adults diagnosed with personality disorders or observed in detention centers have unrecognized or unremediated attention and learning disabilities (Silver, 1990, p. 396). Other researchers have found that when academic remediation is an effective part of the treatment of delinquent behavior, subsequent delinquency is reduced (Keilitz and Dunivant, 1986).

Another possible reason for the social and emotional problems that many students with learning disabilities encounter is a lack of social "savvy." Bryan (1977) has suggested that these students misread the social cues that are usually understood by others. They misinterpret emotional and social communication from others. They may also not comprehend the impact of their own behavior on other people. As Hallahan and Kauffman describe this aspect of the challenges faced by students with disabilities, they may "have difficulty taking the perspective of others, of putting themselves in someone else's shoes" (Hallahan and Kauffman, 1994, p. 177).

Ways of Helping Students with Learning Disabilities in Inclusive Classrooms

THE SUGGESTIONS FOR CREATING more inclusive learning environments for students with learning disabilities presented in this section are focused on the problem areas that were discussed in the preceding pages of this book. These ideas for promoting school success for students with learning disabilities are intended to be a few beginning points for helping these students function well in general classrooms. They are not intended to be an exhaustive menu of teaching strategies. The modifications and techniques presented in each chapter of this book, in fact, are offered in a cumulative spirit. The suggestions in each chapter are intended to build on all of those from previous chapters. There are very few techniques and strategies offered here that will apply to only one form of disability. Although this book is organized in a categorical manner, each student's array of needs will cross these discrete categories.

The suggestions provided here, then, are aimed at addressing the needs of students with learning disabilities that have just been highlighted in this chapter. It is critical to understand, however, that other needs of students with learning disabilities, and strategies for addressing these needs, will be provided in the chapters that follow. Understanding students with special needs requires an analysis of how these students differ in their characteristics and needs. Teaching these students, however, is a cross-categorical process. Effective teaching strategies that work with one type of learning challenge are likely to have potential for the teaching of other students with special needs. Strategies developed for students with disabilities, in fact, often prove to be sound practices in the instruction of all students.

ATTENTION PROBLEMS: INSTRUCTIONAL STRATEGIES

- *Modify the Manner and Rate of Presenting New Material*: Students with attention problems may get lost if material is presented too quickly or if they are overwhelmed with the complexity of the material. It may be helpful to them, therefore, to:

  a. Slow the pace of the presentation of material

  b. Keep students engaged by asking frequent questions as the material is presented to ensure that each step or portion is being comprehended.

  c. Use visual organizers such as transparency outlines on the overhead projector to draw the attention of students to the steps or portions of learning.

- *Have Conferences with the Student*: Students may not be aware of the role that attention plays in learning. They may also be unaware that attention is a particular problem area for them. A conference in which attention is explained in a nonpunitive and nonthreatening manner may be very helpful to students. Both the nature of attention problems and strategies for improving it may be focused on during the conference.

- *Bring the Student Closer to the Teaching*: At times we may, without even being conscious of it, move our own attention away from students who are not doing well. We may, for example, give less eye contact to the student who is not doing well. We may, again unaware, give fewer smiles and other encouraging expressions as a child falls further behind others in the class. Bringing a child "closer to the teaching" through our attitudes and actions can go far toward helping that child focus attention on the work of learning. At times it may be helpful to literally bring a child "closer to the teaching" by moving that student physically closer to you. A seat near you may increase the degree to which the student is in touch with the material being taught. In other words, the student who is most vulnerable to a straying of attention needs to be closest to the teacher and what that teacher is teaching.

- *Provide Frequent and Direct Encouragement*: Let students know when you "catch" them paying attention. Tell students that the eye contact they are giving to you and to the materials you are presenting is noticed and is important. Depending on the level and setting, token rewards for attending may be appropriate. In other settings a verbal commendation, sometimes given quietly and subtly, may be just as effective.

- *Emphasize Sustained Attention Rather Than Rapid Completion of Work*: Students may be discouraged and inattentive when they are penalized for not completing work as rapidly as others. Making adjustments in either the amount of work to be completed or the time allowed for its completion on an individual basis may be extremely helpful and encouraging to some students.

- *Teach Self-Monitoring of Attention*: Students can sometimes be trained to monitor their own attention. By using a timer or watch alarm, they can be taught to record at varying intervals whether or not they are paying attention to the instruction or material to be learned. When they hear the beep or other signal, they record what their attention was focused on (for example, the teacher, a daydream, or another student). These records can help create a greater awareness of the need to focus attention. They can also be used as a basis for student-teacher conferences on strategies for enhancing attention skills.

MEMORY PROBLEMS: INSTRUCTIONAL STRATEGIES

- *Teach Highlighting to Help with Recall*: Students who have problems remembering information should be encouraged to use the tool of highlighting or underlining with a marker. They should be shown how to select headings, key sentences, and key terms for underlining or marker highlighting. It might be very helpful to demonstrate highlighting to the student by reviewing material from a textbook. If necessary, obtain permission from the school to allow the student to mark directly in textbooks.
- *Allow the Use of Memory Aids*: Students who have memory problems should not be required to use their memory skills on unnecessary tasks. The use of calculators, for example, should be encouraged with students who continue to have difficulty remembering multiplication tables. A list of spelling rules taped to a student's desk may be a great help. Daily schedules can also be laminated and placed in an easily accessible location for students who need to remind themselves of what their next activity should be. These aids may serve not only as memory helps but also as teaching devices. A student who regularly uses a calculator for multiplication may learn multiplication facts through using this aid. A child who refers often to spelling rules on his desk will probably be learning them in the process as well.
- *Allow Students with Memory Problems to Take Smaller Steps in Learning*: It may be very helpful to students with memory problems to break down instruction, practice, and testing into smaller units. A student may learn much more effectively if new material that is presented in a textbook as one lesson is divided into two or more lessons. Classwork and homework assignments can also be divided in this way. More frequent testing for skill mastery may be required.
- *Teach Students with Memory Problems to Rehearse and Practice for Remembering*: It may be helpful to students with memory problems to learn to rehearse giving back information that they have just learned. This may be accomplished by having "rehearsal tests" immediately after the student has learned new material. Practice in giving back information either in written form or orally may enhance the student's awareness of the most salient features of what has been presented.

COGNITIVE PROBLEMS: INSTRUCTIONAL STRATEGIES

- *Present Material to be Learned in a "High Meaning" Context*: Because of memory and attention problems, students with learning disabilities may not have as large a knowledge base as many other students. In other words, they may have less background information on which to "attach" new learning. New information that is meaningful to most students may not have meaning for students with learning disabilities. It is, therefore, very important to determine if the student understands the meaning of what is being read, for example, or the meaning of a question about new information. Meaningfulness may be enhanced by using examples, analogies, or contrasts.

- *Delay Summative Testing and Grading*: It is important to provide frequent and encouraging feedback to students with learning disabilities. Evaluations of their work that serve as formative learning experiences can be quite helpful. In other words, a constant awareness of how they are doing helps these students develop confidence in themselves and their abilities. For some students, however, it may be best to delay formal or summative testing (testing for grading purposes) until after these students have acquired a greater mastery of the content they are learning.
- *Place Students in a "No Failure" Learning Context*: Students with learning disabilities often have a long history of failure in school. They may have developed a sense of failing at most of the things they have tried in classrooms and a sense of being "failures" as people. Breaking this chain of failure and creating a new sense of self for these students can be the most important thing a teacher does for them. In any subject or skill, the student should be taken back to the point where work can be done without failing. In reading, for example, this might mean taking a second-grade student back to basic letter recognition and then moving forward. After a baseline level of mastery has been determined, the student should be moved forward in increments that will ensure constant success. Most of us have known the feeling of falling further and further behind after one step in a sequence of learning was not mastered. Some of us have been lucky enough to have someone take us back to the starting point of our difficulties, give us the help needed to understand what we missed before, and provide the encouragement to move confidently ahead. This scenario is perhaps the most important thing to keep in mind when working with a discouraged student.

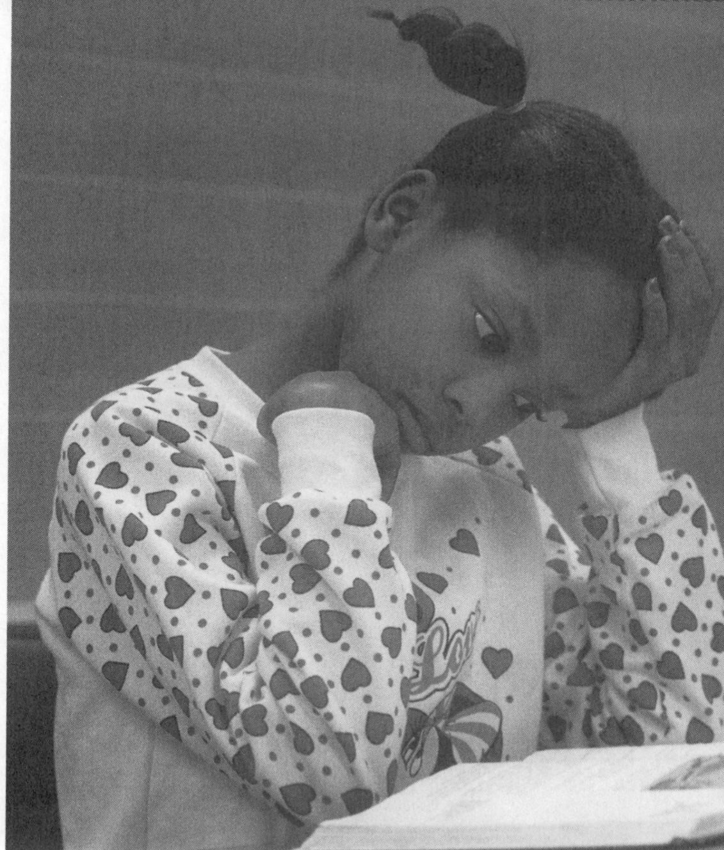
Richard S. Orton/The Picture Cube

BOB DAEMMRICH/STOCK BOSTON

SOCIAL AND EMOTIONAL PROBLEMS: INSTRUCTIONAL STRATEGIES

- *Make the Classroom Reward System Understandable and Accessible*: Students with learning disabilities need to understand the reward system in their classrooms and feel that they are participants in it. Students who have a long history of failure and misbehavior may feel that they are "outlaws" who have no chance to experience the rewards that other students receive. In addition to understanding how they can earn the rewards of good grades, these students need to understand how they can earn the social benefits of positive behavior and good social relationships in the classroom. Some students may need to start with earning points or tokens, but others may respond immediately to praise from teachers and the acceptance of their peers. Again, it is a matter of getting the student started on a path of success, in this case social success.
- *Build Awareness of Self and Others*: Some students with learning disabilities may simply not have a clear awareness of their own behavior and its impact on other people. Helping these students become more insightful about their behavior and its impact on other people may be a significant opportunity for social and emotional growth. Talking honestly and caringly to these students about their behavior may also be an important step in building trusting relationships with them.
- *Teach Positive Behavior*: Once students with learning disabilities become more aware of their own behavior and achieve a better understanding of their interactions with others, they may respond well to instruction on how to construct better relationships and a more positive sense of self. Direct instruction in these matters may be very helpful to them. These students may simply lack the skills they need for getting along with other people. They may not know how to be a friend or how to relate positively to teachers. Help with this kind of direct instruction may be available to teachers from special education resource teachers and from instructional programs that have been developed for the purpose of teaching social skills.
- *Ask for Help*: If the behavior of a student with a learning disability is very inappropriate or if negative behaviors persist when all else has been tried, do not hesitate to ask for help. Seek help first from colleagues in the school who may have the expertise to assist in explaining social and emotional problems, and developing solutions to these problems. This help might come from parents, special educators, counselors, school psychologists, assistant principals, and principals. Some behavioral or social problems may

be severe enough to require outside consultation from other professionals. It is most important that teachers understand that asking for help is not a sign of weakness or incompetence. It is a sign of concern and good judgment.

OTHER STRATEGIES FOR HELPING STUDENTS WITH LEARNING DISABILITIES

A few other strategies for helping students with learning disabilities experience greater school success are listed in Box 2.2. As mentioned earlier, these are strategies that may be helpful to students with other kinds of disabilities as well. Some of these suggestions reinforce the ideas presented earlier in this chapter. Others are general principles that may stimulate specific ideas for working with children in particular settings.

The University of Kansas Center for Research on Learning has developed an instructional strategies approach for teaching students with learning disabilities academic learning strategies, social skills motivation, and self-direction. This approach teaches students techniques for meeting learning demands, and it helps teachers see how they can modify classroom environments to help students use these strategies (Deshler and Lenz, 1989). The approach involves breaking down tasks to be learned into clear, simple, sequential steps. It also emphasizes mastery of each step and having students covertly explain and rehearse to themselves each step they take in the process of learning content or skills (Deshler and Schumaker, 1993). The approach has been adapted for use with students in inclusive classrooms at the elementary, middle, and secondary school levels (Schumaker and Deshler, 1995).

Box 2.3 presents the Corvallis, Montana, Project. It is included here as one model for inclusion of children with learning disabilities in a total school program. The services and components described have the combined effect of creating a more positive environment in which children with diverse characteristics and needs can learn together.

COMPUTER-ASSISTED INSTRUCTION

Computers have become important instructional tools in most educational settings. They have a proven role in helping students with disabilities learn more effectively. Computer hardware and software can be very helpful in creating inclusive learning environments for students with learning, and other, disabilities. Among the functions that computers can serve in promoting successful learning are:

- Providing self-paced math tutorials and math drill-and-practice.
- Providing drill and practice in spelling, and spell-checking functions.
- Promoting writing fluency by allowing for easy revision.

BOX 2.2

Other Strategies That May Be Helpful in Teaching Students with Learning Disabilities

- Look for and emphasize the student's strengths;
- Provide structure, give clear directions, and make sure students understand your expectations;
- Be flexible in classroom procedures (for example, allow tape recorders and calculators);
- Use self-correcting materials, which provide immediate feedback;
- Use computers and other technology;
- Students with learning disabilities often need time to grow and mature—be patient.

- Promoting problem solving and higher-order thinking skills through software exercises and simulations (Hasselbring and Goin, 1988).

Computers have been proven to be effective in improving self-expression and communication skills in students with disabilities (Holzberg, 1994). Their use in inclusive environments has also been shown to create improved communication between general and special educators who work together with students with special needs (Storeygard, 1993). Combining the use of computer-assisted instruction with cooperative learning techniques is an effective way of integrating students with disabilities into general classrooms (Male, 1993). By having students work together on computers, positive relationships and a sense of cooperation may be established that will carry over to other classroom activities.

BOX 2.3

The Corvallis, Montana, Project: A Model for Inclusion

The Corvallis, Montana, Public School District implemented an inclusion program several years ago that has been cited as a model program. It includes the following components:

Consultative Services: Resource teachers meet regularly with general classroom teachers concerning the strengths, weaknesses, and learning styles of students with special needs. Together the teachers decide on alterations and adaptations necessary to facilitate the success of their students.

Team Teaching: Special and general classroom teachers collaborate in teaching classes, making certain that the special needs of students are met through these group activities. This cooperative effort may take the form of one teacher teaching a lesson while the other attends to the special needs of children who require individual attention in order to benefit from that lesson.

Tutorial Sessions: Individual and small-group study sessions are provided for students with learning disabilities or other developmental disabilities. The intent of these sessions is to enhance the student's comprehension level when the same material is taught in the general classroom setting.

In addition to these components, the Corvallis Project also uses other strategies to optimize the probability of student success in inclusive schools:

Cross-Curricular Teaching: School staff members serve students with special needs according to a pervasive philosophy of mutual support. Teachers of different grade levels work together to produce schoolwide projects such as thematic fairs and special event days. Children of different ages, as well as ability levels, are encouraged to work together on these projects.

Cooperative Learning: Within classrooms students are encouraged to work together on assignments. Having children work in groups promotes the development of social and communication skills. Cooperative learning is a powerful means of creating in students a sense of tolerance for others and a sense of the benefits of mutual efforts. The result is often a growth in trust, interdependence, an understanding of responsibilities to others, and increased self-esteem. These are qualities that are critical to the success of inclusive schools.

Peer Tutoring: The schools use both peer tutors and cross-age peer tutors. Age-peer tutoring enhances relationships within a class. A student who can help another student in her/his class benefits in obvious ways, and a more healthy classroom environment is created. Older students acting as teacher assistants may also benefit greatly from the experience.

Assistive Technology: Assistive technology can include such basic aids as adapted spoons and trays that make eating possible for students with severe physical disabilities as well as sophisticated computer equipment. Students with learning disabilities may be able to function much more successfully in inclusive classes by using word processing and programs that facilitate the development of math skills.

Adapted from J. Jakupcak. "Innovative Classroom Programs for Full Inclusion," in J. W. Putnam, *Cooperative Learning and Strategies for Inclusion*. Baltimore, MD: Paul H. Brooks, 1993.

Case Studies and Questions to Consider

STUDENT: NATHAN TATE

SCHOOL: PEACE ELEMENTARY

CURRENT PLACEMENT: SECOND GRADE

AGE: 7 YEARS, 11 MONTHS

Family Structure and Home Environment

Nathan lives with his mother, Caroline Tate. Ms. Tate is thirty-nine years old and is employed by Junior Achievement. Ms. Tate is separated and will soon be divorced from Nathan's father, Lawrence Tate. Mr. Tate is forty-four years old and is a division manager with Success Insurance Companies. Nathan sees his father regularly.

Nathan also lives with his brother, Larry. Larry is seventeen years old and is a popular senior at Peace High School. Nathan, his mother, and his brother live in a rented house.

Parental Perception of the Student's School Program

Ms. Tate is interested in determining if Nathan is in need of special services. She does not feel that Nathan has a learning disability. Ms. Tate has requested help, however, to help clarify that question. She said that reports and comments from school made her feel that it was necessary to resolve the issue.

Earlier this year, Ms. Tate had Nathan evaluated at the Child Development Clinic. The report of that evaluation confirms her opinion that her son falls within normal limits in intelligence, achievement, and all basic learning skills.

Ms. Tate feels that Nathan has experienced some difficulties in school this past year, but she thinks these difficulties are largely situational. She explained by saying that when Nathan came to Peace Elementary last year after attending Rural Elementary for two years, he got off to an unfortunate start. She feels he came to the school having experienced a slightly different curriculum, was separated from the rest of the children in his room, and simply never got into the flow of things with his class. Nathan's mother feels that with a bit more individual attention, he could have done much better work.

Ms. Tate did mention that she believes Nathan shows some weaknesses in concentration and attention. She repeated, however, that the Child Development Clinic report indicated that, even in these areas, he is within normal limits. On the advice of Nathan's pediatrician, he was put on an eight-week trial with Ritalin this past spring. Ms. Tate said that she did note some improvement in his ability to maintain attention during this period. She has not yet decided whether she will resume the medication during the next school year.

Additional Comments

Ms. Tate does not feel that there are any areas of personal or social behavior where her son shows deficiencies. In her opinion, Nathan is a typical seven-year-old boy.

If there is one area where Ms. Tate would wish to see a change in Nathan, it would be in the area of his emotional sensitivity. She thinks that he is too sensitive to the opinions and reactions of others. It concerns her that Nathan is too easily hurt.

On the other hand, Ms. Tate admires Nathan's sensitive nature. She describes him as a loving and expressive child who is a pleasure to be around.

Nathan's teacher feels that his school difficulties are more serious than as perceived by his mother. She says that they go beyond the situation of his transferring from a different school with a slightly different curriculum. Nathan's teacher feels very strongly that he should be evaluated for a possible learning disability.

Questions

1. How might the differences in opinion about Nathan's school difficulties between his mother and his teacher be reconciled?
2. What would be the most important additional information you would want to have about Nathan's school performance in order to help plan an educational program for him?
3. What questions would you want to ask Nathan himself about school?

PUPIL: VALERIE LANG

CURRENT PLACEMENT: DEARLY ELEMENTARY

GRADE: 3

AGE: 8 YEARS, 9 MONTHS

Family Structure and Home Environment

Valerie has difficulties in reading and writing. She was recently moved to a reading group that is working at a lower level. Valerie is described as disliking reading and as having a poor image of herself relative to her work at school. She has also engaged in some inappropriate classroom behavior.

Valerie lives with her parents, Bill and Betty Lang. Mr. Lang is a college graduate and is employed as a banker. Ms. Lang is an attorney in private practice. Valerie also lives with her sister, Ann, who is four years old. Valerie and Ann are described by their parents as being very close.

The Lang family lives in a spacious and well-maintained home. Both the physical and emotional atmosphere of their home is warm and comfortable.

Parental Perception of Child's Developmental Progress and Needs

Mr. and Ms. Lang believe that Valerie's difficulties in school are specific to reading and writing. Mr. Lang has noticed that his daughter misreads words, transposes letters, and writes in what he describes as reverse order. Ms. Lang made the observation that Valerie's problems with reading and writing have much to do with timing. She remarked that when Valerie has, or takes, the time to concentrate and attend to detail, she does much better work than when she rushes or is under tight time constraints.

The Langs feel that Valerie has a number of strengths relative to school. They describe her as an articulate child with very good memory and math skills. They also feel that her social skills are exceptional and have noticed that she has the ability to make other people feel at ease with her.

Mr. and Ms. Lang believe that Valerie's difficulty in reading and writing began to emerge in first grade. They feel that her performance has ebbed and flowed in quality since then depending on the expectations and instruction in her class placements. Valerie's parents are concerned that they not overreact to the realities of her school placement and achievement. To quote them, they do not want to "make a mountain out of a molehill." They do want, however, the most appropriate instructional arrangement that will meet the educational needs of their child.

Additional Comments

Mr. and Ms. Lang feel that their daughter's social and emotional development is within the normal range for a girl her age. They indicate that they believe that any inappropriate behavior she has manifested at school is associated with her feeling of not having done as well academically as she thinks she should. The Langs' primary goal for Valerie is that she grow up to be a happy adult who will seek something that will bring her fulfillment and security. They believe she already has the intelligence and skills that will allow her to achieve these goals. They hope she will develop greater self-motivation. They are most pleased with the friendly and affectionate way that Valerie approaches other people.

Questions

1. In your opinion, do you think Valerie's problems dictate the necessity of special help in a resource room, or could she "make do" with extra help in her general education classroom? Explain your answer.
2. What strategies would you, as a general education teacher, use to help Valerie in reading?
3. What strategies would you use to help Valerie with her image of herself?

References

American Psychiatric Association. *Diagnostic and Statistical Manual of Mental Disorders,* rev. 3d ed. Washington, DC: American Psychiatric Association, 1987.

Bryan, T. "Learning Disabled Children's Comprehension of Nonverbal Communication." *Journal of Learning Disabilities, 10,* 1977: 501–506.

Cone, T. E., L. R. Wilson, C. M. Bradley, and J. H. Reese. "Characteristics of LD Students in Iowa: An Empirical Investigation." *Learning Disability Quarterly, 8,* 1985: 211–220.

Cruickshank, W. M. *A Teaching Method for Brain-Injured and Hyperactive Children.* Syracuse, NY: Syracuse University Press, 1961.

———. *Learning Disabilities in Home, School and Community.* Syracuse, NY: Syracuse University Press, 1977.

Deshler, D. D., and B. K. Lenz. "The Strategies Instructional Approach." *International Journal of Disability, Development and Education, 36,* 1989: 203–224.

Deshler, D. D., and J. B. Schumaker. "Strategy Mastery by At-Risk Students: Not a Simple Matter." *Elementary School Journal, 94,* 1993: 153–167.

Epstein, M. H., W. Bursuck, and D. Cullivan. "Patterns of Behavior Problems Among the Learning Disabled: Boys Aged 12–18." *Learning Disability Quarterly, 9,* 1985: 43–54.

Federal Register. "Procedures for Evaluating Specific Learning Disabilities." Washington, DC: Department of Health, Education, and Welfare, December 29, 1977.

Gibbs, D. P., and E. B. Cooper. "Prevalence of Communication Disorders in Students with Learning Disabilities." *Journal of Learning Disabilities, 22,* 1989: 60–63.

Hagen, J. W., and R. V. Kail. "The Role of Attention in Perceptual and Cognitive Development." In W. M. Cruickshank and D. P. Hallahan (Eds.), *Perceptual and Learning Disabilities in Children: Research and Theory,* Vol. 2, Syracuse, NY: Syracuse University Press, 1975: 165–194.

Hallahan, D. "Some Thoughts on Why the Prevalence of Learning Disabilities Has Increased." *Journal of Learning Disabilities, 25,* 1992: 523–528.

Hallahan, D., and J. Kauffman. *Exceptional Children: Introduction to Special Education.* Needham Heights, MA: Allyn and Bacon, 1994.

Hammill, D. D., J. E. Leigh, G. McNutt, and S. C. Larsen. "A New Definition of Learning Disabilities." *Learning Disability Quarterly, 14,* 1981: 336–342.

Hasselbring, T. S., and L. I. Goin. "Use of Computers." In G. A. Robinson, E. A. Polloway, and L. R. Sargent (Eds.), *Best Practices in Mental Disabilities,* Reston, VA: Division on Mental Retardation, Council for Exceptional Children, 1988: 199–210.

Holzberg, C. S. "Technology in Special Education." *Technology and Learning, 14,* 1994: 18–21.

Jakupcak, J. "Innovative Classroom Programs for Full Inclusion." In J. W. Putnam, *Cooperative Learning and Strategies for Inclusion.* Baltimore, MD: Paul H. Brooks, 1993: 163–179.

Keilitz, J., and N. Dunivant. "The Relationship Between Learning Disability and Juvenile Delinquency: Current State of Knowledge." *Remedial and Special Education,* 7(3), 1986: 18–26.

Kephart, N. *The Slow Learner in the Classroom,* 2d ed. Columbus, OH: Charles E. Merrill, 1971.

Kirk, S. A. "Behavioral Diagnosis and Remediation of Learning Disabilities." In *Proceedings of the Conference on Exploration into the Problems of the Perceptually Handicapped Child.* Chicago: Perceptually Handicapped Children, 1963: 2–8.

Licht, B. B. "The Interaction Between Children's Achievement-Related Beliefs and the Characteristics of Different Tasks." Paper presented at the Annual Meeting of the American Educational Research Association, Washington, DC, April 1987.

Male, M. "Cooperative Learning and Computers in Social Studies Integrating Special Needs Students into General Education Classrooms." *Social Studies Review, 32,* 1993: 56–62.

National Joint Committee on Learning Disabilities. Letter from NJCLD to member organizations regarding modification to the NJCLD definition of learning disabilities, September 18, 1989.

Office of Special Education Programs. *Fifteenth Annual Report to Congress on the Implementation of the Individuals with Disabilities Education Act.* Washington, DC: U.S. Department of Education, 1993.

———. *Seventeenth Annual Report to Congress on the Implementation of the Individuals with Disabilities Education Act.* Washington, DC: U.S. Department of Education, 1995.

Orton, S. *Reading, Writing, and Speech Problems in Children.* New York: W. W. Norton, 1937.

Pearl, R. "Psychosocial Characteristics of Learning Disabled Students." In N. N. Singh and I. L. Beale (Eds.), *Current Perspectives in Learning Disabilities: Nature, Theory, and Treatment.* New York: Springer-Verlag, 1992: 96–125.

Reid, D., and W. Hresko. *A Cognitive Approach to Learning Disabilities.* New York: McGraw-Hill, 1981.

Schumaker, J. B., and D. D. Deshler. "Secondary Classes Can Be Inclusive Too." *Educational Leadership, 52,* 1995: 50–51.

Silver, L. B. "Attention Deficit-Hyperactivity Disorder: Is It a Learning Disability or Related Disorder?" *Journal of Learning Disabilities, 23,* 1990: 394–397.

Storeygard, J. "Making Computers Work for Students with Special Needs." *Teaching Exceptional Children, 26,* 1993: 22–24.

Strauss, A., and L. Lehtinen. *Psychopathology and Education of the Brain-Injured Child.* New York: Grune and Stratton, 1947.

Swanson, H. L., K. F. Cochran, and C. A. Ewers. "Can Learning Disabilities Be Determined from Working Memory Performance?" *Journal of Learning Disabilities, 23,* 1990: 59–67.

Terrell, B. Y. "Some Thoughts on Language-Learning Disabilities and the Preschool Child." *Heresay* (Spring–Summer 1990): 58–59.

Torgensen, J. K. "Cognitive and Behavioral Characteristics of Children with Learning Disabilities: Concluding Comments." *Journal of Learning Disabilities, 22,* 1989: 166–168.

Vogel, S. A. *Syntactic Abilities in Normal and Dyslexic Children.* Baltimore, MD: University Park Press, 1975.

Zukier, H., and J. W. Hagen. "The Development of Selective Attention Under Distracting Conditions." *Child Development, 49,* 1978: 870–873.

Creating Classrooms That Welcome Students with Mental Retardation

Madame Guerin and Victor: La Mere de L'Enfant Sauvage

One of the classic stories in the history of special education is that of Victor, a child who came to be known as the "Wild Boy of Aveyron." In September 1799, a boy who had apparently grown up in the wild of the Caune Woods of southern France was captured by hunters. He was taken to a village nearby and placed in the care of a widow. He soon escaped and returned to his forest home. Six months later he was again found wandering in search of food and shelter. Accounts of the boy spread rapidly, and he was brought to Paris for study. There he was examined by the eminent physician, Philipe Pinel, and was diagnosed as mentally retarded. He was classified as an incurable "idiot."

A young physician who had been working with children with hearing impairments, Jean-Marc-Gaspard Itard, did not agree that the boy's condition was incurable. He asked that he be allowed to attempt to find a way to help him. His request was granted.

Victor, as Itard named the boy, made excellent progress under his teacher's instruction. He learned numbers, colors, and shapes and was eventually able to write a few French nouns and verbs. Victor used gestures for expression, and he understood much of what was said to him. He never learned to speak well enough, however, to communicate verbally.

Victor also developed social skills. He learned how to adapt to an environment where survival was based on meeting the expectations of other people. This was quite a change for him. Up to that point in his life, survival had depended on meeting the challenges of the forest.

Even though Victor made great progress in most of the skills that Itard set out to teach him, Itard was deeply disappointed in his student's failure to develop speech. After five years of working with Victor, Itard decided that it was hopeless. He felt Victor would never learn spoken language. He abandoned his instruction of Victor completely. He had come to the conclusion that the boy was, after all, retarded.

It is ironic that, though Itard believed that he had failed with Victor, he has been admired through the years by special educators. Many feel that his philosophy and the techniques he developed mark the beginning of special education as a discipline. Itard has frequently been referred to as the "father of special education."

There is another person, however, who played a very important role in Victor's life and education. Many people who are well acquainted with the story of Itard and Victor do not recognize her name. In some ways, however, she played an even more important role in Victor's life than Itard. Her name was Madame Guerin.

In his account of how Victor came to be his student, Itard explained that, after his capture in Aveyron, the boy had been exhibited in public, examined by professionals, and judged to be fit only for living in an institution. He said that the prevailing attitude seemed to be that "society had the right to tear a child away from a free and innocent life, and send him to an institution" (Itard, 1962, p. 11). Itard went on to express his belief that more humane treatment was deserved by the boy, "namely, to treat him kindly and to exercise great consideration for his taste and inclinations" (Itard, 1962, p. 11).

The primary source of this needed understanding and kindness was actually to be Madame Guerin, the housekeeper hired to care for Victor on a daily basis. According to Itard, she performed her duties with the "patience of a mother and the intelligence of an enlightened teacher" (Itard, 1962, p. 12). In an extensive and scholarly examination of Victor's discovery and treatment, Roger Shattuck found that Madame Guerin lived with her husband in quarters near the kitchen of the institution for children with hearing impairments where Itard worked. Madame Guerin, according to Shattuck, was around forty years old when she first agreed to care for Victor. She had "no special training, no theories of education, no career to make, no books to write, no fame to win. She was an 'ordinary' person; she must also have been a remarkable human being" (Shattuck, 1980, p. 76).

Throughout his report, Itard comments on the strong relationship between Victor and Madame Guerin. Given the constant care she gave the boy, of course, this is not unexpected. Reading the account of their relationship, however, gives the impression of a depth of relationship based on more than time and proximity. Itard's description of an incident when Victor ran away is illustrative:

> The last time when his memories and his passion for the freedom of the fields led our savage to escape from the house, he turned in the direction of Senlis and gained the forest. He soon came out, however, doubtless driven by hunger and the impossibility of providing for himself any longer. Drawing near to the neighboring fields, he fell into the hands of the police who arrested him as a vagabond and kept him as such for a fortnight. Recognized at the end of this time and again brought to Paris, he was taken to the Temple, where Madame Guerin, his guardian, came to claim him. A number of inquisitive people assembled to witness this interview, which was truly affecting. Scarcely had Victor caught sight of his governess, when he turned pale and lost consciousness for a moment but, as he felt himself embraced and fondled by Madame Guerin, he suddenly revived and showed his delight by sharp cries, convulsive clenching of his hands and a radiant expression. In the eyes of all the assistants he appeared less like a fugitive obliged to return to the supervision of the keeper, than like an affectionate son who, of his own free will, comes and throws himself in the arms of the one who has given him life (Itard, 1962, pp. 89–90).

We might question whether the description of Victor as a "wild boy" was ever accurate or necessary. This is particularly true when we examine the growth in the friendship between the boy and Madame Guerin. In discussing the development of Victor's emotional characteristics, Itard describes an incident that occurred around the time of Monsieur Guerin's death.

> . . . Madame Guerin's husband fell ill and was nursed away from the house without Victor being told of it. Having among his little domestic duties that of setting the table at dinner time, he continued to lay a place for Monsieur Guerin, and although he was made to remove it every day he never failed to set it again the next day. The illness had a sad end. Monsieur Guerin succumbed, and on the day when he died his place was again laid for him. One can guess what an effect such a distressing attention had upon Madame Guerin. Witnessing this scene of grief, Victor understood that he was the cause of it; and, whether he only thought he had done wrong, or whether he penetrated the real reason of his governess' despair and felt how useless and misplaced were the pains he had been taking, he removed the place of his own accord, sadly put the things back in the cupboard, and never again set them (Itard, 1962, pp. 90–91).

Madame Guerin worked with Victor on the educational goals that Itard had laid out for him. She practiced arranging cut-out letters to form words with him. She encouraged his perceptual and motor development. She used the techniques that Itard prescribed for developing Victor's spoken language. The success of these techniques was, indeed, modest. In reports of Victor's progress, however, the only spontaneous speech that he produced was in his relationship with Madame Guerin.

The first example of spontaneous speech produced by Victor was a syllable he spoke on those occasions when Madame Guerin's daughter Julie visited them. The syllable *li* ("lee") was uttered by Victor in response to her presence. In Itard's estimation, this sound was repeated with "an inflection of voice not without sweetness" (Itard, 1962, p. 33).

The other example of spoken language produced by Victor without instruction or provocation seems to have been the result of Madame Guerin's habit of uttering the French for "Oh God": *Oh Dieu.*

> It is the exclamation "Oh God" (Oh Dieu) which he has taken from Madame Guerin, and which he lets escape frequently in moments of great happiness. He pronounces it by leaving out the *u* in Dieu, and laying stress on the *i* as if it were double and in such a way as to be heard to cry distinctly, "Oh Diie! Oh Diie!" The *o* found in this last combination of sounds was not new to him; I had succeeded some time previously in making him pronounce it (Itard, 1962, pp. 33–34).

It was Itard who courageously placed his bets on Victor's ability to learn and develop. It was he who saved the boy from a lifetime of institutionalization. Itard's ideas and experiments provided the source for Victor's education and the inspiration for generations of special educators to follow. Yet it is clear that Madame Guerin was the nurturant source of most of Victor's progress. It was she who implemented and gave life to many of Itard's conceptions of Victor's potential. According to Harlan Lane, who has written a revealing exploration of this study,

> . . . Madame Guerin was probably the source of much of the progress, it was she who fed Victor, who cleaned and caressed him, who was his companion during most of his waking hours. It is a pity that she has not left us an account of her observations and actions, or that Itard, drawing less of a demarcation between lessons and life, did not record more than a few revealing incidents (Lane, 1976, p. 154).

Richard Scheerenberger has described Madame Guerin as the "real heroine of this epic" (Scheerenberger, 1983, p. 77), and Robert Shattuck agrees when he writes:

> We must assign as much credit for the Wild Boy's development to Madame Guerin as to Itard. The doctor could not possibly have gone on without someone like her. She also reported on the boy's behavior—how he slept, his movements and responses, the outings they began to make together to nearby parks and gardens. She was always there, physically and emotionally. Madame Guerin's name should be remembered with as much honor as Itard's in the events that follow. He would surely have agreed (Shattuck, 1980, p. 75).

If Itard is remembered as the father of special education, it seems equally important that we recognize that the field had another parent. Madame Guerin's care of Victor and her encouragement in him of precious human qualities remind us that all teaching is a synthesis of the promotion of independence and the nurturance required for the personal freedom we wish for every student. In this sense Madame Guerin was an inclusive educator. Rather than exclusionary requirements and rigid expectations, she provided the context and care that allowed Victor to grow.

In 1805, Itard ceased his efforts with Victor. The young man's care was turned over completely to Madame Guerin. She was allocated 150 francs a year for her efforts. In 1811 she was granted an additional 500 francs a year so that she and Victor could have more suitable living quarters. Victor died in 1828 at forty years of age. Madame Guerin was there.

Mental Retardation: The History of a Construct

AN OPTIMISTIC BEGINNING

The efforts of Jean Itard and Madame Guerin on Victor's behalf are evidence of the beginning of an important change in social attitudes toward people thought to have mental retardation. During the 1800s in Europe and North America, an optimism about the educability of people who had previously been considered uneducable bloomed.

Edouard Sequin, a student of Itard, established a school for children with mental retardation in Paris in the 1830s. He based his curriculum on the techniques that had been pioneered by Itard. His school emphasized sensory stimulation, positive reinforcement, and modeling. The results of Sequin's work with children with mental retardation were positive enough to impress a team of scientific evaluators. In 1844 his students were examined by the Paris Academy of Sciences, and Sequin was declared to have found the answer to the problem of educating children with retardation (Kanner, 1964).

In 1848 Edouard Sequin left France and emigrated to the United States. For more than thirty years he was the most influential person in the development of educational programs and schools for students with mental retardation in America. He was also central to the encouragement of an attitude of optimism about the potentials of these students. The residential schools that he helped establish were intended to be places where children with mental retardation could receive the education that would prepare them to live their adult lives as independent and contributing citizens of their society.

THE FADING OF OPTIMISM

The optimistic outlook on the potentials of people with mental retardation that was encouraged by Sequin's work faded before the end of the nineteenth century. The schools he helped found had, in fact, become custodial institutions. The prevailing view of mental retardation by the turn of the century was that it was primarily a hereditary defect and that little could be done to improve the lives of people who were born with it. The words of the psychologist and leader in the field, Henry Goddard, are illustrative of the conventional wisdom concerning mental retardation at that time: "[T]hey are feeble-minded and no amount of education or good environment can change a feeble-minded individual into a normal one, anymore than it can change a red-haired stock into a black-haired stock" (Goddard, 1912, p. 53).

Goddard was a strong advocate of institutions for children and adults with mental retardation. He firmly believed that they belonged in segregated facilities that would protect society from the problems they would have created if left in the community. Again, a statement by Goddard is a good example of the attitude of the time.

> If such colonies were provided in sufficient number to take care of all the distinctly feeble-minded cases in the community, they would very largely take the place of our present almshouses and prisons. . . . Such colonies would save an annual loss in property and life, due to the action of these irresponsible people, sufficient to nearly or quite offset the expense. . . . Segregation through colonization seems in the present state of our knowledge to be the ideal and perfectly satisfactory method (Goddard, 1912, pp. 105–106, 117).

EUGENICS AND MENTAL RETARDATION

In addition to institutionalization, proponents of the movement known as *eugenics* (the so-called science of "race betterment") argued that people with mental retardation should be sterilized. Both institutionalization and sterilization were advanced by Henry Goddard's study of a family he called the Kallikaks. He reported on a family with one line of descendants from the union of a Revolutionary War soldier with a tavern maid who Goddard claimed was feeble-minded. This line, he further asserted, was filled with generations of people with mental retardation. A second line, descending from the same soldier and a woman from an upstanding family, was reported to be outstanding in its intellectual, social, and economic accomplishments. Goddard's conclusions about the "bad" Kallikaks helped set the tone of opinion concerning mental retardation for much of the twentieth century:

> We have the type of family which the social worker meets continually and which makes most of our social problems. A study of it will help account for the conviction we have that no amount of work in the slums or removing the slums from our cities will ever be successful until we take care of those who make the slums what they are. . . . If all of the slum districts of our cities were removed tomorrow and model tenements built in their places, we would still have slums in a week's time because we have these mentally defective people who can never be taught to live otherwise than as they have been living. Not until we take care of this class and see to it that their lives are guided by intelligent people, shall we remove these sores from our social life (Goddard, 1912, pp. 70–71).

Schaffer Photography

EUGENICS AND SCHOOLS

The research of Goddard and other eugenicists has been examined and found to be of questionable validity (Smith, 1985). The impact of the eugenics arguments was, however, great and resulted in the institutionalization and sterilization of thousands of people who were inaccurately identified as mentally retarded (Smith and Nelson, 1989). The influence of the eugenics movement was evident in the policies and practices of schools as well. The following comment was publicized in a circular published by the North Carolina Teachers Association and sent to all elementary school teachers in that state in 1912. The statement is stark in its call for the segregation of children with disabilities:

Fellow Teacher:

Rid your room of mental deficients. You owe it to the enormous majority of normal pupils. You owe it to the deficients who are entitled to special education. You owe it to the tax payers on whom these deficients, when adults, unless specially educated, will be a burden. Finally, you owe it to yourself. You can no more do your grade work properly with a deficient child in your room than you could do it were a blind or a deaf and dumb child put into it.

For the protection of your own professional character, take the action which we urge. We need not add that there is even a distinct personal award in the removal of a wholly unwarranted wear and tear upon your nerves (North Carolina State Archives, 1912).

MENTAL RETARDATION AND SEGREGATION

Phillip Ferguson has presented evidence in his book *Abandoned to Their Fate* that whether it was to segregated classes or to residential institutions, American culture has traditionally sought places to "abandon its failures." The "failures" he speaks of are those people who have been judged "unfixable." Through his study of mental retardation in the nineteenth and early twentieth century, he found that it is the judgment of "chronicity" that has the most profound impact on the lives of people with disabilities. To be judged "chronic" has meant to be socially abandoned. The judgment of chronicity is reached when, in Ferguson's own words, "badness becomes incorrigible, ugliness becomes inhuman, and uselessness becomes untrainable" (Ferguson, 1994, p. 16).

James Trent introduces his book, *Inventing the Feeble Mind,* by arguing that mental retardation has sometimes been defined in the name of science, other times in the name of care, and in other instances in the name of social control. These definitions, of course, have usually overlapped. Trent also finds three themes that are woven into the tapestry of mental retardation in American history. First, he finds that institutions (state schools) became places where the goals of care and control were commingled. Second, he argues that institutions shaped the meaning of retardation in ways that diminished resources, status, and power in the lives of the people with retardation. Finally, Trent finds that the economic vulnerability of people with mental retardation, more than their intellectual or adaptive limitations, has shaped the treatment they have been afforded in American society.

Trent argues that even the deinstitutionalization movement—he calls it the "abandonment of the institution"—came from an ironic convergence of the advocacy efforts of individuals and groups truly concerned with the best interests of people with mental retardation, and the efforts of state governments to reduce spending for institutional care. Trent's assessment of the impact of the depopulating of institutions and the placement of people with mental retardation in communities is dramatically stated in the last paragraph of his book.

> As they did in the 1840s, mentally retarded people who have money, supportive relatives, and understanding neighbors and employers do well in American communities. As they did in the 1840s, mentally retarded people who do not have those things, do not. For some, the community has become "the beloved community": for others, "the lonely crowd" (Trent, 1994, p. 268).

A NEW HOPEFULNESS

During the early 1960s, President John F. Kennedy called on the nation to launch a campaign to better address the needs of people classified as having mental retardation. In 1962 the Presidents' Panel on Mental Retardation issued a report that recommended the development of educational services to meet the needs of children with mental retardation. This report defined a national policy on mental retardation that marked a dramatic shift in the treatment of people with this disability.

Throughout the 1960s, funding for services for people with mental retardation increased. Growing awareness of the shortcomings of residential institutions created the beginnings of reform within those institutions (often referred to as *normalization*) and the movement of many people out of those institutions (deinstitutionalization). During this period there was also growth in the number of school programs for children with mental retardation. These programs continued to be completely voluntary for school systems but were encouraged by the availability of federal funds to support them.

MENTAL RETARDATION AND REFORM

It was largely during the 1970s, however, that the rights of people with mental retardation were recognized by courts and legislative bodies. In Washington, D.C., the decision in *Mills* v. *Board of Education* (1972) established that no child could be excluded from public education because of mental retardation or other disabilities. The ruling in *Pennsylvania Association for Retarded Children (PARC)* v. *Commonwealth of Pennsylvania* (1971) said that all children with mental retardation had a right to an education regardless of how severe the disability. These court actions, and others, laid the foundation for the enactment in 1975 of Public Law 94-142 (the Education of All Handicapped Children Act). As discussed in Chapter 1, this law provided for increased special education services so that all children with special needs would receive appropriate educational services, but it also called for the integration of children with special needs with other children through the principle of the *least restrictive environment.*

MENTAL RETARDATION AND PL 94-142: AN IRONY

The passage of PL 94-142 has been hailed as a landmark event in special education and in the overall movement to secure the rights of people with disabilities. This designation is well deserved. It is ironic, therefore, that since the enactment of that law there has actually been a decrease in the number of children with mental retardation receiving the benefits of its provisions. Between the school years 1976–77 and 1980–81 the number of students in mental retardation programs decreased nationally by 12.9 percent. This is particularly striking since these were the years that followed the passage of PL 94-142. Thus, this decline came in spite of the federal mandate to identify and serve more students with disabilities. This decline in the number of students with mental retardation being served in public schools has continued (Polloway and Smith, 1988).

One reason for the decreasing numbers of students with mental retardation in public school programs is that many children who would have been classified as mildly mentally retarded in the past are now diagnosed as having learning disabilities and are served on that basis. Other students are not classified as retarded because of professional and parental reluctance to use that term because of the stigma associated with it. Unfortunately, many of these children, although not classified, are also not given the services they need to succeed in school. Many end up in the ranks of children who are considered "slow learners" and are unfortunately not eligible for help on that basis. This trend has also contributed to the fact that the students who remain in special education classes for those with mild mental retardation tend to have more serious disabilities and greater needs than those who were in these classes twenty years ago (Polloway and Smith, 1988).

MENTAL RETARDATION AS A SOCIAL CONSTRUCT

The fact that changes in attitudes and policies can determine to such a large extent the numbers of people considered to have mental retardation illustrates the degree to which mental retardation is a social construct. As Sarason observed, "Mental retardation is never a thing or a characteristic of an individual, but rather a social invention stemming from time-bound societal values and ideology that make diagnosis and management seem both necessary and socially desirable" (Sarason, 1985, p. 233). Given the social meaning of the term *mental retardation* and its application to people with varied physical, social, and personal circumstances in their lives, it is important to review some of the causes of these circumstances.

The Characteristics and Needs of Students with Mental Retardation

MENTAL RETARDATION: THE ENVIRONMENT AS CAUSE

Nearly four hundred causes of mental retardation have been identified by the American Association on Mental Retardation (1992). These include genetic causes, factors during pregnancy, birth trauma, disease, and injury during childhood and adolescence. Most children with mental retardation are not, however, the victims of genetics, diseases, or accidents. Instead, they are more likely to be the victims of environments that harm or hinder their mental development, or they are children who come to school with environmental experiences that put them at a disadvantage in meeting the expectations they encounter as students.

Harold Skeels was a pioneer in research on the role of early social and psychological influences on intellectual development. In 1939 Skeels and Dye reported on research with very young children who had been placed in an orphanage and who had been found to have low intelligence test scores. These thirteen children had an average IQ of 64. They had been designated as being not suitable for adoption. These children were, however, transferred to an institution where each was assigned a surrogate mother. These surrogate mothers were themselves classified as retarded but were encouraged to give their full care and attention to their "adopted" children. They were given training in how to care for, talk to, and otherwise enrich the lives of these infants and toddlers. Two years later these children were tested again and showed an average IQ gain of 28 points. Eleven of them had scores high enough to make them eligible for adoption (Skeels and Dye, 1939).

More than twenty-five years later, Skeels did a follow-up study of these young people. He found that their average level of education was twelfth grade and that four had attended college. All of them were responsible adults. Their occupations ranged from being homemakers to having professional and business careers. Their incomes were consistent with national averages. Most of them were in apparently stable marriages (Skeels, 1966).

In the original 1939 study, Skeels tested a contrast group of children at the orphanage who were not transferred to the institution and did not, therefore, receive surrogate mothers. These twelve children were of comparable ages but had a higher average IQ of 86. After two years the initial follow-up of this group of children showed that they *dropped* an average of 26 IQ points. Skeels and Dye attributed this drop to the unstimulating environment of the orphanage. In his 1966 article, Skeels reported that these young people had an average educational attainment of third to fourth grade. The employment level of this group was very low, and four of them were in institutions (Skeels, 1966). Skeels concluded his follow-up report with the following statement:

> It seems obvious that under present-day conditions there are still countless infants with sound biological constitutions and potentialities for development well within the normal range who will become retarded and noncontributing members of society unless appropriate intervention occurs. It is suggested by the findings of this study and others published in the past 20 years that sufficient knowledge is available to design programs of intervention to counteract the devastating effects of poverty, sociocultural, and maternal deprivation (Skeels, 1966, pp. 54–55).

MENTAL RETARDATION AND THE SOCIAL ENVIRONMENT: A LEGACY CONTINUED

Unfortunately, Skeels' optimism concerning programs of intervention has not come to fruition in the lives of many children. Thirty years after his remarks, there are still children whose development becomes needlessly retarded because of environmental deprivation.

The risk of damage to children through a nonnuturing social environment is perhaps nowhere more evident than within the increasing numbers of homeless families. In his book, *Rachel and Her Children,* Jonathan Kozol (1988) describes the realities of homelessness through interviews he conducted with people he describes as "ordinary people" who have no homes. He portrays in stark terms the dimensions of this problem for children and their families:

> By the time these words are printed there will be almost 500,000 homeless children in America. If all of them were gathered in one city, they would represent a larger population than that of Atlanta, Denver, or St. Louis. Because they are scattered in a thousand cities, they are easily unseen. And because so many die in infancy or lose the strength to struggle and prevail in early years, some will never live to tell their stories.
>
> Not all homeless children will be lost to early death or taken from their parents by the state. Some of their parents will do better. . . . Some will be able to keep their children, their stability, their sense of worth. Some will get back their vanished dreams. A few will find jobs again and some may even find a home they can afford. Many will not (Kozol, 1988, p. 3).

Kozol has also examined the unequal educational opportunities that exist for children and adolescents in the poorest communities of our country and contrasts these with the wealth of educational resources and opportunities in the nation's most affluent communities. His book, *Savage Inequalities: Children in America's Schools* (1991), profiles specific schools and illustrates the differences in resources, talent, and support for students in rich and poor schools and school districts. In speaking of the odds against success for students in Chicago's South Side, Kozol states:

> In strictly pedagogic terms, the odds of failure for a student who starts out at Woodson Elementary School, and then continues at a nonselective high school, are approximately ten to one. The odds of learning math and reading on the street are probably as good or even better. The odds of finding a few moments of delight, or maybe even happiness, outside these dreary schools are better still. For many, many students at Chicago's nonselective high schools, it is hard to know if the decision to drop out of school, no matter how much we discourage it, is not, in fact, a logical decision (Kozol, 1991, p. 59).

Although most instances of mental retardation cannot be attributed to a physiological cause, it is important to understand the kinds of medical conditions that may result in this disability. While mental retardation has long been recognized as a condition that inordinately affects children who are placed at risk because of poverty or other social risk factors, some causes of retardation are found to touch the lives of children of all social and economic groups. While there are hundreds of different biological causes of mental retardation and a discussion of all of them would not be appropriate or helpful, it is important for educators to understand the kinds of factors that may result in mental retardation. The following categories and examples are provided as helpful ways of comprehending the complex nature of this disability.

GENETIC AND CHROMOSOMAL CAUSES

There are a number of forms of mental retardation that are caused by genetic factors. Phenylketonuria (PKU) is a condition caused by the inheritance of two recessive genes from parents who are carriers of the condition. Because the PKU gene results in the lack of production of an enzyme that processes proteins, there is a buildup of an acid called phenylpyruvic acid. This buildup causes brain damage. The damage can be prevented by early detection and the use of a special diet low in phenylalanine. Box 3.1 presents a history of the successful discovery of the cause and prevention of PKU.

Tay-Sachs disease is also caused by recessive genes inherited from parents who carry these genes. Unfortunately, however, no preventative measures have been discovered for the rapidly progressing brain damage that results from this condition. It leads to severe retardation, and the life expectancy of a child with Tay-Sachs is less than school age. The disease occurs almost exclusively among

BOX 3.1

PKU: The Process of Discovery of a Cause and the Prevention of Mental Retardation

- Understanding of PKU came in the 1930s.
  a. In 1934 a musty body odor in young children associated with their mental retardation was detected by Dr. Ivar Folling, a Norwegian physician.
  b. Dr. Folling found that phenylpyruvic acid caused the body odor.
  c. In 1937 Dr. Folling identified the disorder as phenylketonuria, a genetically caused metabolic dysfunction.
- Approximately one child in fifteen thousand is born with PKU.
- In 1953 Dr. Horst Bickel discovered that a diet low in phenylalanine could prevent or reduce retardation in children with PKU.
- In 1963 Dr. Robert Guthrie reported on a blood test that could detect PKU in newborns.
- State laws now require PKU screening of all newborns.

BOX 3.2

Down's Syndrome: The Social Meaning of an Extra Chromosome

- 1860s: J. Langdon Down describes the condition and calls it *mongolism*. The term *mongoloid* is derived from the association of the eye folds of people with Down's syndrome with the Asian races. The condition is thought by Down and others who viewed retardation from the perspective of social Darwinism to result from an evolutionary regression.
- 1920s–1950s: The best treatments for people with Down's syndrome were thought to be institutionalization and sterilization. Parents were often counseled by physicians to institutionalize infants to prevent family disruption.
- 1959: Jerome Lejeune discovers that Down's syndrome is caused by extra chromosomal material.
- 1960s and 1970s: Deinstitutionalization, normalization, the growth of special education services, and the changing civil rights atmosphere create reforms in the treatment of people with Down's syndrome.
- 1980s and 1990s: There is continuing growth in the recognition of the abilities and rights of people with Down's syndrome. At the same time, Down's syndrome infants have been at the center of controversy concerning "right to treatment" and "quality of life" issues.

children of Jewish parentage. People who are carriers of the gene can be identified through genetic screening, and the condition may also be detected through prenatal testing.

Down's syndrome is a form of mental retardation familiar to most people. It is caused by the presence of extra chromosomal material in the cells. The most common form is called Trisomy 21 because of an extra chromosome that is attached to the twenty-first chromosome pair. Two other forms of Down's syndrome also result from chromosomal material that moves from one location to another (translocation) and extra chromosomal material in only some cells (mosaicism). There are distinct physical characteristics associated with Down's syndrome that make it recognizable to so many people. These include folds in the corners of their eyes that J. Langdon Down described as appearing "Oriental" and led to their being described by the unfortunate term *mongoloid*. An historical outline of the understanding and treatment of people with Down's syndrome is contained in Box 3.2.

PRENATAL CAUSES

Genetic and chromosomal causes of mental retardation are present from the moment of conception. Prenatal causes, however, have their origins sometime after conception but before birth. The most damaging effects of rubella (German measles) on a fetus, for example, come during the first trimester of pregnancy when the developing brain is most vulnerable. Following the last large rubella epidemic in the United States in the late 1960s, thousands of children were born with mental retardation. Others were born with hearing disorders, vision problems, or damaged hearts. As immunization against rubella has become widespread, this form of mental retardation has decreased in occurrence.

While untreated syphilis and other venereal infections can also cause brain damage during pregnancy that results in retardation, a greater threat to healthy pregnancies comes from toxins that our society has not found the means for managing as successfully as problems like rubella and PKU. These are the toxins of alcohol and drugs.

Pregnant women who are heavy drinkers are at a marked risk for damaging their developing fetuses. Children with fetal alcohol syndrome are at increased risk for being born with a variety of problems including mental retardation. Drugs, even some prescription medications, can also cause fetal mental retardation when used by pregnant women. It is widely recognized that use of illegal drugs such as heroin and cocaine can have very detrimental effects on a developing fetus. It is becoming more known, as well, that smoking may result in premature and low-birth-weight babies (Hetherington and Parke, 1986). It is evident that the only drugs that should be considered safe for use during pregnancy are those prescribed by a physician who is familiar with the status of that pregnancy.

CAUSES AT BIRTH

The most common problem at the time of birth that may cause mental retardation is prematurity. Infants born very premature are at risk for a variety of physical difficulties that may be associated with damage to the brain. Many premature infants, however, eventually thrive and suffer no damage. The greater the prematurity, the greater the risk (since prematurity is usually gauged by birth weight, five pounds is often used as the point below which a baby is considered premature). Although fetal alcohol syndrome and the effects of other substances may cause low birth weight, prematurity may occur with even the healthiest of pregnancies.

Mental retardation may also result from problems during labor and delivery. One of these is breech presentation. If the infant is not in a head-down position for delivery, the birth process may be slowed and oxygen deprivation may occur. Caesarean deliveries are often used as a measure to avoid the risk of damage that otherwise accompanies delivery by breech presentation.

CAUSES DURING CHILDHOOD AND ADOLESCENT DEVELOPMENT

Mental retardation may occur at any point during childhood or adolescence. Illnesses such as meningitis or encephalitis, especially when not treated early and aggressively, may damage the brain. Accidents that cause injury to the brain can result in retardation as a disability during a child's development. Poor nutrition or poisoning can also damage the brain. Lead poisoning, especially, is a threat to children from a number of environmental sources, including old paint and water pipes.

As mentioned earlier in this chapter, there are hundreds of different causes of mental retardation delineated by the American Association on Mental Retardation. It is important to note that these causes are very diverse and that the only common factors in mental retardation tend to be the social and intellectual meanings assigned to this disability.

MENTAL RETARDATION: LABELS AND DEFINITIONS

People with mental retardation have been labeled in various ways over the centuries and decades. The words used to describe them have ranged from pejoratives such as *dumb* and *stupid* to words that were originally used for medical classification such as *idiot* (used to describe severe retardation) and *imbecile* (a term used for less severe retardation). Henry Goddard coined the term *moron* from a Greek word meaning "foolish." This label came to be widely applied during the first half of the twentieth century to people who were considered to be "high-grade defectives"—individuals who were characterized as not being retarded severely enough to be obvious to a casual observer and who had not been brain damaged by disease or injury. These were people whose retardation was considered to be hereditary (Smith, 1985). Generic terms like *feebleminded, mentally defective, mentally deficient,* and *mentally retarded* have often been used until the stigma associated with them became great. A new term was then created. A current trend, for example, is to use the term *developmental disability* rather than mental retardation.

As the provision of educational services for students with mental retardation expanded during the 1950s and 1960s, special educators increasingly used terms to describe their students according to educational classifications. These classifications were used to describe both the anticipated level of educational achievement of these students and the corresponding educational placements to which they were assigned. Students who were labeled *educable mentally retarded* were expected to be able to learn to read and write at the elementary school level but at a much slower pace. Students described as *trainable mentally retarded* were considered capable of learning only a few isolated words and very limited counting skills. They were considered capable of becoming semi-independent at best. Children and adults who were perceived to be unable to function at the trainable level were often referred to as *subtrainable* or *custodial*. They were thought of as being below a level that made them the responsibility of schools and educators.

Another classification system has been used more frequently by psychologists and physicians. *Mild mental retardation, moderate mental retardation, severe mental retardation,* and *profound mental retardation* have been used to classify people according to their performance on IQ tests. Although these classifications and the tests they are based on have been criticized for many years, they have remained in widespread use. This is primarily because of the efficiency of IQ tests and the structured system of categories that their scores provide. Although criticism has been countered by an increasing emphasis on the assessment of social, self-care, communication, and vocational skills and other adaptive behavior, IQ measures have continued to be dominant in the classification of mental retardation (Smith and Polloway, 1979).

In 1992 the American Association on Mental Retardation (AAMR) published a revision of its manual on the definition and classification of mental retardation. That revision focuses much more attention on the needs of people with mental retardation than on their deficits. The AAMR revision specifies four levels of need for support that may be required by people with mental retardation. These levels are *intermittent needs* that are episodic in nature and do not always require support, *limited needs* that are consistent over time but are limited in intensity, *extensive needs* that are long-term and serious, and *pervasive needs* that are constant and intense throughout life (Luckasson et al., 1992). The 1992 definitions place more emphasis on adaptive behavior as a measure of mental retardation and less emphasis on IQ. The definition describes ten categories of adaptive behavior ranging from communication skills, to social skills, to work skills. A criticism of the definitions, however, has been that they do not provide ways of measuring a person's abilities and needs in each of these adaptive behavior categories. Although there are some difficulties in implementing this conception of mental retardation in educational settings, it is a promising way of looking at what students with mental retardation need in order to be most successful in school and as independent in life as possible (Smith, 1994).

MENTAL RETARDATION: CHANGES IN NAMES AND NUMBERS

Revisions in the definition of mental retardation have been accompanied by changes in the numbers of people thought to have the condition. For decades the estimate of the number of people in the United States with mental retardation was approximately 3 percent. As the definition changed, however, the estimate decreased to approximately 1 percent of the population (Ramey and Finkelstein, 1981). In particular, the number of children identified as having mental retardation has decreased significantly. During the 1976–77 school year, approximately 820,000 students were classified as having mental retardation. In the 1993–94 school year, that number had dropped to less than 554,000 (Office of Special Education Programs, 1995). The decline in the number of students identified as having mild levels of retardation and the rise in the number of students identified as having learning disabilities have been associated with the overall reduction in the category of retardation (Baumeister, 1987; Forness and Polloway, 1987).

The decrease in the number of children identified as having mental retardation is complex, however, with a number of contributing factors. Polloway and Smith have examined these factors in detail. Among the most important reasons for the changes in the number of students considered to have mental retardation that they discuss are: 1) the impact of changes in the AAMR definition; 2) the effect of legislation challenging the use of IQ tests and increasing the caution that is necessary before identifying minority children as having mental retardation; 3) the positive effect of early childhood intervention programs; and 4) the increasing sensitivity of parents and school personnel to the stigma associated with retardation (Polloway and Smith, 1988).

Even with these changes in the ways that mental retardation is thought of and the greater care that is taken in identifying children as having this condition, much mental retardation is still associated with poverty. A study of identification patterns in one state, for example, indicates that while more severe forms of mental retardation are distributed across families of various socioeconomic backgrounds, mild retardation is inordinately associated with low socioeconomic status. In this study, some school districts almost exclusively categorized students with learning problems as mildly mentally retarded. Other districts categorized almost all of these children as learning disabled. The districts characterizing children as having mental retardation tended to have large numbers of families living in low socioeconomic conditions. They also had low tax revenues to support the schools and, therefore, lower expenditures for students (McDermott, 1994).

J. Berndt/Stock Boston

STUDENTS WITH MENTAL RETARDATION: THEIR NEEDS

Students with mental retardation have the potential to learn and develop in all areas of their lives. Most researchers have found that the developmental disabilities created by mental retardation cause people to learn at a slower rate but that they learn in basically the same ways as others. Some research, however, indicates that people with mental retardation, particularly those with more extensive disabilities, develop very differently in the cognitive, social, and even physical domains of their lives. They may have difficulties in school, in working, and in living in the community that require very special types of intervention.

Thus, some children and adults with mental retardation may need only the same basic services that all students need for educational development. What they require in addition is the understanding of their teachers and peers of the time and assistance they need to be successful in regular classrooms.

Other students with mental retardation will require very special services if they are to succeed educationally, socially, and vocationally. These services may include infant stimulation programs, early childhood special education services, physical therapy, occupational therapy, speech therapy, the teaching of self-care skills, instruction in functional academics (for example, learning to read the word *hot* or learning to recognize coins), and special preparation for employment and community living.

There are, however, some areas of common concern for all students with mental retardation that must be considered in planning for the most appropriate educational placement and program for each student.

Cognitive Abilities

One of the most important characteristics of students with mental retardation is, by definition, the way that they learn. There are basic considerations that teachers need to be aware of regardless of whether they are planning for a student with milder or more severe disabilities.

- *The Pace of Learning*: Students with mental retardation may need more time to learn the information that is acquired more readily by other students.
- *Levels of Learning*: Students with mental retardation may not be able to go as far as other students in some skills or subjects. It is important to remember, however, that they are capable of achieving mastery of information and skills at their own levels. They should be recognized and encouraged for doing so. It is also important to remember that students with mental retardation may excel in specific skills or abilities, and that the difficulties in learning that they experience may be experienced by any student.
- *Levels of Comprehension*: Students with mental retardation may have the greatest difficulty with learning material that is abstract. Teaching techniques that employ concrete materials and clear examples may be most effective in helping these students learn.

Research has indicated that the following factors may also interfere with the effective learning of students with mental retardation:

1. Students with mental retardation may have difficulty focusing their attention on a task for an extended period.
2. Students with mental retardation may have difficulty recognizing and focusing on the most important aspects of a task.
3. Students with mental retardation may have difficulty transferring and generalizing skills from one context to another.
4. Students with mental retardation may not easily acquire information that is incidental to the main point. They may miss the implied meaning of a story or lesson.
5. Students with mental retardation may forget information much more quickly than other students (Espin and Deno, 1988).

Language Abilities

Delayed language or difficulties with language often accompany mental retardation (Warren and Abbeduto, 1992). It appears that people with mental retardation develop language according to the same pattern as others. The difference is in the rate of development and the level of development achieved. It is important for teachers to recognize that language development is slower for these students and may be the source of much of their academic difficulties.

Language difficulties may cause a student's abilities to be misunderstood and underestimated. Kernan and Sabsy (1993), for example, found that students with mental retardation can produce stories that have the same structure as those of students without disabilities. Given the proper context and orientation, these students crafted stories that demonstrated a degree of creativity and sensitivity that would not have otherwise been recognized.

Social Abilities

Very important arguments have been made that mental retardation is primarily a social disability. This perspective emphasizes that the inability to assume social roles in the family, school, and community is much more disabling to an individual across a life span than is the inability to master certain academic skills (Greenspan and Granfield, 1992).

When social interactions between adults with mental retardation are observed, four concerns emerge that demonstrate the impact of this disability. In these interactions, the following needs become evident:

1. The need to belong.
2. The need to find refuge from negative attitudes and labels.
3. The need for social support and comfort.
4. The need to escape boredom and find social stimulation (Turner, 1983).

These social needs speak directly to the importance of encouraging positive social interactions among students with mental retardation and their nondisabled peers. They speak to the need for inclusive school environments for these young people.

It is also important to recognize that students with mental retardation may also bring personal and social assets to an inclusive classroom that add to the quality of the learning environment. Wolfensberger (1988) has identified a number of strengths that people with mental retardation may bring to their relationships with others. These positive attributes include:

- A natural and positive spontaneity.
- A tendency to respond to others generously and warmly.
- A tendency to respond honestly to others.
- The capacity to call forth gentleness, patience, and tolerance from others.
- A tendency to be trusting of others.

Ways of Helping Students with Mental Retardation Succeed in Inclusive Schools

MENTAL RETARDATION: THE CURRENT STATUS

The issue of inclusive classrooms is very important for students with mental retardation. More than any other group of students with disabilities, they continue to be excluded from regular classrooms. During the 1993–94 school year, there were more than half a million students with mental retardation in school programs. Only 7.1 percent of these students, however, were being served in regular classrooms. Almost 57 percent of these students were served in separate classrooms, and more than 9 percent were placed in even more restrictive settings. Table 3.1 provides more detail on the educational placement of students with mental retardation.

TABLE 3.1

Students with Mental Retardation in School Year 1993–94: Number and Placement Percentages

Number	553,992
Resource Room	26.8%
Separate Class	56.8%
Separate School	7.9%
Residential Facility	0.9%
Homebound/Hospital Setting	0.5%

Source: Office of Special Education Programs. *Seventeenth Annual Report to Congress on the Implementation of the Individuals with Disabilities Education Act.* Washington, DC: U.S. Department of Education, 1995, pp. 11, 17.

TABLE 3.2

Students with Mental Retardation in School Year 1992–93: Basis for Leaving School

	Number	Percent
Received Diploma	14,088	36.1
Certificate (no high school diploma awarded)	10,797	27.7
Reached Maximum Age for Attendance	2,359	6.0
Dropped Out	7,650	19.6
Status Unknown	4,099	10.5

Note: Percentages do not total 100 percent because of rounding.
Source: Office of Special Education Programs. *Sixteenth Annual Report to Congress on the Implementation of the Individuals with Disabilities Education Act.* Washington, DC: U.S. Department of Education, 1994, p. 19.

Information on the conditions under which students with mental retardation leave school also points to the need for more inclusive schools for these students. Only 36 percent of these students left school in 1992–93 with a diploma. Almost 20 percent dropped out of school before graduating. A significant number were unaccounted for and may have also dropped out. These facts, and the other information presented in Table 3.2, point to the necessity of meeting the needs of these students in a more appropriate manner.

In 1992 the ARC (formerly known as the Association for Retarded Citizens), a national advocacy organization originally formed by parents of children with mental retardation, issued a report that criticized a majority of the states for their poor practices in inclusive schooling. The report referenced documentation of the benefits of inclusion for students with disabilities as well as their nondisabled peers. The documentation included the following points:

- Students with disabilities meet a greater number of their Individualized Educational Program (IEP) goals when they are placed in inclusive settings.
- Students with disabilities are more motivated to learn in inclusive settings.
- Inclusive classrooms provide better access to peer models for the facilitation of learning appropriate social behaviors.
- In inclusive settings, students with disabilities encounter the real expectations and diversity of society.
- Graduates from inclusive schools are more successful as adults.

- More friendships between classmates with and without disabilities develop in inclusive settings.
- Students without disabilities learn to appreciate and accept individual differences.
- Students without disabilities learn to appreciate the abilities and strengths of their classmates with disabilities (Davis, 1992).

The ARC reported that during the 1989–90 school year fewer than 7 percent of students with mental retardation received their education in regular classrooms and that fewer than 30 percent of these students had any regular interactions at all with nondisabled peers. The report also showed that only two states educated more than 50 percent of their students with mental retardation in regular classrooms, two others educated between 26 and 50 percent in regular classrooms, and four additional states served between 10 and 25 percent of students with mental retardation in regular classrooms. All of the remaining states served fewer than 10 percent of these students in regular classrooms.

As a result of these findings, the ARC's report card assigned a grade to each state. No "A"s or "B"s were awarded. Two states earned a "C," and there were six "D"s. All of the other states received an "F" (Davis, 1992).

An update of the ARC report card pointed out that in the 1991–92 school year even fewer students with mental retardation were being educated in regular classrooms (5.1 percent). The update emphasized the need for administrative support for the implementation of inclusive classrooms. It also stressed the importance of providing the preparation for teachers that is necessary to make truly inclusive classrooms a reality (Davis, 1992). In its 1995 report, the ARC continued to criticize the unsuccessful efforts being made to place students with mental retardation in more inclusive school environments (LRP, 1995).

EFFECTIVE TEACHERS FOR STUDENTS WITH MENTAL RETARDATION

It has long been recognized that "good teaching" cuts across subjects or grade levels. The principles of good teaching are basically the same regardless of the content being taught or the students who are being taught. Good teachers tend to be people who think of themselves as teachers of students, not as specialists focusing entirely on one subject or a particular grade level.

Many people who have studied the question of inclusive schools feel that what children with disabilities need most for success in regular classrooms is simply good teaching. "Good" teachers who have had a chance to learn some basic information about disabilities and who have been made aware of the fact that they have much to offer children with special needs are the foundation for successful inclusion of students with mental retardation.

Wong, Kauffman, and Lloyd (1991) have characterized the behaviors and attitudes of effective teachers of students with disabilities in regular classrooms. Their list of attributes includes the following:

1. The expectation that children will succeed.
2. Frequent monitoring of student work and frequent feedback.
3. Clarity of standards, directions, and expectations.
4. Flexibility in working with students.
5. A commitment to treat each student fairly.

6. Responsiveness to student questions and comments.
7. Warmth, patience, and humor with students.
8. A highly structured approach to teaching.
9. Firmness and consistency in behavior expectations.
10. Having a variety of behavior management approaches.
11. An open and positive attitude toward diversity and differences in children and adults.
12. A willingness to work with special education teachers and a responsiveness to help from others.
13. A sense of confidence and competence as a teacher.
14. A high sense of professional involvement and professional satisfaction (Wong, Kauffman, and Lloyd, 1991, pp. 108–115).

Larrivee (1985) has also identified teacher characteristics and classroom conditions that lead to the effective inclusion of students with disabilities. These are important considerations for the placement of students with mental retardation in regular classrooms. The following guidelines are based on Larrivee's observations:

CLASSROOM MANAGEMENT AND DISCIPLINE

- The teacher and students make efficient use of time.
- Students seldom have to wait for help.
- Students spend very little time off task.
- Students do not spend much time making transitions from one activity to another.

Therefore:

- There is not much need for discipline.
- The teacher seldom uses punishment.
- Other special interventions to manage behavior are rarely needed.

FEEDBACK DURING INSTRUCTION

- The teacher provides frequent positive feedback to students for appropriate behavior and achievement.
- The teacher helps students find the correct answer when an incorrect answer is given.

Therefore:

- The teacher avoids negative feedback to students, and avoids criticism of students and their work.

DEVELOPMENTALLY APPROPRIATE INSTRUCTION

- The teacher assigns tasks of an appropriate level of difficulty for each student.
- Students can perform each task with a low error rate.

Therefore:

- Students give a high rate of correct responses to tasks and teacher questions.
- The teacher and students interact very positively in relation to learning tasks.

A SUPPORTIVE LEARNING ENVIRONMENT

- The teacher uses supportive rather than judgmental interventions.
- The teacher responds with care and understanding to students with lower abilities.

- The teacher becomes more supportive when students have a learning problem.

Therefore:

- Students trust the teacher and are willing to ask for help.
- Students' confidence in their ability to learn is increased.
- The rate and quality of student learning is enhanced.

PREPARING STUDENTS FOR THE TRANSITION FROM SCHOOL TO WORK AND COMMUNITY LIVING

In 1987 the National Longitudinal Transition Study of Special Education Students (NLTS) was initiated under the auspices of the Office of Special Education Programs of the U.S. Department of Education. This research was deemed critical by the Department of Education because of reports from some states and localities that the graduation rates of students with disabilities were low. Various reports had also indicated that the subsequent employment rates and wage levels of these students were low. The NLTS focused on four postschool factors:

- Participation in postsecondary education.
- Employment.
- Residential arrangements.
- Community participation.

POSTSECONDARY EDUCATION

The study found that young adults with disabilities were less likely to participate in postsecondary education than other young adults. NLTS data indicate that "among youth with disabilities out of secondary school up to three years, 16.5 percent enrolled in academic postsecondary programs, and 14.7 percent in vocational postsecondary programs" (Office of Special Education Programs, 1995, p. 77). Young people with mental retardation were the least likely of those with disabilities to enroll in postsecondary programs: Only 2.5 percent enrolled in postsecondary academic programs, and only 5.7 percent enrolled in postsecondary vocational programs (Office of Special Education Programs, 1995). The study found that students with disabilities who had been in more inclusive high school programs were more likely to enroll in postsecondary programs. Over 70 percent of these students who enrolled in postsecondary academic programs had spent at least 75 percent of their high school program in general classrooms. Over 53 percent of these students who enrolled in postsecondary vocational programs had been in general high school classrooms at least 75 percent of the time.

EMPLOYMENT

The NLTS found that there were several variables that influence successful employment of young people with disabilities after they leave school. These variables are:

1. Time in General Education: Students who had spent more time in general education courses in high school were more likely to be employed and to earn higher salaries than students who had taken fewer general education courses.
2. Work Experience During High School: Paid work experience during high school increased the likelihood of employment after high school for students with disabilities. This seems to be a result of the work-related skills developed in real work situations.

Bob Kramer/The Picture Cube

3. Vocational Education During High School: Vocational training during high school contributed significantly to the probability that students with disabilities would be competitively employed.

RESIDENTIAL ARRANGEMENTS

The NLTS found that 28 percent of youth with disabilities three years or less out of high school were living independently. Only 15 percent, however, of those students with mental retardation were living independently. Two-thirds of the young adults with disabilities living independently had been in general education classes 75 percent or more of their time in high school. Only 9 percent of these students had been in general education classes 25 percent or less of their high school time (Office of Special Education Programs, 1995).

COMMUNITY PARTICIPATION

The NLTS developed a composite measure of adult independence that profiled social activities, employment status, residential arrangement, and participation in postsecondary education. This composite was used as an indication of the social engagement or social isolation of young adults with disabilities. The study found that those students who had spent 75 percent or more of their high school time in general education settings were much more likely to be socially engaged in their communities. The opposite was true of those who had spent 25 percent or less of their time in high school in general classrooms.

ENHANCING INCLUSIVE LEARNING ENVIRONMENTS FOR STUDENTS WITH MENTAL RETARDATION

Children and adults with mental retardation need the same opportunities and environments for development that are needed by all people. As indicated earlier in this chapter, when the needed opportunities for learning are offered to students with special needs in general classrooms, the outcomes are most positive. The debate between excellence and equity has been described by some observers as a false dichotomy. Skirtic (1991) argues that "successful schools" are founded on the values, expectations, and actions of people who work to make those schools both excellent and equitable for their students. He observes that such schools are effective and adaptable places that encourage the educators who work in them to be problem solvers. This chapter has outlined some of the qualities and skills teachers need in order to be problem solvers of this kind. There are also principles and practices that must characterize schools as institutions if teachers are to be able to teach inclusively in them. Inclusive schools for children with mental retardation must be committed to:

- Providing every student with mental retardation a "home" in a regular classroom even if some of those students must be served for substantial periods each day outside of that classroom. Every student must spend enough time each day in a general classroom to consider that classroom a "home."
- Meeting the needs of students with mental retardation as a responsibility of the total school and not as the sole responsibility of special education or special teachers.
- Providing education programs for all children that are individualized and organizing teaching as a team effort.

LRE OR MEE?

One criticism of the least restrictive environment (LRE) approach to determining the most appropriate educational placement for students with disabilities has been the claim that it has resulted in students being required to demonstrate that they *deserve* acceptance into a general classroom. Kunc (1992) has argued that the LRE approach has meant that many students with disabilities never *earn* the *right* to be *included* in the life of a class or school. As a result, they are never considered "normal" enough to belong with other students. In commenting on the movement toward more inclusive schools, Kunc states:

> As a collective commitment to educate *all* children takes hold and "typical" students realize that "those kids" do belong in their schools and classes, typical students will benefit by learning that their own membership in the class and society is something that has to do with human rights rather than academic or physical ability (Kunc, 1992, p. 39).

Kunc believes that it is possible that this commitment may liberate all students of inclusive schools from the tyranny of thinking that they must earn the right to belong. He argues that, in this sense, students with disabilities may guide us to the overall creation of more positive school environments.

An alternative concept to LRE has been offered by Witkin and Fox (1992). They argue that although LRE has been an important criterion for assessing the appropriateness of school placement for students with disabilities, it has also been used to justify continued and unnecessary segregation in some cases. They observe that a separate structure of schooling has been maintained for some students with disabilities. This appears to be the fact for many students with mental retardation.

Witkin and Fox suggest that a new term and concept be adopted to replace *least restrictive environment.* They think that a commitment to the *most enabling environment* (MEE) shifts the focus from the student's qualifications to those measures that are necessary to make the learning environment of the inclusive classroom more facilitative of each student's development regardless of disabilities. The MEE begins with the idea of an optimal school environment that honors individual rights and is committed to the achievement of the most positive learning outcomes for each student. Witkin and Fox believe that the concept of MEE will allow "schools to function as a unitary educational system for all children . . . rather than a dual system of 'regular' and 'special education'" (Witkin and Fox, 1992, p. 332).

BRICKS AND MORTAR: THE CONSTRUCTION OF A CHANGE FOR STUDENTS WITH MENTAL RETARDATION

There are suggestions throughout this text that may have applicability to the education of individual students with mental retardation. For students with milder disabilities, for example, some of the ideas presented in the chapter on learning disabilities may be relevant. For students with more severe disabilities, some of the suggestions in the chapters on physical disabilities and communication disorders may be useful.

Regardless of the level of disability, however, students with mental retardation deserve an education that is as inclusive as possible given their individual needs. Thousand and Villa believe that the *bricks* and *mortar* of inclusive schooling are available and should be put to use. The *bricks* for building more inclusive educational environments are: 1) peer tutoring and children learning through partnerships, 2) collaborative and cooperative learning, 3) teaching by teams, and 4) mentoring and professional support among educators. The *mortar,* they believe, is the creation of a climate of truly shared responsibility for all students in schools and in communities (Thousand and Villa, 1991).

Case Studies and Questions to Consider

PUPILS: MARK AND MATTHEW RUSS

SCHOOL: DUNN MIDDLE

CURRENT PLACEMENT: SELF-CONTAINED CLASSROOM—EDUCABLE MENTALLY DISABLED

AGES: 11 YEARS, 7 MONTHS

Family Structure and Home Environment

Mark and Matthew live with their parents, Ross and Sherry Russ. Mr. Russ is forty-four years old and is temporarily employed as an equipment operator with the Dunn City Department of Sanitation. Ms. Russ is forty-one and is a homemaker. The twins also live with their two older brothers and an older sister. Ross Jr. is twenty years old and is unemployed. Jacob is eighteen and is currently working as a dishwasher. Their sister, Joy, is fifteen and is a student at Dunn High School. All of the Russ children either have been or currently are enrolled in special education classes.

The Russ family lives in a very small house for a family of seven. Their home is modest but appears to be cared for and respected by the whole family.

Parental Perception of the Child's Developmental Progress and Needs

Mr. and Ms. Russ feel that neither Matthew nor Mark is making much progress in basic academic skills. Their observation is that the twins are still unable to read and write for any practical purposes. Neither of the parents can read. Both say they never had the opportunity to learn to read when they were "growing up in the country and working on the farm." They are less concerned about reading, however, than they are about the speech of their sons. They feel that this is their sons' major problem area. They mentioned that other children make fun of Matthew's and Mark's speech and that they are hurt by this teasing. Mr. and Ms. Russ feel that Matthew's and Mark's social development is significantly behind that of other children their age. Again, speech is the focus of concern. Mr. Russ says that he would like to see Matthew and Mark be able to "talk better."

Additional Comments

Mr. and Ms. Russ have only one long-range goal for their twin boys, that they grow up to be "able to work." They are willing to do all that they are able to do to help their sons.

Questions

1. Put yourself in the special education teacher's place. Do you think the twins could benefit from a more inclusive educational environment?

2. Do you think Mr. and Ms. Russ could do anything more to help Matthew and Mark with their speech problems?
3. What do you think the faculty of Dunn Middle School could do to promote acceptance and tolerance of these boys among the middle school population?

STUDENT: LANIEL SWEET

SCHOOL: PROJECT INFANT

CURRENT PLACEMENT: PRESCHOOL SPECIAL EDUCATION—HOME-BASED

AGE: 2 YEARS, 2 MONTHS

Family Structure and Home Environment

For the past two years, Laniel and her mother, Gail Sweet, have been receiving services from Project Infant, an early intervention program. Laniel was born with Cornelia de Lange Syndrome. The developmental implications of this condition are such that Laniel requires an array of educational and therapeutic services to optimize her physical, psychological, and social growth. Ms. Sweet feels that Laniel's best interests would be served at this time by involvement next year in Project Toddler, an early childhood special education program. Ms. Sweet, who is thirty-three years old, is a single parent. For the past two years, Ms. Sweet has not worked outside her home. She remarked that she had felt the need to devote herself entirely to Laniel's development. Ms. Sweet completed the ninth grade in school. She subsequently earned a GED certificate. She has also taken courses at National Business College and Eastern Community College. She hopes to return to Eastern next year.

Laniel and her mother live in a five-room apartment. Their home is pleasant and well kept. Ms. Sweet is obviously proud of the efforts she is making on Laniel's behalf. She has collected extensive material on Cornelia de Lange Syndrome. She remarked that she would be glad to share this information with the staff of Project Toddler who might not be familiar with this rare disorder. She also explained that for a while she and Laniel were visited by a social worker from Child Protective Services. She commented with satisfaction that she had now been "closed out" because the social worker felt things were going so well.

Parental Perception of the Student's School Program

Ms. Sweet is pleased with the progress Laniel has made during the past two years. She speaks with gratitude of the help her daughter has received at Project Infant. Tears came to her eyes when she mentioned Laniel's last day in the program. She mentioned that a recent assessment indicated that Laniel's greatest area of strength is "self-help skills." This obviously pleased her very much.

Ms. Sweet expressed the hope that Laniel will be placed in Project Toddler, a five-day-a-week, center-based program. She feels that the extensive help her daughter needs can be best delivered in such a program.

Additional Comments

Ms. Sweet is a committed advocate and helper for her daughter. She communicates a willingness to grow in any way that would in turn promote growth in Laniel. She feels very strongly that Project Toddler is the appropriate placement for Laniel for next year.

The staff of Project Infant, the home-based program of services that Laniel and Ms. Sweet have been receiving for the last two years, agrees that the most appropriate next step in Laniel's education should be Project Toddler.

Questions

1. Look up Cornelia de Lange Syndrome in a medical or mental retardation reference book. What are the most important educational implications of the syndrome?
2. If Laniel is placed in Project Toddler for three years, what measures can be taken to provide her with exposure to and experiences with children who do not have disabilities?
3. What kinds of services might be appropriate to support Ms. Sweet's own development and her commitment to Laniel?

References

American Association on Mental Retardation. *Mental Retardation: Definition, Classification, and Systems of Support*, 9th ed. Washington, DC: American Association on Mental Retardation, 1992.

Baumeister, A. "Mental Retardation: Some Conceptions and Dilemmas." *American Psychologist, 42,* 1987: 796–800.

Davis, S. *Report Card to the Nation on Inclusion: An Update.* Arlington, TX: ARC, 1992.

Espin, C. A., and S. L. Deno. "Characteristics of Individuals with Mental Retardation." In P. J. Schloss, C. A. Hughes, and M. A. Smith (Eds.), *Mental Retardation: Community Transition.* Boston: College-Hill, 1988: 35–55.

Ferguson, P. *Abandoned to Their Fate: Social Policy and Practice Toward Severely Retarded People in America, 1820–1920.* Philadelphia: Temple University Press, 1994.

Forness, S. R., and E. A. Polloway. "Physical and Psychiatric Diagnoses of Pupils with Mild Mental Retardation Currently Being Referred for Related Services." *Education and Training in Mental Retardation, 24,* 1987: 7–16.

Goddard, H. H. *The Kallikak Family: A Study in the Heredity of Feeble-Mindedness.* New York: Macmillan, 1912.

Greenspan, S., and J. M. Granfield. "Reconsidering the Construct of Mental Retardation: Implications of a Model of Social Competence." *American Journal on Mental Retardation, 96,* 1992: 442–453.

Hetherington, E. M., and R. D. Parke. *Child Psychology: A Contemporary Viewpoint,* 3d ed. New York: McGraw-Hill, 1986.

Itard, J. M. G. *The Wild Boy of Aveyron.* G. Humphrey and M. Humphrey, Trans. Englewood Cliffs, NJ: Prentice-Hall, 1962. (Orig. pub. 1894.)

Kanner, L. *The History of the Care and Study of the Mentally Retarded.* Springfield, IL: Charles C. Thomas, 1964.

Kernan, K. T., and S. Sabsy. "Discourse and Conversational Skills of Mentally Retarded Adults." In A. M. Bauer (Ed.), *Children Who Challenge the System.* Boston: Ablex, 1993: 145–184.

Kozol, J. *Rachel and Her Children: Homeless Families in America.* New York: Crown, 1988.

———. *Savage Inequalities: Children in America's Schools.* New York: Crown, 1991.

Kunc, N. "The Need to Belong: Rediscovering Maslow's Hierarchy of Needs." In R. Villa, J. Thousand, W. Stainback, and S. Stainback (Eds.), *Restructuring for Caring and Effective Education: An Administrative Guide to Creating Heterogeneous Schools.* Baltimore, MD: Brooks, 1992: 25–39.

Lane, H. *The Wild Boy of Aveyron.* Cambridge, MA: Harvard University Press, 1976.

Larrivee, B. *Effective Teaching for Successful Mainstreaming.* New York: Longman, 1985.

LRP. "Little Progress Made in Including Students with MR, the ARC Says." *Inclusive Education Programs, 2,* 1995: 3.

Luckasson, R., D. L. Coulter, E. A. Polloway, S. Reiss, L. L. Schalock, M. E. Snell, D. M. Spitalnik, and J. A. Stark. *Mental Retardation: Definition, Classification, and Systems of Supports.* Washington, DC: American Association on Mental Retardation, 1992.

McDermott, S. "Explanatory Model to Describe School District Prevalence Rates for Mental Retardation and Learning Disabilities." *American Journal on Mental Retardation, 99,* 1994: 175–185.

Mills v. Board of Education, Civil Action No. 1939-71 (U.S. District Court of the District of Columbia, 1972).

North Carolina State Archives. Department of Public Instruction. Office of the Superintendent, 1912–1917. Correspondence, 1912. Cited in J. W. Trent, *Inventing the Feeble Mind: A History of Mental Retardation in the United States.* Berkeley, CA: University of California Press, 1994.

Office of Special Education Programs. *Sixteenth Annual Report to Congress on the Implementation of the Individuals with Disabilities Education Act.* Washington, DC: U.S. Department of Education, 1994: 19.

———. *Seventeenth Annual Report to Congress on the Implementation of the Individuals with Disabilities Education Act.* Washington, DC: U.S. Department of Education, 1995: 11, 17.

Pennsylvania Association for Retarded Children v. Commonwealth of Pennsylvania, Civil Action No. 71-42, 3-Judge Court (E. D. Pennsylvania, 1971).

Polloway, E. A., and J. D. Smith. "Current Status of the Mild Mental Retardation Construct: Identification, Placement, and Programs." In M. Wang, M. Reynolds, and H. Walberg (Eds.), *The Handbook of Special Education: Research and Practice.* Oxford, England: Pergamon Press, 1988: 1–22.

Ramey, C. T., and N. W. Finkelstein. "Psychosocial Mental Retardation: A Biological and Social Coalescence." In M. J. Begab, H. C. Haywood, and H. L. Garber (Eds.), *Psychosocial Influences in Retarded Performance: Issues and Theories in Development,* Vol. 1. Baltimore, MD: University Park Press, 1981: 65–92.

Sarason, S. *Psychology and Mental Retardation: Perspectives in Change.* Austin, TX: Pro-Ed, 1985.

Scheerenberger, R. C. *A History of Mental Retardation.* Baltimore, MD: Paul H. Brookes, 1983.

Shattuck, R. *The Forbidden Experiment.* New York: Farrar Straus, 1980.

Skeels, H. "Adult Status of Children with Contrasting Early Life Experiences: A Follow-Up Study." *Monographs of the Society for Research in Child Development, 31* (Serial No. 105), 1966.

Skeels, H., and H. Dye. "A Study of the Effects of Differential Stimulation on Mentally Retarded Children." *Journal of Psycho-Asthenics, 44,* 1939: 114–136.

Skirtic, J. M. "The Special Education Paradox: Equity as the Way to Excellence." *Harvard Educational Review, 61,* 1991: 148–206.

Smith, J. D. *Minds Made Feeble: The Myth and Legacy of the Kallikaks.* Rockville, MD: Aspen, 1985.

———. "The Revised AAMR Definition of Mental Retardation: The MRDD Position." *Education and Training in Mental Retardation and Developmental Disabilities, 29,* 1994: 179–183.

Smith, J. D., and K. Nelson. *The Sterilization of Carrie Buck.* Far Hills, NJ: New Horizon Press, 1989.

Smith, J. D., and E. A. Polloway. "The Dimension of Adaptive Behavior in Mental Retardation Research: An Analysis of Recent Practices." *American Journal of Mental Deficiency, 84,* 1979: 203–206.

Thousand, J., and R. Villa. "A Futuristic View of the REI: A Response to Jenkens, Pious, and Jewell." *Exceptional Children, 57,* 1991: 556–562.

Trent, J. W. *Inventing the Feeble Mind: A History of Mental Retardation in the United States.* Berkeley, CA: University of California Press, 1994.

Turner, J. L. "Workshop Society: Ethnographic Observations in a Work Setting for Retarded Adults." In K. T. Kernan, M. J. Begab, and R. B. Edgerton (Eds.), *Environments and Behavior: The Adaptation of Mentally Retarded Persons.* Baltimore, MD: University Park Press, 1983: 147–171.

Warren, S. F., and L. Abbeduto. "The Relation of Communication and Language Development to Mental Retardation." *American Journal of Mental Retardation, 97,* 1992: 125–130.

Witkin, S., and L. Fox. "Beyond the Least Restrictive Environment." In R. Villa, J. Thousand, W. Stainback, and S. Stainback (Eds.), *Restructuring for Caring and Effective Education: An Administrative Guide to Creating Heterogeneous Schools.* Baltimore, MD: Brooks, 1992: 325–334.

Wolfensberger, W. "Common Assets of Mentally Retarded People That Are Commonly Not Acknowledged." *Mental Retardation, 26,* 1988: 63–70.

Wong, K. L. H., J. M. Kauffman, and J. W. Lloyd. "Choices for Integration: Selecting Teachers for Mainstreamed Students with Emotional or Behavioral Disorders." *Intervention in School and Clinic, 27,* 1991: 108–115.

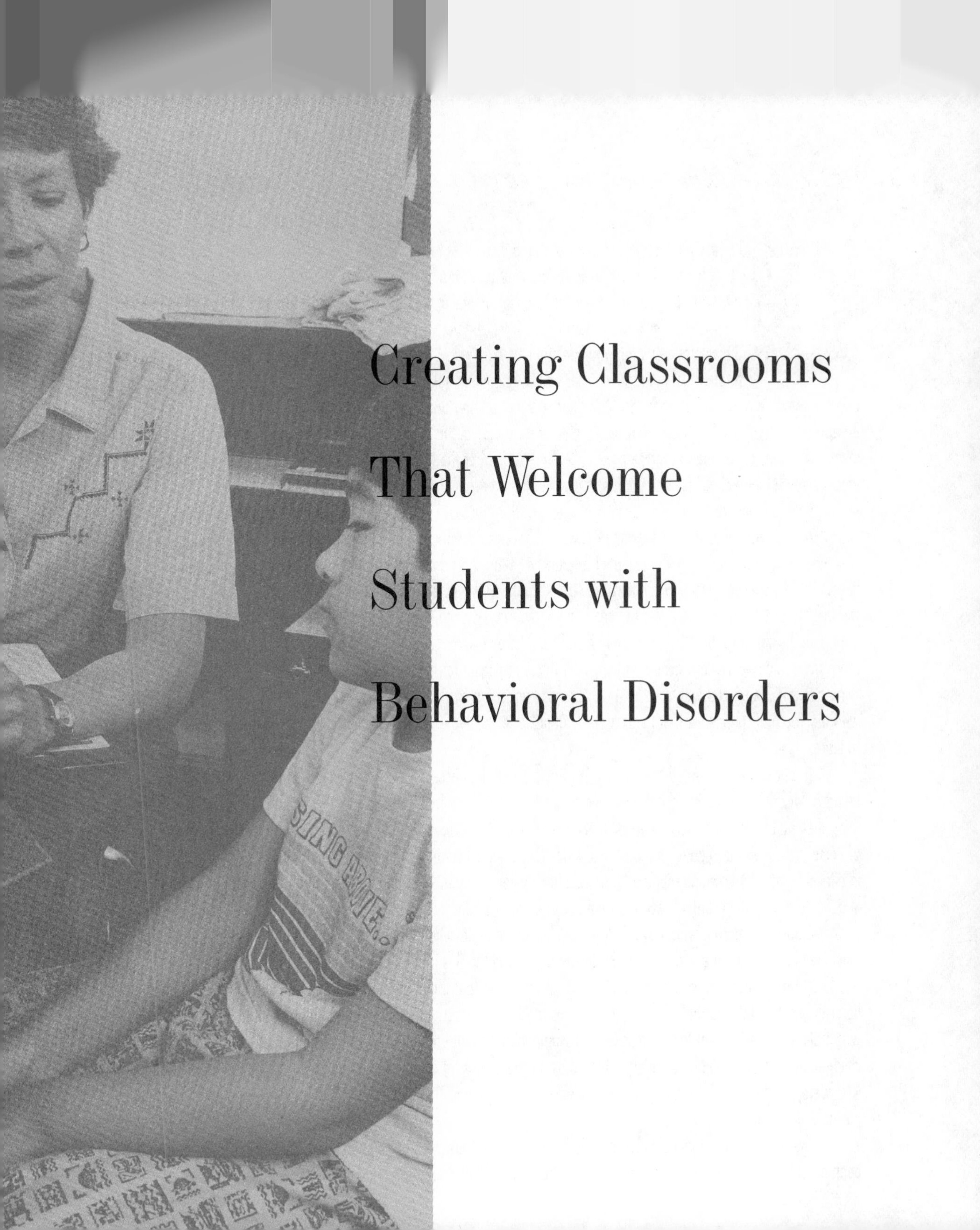

Creating Classrooms That Welcome Students with Behavioral Disorders

Mike and the Clown Faces: Learning to Love, Loving to Learn

The first year in the classroom is memorable for most teachers. For some new educators, it can be a year of such painful memories in the making that a career has ended before June. For others, it is a year that provides war stories and lessons in survival upon which is built a lifetime of continued learning.

Frankly, my first year of teaching came as the result of avoidance. I was in graduate school, draft deferments for graduate students had ended, and I was seeking a way of serving other than through the military. In other words, and again quite frankly, I did not want to be drafted. I had been asked to work in a rehabilitation facility. The director wrote a letter on my behalf, but my draft board would not grant a deferment on that basis. I made a personal appearance to appeal this decision. The appeal was unsuccessful, but the lawyer who was appointed to represent me called me aside after the hearing and suggested that I could be deferred for work with children with disabilities, that is, if I could find a teaching job. Deferments were still being granted for teachers in critical need areas, and special education was one of those areas. I immediately began my search for a position.

My first day of seeking a teaching job was illusively successful. I went to the school system's personnel office and was greeted with enthusiasm. The receptionist glanced at the short application form I had filled out. It indicated that I was interested in a special education position. She asked that I wait for just a moment. When she returned, she told me that the Director of Personnel would like to interview me right away. Within twenty minutes he had offered me a job and was urging me to sign a contract before leaving his office. There was an opening for a teacher of children with "emotional problems," and he was convinced that I was just the right person for the position. I asked to have a little more time to think about it. He agreed and said that I could come back the next day with my decision. I will admit that I left his office with the youthful confidence that I was a pretty impressive candidate. I had been offered a job on the spot! I had a lot to learn.

The next day I accepted the position. I completed all the necessary paperwork, and was told when and where to report before the opening of school. I learned that my class was made up of all boys. They varied in age, and the only thing they had in common was the label *serious emotional disturbance*. In fact, once I had signed the contract, the Director of Personnel called these boys "the dead-end kids." They had all been expelled from their schools. Most of them had been in difficulty with the law, and many of them had been given up by their families to foster care. I would be teaching them in a "special education center," which turned out to be an old house with four other classes of "dead-end kids."

During the teacher work days, before the children came to school, it became obvious to me why the Director of Personnel had greeted me with such enthusiasm and offered me this job on the spot. The veteran teachers of the "dead-end kids" bombarded me with horror stories and informed me that the class I would have had been through two teachers before Christmas the year before. My qualifications for the job, it became obvious, were my naïveté, and the fact that I was male and over six feet tall. I suppose the assumption was that I might have a better chance of controlling these children because I was likely to be larger than most of them. This, of course, was a bad assumption. These were children who were, for the most part, unintimidated by size, age, or gender. They had become experts at finding ways of winning power struggles of all kinds.

The first day of school came too quickly for me. I knew that I was not prepared to deal with the boys who had been described to me. Even though there were to be only eight of them, and I had a full-time teaching assistant, I knew that I was unprepared to meet the educational needs of the students. I had even begun to doubt my ability to survive as their teacher. I was a psychology major in college, and I did graduate work in clinical psychology. This background was helpful to me as I read the case histories of the boys. Nevertheless, I had no idea of where to begin as their teacher. The records showed that they ranged in age from seven to fifteen. There were both nonreaders and excellent readers in the group, and their levels of skill did not necessarily correspond to their ages. Some of the older boys had weaker academic skills than the younger ones.

I tried to prepare for them as best as I could. My few teacher work days before the opening of school, however, were not enough to allow me to make up for my lack of training. It was not enough time for me to be ready to teach the skills that the boys needed to develop in academics. It was not enough time to devise a strategy for helping them develop the sense of self and the social skills that they would need to have a chance to be something other than "dead-end kids." I used the time I had to do what I could to make the environment of the classroom (actually two converted bedrooms) as orderly and attractive as possible.

I cleaned the desks and arranged the rest of the furniture in the larger of the two rooms into what I thought was a pleasant configuration. I moved some of the extra desks and what appeared to be leftover supplies into the room next door. The director of the center had told me that I could use the room as I saw fit. It was as large as my classroom and was the perfect place for stashing everything I wanted to get out of the way. I envisioned, even then, that it might also become a place for "cooling down," either for the boys or for myself.

I had excellent help in getting the room ready. In fact, my most encouraging discovery after reporting for work was that my teaching assistant was a person of calm confidence. She had just graduated from college as an art major. Although she shared my inexperience and lack of training as a teacher, she was filled with optimism about what we would be able to accomplish with the children we were about to meet. She had lots of ideas for decorating the room for the opening of school and ways that we could make each boy's desk personally welcoming. Soon we had filled the walls with her creations and stocked each boy's desk with paper and other supplies. Each desk had a laminated nameplate across the front. After a week of preparation and planning, the teaching assistant, Miss Bowyer, and I were as ready as we were going to be to meet our students.

On Monday morning, the first boy to arrive was Mike. He was very early. His mother brought him on her way to work and dropped him off about twenty minutes before any of the other children arrived. This pattern would persist throughout the school year. Mike would also persist in calling me "Smith." Although I introduced us to Mike as Mr. Smith and Miss Bowyer, I would be "Smith" for the rest of the year not only to Mike but to the other boys, who soon picked up on this name for me. Miss Bowyer would be referred to by her complete name.

As soon as Mike entered the room, the atmosphere changed. Mike was in constant motion and seemed to create energy even in inanimate objects. Everything he touched, and that seemed to be everything, was energized. I directed Mike to his desk and showed him the supplies we had placed there for him. He immediately asked if he could draw a picture on one of the large pieces of drawing paper.

The picture that Mike drew was of a clown. It was drawn quickly and with movements that were mechanical. It appeared that Mike had drawn this picture before. The clown face consisted of a large circle with semicircles for ears, smaller circles for eyes, a round nose, and a crescent mouth. A bowler hat with a broad brim topped it.

When Mike finished the clown, he asked if he could use another piece of paper from his desk. He changed the color of the marker he used, but the image was the same. He drew the clown again in exactly the same sequence of parts. First, he drew the round head, then the ears, then the eyes, nose, and mouth. He finished with the bowler hat and immediately asked to use yet another piece of paper.

Before the other boys arrived, Mike produced a stack of clown faces that he placed in a neat pile on his desk. As the other students came, and Miss Bowyer and I were greeting them, Mike requested and was given more drawing paper. He produced even more clown faces.

The next few weeks were some of the most difficult of my life. I came home at the end of each day with an amalgam of negative feelings. The boys exhausted me; I felt absolutely ineffectual as their teacher, and I disliked them and myself. I doubted that I could make it to Thanksgiving. Christmas, I was certain, was an impossible goal.

The boys became increasingly disruptive and aggressive as the weeks went by. The language that they used was truly creative in its vulgarity. The academic progress that we could make with them was practically nil. Each boy had developed his own way of avoiding the failure that he had come to associate with schoolwork. Some would explode with anger when they were unable to do their work. Others would become clowns in an attempt to show that they really did not care if they could not do the work. Mike simply drew his clowns. Regardless of the task that I gave him or the material I put before him, he ended up drawing the same clown face with exactly the same sequence of movements of his marker. It never varied. I came to understand that it was the one thing he knew he could do well, and he drew the face as a comforting compulsion to avoid the pain of not being able to read, write, or do math.

I reached a point of absolute desperation in my work with the boys, and I finally sought help. I literally put myself in the doorway of a professor's office at the university where I had previously studied, pleading for assistance. He was a professor of special education, and one of my former psychology professors had recommended him as a possible source of ideas for bringing some order and rationality to what I was doing as a teacher. This man allowed me in, listened to my plight, and, most importantly, gave me several simple guidelines to think about. He also gave me a book that proved to be very helpful.

The pieces of advice were these: First, in all academic subject areas, take each student back to the point where he can show mastery of a skill. Sometimes this meant taking an older student back to letter or number recognition before proceeding with any further reading or math instruction at all. This, of course, had to be accomplished in a way that allowed the student to preserve his dignity; he could not feel that you were giving him "baby work." Second, proceed with instruction in small steps—small enough, in fact, that you can be sure that the student will be successful. Students who have been hurt by failure must come to trust that you will not give them work that they cannot do. They must know that you are a teacher who will not let them fail. Third, you must make their successes dramatically obvious to them. Their success must be concretely and vividly displayed to them. Their victories must be immediately and enthusiastically acknowledged.

The book that the professor gave me was helpful to me in rethinking the use of the space that we had. As a result of reading it, Miss Bowyer and I moved all of the desks into the room that we had been using for storage. We placed the desks along the walls, and we built cardboard partitions between them. We thereby gave the boys "offices" for doing the work that we thereafter completely individualized. In their offices, the boys did the reading, language arts, and math that most of them had experienced failure with previously. In the privacy of their offices, however, Miss Bowyer and I were able to follow the professor's advice. We took each boy back to the level where success was a certainty, and we moved ahead in increments that also ensured success. The work and office schedule of each boy was personalized and private. There was no stigma of "baby work" associated with what was done in the offices. Miss Bowyer and I moved from office to office as "consultants" helping each boy individually.

Our larger classroom became a group activity area. We started and ended each day there as a class. We also used it for social studies, art, and other activities that the boys could share regardless of their level of academic ability. Daily, we posted schedules in this room so that when the boys arrived in the morning each could check for any variations in his daily routine. There were few variations, however; the boys liked the certainty of their schedules.

We also began a simple token economic system that allowed the boys to earn extra free time, pencils, drawing paper, and markers through points they earned for the focused work time in their offices and the successful completion of assignments. In addition, we made sure that we used traditional ways of recognizing good work. Papers were graded immediately upon completion and were marked with number grades, letter grades, and comments.

Mike responded very well to our new system of rewards. At first, as might be expected, he used the points he earned to buy drawing paper and markers. These were used in turn for the production of lots of clown faces. At least, however, he was now doing his work in order to have the satisfaction and comfort of the familiar drawings. After a while, however, Miss Bowyer and I noticed a diminishing interest in paper and markers on Mike's part. We also noticed that he was producing far fewer of the clown drawings that he had taken home earlier in the year in stacks. He seemed instead to be more interested in taking home the math and reading papers that we carefully graded in bold markers with "100," "A," and "Good Work." We shared Mike's gratification of having these papers now going home in stacks with him.

I do not mean to give the impression that suddenly everything was perfect in our class. There were still arguments and blowups. There were still harsh expressions of frustration. Yet, as we became better organized in our learning environment and schedules, and as the boys experienced greater success academically, their behavior improved. They became children who were more pleasant to be with. They had more positive attitudes toward themselves and about their abilities to learn. Miss Bowyer and I also felt a change in the ways the boys behaved toward us. They were clearly happy to see us each morning, and even the "toughest" showed signs of affection for us on occasion.

One December morning, I gave the boys some exciting news. The afternoon before, I had been told as I was leaving school that a civic group would be coming the next morning to give a party for the children. We would gather in the lunchroom (a converted area in the basement of the building) at 10:30 for ice cream, candy, and gifts. When we gathered for our morning group meeting, I told the boys about the party. Most were excited about the news. Mike, however, protested immediately that he could not go to the party. When I asked why, he said, "Smith, you know I have math to do at 10:30. I will be in my office then." When I explained that today was special and that we were changing the usual morning schedule, he protested even more loudly, "Smith, I'm not going to the damn party till I finish my math."

At 10:30 Miss Bowyer took the other boys to the party. Mike stayed in his office, I brought him his math assignment, and he worked diligently on it for fifteen minutes. When he was finished, I congratulated him and suggested that we join the others at the party. He agreed, but said, "Smith, you forgot something." I looked down and realized that he was waiting for me to grade his work. I reviewed it and marked it "100," "A," "Good Work." Mike smiled, filed his work away, and said, "Now, Smith, we can go to that party."

On our way down the hall, Mike explained why following his schedule was so important to him. "Smith," he said more openly than I had ever heard him speak before, "My mama loves the papers I bring home. She hugs me and tells me I'm getting smarter all the time. She saves my papers. She says you and Miss Bowyer are good teachers. I think so too. My uncle teaches good too. He taught me how to draw clowns, but I like math better now."

Learning to love to learn; I think often of Mike and the others. I am grateful for all that I learned from them on my journey to becoming a teacher. I'm glad they helped me take the first few steps.

Behavioral Disorders: Ways of Viewing Students and Their "Disturbing" Behavior

THE "RISK" OF BEHAVIORAL DISORDERS

In the field of special education, and in education in general, the term *at risk* is used frequently to describe students who are vulnerable for developing a particular problem or disability. It is not unusual to hear educators in early childhood settings, for example, describe certain children as being "at risk" for the development of school difficulties. Educators in secondary settings may view some students as being "at risk" for school dropout. Medical professionals use the term to diagnose "at risk" pregnancies that may lead to the birth of a child with a developmental disability.

Richard Whelan has asked the question: "What is the risk of developing an emotional disturbance? Is it one out of 100, one out of 20, one out of 10?" (Whelan, 1995, p. 273). In answering his own question, Whelan comes to the conclusion that the risk of becoming a person with an emotional disturbance is much higher than any of these ratios would suggest. He believes that the risk is one out of one. His reason for placing this risk figure on the chance of developing an emotional disturbance is simple. If external and internal stresses become great enough for any individual, that person's ability to cope will become impaired. If stresses become extreme, a person's behavior may, in turn, become extreme or desperate. If stresses become unbearable, they will shatter the person. The hope that Whelan offers in these instances, however, is that people who are impaired or shattered may be restored by changes in their environments and with the help of others (Whelan, 1995).

SHAFFER PHOTOGRAPHY

THE ECOLOGY OF EMOTIONS AND BEHAVIOR

Central to the question of why certain persons are thought to have emotional or behavioral disorders is the fact that people respond to different types and degrees of stress in their lives in diverse and often unexpected ways. A seemingly small amount of stress may trigger a major reaction in some people. What appears to be overwhelming stress may be borne, or at least appear to be, by another person with little noticeable effect.

Whelan also points out that it is not always a person's overt response to stress that leads to the characterization of that person as having an emotional or behavioral disorder. Although behavior *excess* may cause a person difficulty, so too may a *deficit* in behavior (Whelan, 1979). For example, a child who does not do the appropriate or expected things may be viewed as having just as serious a problem as a child who engages in excessively strong reactions to people and events in her/his life.

William Rhodes was an early proponent of an ecological understanding of the meaning of behavioral disorder. In a classic statement, he described emotional and behavioral disturbances as being as much or more a product of the cultural, community, and family environment in which the person exists as a production of that individual (Rhodes, 1967). Cultural anthropologists have long recognized that normal behavior in one culture may, in fact, be considered abnormal in another. On the other hand, people who have been identified as abnormal in their own culture may find acceptance in a different one. Even within a culture, the definitions of normal and abnormal behavior are constantly shifting with time and vary in different subcultural settings. Behavior that was unacceptable twenty-five years ago may be considered a sign of sophistication today. Behavior that would be condemned in one social group based on age or social class might be the key to admiration in another age or social group.

DEFINING BEHAVIORAL DISORDERS

As with many other disabilities (for example, mental retardation and learning disabilities), controversy continues over the definition of behavioral/emotional disorders. Most fundamental to this controversy is the term to be used. The term ***emotionally disturbed*** is often preferred by those concerned about the internal psychological factors that lead to disordered behavior. The term ***behavioral disorder*** is most often preferred by those who think it is more important to describe and modify the overt behaviors that are the real problems rather than searching for underlying psychological causes. Proponents of this term tend to de-emphasize the internal, psychodynamic aspects of this disability.

Going beyond the term to a definition of the term is equally controversial. All children engage at times in behaviors that might be considered disturbed or disordered if they come to the attention of people in a position to pass judgment on them. These behaviors may go unnoticed, however, or they may not be considered problematic unless they are performed too often, too intensely, or in the wrong place. These judgments, of course, involve a great deal of subjectivity. It is also difficult to develop a means for fairly assessing whether a person's behavior is sufficiently characterized by abnormally intense, excessively repeated, or contextually inappropriate actions. The potential harm of inaccurate labeling in a person's life obviously requires that great caution be exercised in developing a definition of behavioral disorders.

When Public Law 94-142 was passed, the term *serious emotional disturbance* (SED) was adopted for this category of disability. It was selected, at least in part, because it emphasized that emotional disturbances are a normal part of everyone's experience. In order for a student to be categorized as having a disability in her or his life, there must be evidence that there is a *serious emotional disturbance*. This wording continues to be used in the federal definition. SED, as it is defined for the Individuals with Disabilities Education Act (IDEA), says of serious emotional disturbance:

(i) The term means a condition exhibiting one or more of the following characteristics over a long period of time and to a marked degree, that adversely affects educational performance:

(A) An inability to learn that cannot be explained by intellectual, sensory, or health factors;

(B) An inability to build or maintain satisfactory interpersonal relationships with peers and teachers;

(C) Inappropriate types of behavior or feelings under normal circumstances;

(D) A general pervasive mood of unhappiness or depression; or
(E) A tendency to develop physical symptoms or fears associated with personal or school problems.

(ii) The term includes schizophrenia. The term does not apply to children who are socially maladjusted, unless it is determined that they have a serious disturbance (U.S. Department of Education, 1993).

Thus, the definition used for the purposes of IDEA, in describing the meaning of serious emotional disturbance, includes the factors of A) educational needs, B) interpersonal needs, C) and D) behavioral and emotional needs, and E) school-related physical needs and personal problems.

Critics of the federal definition have long pointed out shortcomings of this way of defining emotional disabilities. A primary complaint has been that it places too heavy an emphasis on academic performance in subject areas instead of looking at the broader meaning of school performance. The term *serious emotional disturbance* has also lost favor among professional organizations (Forness, 1992). The Council for Children with Behavioral Disorders (CCBD) has joined with other professional groups in proposing a new definition. It reads:

(i) The term *emotional* or *behavioral disorder* means a disability characterized by behavioral or emotional responses in school programs so different from appropriate age, culture, or ethnic norms that they adversely affect educational performance. Educational performance includes academic, social, vocational, or personal skills. Such a disability is more than a temporary expected response to stressful events in the environment; is consistently exhibited in two different settings, at least one of which is school-related; and is unresponsive to direct intervention applied in the general education setting, or the child's condition is such that general education intervention would be sufficient.
(ii) Emotional or behavioral disorders can co-exist with other disabilities.
(iii) This category may include children or youth with schizophrenic disorders, affective disorders, anxiety disorders, or other sustained disorders of conduct or adjustment when they adversely affect educational performance in accordance with section (i) (Forness and Knitzer, 1992).

Hallahan and Kauffman (1994) have pointed out that this proposed change in the definition of behavioral and emotional disorders is desirable for several reasons, including the following:

- It recognizes that the category includes students with both emotional and behavioral disorders.
- It recognizes that emotional and behavioral disorders may exist separately or may interact in the life of a student.
- It recognizes the importance of cultural and ethnic diversity in the defining of behavioral or emotional disorders.
- It recognizes that students may have multiple disabilities.

Thus far, however, the proponents of this alternative definition have been unsuccessful in convincing the U.S. Congress to adopt it for use in IDEA.

THE SEARCH FOR CAUSES

Human behavior is so complex that it is almost impossible to isolate a simple cause-

and-effect relationship for emotional or behavioral disturbances. Some physical or environmental factors may increase the likelihood of a problem developing. A hereditary *predisposition* for depression may, for example, increase the probability that a person may have problems with depression. This may not occur, however, if the individual does not encounter the life events that could *precipitate* the depression. Predisposing and precipitating factors may be important in the development of positive characteristics as well. A child may have strengths that predispose her/him to high academic achievement. If that child is not provided with the necessary opportunities and encouragement to nurture that achievement, it may not become a reality in that child's life.

The predisposing and precipitating causes of emotional disturbance may include the interaction of genetics, disease, injury, family relationships, community forces, school influences, and many other factors. One way of categorizing these causes is according to whether these factors appear to be primarily *physiological* or *social/interpersonal* in nature.

The *physiological* factors that may cause emotional and behavioral difficulties for an individual include neurological problems, problems with body chemistry and metabolism, and certain hereditary predispositions. Alcohol and drug abuse are also important physiological influences in many emotional and behavioral disturbances. Obviously, these physiological factors may interact with each other, and with the personal and cultural features of a person's life, to create an intricate network of influences that result in the individual's emotional experience and behavioral repertoire.

The *social* and *interpersonal* forces that may cause or contribute to the development of emotional and behavioral disorders include the family environment, the interaction that a student has with teachers and peers at school, and the influence of the community on children and adolescents. The relationship between child abuse and the development of disabilities has also been well established (Zirpoli, 1986). Both the positive and negative consequences of teacher and peer relationships in school for emotional and behavioral development are thoroughly documented as well (Ormond, 1995).

Kotlowitz (1991), in *There Are No Children Here,* portrays in stark terms the impact that poverty and community disintegration may have on the development of children. This book provides a shocking account of the lives of two young boys growing up in a public housing project in Chicago. The boys face daily the physical and psychological dangers of a predatory environment. Kotlowitz derived the title of his book from a comment made by the mother of the boys when she was asked to describe what life was like for children living in an environment of poverty, crime, drugs, explicit sexual behavior, and violence. Her response was, "Mister, there are no children here." Kotlowitz was moved and disheartened by the attitudes of children in the projects about their hopes for the future. He found that these children, who had seen playmates killed by gang members, drug dealers, and the police, spoke of their plans tentatively in terms of "if I grow up" rather than "when I grow up." The psychological toll and behavioral consequences of community disintegration are a growing source of emotional disorders.

TYPES OF PROBLEMS

Although there are a number of classification systems used to categorize people with emotional and behavioral problems, these systems

Bob Daemmrich/The Image Works

have very limited value in educational settings. A psychiatric diagnosis applied to a student's difficulties, for example, may have little relevance for the educational needs of that student. A more helpful approach to understanding the needs of these students has been found in focusing on the categories or dimensions of behavior that have the greatest implications for the understanding of a student's behavior in a classroom.

Quay (1986) has developed a helpful conceptualization of the problems that students with behavioral and emotional disabilities encounter. According to this conceptualization, the two categories of disordered behavior are the *externalizing* and the *internalizing* dimensions. The externalizing dimension encompasses behavior that is directed toward other people, including aggressive and hostile actions. The internalizing dimension involves emotions that are turned inward and behavior directed toward the self. Depression and a poor concept of self are examples of internalized emotional conflict. Some behaviors have both internal and external components. A child, for example, may have a poor self-concept accompanied by anxiety and self-doubt. The same child, however, may also strike out against other people with hostile language and aggressive acts.

Quay and Peterson (1987) describe six classes of behavior that may involve either external or internal dimensions:

- *Conduct Disorder*: Highly disruptive, extreme attention- seeking behavior, tantrums.
- *Socialized Aggression*: Marked rejection of general and social values, acceptance of values and rules of a peer group (for instance, a gang or subculture), delinquency, truancy, drug abuse.
- *Anxiety/Withdrawal*: Extreme self-consciousness, generalized fearfulness, high anxiety, extreme depression, overly sensitive, and easily embarrassed.
- *Attention Problems/Immaturity*: Extremely short attention span, poor concentration, high distractibility, impulsivity.
- *Motor Excess*: Restless, unable to relax, high level of tension, extremely talkative.
- *Psychotic Behavior*: Expresses strange ideas, engages in repetitive and nonsensical speech, exhibits bizarre behavior.

The first five of the classes identified by Quay and Peterson include behavior or emotions that may be considered developmentally normal when expressed within expected limits. Behavior becomes problematic when it requires further designation as *extremely*, *highly*, or *overly*. Aggression, anxiety, and restlessness, for example, are all behaviors that are expected in every child. The difference lies in the degree of the behavior, how long it lasts, how often it occurs, or where it occurs.

This relativism does not apply to the final class of behavior in the Quay and Peterson list. Psychotic behavior is clearly different from the behavior observed in most children. Children with psychoses (often referred to as *pervasive developmental disorders*) are strikingly different in the quality of their behaviors. The description of these children as "living in their own world" illustrates the separateness and baffling nature of their behavior.

Autism

A condition called *autism* was formerly included under the category *seriously emotionally disturbed*. In the 1990 revisions that created IDEA, a separate category for autism was added. This addition resulted, in part, because the disorder is so clearly different in etiology and characteristics from other disorders included in the seriously emotionally disturbed category.

Autism is a neurological disorder that often results in disabilities in communication and social interaction. It is three times more common in boys than in girls. Although it is considered to be a physiological, not a psychological, disorder, the specific cause is unknown in most cases.

Children with autism often exhibit the characteristics of the disorder beginning in infancy. Some of these characteristics are:

- unresponsiveness to other people,
- repetitive movements such as rocking, spinning, and hand twisting,
- avoidance of eye contact with others,
- insistence on routines,
- bizarre and ritualistic behaviors (National Information Center for Children and Youth with Disabilities, 1993).

United Artists Pictures, Inc./Motion Picture & TV Archives

Any of these characteristics may, of course, be observed in children who do not have autism. It is when these characteristics are pervasive and chronic that they may be manifestations of autism.

The Characteristics and Needs of Students with Behavioral Disorders

Students with emotional and behavioral disorders are at very high risk for failure in school. They make lower grades than other groups of students with disabilities. They fail more often and pass required competency tests less frequently than other students with disabilities (Office of Special Education Programs, 1994). Students with emotional and behavioral disorders have an average high school GPA of 1.7, compared with an average of 2.6 for all students. Of those taking minimum competency tests, 63 percent failed at least some part (Wagner et al., 1991).

As illustrated in Table 4.1, only 19.6 percent of students with emotional and behavioral disabilities were in regular class placements during the 1992–93 school year. A total of 53.7 percent of these students were placed in separate classrooms or even more restrictive settings.

Table 4.2 illustrates that the dropout rate for students with emotional and behavioral disabilities is high and the graduation rate is low. During the 1991–92 school year, for example, only 28.1 percent of these students leaving school received a high school diploma. At least 35 percent of these students dropped out, and another 29.4 percent left school and were listed as "status unknown."

TABLE 4.1

Students with Serious Emotional Disturbance in School Year 1992–93: Number and Placement Percentages

Number	401,659
Regular Class	19.6%
Resource Room	26.7%
Separate Class	35.2%
Separate School	13.7%
Residential Facility	3.5%
Homebound/Hospital Setting	1.3%

Source: Office of Special Education Programs. *Seventeenth Annual Report to Congress on the Implementation of the Individuals with Disabilities Education Act.* Washington, DC: U.S. Department of Education, 1995, pp. 11, 17.

TABLE 4.2

Students with Serious Emotional Disturbance in School Year 1991–92: Basis for Leaving School

	Number	Percent
Received Diploma	9,557	28.1
Certificate (no high school diploma awarded)	2,217	6.5
Reached Maximum Age for Attendance	338	1.0
Dropped Out	11,894	35.0
Status Unknown	9,995	29.4

Source: Office of Special Education Programs. *Sixteenth Annual Report to Congress on the Implementation of the Individuals with Disabilities Education Act.* Washington, DC: U.S. Department of Education, 1994, p. 19.

THE DEMOGRAPHICS OF EMOTIONAL AND BEHAVIORAL DISORDERS

Demographic studies of students with emotional and behavioral disabilities have repeatedly shown that this category of disability is disproportionately male. Marder and Cox (1991), for example, found that 76.4 percent of students identified as having these disabilities were male. This appears to confirm an earlier study that found that educators are more likely to perceive boys as more "disturbing" than girls. Boys are, therefore, more likely to be identified as emotionally disturbed (Kelly, Bullock, and Dyes, 1977).

Students of African-American heritage are also more likely to be identified as having serious emotional disturbance (SED). Marder and Cox (1991) reported that 25 percent of all students with SED were African-American.

According to the Office of Civil Rights, however, African-American students represent only 16 percent of the student population as a whole (Office of Civil Rights, 1993). In an earlier study, Kelly, Bullock, and Dyes (1977) found that teachers were more likely to perceive and identify African-American students as having emotional disturbances. Prieto and Zucker (1981) found that Hispanic students were also disproportionately identified as having emotional and behavioral disabilities.

Students with emotional and behavioral disabilities are disproportionately from lower socioeconomic groups (Frazier and DeBlassie, 1984). This finding agrees with the report by Marder and Cox (1991) that, when the socioeconomic backgrounds of all students with disabilities are examined, 68 percent live in homes with total annual incomes of less than $25,000.

Age may be an important factor in determining the kind of educational placements students with behavioral and emotional disabilities receive. Younger students tend to be placed in inclusive settings. Older students with more externalizing characteristics tend to be placed in restrictive settings (Glassbery, 1994).

The number of students with emotional and behavioral disabilities in regular schools has actually decreased by approximately 4 percent since the 1977–78 school year (Office of Special Education Programs, 1993). This decrease may be the result of the increasingly complex needs of these students, the increasing demand for school resources to meet other needs, or both. Whatever the source of the problem, Kauffman and Lloyd (1992) have argued that it is the inadequacy of public school programs that provide effectively designed interventions that leads to more restrictive placements for these students.

THEORETICAL APPROACHES TO THE NEEDS OF STUDENTS WITH EMOTIONAL AND BEHAVIORAL DISORDERS

The theoretical approach taken in attempting to meet the needs of students with emotional and behavioral disabilities does much to determine whether a student is viewed as a part of the life of a regular classroom. Some approaches do not lend themselves to classroom use. Others involve techniques that teachers can use and that may, in fact, be best implemented in a classroom environment. In considering these approaches and their applicability in schools, the observation of James Kauffman, a leader in the field of special education for students with emotional and behavioral disorders, is important: "The focus of the special educator's concern should be on those contributing factors [to the emotional or behavioral disability] that can be altered by the teacher" (Kauffman, 1977, p. 263). An overview of these approaches and their applicability to classrooms may be helpful in illuminating which are relevant to the teacher's focus on altering the factors that contribute to the student's disability.

The Biomedical Approach

This approach attempts to explain and treat emotional and behavioral disabilities from the perspective of the field of medicine. It emphasizes biochemical imbalances, neurological abnormalities, and neurological injuries as the causes of these disabilities. The intervention strategies emphasized in this approach are the use of medication and other medical interventions.

Although the intervention in this approach is largely medical, there is a role for the teacher. It may be important for the teacher to be aware of and understand the

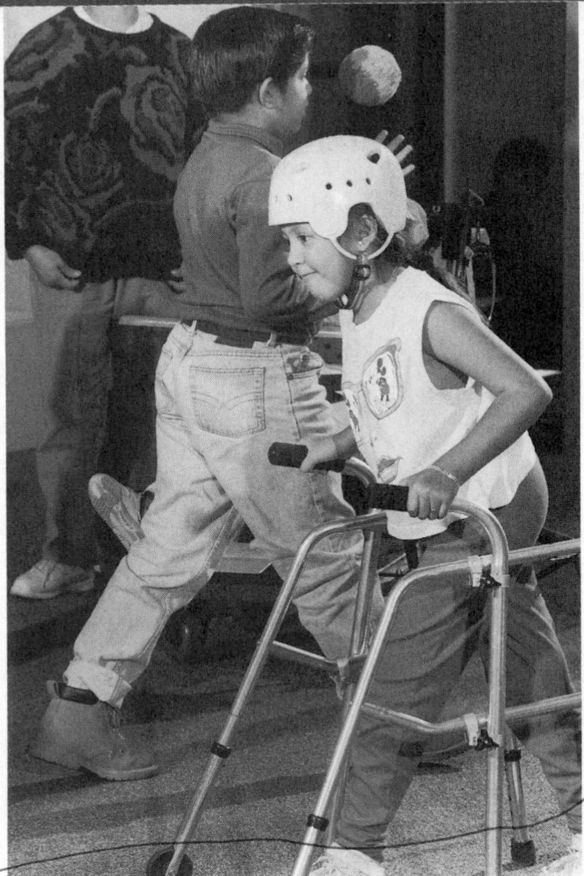

Spencer Grant/The Picture Cube

medical treatment a student is receiving. This may be an important part of the overall program of help that a student needs. The teacher may need to help the student and parents to regulate medication. The teacher may also help with monitoring and recording behavior changes following medical interventions.

The Psychodynamic Approach

This approach emphasizes the internal psychological life of the student. Those who attempt to help this person understand and resolve these difficulties focus on the underlying causes of the disability. Insight into one's own internal life is assumed to be the work of the person with the emotional disability. The helper in this process may be a psychiatrist, psychologist, counselor, social worker, or other professional. Teachers may also be part of a therapeutic team that uses a psychodynamic approach. There are many variations of the psychodynamic approach, and the teacher may be more or less involved in a student's therapy depending on the particular variation employed.

There may be limitations to the amount of individual counseling a teacher can do because of time constraints, other classroom demands, or lack of training. It is important to realize, however, that the relationships that teachers establish with students with emotional and behavioral disabilities are often, in themselves, therapeutic. Teachers who are trusted by students may be central to the process of positive change in the lives of those students.

The Behavioral Approach

This approach focuses on observable behavior. Rather than trying to understand the underlying causes of behavior, it attempts to make changes in the behaviors that are socially and personally problematic for the student. The central goal of this approach is to eliminate problem behaviors and replace them with behaviors that are more socially appropriate and, therefore, more personally satisfying. This is accomplished primarily by the reinforcement of appropriate behaviors and the withholding of reinforcement for inappropriate behaviors.

There is a large and important role for the teacher in this approach. Teachers spend more time with students than any other professional. In some cases they may spend more time with children than the children's parents do. Teachers are also more likely to encounter the full range of a student's behavior in the social context of the classroom than professionals working with students in a more isolated and removed setting.

Behavior-modification techniques and programs have become common in all kinds of classrooms. Their applicability and potential for effective "alteration" by teachers are particularly important in choosing ways to work with students with emotional and behavioral disabilities.

The Educational Approach

Educators have long pointed out that emotional and behavioral disabilities are almost always intricately intertwined with problems in learning. It is rare to find a student with these disabilities who is doing very well academically. Students who are upset and unhappy rarely escape the educational deficits that come with being unable to focus and organize for learning.

On the other hand, educational interventions that help students succeed academically are likely to have an impact on the emotional life and behavior of these students as well. Well-organized instructional programs with clearly articulated expectations can be central to a student's school success. That success can be central, in turn, to a student's progress in overcoming an emotional or behavioral disability. Good classrooms can truly be therapeutic environments.

The Ecological Approach

This approach emphasizes the interaction of factors and forces in the total community of a student's life. Emotional and behavioral disabilities do not exist in only certain sectors of a student's life. They arise in and have an impact on every facet of a student's life. Problems at home interact with problems at school. The influence of peers and the environment of the community is felt in both the family and the classroom. The ecological approach emphasizes the necessity of understanding students within the total context of their lives. It also emphasizes that helping students with these disabilities must come through the collaborative efforts of families, schools, peers, and communities.

Ways of Helping Students with Behavioral Disorders Succeed in Inclusive Classrooms

PREVENTING EMOTIONAL AND BEHAVIORAL PROBLEMS

The most effective techniques for dealing with emotional and behavioral problems in the classroom are those that prevent these problems from occurring. While not all emotional and behavioral problems can be prevented, a proactive approach can be much more effective than one that is merely responsive to problems. It may also allow for a mutually satisfying relationship between a teacher and a student who might otherwise be perceived much more negatively. Some techniques that have been suggested for creating a classroom environment that promotes positive behaviors and helps prevent negative behaviors are:

- Make your academic and behavioral expectations of students very clear to them.
- Show your students that you are fair in your relationships with them.
- Give attention and recognition to students for their positive attributes and accomplishments. A good rule of thumb is to find something positive to say about each student every day.
- Be a positive model of attitudes, work habits, and relationships.
- Be prepared for instruction and provide a highly structured curriculum.
- Make the classroom a physically and socially appealing place to be (adapted from Sabatino, 1987).

It should be noted here, once again, that the educational approaches introduced in this chapter may have relevance and applicability to students with disabilities other than behavioral disorders. In addition to being helpful and effective in working with students with other disabilities, these are techniques that may have applicability to students with no identifiable disability. Any student may at times need the kind of instruction and support described in this and other chapters of this book.

SELF-MANAGEMENT SKILLS

Teaching students to take responsibility for their own behavior can be an effective intervention for helping these students improve their social skills. This approach may also help them to function more effectively in inclusive classrooms. Alberto and Troutman (1995) have also found that teaching self-management skills may promote more independence in students. Some of the techniques for self-management that can be tried with students in inclusive classrooms are:

Self-Monitoring

Self-monitoring techniques have been used in a variety of ways as strategies for modifying an array of classroom behaviors. These include teaching students to become aware of and record how frequently they are out of their seats, the number of times they speak out in class, the number of times they act aggressively toward others, and the amount of time they attend to academic tasks (Alberto and Troutman, 1995). Self-monitoring approaches teach students to focus on specific behaviors and record their frequency and/or duration on a chart over a given period of time. Students may then be taught to set goals for decreasing negative behaviors or increasing positive behaviors. By setting goals for these changes and recording their progress toward these goals, students become central to the process of change in their own lives.

A systematic approach to self-monitoring has been developed by Kaplan (1991). This system explains in cartoon form what behavior the student is to monitor, how he/she is to record the target behavior, and what the positive results of changes in that behavior are to be.

Self-Intervention

After students have become more aware of their own behavior and its impact on others, it may be important to teach them how to systematically reward themselves for positive changes in those behaviors. As part of the behavior-change goals they set for themselves, students should select appropriate positive reinforcements as rewards for those changes. Students might be taught to give themselves free time, award charts (for example, gold stars), certificates of achievement that can be taken home to parents, and other forms of concrete rewards for their achievements in academic and interpersonal behaviors.

Self-Instruction

Training students to teach themselves to solve problems may also be conducive to success for them in inclusive classrooms. Self-instruction, as a technique for analyzing problems and developing appropriate solutions to those problems, involves: 1) identifying the problem (What have I been asked to do?), 2) generating possible solutions (What are some ways I can do what I have been asked to do?), 3) analyzing the possible solutions (Which of the solutions seems to be best for the particular thing I have been asked to do?), 4) attempting to solve the problem (How do I select a solution for getting done what I have been asked to do?), and 5) determining if the solution worked (Did it help me complete successfully what I was asked to do?) (Mastropieri and Scruggs, 1987; Salend, 1994).

APPLIED BEHAVIORAL ANALYSIS

In some cases, the inappropriate behaviors of students with emotional and behavioral disorders may require the intervention of a special education consultant, who can help the classroom teacher analyze the nature of those behaviors and provide assistance in developing intervention strategies. The kinds of questions that may be asked during this process are:

- How often does this behavior occur? How long does it last when it occurs? How different is this behavior in frequency and duration than in other children in the class?
- What stimulates or elicits this behavior? Are there factors that intensify this behavior? Are there factors that lessen it?
- What is the history of this behavior? Has the student been engaging in it for a long time? Has it developed recently? Has it arisen or intensified recently because of changes in the student's situation?
- Is this behavior related to particular subjects or activities in school? Does it appear to be related to particular anxieties or patterns of academic failure?

As a result of asking these questions, a picture may emerge of the problems and patterns that need to be addressed in order to facilitate more appropriate and successful classroom functioning. An intervention plan may be developed that includes the control of the consequences of the behaviors that have been identified as being problematic. The selection of positive reinforcements to increase desirable behaviors or the decision to withhold reinforcement of undesirable behaviors may, for example, be based upon this analysis.

SHAFFER PHOTOGRAPHY

SOCIAL SKILLS TRAINING

Direct training in social skills may be helpful for students with behavioral and emotional disabilities who are learning how to succeed in inclusive classroom environments. A program called *Skillstreaming* uses a structured learning approach to teaching social skills. The program includes the following elements: 1) modeling, 2) role-playing, 3) performance feedback, and 4) transfer of training.

Prior to the implementation of these activities, an assessment is made of the strengths and weaknesses in the student's repertoire of social skills. In the first phase of the program, the student is provided with models of positive social behaviors. This modeling is sometimes provided by a trained peer and sometimes by a teacher. Positive and effective social behavior in difficult and provocative situations is modeled. The modeling is

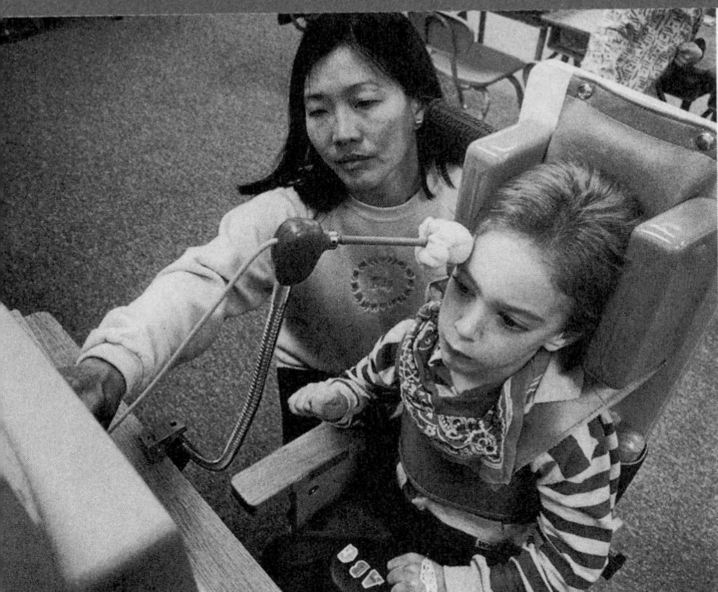

Bob Daemmrich/Stock Boston

followed by role-playing, during which the student practices the behaviors that have been modeled. Feedback on the role-playing allows the student to know how well he/she is approximating the social behavior that has been modeled. The student is then supported in using the newly acquired social skill in the natural setting of the classroom and at home (McGinnis, 1990).

FAMILY PARTICIPATION

The participation of families in the inclusion of students with behavioral and emotional disabilities in regular classrooms is critical to the success of this effort. Families may differ in their degrees of willingness and ability to participate in the education of their children. Every family, however, should be invited to and supported in becoming involved in inclusive schools and classrooms.

Welkowitz et al. (1993) found that when parents perceive themselves as full members of collaborative educational teams, they report that this collaboration has a beneficial impact on the education of their children. Critical to this perception of being a full team member, however, is the sense that they have an equal voice in decision making about their children's school programs.

Parents also report that, with the increased communication and the sharing of information, the teaming process allows them to follow through at home on their children's school program. The teaming process also allows teachers to learn from parents (Welkowitz et al., 1993).

COGNITIVE-BEHAVIORAL TRAINING

Cognitive-behavioral training is a synthesis of behavior-modification techniques and other teaching strategies. It focuses on using verbal mediation to improve behaviors (Meichenbaum, 1977). An example of cognitive-behavioral training is the following steps in an instructional sequence:

Step 1: Stop and think before you act; delay your impulse to act without thinking.

Step 2: Say to yourself how you feel and what the problem is for you; define what the problem is.

Step 3: Think of as many possible solutions to this problem as you can; look at the alternatives to the way you have reacted before.

Step 4: Think ahead to what might happen if you use different alternatives; look at the possible consequences of your behavior.

Step 5: When you think you have come up with the best alternative, try it; put it into action (Etscheidt, 1991, p. 11).

This approach shows much promise for students who have limited awareness of the impact of their behaviors on others and the consequences of those behaviors for themselves. It may promote more satisfying social interaction and increased self-esteem for these students.

PEER COLLABORATION

Students can have a very positive influence on each other in terms of both academics and social skills (Berndt, 1989). This is an important consideration in working with students with emotional and behavioral disabilities on their relationships with their peers without disabilities.

One means for promoting positive relationships between peers in inclusive classrooms is peer tutoring. One study of peer tutoring showed that when peers without disabilities tutored those with emotional and behavioral disabilities, the class test scores of the students with disabilities increased significantly. Equally important, however, the test scores of the tutors also increased significantly (Bell, 1990).

Another form of peer collaboration that may be helpful to students in inclusive classrooms is peer mediation. This technique involves training students to mediate differences among their peers. The mediators are trained in techniques of conflict resolution. They learn how to conduct mediation sessions in a fair and neutral manner. They also learn how to gather information about conflicts and how to promote communication between disagreeing parties. They are trained in how to help these parties find solutions to their disagreements and how to help them agree on a solution (Schrumpf, 1994).

Peer collaboration may serve as an excellent way for students to become actually involved in improving the academic and social "quality of life" in their classrooms. It may also result in a greater share of responsibility between teachers and students.

TEACHER ATTITUDES

Critical to the successful inclusion of students with emotional and behavioral disabilities in regular classrooms are the attitudes of the teachers who lead those classrooms. The academic and social growth of these students seems to be particularly contingent on several attitudinal factors. The attitudes that have been identified as most helpful are:

- Flexibility in academic expectations; recognizing that students learn differently and at different rates.
- Flexibility in behavioral expectations; being willing to work with students toward improved behavior and social skills.
- A willingness to interact personally with students rather than always teaching students as a group.
- Humor; being able to see humor in the classroom and being able to laugh with students at this humor (Crowley, 1991).

Teachers need to be aware that the problems they will encounter in students with emotional and behavioral disabilities will be both academic and social. Smith (1995) found that 80 percent of his sample of students with these disabilities exhibited poor peer interaction skills at the time they were placed in regular classrooms. Of these same students, however, 69 percent also showed a pattern of failure in completing their classwork. He also found that these students had most often been dealt with through suspension and expulsion and had least frequently had their social and learning problems dealt with through curricular modifications. There is clearly a need for attempting to find ways of better welcoming these students into inclusive classrooms.

Case Studies and Questions to Consider

STUDENT: LILLY MATT
SCHOOL: PERRY ELEMENTARY
CURRENT PLACEMENT: REGULAR THIRD GRADE
AGE: 10 YEARS

Family Structure and Home Environment

Lilly is described by her parents and teachers as constantly expressing feelings of anger and hostility. Lilly also experiences difficulty in academic performance and had to repeat the second grade.

Lilly lives with her mother, Theressa Wiley, and with her father, Charles Matt. Ms. Wiley is thirty years old and is a service coordinator at a fast-food restaurant. She received her GED certificate and attended American Business College. Mr. Matt is currently unemployed. He is thirty-eight years old and completed the tenth grade. Lilly does not have siblings.

Ms. Wiley reports that Lilly likes to be active and that she particularly enjoys roller skating, swimming, and riding her bike. She prefers to play outside whenever weather permits. She also likes to read. Ms. Wiley says that she and Lilly take turns reading to each other at night.

Ms. Wiley and Mr. Matt say that they frequently discipline Lilly by taking away things she likes and by sending her to her room. More often, however, they talk with their daughter about problems and encourage her to do better. Lilly has household responsibilities, including keeping her room neat, doing dishes, and helping clean the house.

Parental Perception of Student's Developmental Progress and Needs

Ms. Wiley and Mr. Matt feel that Lilly's problems in school are the result of her attitude, not her inability to do her work. They say that Lilly does not like to be criticized and will do anything to save face. They say that Lilly puts up a tough front that hides the feelings she has inside. Lilly fears defeat, they think, and will do things to draw attention away from anything she perceives to be a shortcoming.

Ms. Wiley and Mr. Matt believe that in most domains, Lilly's personal and social behavior is within normal limits for a girl of her age. They feel, however, that being overweight is an important part of their daughter's problems. They see it as a primary reason why Lilly is teased by other children. They say that Lilly is now thinking about losing weight, but that it must be her own responsibility to do so.

Additional Considerations

Ms. Wiley and Mr. Matt say that when Lilly lets down her emotional barriers, she is a loving and considerate child. More than anything else, they hope that their daughter will grow into a person who is happy with herself.

Questions

1. As a regular education teacher, what do you think you could do in order to promote class tolerance regarding Lilly's weight?
2. What could you, as Lilly's teacher, suggest to her parents to help her control her anger and hostility?
3. In what way could Lilly's parents help her improve her self-concept?

STUDENT: TONY MAX

SCHOOL: BASS ELEMENTARY

CURRENT PLACEMENT: REGULAR SIXTH GRADE

AGE: 12 YEARS, 11 MONTHS

Family Structure and Home Environment

Tony has been living between two homes for a number of months. His parents, Glen and Linda Max, are separated. Tony has spent some time with his father at Lyon Trailer Park and the rest of the time with his mother in a rented house on Carter Street. His switching back and forth between homes has apparently been frequent and not according to any pattern.

Mr. and Ms. Max are now discussing the possibility of reconciliation. The effect that their coming back together would have on Tony's life, however, is unclear. Glen Max is forty years old and has not worked regularly for several years. Linda Max is thirty-nine years old and is also not employed. Both parents describe themselves as being disabled and unable to work at this time. The nature of the family's income is unclear, but at least some support comes from a death benefit that Ms. Max receives as the heir of her former husband. Virginia Hunt, a social worker with the Department of Social Services, has worked extensively with the Max family.

In addition to his parents, Tony also lives with a brother, Kenny, who is eleven, and a sister, Lisa, who is eight. He also has a sister, Doreen, and a brother, Joe, who are twenty and seventeen, respectively. They both live on their own.

Tony lives in an atmosphere that is characterized by frequent change and uncertainty. In addition to his parents' separation, he has also recently experienced his mother being incarcerated and her being absent from the home while receiving residential treatment for alcohol abuse. It appears that at times Tony must assume responsibility not only for himself but for other family members as well.

Social Worker's Perception of Student's Developmental Progress and Needs

From her perspective as a social worker, Ms. Hunt believes that the major problem areas for Tony are his poor self-image and his difficulty in relating well with others. She believes that his poor image of himself is easily understood given a life situation that does not encourage him to feel good about himself. She feels that he has a "rock-bottom" concept of his abilities, his school performance, and his family circumstances. This poor self-esteem carries over into his relationships with others. He lacks both the confidence and the skill to interact well with other children and adults. This is particularly true in his relationships with people from social backgrounds different from his own. This is usually the case for Tony in school. Most of the other children Tony meets come from more stable home environments than his own.

Additional Considerations

Tony's social worker feels that school is one of the few avenues of hope still open for him. Even with the difficulties he has experienced in relating positively to the people and programs in school, she hopes that further help will be forthcoming. It is her opinion that the school's continuing efforts with Tony are important and critical to his development. She says that she hopes that the school won't give up on Tony even if it appears that he has given up on school.

Questions

1. How do you think Tony could become better able to socialize with his peers at school? What could you as his teacher try in this regard?
2. As a classroom teacher, would you want to see Tony referred for special education for his behavioral problems? Why or why not?
3. Do you think the ambiguity of the relationship between his mother and father has caused irreparable damage to Tony's self-concept? Why or why not?

References

Alberto, P. A., and A. C. Troutman. *Applied Behavior Analysis for Teachers.* New York: Merrill/Macmillan, 1995.

Bell, K. "Facilitating Mainstreaming of Students with Behavioral Disorders Using Classwide Peer Tutoring." *School Psychology Review, 19*(4), 1990: 564–573.

Berndt, T. J. "Contributions of Peer Relationships to Child Development." In T. J. Berndt and G. W. Ladd (Eds.), *Peer Relationships in Child Development.* New York: Wiley, 1989: 127–139

Crowley, E. "Mainstreamed Behavior Disordered Adolescents' Perceptions of Teacher Interventions." Paper presented at the 69th Annual Conference of the Council for Exceptional Children, Atlanta, GA, April 1991. ED 335 814.

Etscheidt, S. E. "Reducing Aggressive Behavior and Improving Self-Control: A Cognitive-Behavioral Treatment Program for Behaviorally Disordered Adolescents." *Behavioral Disorders, 16*(2), 1991: 107–115.

Forness, S. "Proposed EBD Definition Update." *CCBD Newsletter,* February 1992: 4.

Forness, S., and J. Knitzer. "A New Proposed Definition and Terminology to Replace 'Serious Emotional Disturbance' in the Individuals with Disabilities Education Act." *School Psychology Review, 21,* 1992: 12–20.

Frazier, D., and R. DeBlassie. "Diagnosing Behavior Disordered Early Adolescents as a Function of Cultural Differences." *Adolescence, 19,* 1984: 381–390.

Glassbery, L. A. "Students with Behavioral Disorders: Determinants of Placement Outcomes." *Behavioral Disorders, 19,* 1994: 181–191.

Hallahan, D., and J. Kauffman. *Exceptional Children: Introduction to Special Education.* Needham Heights, MA: Allyn and Bacon, 1994.

Kaplan, J. S. *Beyond Behavior Modification: A Cognitive- Behavioral Approach to Behavior Management in the School.* Austin, TX: Pro-Ed, 1991.

Kauffman, J. M. *Characteristics of Children's Behavior Disorders.* Columbus, OH: Charles E. Merrill, 1977.

Kauffman, J. M., and J. W. Lloyd. "Restrictive Educational Placement of Students with Emotional or Behavioral Disorders: What We Know and What We Need to Know." In R. B. Rutherford and S. R. Mather (Eds.), *Severe Behavior Disorders of Children and Youth, 15.* Reston, VA: Council for Children with Behavioral Disorders, 1992: 35–43.

Kelly, T. J., L. M. Bullock, and M. K. Dyes. "Behavioral Disorders: Teacher's Perceptions." *Exceptional Children, 43,* 1977: 440–444.

Kotlowitz, A. *There Are No Children Here: The Story of Two Boys Growing Up in the Other America.* New York: Anchor, 1991.

Koyangi, C., and S. Gaines. *All Systems Failure: An Examination of the Results of Neglecting the Needs of Children with Serious Emotional Disturbance.* Washington, DC: National Mental Health Association, 1993.

Marder, C., and R. Cox. "More Than a Label: Characteristics of Youth with Disabilities." In M. Wagner, L. Newman, R. D'Amico, E. D. Jay, P. Butler-Natlain, C. Marder, and R. Cox, *Youth with Disabilities: How Are They Doing?* The first comprehensive report from the National Longitudinal Transition Study of Special Education Students. Menlo Park, CA: SRI International, 1991: 9–16.

Mastropieri, M. A., and T. E. Scruggs. *Effective Instruction for Special Education.* Boston: College Hill Press, 1987.

McGinnis, E. *Skillstreaming in Early Childhood: Teaching Prosocial Skills to the Preschool and Kindergarten Child.* Champaign, IL: Research Press, 1990.

Meichenbaum, D. H. *Cognitive-Behavior Modification: An Integrative Approach.* New York: Plenum, 1977.

National Information Center for Children and Youth with Disabilities. *Autism* (Fact Sheet No. 1 [FS1]). Washington, DC: National Information Center for Children and Youth with Disabilities, 1993.

Tony's special needs.

Office of Civil Rights. *User's Guide for National Estimates.* Fall 1990 Elementary and Secondary School Civil Rights Survey. Revised National Estimates. U.S. Department of Education, Office of Civil Rights, 1993.

Office of Special Education Programs. *Fifteenth Annual Report to Congress on the Implementation of the Individuals with Disabilities Education Act.* Washington, DC: U.S. Department of Education, 1993.

———. *Sixteenth Annual Report to Congress on the Implementation of the Individuals with Disabilities Education Act.* Washington, DC: U.S. Department of Education, 1994.

———. *Seventeenth Annual Report to Congress on the Implementation of the Individuals with Disabilities Education Act.* Washington, DC: U.S. Department of Education, 1995.

Ormond, J. *Educational Psychology: Principles and Applications.* Columbus, OH: Merrill, 1995.

Prieto, A. G., and S. H. Zucker. "Teacher Perception of Race as a Factor in the Placement of Behaviorally Disordered Children." *Behavioral Disorders, 7,* 1981: 34–38.

Quay, H. "Classification." In H. C. Quay and J. S. Werry (Eds.), *Psychopathological Disorders of Childhood,* 3d ed. New York: Wiley, 1986: 49–61.

Quay, H., and D. R. Peterson. *Manual for the Revised Behavior Problems Checklist.* Coral Gables, FL: H. C. Quay and D. R. Peterson, 1987.

Rhodes, W. C. "The Disturbing Child: A Problem of Ecological Management." *Exceptional Children, 33,* 1967: 449–455.

Sabatino, D. A. "Preventive Discipline as a Practice in Special Education." *Teaching Exceptional Children, 19,* 1987: 8–11.

Salend, S. *Effective Mainstreaming: Creating Inclusive Classrooms.* New York: Macmillan, 1994.

Schrumpf, F. "The Role of Students in Resolving Conflicts in Schools." In J. S. Thousand and A. J. Nevin (Eds.), *Creativity and Collaborative Learning: A Practical Guide to Empowering Students and Teachers.* Baltimore, MD: Paul H. Brookes, 1994.

Smith, C. "Behavior Disorders and LRE." *Inclusive Education Programs, 2*(7), 1995: 9–10.

Wagner, M., L. Newman, R. D'Amico, E. D. Jay, P. Butler-Natlain, C. Marder, and R. Cox. *Youth with Disabilities: How Are They Doing?* The first comprehensive report from the National Longitudinal Transition Study of Special Education Students. Menlo Park, CA: SRI International, 1991.

Welkowitz, J., R. Hamilton, K. Topper, and L. Inatsuka. "Perceptions of Parents Regarding Their Involvement and Experience with Collaborative Educational Teams for Students with Emotional and Behavioral Disorders." In C. Liberton (Ed.), *System of Care for Children's Mental Health: Expanding the Research Base.* 6th Annual Research Conference Proceedings, Tampa, FL, March 1993. ED 372 524.

Whelan, R. "The Emotionally Disturbed." In E. L. Meyen (Ed.), *Basic Readings in the Study of Exceptional Children and Youth.* Denver, CO: Love, 1979: 329–330.

———. "Emotional Disturbance." In E. L. Meyen and T. Skirtic (Eds.), *Special Education and Student Disability: An Introduction.* Denver: Love, 1995: 271–336.

U.S. Department of Education. "Rules and Regulations." *Federal Register, 58*(145): 40961–40973 (34 C.F.R., Ch. III, Sec. 300.7), July 30, 1993.

Zirpoli, J. "Child Abuse and Children with Handicaps." *Remedial and Special Education,* 7(2), 1986: 39–48.

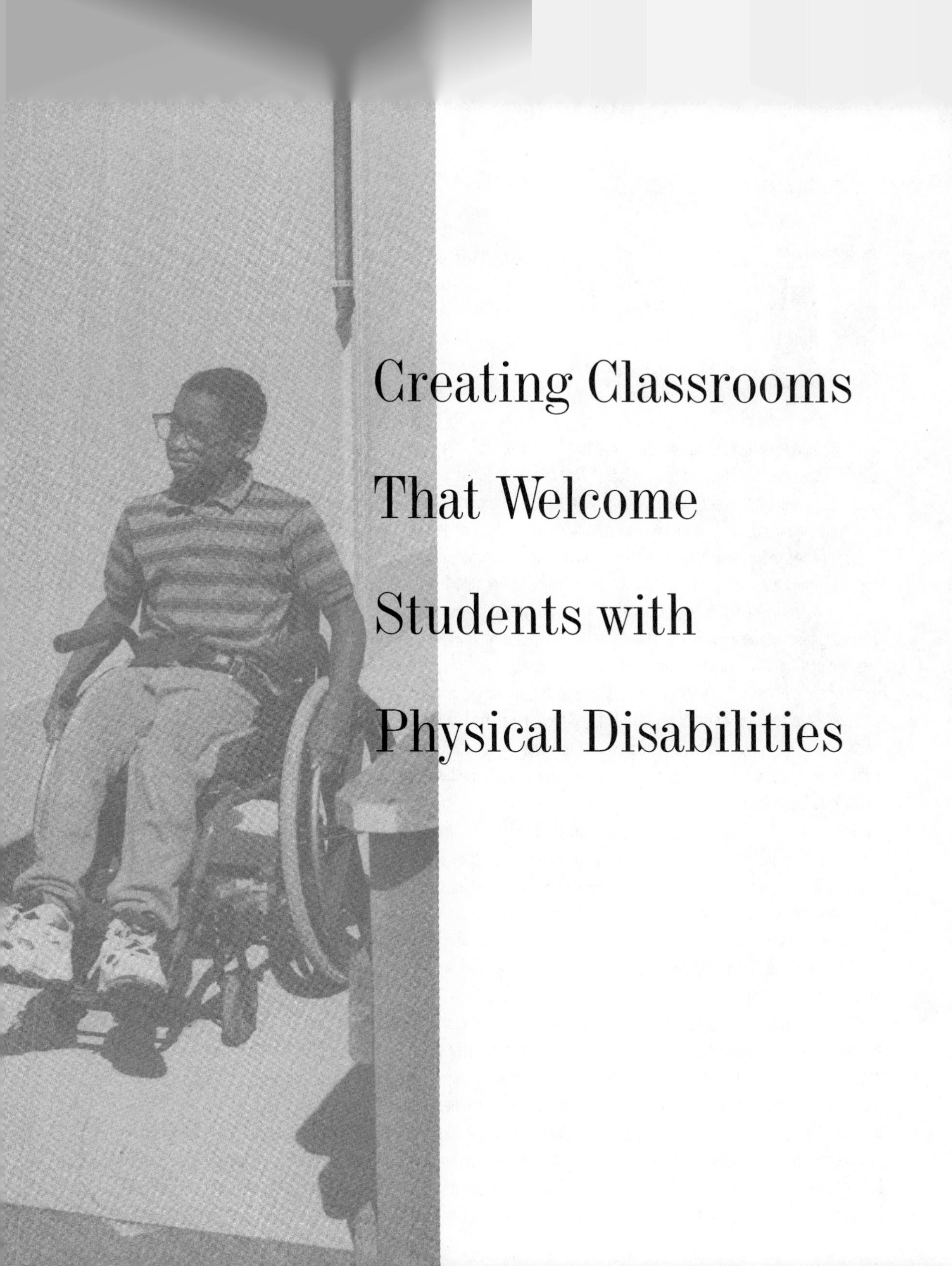

Creating Classrooms That Welcome Students with Physical Disabilities

Finding a Voice: The Story of Bill

The following story was told to me by one of my own professors when I was a student preparing to become a teacher. It is about one of his former students. It is a story that has strengthened and sustained my belief in the critical difference that one teacher can make in the life of a student. It has served to remind me for many years now of the importance of hope, sensitivity, and innovation in the work that we do as teachers. I have shared this story with generations of my own students. I am pleased to share it with you.

Amy, a special education major at a small college, had reached her senior year. She told her adviser that she very much wanted to do her student teaching in a nearby residential facility operated by the state for adults with mental retardation. Amy explained that she preferred that kind of placement rather than student teaching in a public school. Her career goal was to teach adults with mental retardation. And so her adviser, later my professor, made the arrangements. Amy had also requested that she be assigned to work with people with more severe disabilities. Accordingly, she was given a small number of people with multiple disabilities to work with on an individual basis. She was assigned four people to develop and implement programs for during the 15-week period of her student teaching.

One of the men she was assigned to work with was thirty-five years old. He had severe cerebral palsy and had been diagnosed as being severely mentally retarded. He was in a wheelchair. He had no control over the movement of his legs. He had some voluntary movement in his arms, but he could not control them very well. He was also able to move some of the muscles in his neck and face. He could not, however, speak. The assumption noted in his records was that he was unable to speak because of his retardation. After Amy started working in the institution, something about this man, whose name was Bill, gave her the impression there was more within him than had been recognized. There was something about the way he moved his eyes, she said. There was something about the way he seemed to react to the things she said to him. She was told by people who worked at the facility that Bill loved being read to. One person commented, "We don't think he understands anything, but he just loves to hear the sound of a voice reading to him." She tried it and sure enough he did react very positively the minute he saw the book in her hand. "His eyes brightened up," she said.

Bill had been in the institution since he was an infant, having been brought there by parents who felt that they could not take care of him. Amy decided, "Here's a man who has no way of communicating. The only semblance of communication we have is when I watch his face, like when I bring a book into the room and his eyes seem to light up." She later reflected "I didn't know what that meant—'his eyes lighting up.' I just wanted to find some way of beginning to teach him to communicate."

In college, Amy had learned about communication boards and how they can be helpful to people who are unable to speak. This was before the development of the various computer keyboards, voice synthesizers, and other augmentative devices that have become so important today in enabling people with severe disabilities to communicate. But Amy's professors had encouraged her to be resourceful and creative. So, she made a very simple communication board one evening after work. She took a big square of cardboard, divided it into four sections, and put a picture in each section. In one section she put a picture of a glass of orange juice, another section had a picture of a bathroom door, the third section had a picture of a book, and the last section contained a picture of a park bench and a tree. Bill had enough movement in his arms and hands to point to these pictures, and she wanted to teach him that if he wanted a drink of orange juice, his favorite, he should point to the glass of orange juice on the board. If he needed to use the bathroom, she wanted to teach him that he could point to the picture of the bathroom door, and so on. She brought the board in and demonstrated it to him. Amy placed his hand on the picture of the tree and then she took him outside to the bench, a special place, it seemed, for Bill. She came back inside and put his hand on the picture of the book and then opened a book and read to him. In the process, she thought, "I'll try this for several days and see if I can get him to catch on."

Bill's response, however, proved to be immediate. Amy finished reading and was going to take his hand and point to the glass of orange juice, but he shook his head and grunted. She wasn't sure, but it seemed that he wanted her to continue reading.

She read a few more pages and Bill seemed pleased. When she placed the communication board on his wheelchair again, Bill pointed first to the book and then to the bench. She corrected him by placing his finger on only one of the pictures, the bench. When she gave him another trial, however, he repeated the sequence of touching the book and the bench. She wasn't certain but thought perhaps he was trying to say he wanted to go outside and read. She pushed his wheelchair toward the exit door, and as they passed through it she thought she heard Bill giggle with delight.

That night Amy made a larger communication board with more pictures and thus more alternatives. What she saw from Bill the next day was immediate comprehension of how to use the bigger board. She then decided to make a communication board with all the letters of the alphabet, thinking maybe she could begin teaching him to spell words. She brought it to work and began using it by trying to teach him the word *book*. She felt that his love of being read to might be very motivating to him in learning *book* as his first word. She held his finger and pointed to "B," then to "O," to another "O," and finally to "K." She repeated the word *book* and put his hand on the one she had been reading from. She then encouraged Bill to point to the letters on his own. His finger went immediately to the letter "T." She corrected him by placing his finger again on the "B" and calling out the name of the letter. When he was again given the freedom to point, however, his finger went in a seemingly deliberate manner to the "T." Amy decided to let him proceed. Bill in a slow, labored, and careful way, pointed to the sequence of letters that communicated to her his message of choice. He said to his teacher, "T" "H" "A" "N" "K" "Y" "O" "U." Amy was astounded.

Bill had never been taught to read or write; he had never had academic instruction of any kind. Apparently over the years, however, when people had read to him, Bill watched carefully. He had taught himself to read. Amy began to work with Bill on the communication board with great intensity. She spent her evenings and weekends "listening" to him through his pointing to letters. He "spoke" with her about a lifetime of unexpressed perceptions and silent frustrations. Once she understood how deeply he could communicate with the spelling board, she told others at the institution. Many of them said, "There must be some misunderstanding—Bill is severely retarded." She finally convinced a psychologist to watch as she asked questions of Bill, to which he responded by pointing to the letters of the alphabet. The psychologist was absolutely amazed. He decided to give Bill some sections of an IQ test through his communication board. Not only did he find that Bill was not severely mentally retarded, the psychologist estimated that his IQ fell into the superior range. He had been locked into his body for thirty-five years and treated as if he were severely retarded. He had no way of telling the world he wasn't. Amy had given him a key—she had given him a means of communicating and demonstrating the depth of his comprehension and insight.

By this time, Amy was nearing the completion of her student teaching. She asked special permission, however, to remain at the facility that summer and work with Bill. This was allowed. As a result of Amy's efforts and the world that had opened to him through the communication board, Bill moved out of the institution the next year and into a group home. Amy continued to work with him and taught him to type on an electric typewriter. It was a slow process, but he mastered it. A new freedom of expression came to him with the keyboard.

Bill developed friendships in the community that surrounded the group home. He became an active member of a local church. He loved going to community theater performances. He was invited to join a civic organization. Unfortunately, he died of a stroke when he was in his late forties. It is sad to think that until he was thirty-five years old he was treated as severely disabled by everyone who knew him. He had so few years of "liberation" from his disability. His friend and teacher Amy, however, found a way of helping him break through, so for at least ten years of his life he was recognized as a person, not as a disability.

We all need to be very careful with the assumptions we make about people, and extremely careful about the assumptions we make about people who have trouble communicating. We often jump to conclusions when people can't communicate effectively, and we sometimes have lower expectations of them. Bill and Amy come to my mind when I am tempted to make judgments about the potentials of others. I'm glad Bill found a voice. I'm glad that I know their story.

Students with Physical Disabilities: Causes and Characteristics

STUDENTS WITH PHYSICAL DISABILITIES constitute a relatively small percentage of the total number of students who are identified as having special education needs under the provisions of IDEA. According to the *Sixteenth Annual Report to Congress on the Implementation of the Individuals with Disabilities Act*, 2.5 percent of the students being served under that act during the 1992–93 school year were identified on the basis of a physical disability (Office of Special Education Programs, 1994). The term *physical disability* is not actually used, in fact, in the definitions employed for the implementation of IDEA. The terms used for that act are *orthopedic impairment* and *other health impairment*. These terms are defined in the following ways in the *Federal Register*.

> Orthopedic Impairment means a severe orthopedic impairment that adversely affects a child's educational performance. The term includes impairments caused by congenital anomaly (e.g., clubfoot, absence of some member, etc.), impairments caused by disease (e.g., poliomyelitis, bone tuberculosis, etc.), and impairments from other causes (e.g., cerebral palsy, amputations, and fractures or burns that cause contractures).
>
> Other Health Impairment means having limited strength, vitality, or alertness, due to acute health problems such as heart condition, tuberculosis, rheumatic fever, nephritis, asthma, sickle cell anemia, hemophilia, epilepsy, lead poisoning, leukemia, or diabetes, that adversely affects a child's educational performance (*Federal Register*, 1990).

Concerning these definitions, it should be noted that with both orthopedic impairments and other health impairments, the assumption is that these are primary disabilities. Students who are identified as having these disabilities may have other, secondary disabling characteristics. A child with cerebral palsy may, for example, have mental retardation. A child with epilepsy may also have a learning disability. In both of these examples, however, the physical disability must be identified as the primary disabling condition if the student is to be placed in the categories of either orthopedically impaired or other health impaired.

The types and causes of physical disabilities vary greatly. Some children are born with *congenital* disabilities. The implications of having a disability from birth can be quite different from having a disability that is *acquired* later in childhood as a result of disease or injury. Some physical disabilities may be relatively mild and manageable (for example, some cases of diabetes), or they may be severe and require multiple sources of support (for example, some cases of spastic quadriplegia cerebral palsy). Some physical disabilities may be progressive (for example, muscular dystrophy) and some may be fatal (for example, AIDS).

The number of different physical disabilities makes it impractical to discuss all of them in a book of this kind. An attempt to do so would end in nothing but a list of terms and brief descriptions. Instead, this chapter will include a discussion of a few physical disabilities that are representative of many different types of orthopedic and other health impairments.

CEREBRAL PALSY

Cerebral palsy is a disability that is one of the most common of the orthopedic impairments.

BOX 5.1

Cerebral Palsy: Movement Disorders

Spasticity: sudden contractions of muscles; labored and awkward voluntary movement; general tightness of muscles; also called *hypertonia*.

Athetosis: irregular, involuntary movements; these movements become more pronounced under stress; also called *dyskinesia*.

Ataxia: poor balance; the gait may be unsteady and jerky; poor control of fine motor movements.

Rigidity: very rigid movement of the limbs; movement capability may be lost.

Tremor: constant shaking of the affected limbs; repetitive, rhythmic movements.

Most teachers will have a child in their classrooms at some time in their careers who has some degree and some form of this disability. The words *degree* and *form* are very important here because cerebral palsy is not a specific disease or disorder. It is a general term used to designate the various effects that damage to the brain may have on movement. These effects may be mild or severe. They may be specific to a very small region of the body, or they may involve most of the body. Cerebral palsy is defined simply and accurately as "a disorder of movement and posture due to damage to areas of the brain that control motor function" (Bigge, 1991, p. 3). The brain damage that causes cerebral palsy may occur before birth, during the birth process, or shortly after birth. Brain damage that occurs later, although it may have many of the same consequences for movement, is not usually referred to as cerebral palsy. Cerebral palsy is not a progressive disorder. Without intervention, however, the muscles affected by cerebral palsy may lose strength and tone. It is important, therefore, to intervene early and continuously to promote the greatest use of the muscles that are weakened by the condition.

Box 5.1 and Figure 5.1 present two dimensions of cerebral palsy. In Figure 5.1 the types of disorders in movement that may be caused by cerebral palsy are listed and described. Because cerebral palsy is a descriptor for a general category of movement disorders, the type of effects may vary greatly. Although Box 5.1 describes these effects, a few supplemental comments may be helpful. Some people may show spastic movement that is tight, labored movement. It may be helpful to think of *spasticity* as *disturbed movement*. Cerebral palsy may also result in athetosis. *Athetosis* may be thought of as *unwanted movement. Rigidity*, in its most serious degree, may be thought of as the *absence of movement*. Figure 5.1 illustrates the sites of the body that may be impaired by cerebral palsy. These range from a single limb to all four limbs. It is important to remember, however, that it is not only the limbs that may be disabled by this condition. Other muscles may also be impaired. Facial muscles and the tongue may be disabled in ways that make speech difficult or impossible. Muscles of the trunk of the body may be impaired and thereby create postural problems for the individual. The impairment of muscles of the neck can result in serious problems in controlling the movement of the head.

The severity of problems in movement may vary from mild to very severe. Some people with cerebral palsy may show only some difficulty with fine motor coordination and perhaps a slight speech disorder. Others may be able to support themselves and walk only with the assistance of braces and crutches. People with more serious disabilities may need to use a wheelchair for mobility. There are some people who cannot move independently even with the best assistive devices.

FIGURE 5.1

Cerebral Palsy: Body Areas That May Be Affected

Monoplegia: One limb (may be an arm or leg).

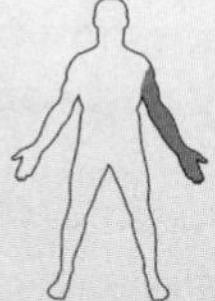

or

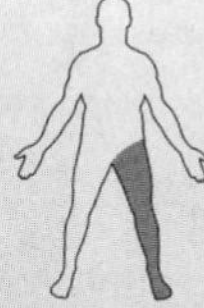

Hemiplegia: One side of the body (an arm and leg on one side).

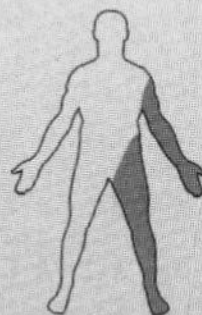

or

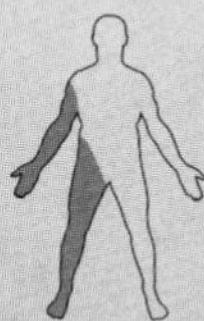

Paraplegia: Both legs.

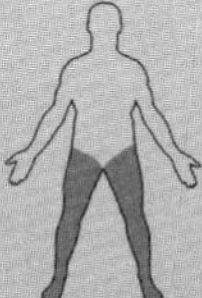

Triplegia: Three limbs (most often both legs and one arm).

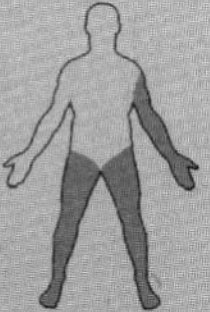

or

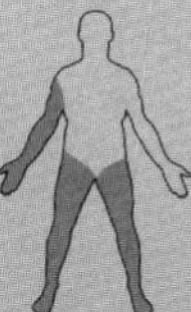

Quadraplegia: All limbs involved.

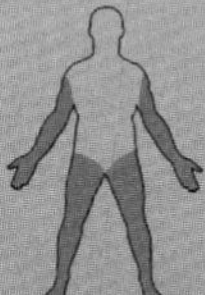

Diplegia: All limbs involved but greater involvement in the legs.

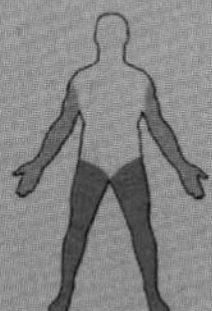

Michael Siluk/The Picture Cube

Children with cerebral palsy may have other problems associated with their primary disability. They are at increased risk for learning disabilities, mental retardation, epilepsy, speech disorders, and vision and hearing problems. These secondary disabilities, when combined with the primary disability of cerebral palsy, may create the need for very intense and varied services to meet the needs of a student. Physical therapy, occupational therapy, speech therapy, other intensive medical services, counseling, and special education services may be necessary if the child is to eventually reach her or his optimal potential.

A critical fact to remember about students with cerebral palsy is that approximately 40 percent of all children and adults with this disability have average or above average intellectual abilities (Batshaw and Perret, 1992). The more severe the cerebral palsy, the greater the chance that mental retardation may be present. It is important to recognize, however, that individuals with very severe limitations in movement and communication may have average or above average intellectual abilities.

The story of Bill earlier in this chapter and the example of a person like the brilliant physicist Steven Hawking should serve to remind us that there is not a direct relationship between conventional communication abilities, appearance, and mobility, and the potential for strong and complex cognitive capacities.

EPILEPSY

Epilepsy is a neurological condition that has a history of various names. People who have seizures have been described in the past as having "fits" or "convulsions." Even today it is not uncommon to hear someone refer to a seizure as an "epileptic fit." These unfortunate terms represent an even more unfortunate attitude of fear and avoidance. Earlier in this century, it was a common practice to institutionalize people with epilepsy. As medication and other interventions have brought seizures under greater control, the lives of people with epilepsy have become less restricted. However, many restrictive attitudes continue to persist.

Epilepsy is a condition that involves rapid and usually brief changes in consciousness accompanied by involuntary movements. Changes in consciousness are experiences we all have every day. Falling asleep is a process in which the level of consciousness changes. Falling asleep, however, is usually not a sudden change. Perhaps that is what distinguishes it from the fearful experience of fainting. A seizure, like fainting, is disturbing to others as well as to the person who has the seizure. This may be the reason, at least in part, for the fear and prejudice that have surrounded epilepsy.

The involuntary movements that occur during a seizure are not unlike the involuntary movements or twitches that happen while people are sleeping or the muscle spasms that may occur due to fatigue. The occurrence of these movements in a person who has suddenly lost consciousness, however, may add to the dramatic effect of a seizure on those who witness it. It might be helpful for teachers, however, to keep in mind that a seizure involves two understandable and not unfamiliar human events, a change in consciousness and the involuntary movement of muscles.

Seizures can be symptomatic of illness. Many children, for example, have seizures as a result of high fevers; these are called *febrile seizures* and are not considered to be epilepsy. Seizures may also result from imbalances in body chemistry. A single seizure, particularly during childhood, is not indicative that a person has epilepsy (Kobrin, 1991).

When seizures are recurring and are not associated with some other illness, a diagnosis of epilepsy may be made. When a cause can be determined for the epilepsy—a malformation or injury to the brain, for example—it is referred to as *symptomatic epilepsy.* When no specific cause can be determined, it is referred to as *idiopathic epilepsy.*

Once a diagnosis of epilepsy has been made, an effective treatment can usually be found. There are many different medications that can be used to control seizures. Physicians seek the drug that is best for the individual in reducing seizure frequency and that produces the least number of side effects (White, 1995). In more than 70 percent of all cases of epilepsy, the seizures can be controlled by medication (Freeman and Vining, 1990). This fact, combined with the reality that most students with epilepsy have average or above average intellectual ability, makes the importance of inclusive school environments and teachers who are informed about this condition compelling (Batshaw and Perret, 1992).

Box 5.2 provides guidelines for helping a student who has a seizure. It is critical to note that the most important measure is to help the student to an area that is free of objects that might be dangerous. Because the muscle contractions during a seizure may cause forceful movements, the area should be free of objects that the student might hurt her or his arms or legs on. It is also important to know that nothing should be placed in the student's mouth. There has long been the misconception that the first thing that should be done for a person having a seizure is to place something in the mouth to prevent the tongue from being swallowed. Objects in the mouth actually pose a hazard. They may cut the mouth or tongue, or damage teeth. There is also the danger of being bitten while attempting to place an object in the person's mouth, as the muscles of the jaw contract during the seizure.

BOX 5.2

Helping a Student Who Has a Seizure

- Help the student to a clear area on the floor away from immovable objects. Move any objects that might cut, burn, or bruise the student during the seizure.
- Turn the student on her or his side if possible. This will help prevent choking on saliva or vomitus.
- Stay by the student. Be comforting as the student regains consciousness. Try to ease the student's embarrassment.
- Don't try to force the student's mouth open, and *do not* place anything in the student's mouth.
- Watch the student during the seizure. Take note of how long it lasts.
- If this is the student's first seizure and/or
  - the seizure lasts longer than ten minutes
  - seizures come one after another
  - the student turns blue or stops breathing

Call for emergency medical help.

It is very important to remember that a seizure may cause a great deal of embarrassment for the student. The teacher should do everything possible to comfort and reassure the student as consciousness is regained. The student will probably be sleepy and should be given the opportunity to rest following the seizure. This may also be a time when the seizure can be explained to other students and their help enlisted in reassuring the student who had the seizure. Parents of a child who is subject to seizures should be consulted concerning other procedures that should be followed if a seizure occurs at school. Parents should, of course, always be informed that a seizure has occurred. Parents should also be consulted about informing the student's classmates about epilepsy. If other students understand what a seizure is, their reactions and feelings toward their classmate with epilepsy may be more encouraging and supportive.

The procedures described in Box 5.2 and the preceding paragraphs apply to the type of seizure called *generalized tonic-clonic.* This type of seizure has also been called *grand mal.* There are other types of seizures, however, that do not require these procedures. These forms of epilepsy may not require any special actions or treatment at all, other than the understanding of the teacher of what the student is experiencing. One form of more subtle epilepsy is called *absence seizure.* It may be noticeable only as a sudden blank stare. It may also be accompanied by chewing movements or blinking. A student who is subject to absence seizures (formerly call *petit mal* seizures) may have a tendency to become confused or may appear to daydream and not pay attention in class. There are other forms of epilepsy that may result in strange behavior in a person who appears to be completely conscious. Jerking muscle spasms, sudden roaming, or other unusual behavior may be symptoms of these kinds of seizures. The most important guideline for any type of seizure, however, is the same. People who have seizures need to be reassured that they are accepted and cared for by others.

SPINA BIFIDA

The term *spina bifida* in its literal sense refers to an open or divided spine. Like cleft palate or cleft lip, it is a failure in midline body fusion during the early weeks of fetal development. A portion of the spinal column does not grow together, and the spinal cord may be exposed and vulnerable to damage. There may, however, be small openings in the spinal column without any damage to the spinal cord. Approximately 40 percent of all Americans have these small openings in the spine, which are called *spina bifida occulta.* Since they cause no problems, most people are unaware that they have them (National Information Center for Children and Youth with Disabilities, 1993). If the spinal cord actually protrudes through the opening in the spinal column the damage to the nerves of the cord is likely to be very serious. A sac with the exposed portion of the spinal cord forms on the back. This is called a *myelomeningocele.* It is the most serious form of spina bifida.

The disabling effects of spina bifida increase with the amount of damage done to the spinal cord and depend on the location on the spinal cord where the damage occurs. Some children with spina bifida can walk without assistance. Others need to use braces and crutches for mobility. Some must use a wheelchair. Lack of bowel and bladder control is common with these children. They must be taught techniques for attending to their own toileting and hygiene needs. Spina bifida is often complicated by the presence of excessive fluid pressure around the brain, a condition called *hydrocephalus.* The increased pressure can cause enlargement of the skull and mental retardation. This condition must be treated by implanting a shunt that drains the excess fluid from the brain and into the bloodstream.

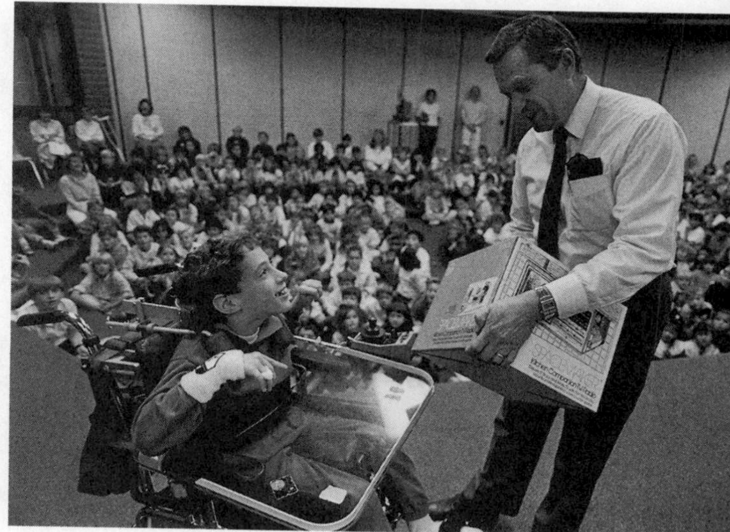

Spencer Grant/Stock Boston

MUSCULAR DYSTROPHY

Muscular dystrophy is actually a group of disorders characterized by progressive deterioration of muscles. The most common form of this disabling condition is *Duchenne muscular dystrophy.* It involves the very rapid deterioration of muscles during childhood. By adolescence, most children with this disorder are unable to walk. It usually proceeds to the point where children with the disorder are totally unable to use their arms and hands, and it may be difficult for them to move or support their heads. Muscle deterioration eventually damages the heart and the muscles that facilitate breathing. The life expectancy of children with Duchenne muscular dystrophy is short. Most will die in adolescence or young adulthood of heart failure or pneumonia.

Muscular dystrophy is a hereditary disorder. It is more often inherited by boys than girls. The other forms of muscular dystrophy are more likely to appear later in childhood, adolescence, or adulthood, and they may progress more slowly than Duchenne. In general, however, the characteristics of these disorders are the same as those of Duchenne.

TRAUMATIC BRAIN INJURY

In recent decades there has been a dramatic increase in the incidence of *traumatic brain injury.* Most of these cases are the result of car, motorcycle, or motorbike accidents. Other cases result from gun wounds and child abuse. The age range of greatest risk for traumatic brain injury is adolescence to young adulthood. According to IDEA, a traumatic brain injury is

> an acquired injury to the brain caused by an external physical force, resulting in total or partial functional disability or psychosocial impairment, or both, that adversely affects a child's educational performance. The term applies to open or closed head injuries resulting in impairments in one or more areas, such as cognition; language; memory; reasoning; abstract thinking; judgement; problem solving; sensory, perceptual, and motor abilities; psychosocial behavior; physical functions; information processing and speech. The term does not apply to brain injuries that are congenital or degenerative, or brain injuries induced by birth trauma (*Federal Register,* 1990).

The disabilities resulting from traumatic brain injury may vary from mild to severe. They may be temporary or permanent. The severity and permanence of a disability from traumatic brain injury is related to the age of the individual when the damage occurs. An adult is less likely to be severely disabled by the same injury than a child. Older children are less likely to be as severely disabled by an injury that would severely disable an infant or toddler (Mira, Tucker, and Tyler, 1992).

TABLE 5.1

Students with Traumatic Brain Injury, Number and Placement Percentages: School Year 1992–93

Number	3,960
Regular Class	16.4%
Resource Room	19.8%
Separate Class	28.4%
Separate School	28.4%
Residential Facility	4.4%
Homebound/Hospital Setting	2.6%

Source: Office of Special Education Programs. *Seventeenth Annual Report to Congress on the Implementation of the Individuals with Disabilities Education Act.* Washington, DC: U.S. Department of Education, 1995, pp. 11, 17.

TABLE 5.2

Students with Traumatic Brain Injury, Basis for Leaving School: School Year 1991–92

	Number	Percent
Received Diploma	41	64.1
Certificate (no high school school diploma awarded)	5	7.8
Reached Maximum Age for Attendance	4	6.3
Dropped Out	8	12.5
Status Unknown	6	9.3

Source: Office of Special Education Programs, *Sixteenth Annual Report to Congress on the Implementation of the Individuals with Disabilities Education Act.* Washington, DC: U.S. Department of Education, 1994, p. 19.

Although the number of students with traumatic brain injuries in schools is relatively small, it is important to note that only a small percentage of these students is served in regular school settings (see Table 5.1). It is also important to recognize that more than 35 percent of students with traumatic brain injury leave school without a high school diploma (see Table 5.2).

OTHER HEALTH IMPAIRMENTS

There are, of course, many other physical conditions, disorders, and diseases that may have serious consequences in an individual's life. A few examples may help as reminders of the sensitivity to the health status of students that teachers must bring to their work.

Juvenile diabetes is the result of inadequate insulin production. This causes the body to be unable to metabolize starches and sugars in the ways needed for normal functioning. Common symptoms of juvenile diabetes include chronic thirst and frequent urination. The more serious symptoms, however, result from the improper level of the insulin that people with this disorder must take in order to control it. *Hypoglycemia* occurs when there is too much insulin in the body. It causes headaches, vomiting, heart palpitations, and problems in breathing. The skin becomes cold and clammy. Orange juice, candy, or sugar may be used to reduce the insulin level. *Ketoacidosis* occurs when there is not enough insulin in the body. Fatigue, excessive thirst, and deep breathing may be signs that the insulin level of the body is too low. People with juvenile diabetes must learn to monitor their insulin levels, exercise regularly, and control their diets.

Cystic fibrosis is a recessive gene disorder. The primary symptom of cystic fibrosis is the secretion in the body of very thick mucus. The mucus causes difficulties for the person with this disorder by disturbances in digestion, respiration, and other body functions. Students with cystic fibrosis will often have a chronic cough and increased thirst, and may need to be allowed special toileting arrangements. Otherwise, they should be encouraged to engage in all school activities. The life expectancy of children with cystic fibrosis has been increased significantly in recent years by newer medications and therapies.

AIDS (acquired immunodeficiency syndrome) is a condition that impairs the ability of a person's body to resist and combat infections. It develops after a person has contracted the human immunodeficiency virus (HIV). HIV may be transmitted from person to person by sexual contact, intravenous drug use, and blood transfusions. It is not spread by insects, tears, kissing, or touching an infected person. It may be transmitted from infected mothers to their babies before or during birth (U.S. Department of Health and Human Services, 1988). The incidence of AIDS in children has increased in recent years to the point that it is approximately the same as the incidence of Down's syndrome or myelomeningocele (Anderson, Hinojosa, Bedell, and Kaplan, 1990). Children with AIDS are included under the protections of IDEA. They have, therefore, the right to both an education appropriate to their individual needs and an education in the least restrictive environment appropriate to those needs. Most children with AIDS do not pose a risk to their teachers or to other students. They are best served in regular classroom placements. In some cases, however, it may be in the best interests of the student who is ill with AIDS to be served in a more restrictive, individualized environment. This may be particularly true for a child in the advanced stages of the disease. The Centers for Disease Control has developed a set of guidelines for serving children with AIDS (Centers for Disease Control, 1985). These guidelines emphasize that the risk of infection from most children with AIDS to teachers and other students is virtually nonexistent. More restrictive school settings are necessary only when children with AIDS lack control of body secretions or engage in biting behaviors.

The Classroom Needs of Students with Physical Disabilities

STUDENTS WITH PHYSICAL DISABILITIES and other health impairments do not usually require a curriculum that is different from that of other students. Most of them have the cognitive ability to function well in a classroom of their age peers. It is important to recognize, however, that most of these students are not in regular classrooms. Tables 5.3 and 5.4 show that large numbers of these

TABLE 5.3

Students with Orthopedic Impairments, Number and Placement Percentages: School Year 1992–93

Number	52,588
Regular Class	35.1%
Resource Room	20.0%
Separate Class	34.1%
Separate School	6.7%
Residential Facility	0.6%
Homebound/Hospital Setting	3.5%

Source: Office of Special Education Programs. *Seventeenth Annual Report to Congress on the Implementation of the Individuals with Disabilities Education Act.* Washington, DC: U.S. Department of Education, 1995, pp. 11, 17.

students are being educated in separate classes and separate schools. There are also large numbers of students with physical disabilities and other health impairments who leave school without diplomas (see Tables 5.5 and 5.6). These facts bring into focus the need to create classrooms and schools that are more truly inclusive of these students.

The categories of physical disabilities and other health impairments are so broad that it is very difficult to speak in generalities about the needs of students with these disabilities. Their classroom needs will vary greatly depending on the age of the student, the type of disability that the student has, and the severity of that disability. There are, however, four important areas of consideration in seeking the best educational accommodations for these students.

TABLE 5.4

Students with Other Health Impairments, Number and Placement Percentages: School Year 1992–93

Number	66,063
Regular Class	40.0%
Resource Room	27.4%
Separate Class	20.6%
Separate School	2.5%
Residential Facility	0.5%
Homebound/Hospital Setting	9.0%

Source: Office of Special Education Programs. *Seventeenth Annual Report to Congress on the Implementation of the Individuals with Disabilities Education Act.* Washington, DC: U.S. Department of Education, 1995, pp. 11, 17.

TABLE 5.5

Students with Orthopedic Impairments, Basis for Leaving School: School Year 1991–92

	Number	Percent
Received Diploma	1,379	50.2
Certificate (no high school diploma awarded)	439	16.0
Reached Maximum Age for Attendance	123	4.5
Dropped Out	252	9.2
Status Unknown	556	20.1

Source: Office of Special Education Programs. *Sixteenth Annual Report to Congress on the Implementation of the Individuals with Disabilities Education Act.* Washington, DC: U.S. Department of Education, 1994, p. 19.

MOVEMENT AND POSITIONING

Movement difficulties can range from mild to severe. Some children with physical disabilities may require electric wheelchairs. Others may use braces, crutches, or walkers. Still others may move without assistance but will require more time for moving about in the classroom and school. The ability to move must also be considered within the context of the degree of effort required of the student for movement. A student may be able to walk, for example, but the energy and time required for walking may be so tiring to that student that a wheelchair becomes a needed form of assistance (O'Connell, Barnhart, and Park, 1992).

The proper positioning of a child in a wheelchair may be very important to that child's ability to move her or his arms and the upper body. Positioning may also be important for proper breathing and swallowing. Some children may require frequent changes of position to help with the prevention of cramps and skin problems.

Teachers may require the assistance and consultation of physical therapists, occupational therapists, and physicians on matters relating to movement and positioning. These are issues that must be viewed as the shared responsibility of a number of different professionals working as a team on the student's behalf.

The most important considerations that must be addressed concerning mobility for students with physical disabilities have more to do with the physical environment of the school than with the students themselves. It is very important that schools are as accessible as possible for students using wheelchairs or other aids to mobility. The primary accessibility questions have to do with access to the school building, individual classrooms, and other school facilities (for example, the library, auditoriums, and gymnasiums), and access to toilets. Are sidewalks wide enough and smooth enough for wheelchair use? Do the sidewalks have curb cuts? Are entrances to the building at ground level, or do they have ramps? Are doorways wide enough to accommodate wheelchairs? Is at least one bathroom stall available that is wide enough and deep enough for wheelchair use? Does it have handrails?

The answers to these questions have increasingly become affirmative in recent years. New buildings are designed for accessibility. The modification of old buildings for accessibility has become common. It is important, however, to assess the needs of each individual student with physical disabilities and to make certain that a match exists between that student's needs and the physical characteristics of the school environment.

TABLE 5.6

Students with Other Health Impairments, Basis for Leaving School: School Year 1991–92

	Number	Percent
Received Diploma	1,771	48.6
Certificate (no high school diploma awarded)	614	16.9
Reached Maximum Age for Attendance	67	1.8
Dropped Out	606	16.6
Status Unknown	584	16.1

Source: Office of Special Education Programs. *Sixteenth Annual Report to Congress on the Implementation of the Individuals with Disabilities Education Act.* Washington, DC: U.S. Department of Education, 1994, p. 19.

COMMUNICATION

Students with physical disabilities have varying capacities for the development of speech, reading, and writing skills. Some children will have no difficulties in acquiring language skills and may excel in all verbal areas. Other students may require the availability of alternative modes of communication. Children with severe cerebral palsy, for example, may be unable to effectively use the muscles that are required for speech and writing. They may also have difficulty with the head and eye movements required for reading. These students must be provided with alternative means of communication.

There are many types of communication devices that can be of invaluable assistance to students with physical disabilities. A simple communication board can be made that enables the student to point or move her/his eyes to a picture, symbol, letter, or word. This was the kind of assistance that gave Bill a "voice" in the introductory story of this chapter. There are also now available a wide variety of electronic and computerized communication devices. Because of the remarkable development of microcomputers during the last two decades, it is now possible for persons without speech capabilities to produce intelligible speech through speech synthesizers and other devices that augment communication for people with disabilities (Mirenda and Iacono, 1990).

Computer hardware and software are now available that provide a variety of modes of input and output to help facilitate the language capabilities of people with physical disabilities. Voice-activation devices, for example, allow students to have greater access to information and greater control of their personal environments.

Communication is also an area that requires collaboration in the best interests of the student. Therapists, psychologists, physicians, and educators must work together to find the best modes of communication and the most effective means of instruction for the individual student with physical disabilities.

SELF-HELP SKILLS

Students with physical disabilities may need training and/or assistance in several self-help areas. Self-help needs like communication difficulties have often been viewed as barriers to the involvement of these students in regular classrooms. With the correct support, however, these are areas of life that need not lead to unnecessary segregation.

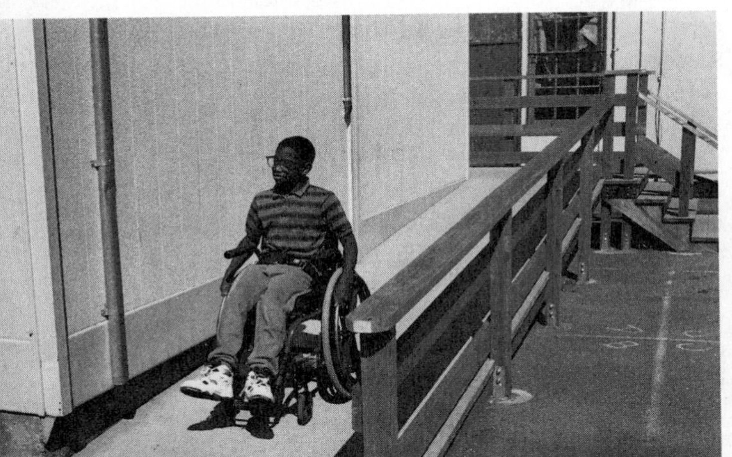

ELIZABETH CREWS/STOCK BOSTON

Some of the same muscle problems that cause communication difficulties for children and adults with physical disabilities may cause difficulties in eating. Movement problems of the trunk, arms and hands, and mouth may result in difficulties in getting food to the mouth, chewing, and swallowing. There are a number of devices and modifications that may be helpful for a student who has these disabilities. The handles of silverware can be changed to make gripping them easier. The angles of the handles can also be changed to meet individual needs. Plastic drinking straws and cup holders may also be helpful. Computer keyboards and the switches for televisions and other devices can be modified so that they can be used with finger or head pointing, mouthsticks, and eye or breath control.

Toileting is a special concern for some students with physical disabilities. Some children with spina bifida, for example, do not have the ability to control their bladders. These children are sometimes fitted with a bag that is attached to a surgically created opening (an ostomy) on the lower abdomen. Urine accumulates in the bag, and it is emptied at regular intervals during the day. This allows the child to stay dry and avoid the odor of urine. Other routines are established for bowel management. These modifications and routines are very important for children in both a physical and social-personal sense. In most instances all that is required of a teacher is an understanding of and sensitivity to these special arrangements in a student's life.

Students with physical disabilities are often on regimens of special medications. These students may be fully aware of and responsible for the schedules of their medications. They may need no special assistance with this matter. In other cases, students may need the assistance of a school nurse for medications and/or other medical matters.

In some cases, teachers may be asked to dispense medication or attend to some other minor medical need. This has been a matter of some controversy, and teachers must know the policies of their state and locality on this issue (McCoy, 1995). Before performing any medical function or teaching a student to perform a medical function for herself or himself, a number of questions need to be asked by the team that develops a student's IEP. These questions are:

- Who has the legal right or responsibility to perform this task?
- Who has the skill or expertise to perform this task or to teach the student to perform it independently?
- Who else could be trained to perform this task?
- Who is consistently available to perform this task or to teach the student to perform this task?
- When, where, and how is it appropriate to teach this task to a student?
- How quickly can it be expected that the student will learn to perform this task independently? (Kirk, Gallagher, and Anastasiow, 1993)

PSYCHOSOCIAL NEEDS

The diversity of physical and self-care needs that is to be found among students with physical disabilities is also true of their psychosocial needs. For some students, the existence of a physical disability may not significantly affect their psychological development or their social interactions. They may only experience the same challenges and have the same needs in growing up as other children and adolescents.

For some students with disabilities, however, growing up with these disabilities presents special challenges. Some researchers, for example, have found that children with physical disabilities have more difficulty in establishing a positive sense of self-esteem and experience more anxiety than other children (Harvey and Greenway, 1984). A variety of psychosocial responses to disabilities by the individuals who have them has been observed. Some children and adults with disabilities develop successful strategies for coping with those disabilities. Others have more negative experiences related to their disabilities (Wright, 1983). It is evident, however, that the attitudes and behavior of those people around the person with a disability determine, in part, the psychosocial consequences of that disability. When family members, friends, teachers, and classmates are supportive and accepting of students with disabilities, these students are more likely to be accepting of themselves (Best, Carpignano, Sirvis, and Bigge, 1991; Heinemann and Shontz, 1984). Creating a school environment that does support and accept students with physical disabilities is the focus of the next section of this chapter.

Ways of Helping Students with Physical Disabilities Succeed in Inclusive Classrooms

THE MOST CONDUCIVE ENVIRONMENT for learning for most students with physical disabilities is the regular classroom. In order to learn best how to live in a diverse and integrated community environment as adults, children and adolescents need to be in the most inclusive schools and classrooms that are appropriate to their educational, social, and physical needs. As discussed in the preceding section, modifications to the physical environment may be necessary. The integration of these students may also require the effective use of consultants in the classroom. Of equal importance, however, to physical adaptations and therapeutic/medical consultation is, as was discussed, the attitudinal atmosphere of the classroom. An attitude of acceptance in the classroom creates the proper context for fostering the independence that will be required of the student with physical disabilities in the adult world.

TEACHING FOR OPTIMAL INDEPENDENCE

The emphasis on instruction for these students, then, must be on optimal independence and self-determination. Through teaching them the skills needed for personal independence, confidence and self-esteem can also be enhanced. Thereby, a student's ability to establish social relations may also be increased as he/she becomes more independent.

Some ways of encouraging self-determination in students with physical disabilities have been suggested by Brotherson et al.:

- Teach choice, decision-making, and self-advocacy skills.
- Structure the school environment to ensure opportunities for choice.
- Serve as a resource for both home and community environments.
- Be advocates for community change and support parent advocacy.
- Support the community in accommodating to the needs of these children.
- Build partnerships with business and community leaders (Brotherson et al., 1995, p. 11).

GROUPING PATTERNS

Grouping of students in schools has often been a practice aimed at creating greater homogeneity of skills or abilities. As will be discussed in the chapter on students with special gifts and talents, this has created in some schools a degree of segregation of students that is not in the best interests of those students or of creating a positive school environment for all students. There are other patterns of grouping, however, that may actually promote more positive school environments and that may create more inclusive contexts for the education of students with disabilities.

Flexible grouping is a technique that may allow students with and without disabilities to work together toward the achievement of specific goals. These groupings of students can be formed and changed as learning or project goals are met and new ones are developed. Flexible groupings may include as few as two students or as many as ten. Each member of the group is encouraged to contribute to the specific task at hand according to his or her individual abilities (Unsworth, 1984). Flexible groups may be an excellent way to involve students with physical disabilities in art projects, research projects for social studies, or other activities that allow for individual differences in the contributions made to a group effort.

Cooperative grouping involves creating small groups of students of varying skills and abilities. These groups of four or five students each may be formed on the basis of shared interests or friendships. Members of the group help each other meet the goals that are set for learning. Group members are encouraged and recognized for helping one another. Cooperative grouping may be used for instruction in reading and math skills. Studies have indicated that cooperative grouping results in both stronger relationships among students and higher academic achievement (Slavin, 1987).

Groupings may provide students with the satisfaction of tutoring and encouraging one another. Even more important, however, it may facilitate the establishment of friendships that might not otherwise develop. Strully and Strully (1989), in fact, have advocated the direct training of students who do not have disabilities in ways to be a friend to students with disabilities in classroom work and other school activities.

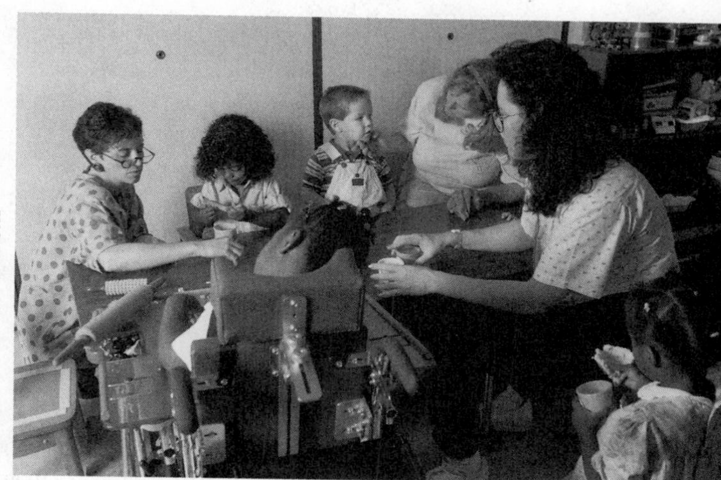

CAROL PALMER BRILLIANT/THE PICTURE CUBE

TEAM TEACHING

It is essential for the creation of more inclusive schools and classrooms that educators work together more cooperatively to provide conducive learning environments and effective instruction for all their students. Cooperative efforts of teachers may not only benefit children with disabilities but may result in improved learning for other students. It has been demonstrated that with careful planning and scheduling, and with the creation of clearly articulated goals, students with disabilities can be taught effectively alongside students who do not have disabilities (Jones and Carlier, 1995).

Among the benefits of team teaching that accrue to both students with and those without disabilities are: the development of better planning skills, the promotion of problem-solving skills, increased self-esteem, improved communication skills, more satisfying and effective social skills, and an increase in academic learning (Cohen, 1986; Putnam, 1993).

Teaching partnerships must be built upon cooperation, trust, and communication. They ultimately require change and compromise between the partners. Teachers in one pilot team-teaching program emphasized the need for developing collaborative values and observed that partners must have adequate opportunities to come to know each other and ask each other lots of questions (Janney et al., 1995). It has been pointed out, in fact, that teams of teachers often refer to their partnerships as "marriages" (Working Forum on Inclusive Schools, 1994). The "marriage" of a regular classroom teacher and a special education teacher built on the strength of their differences may be a strong and productive one. A regular education teacher may bring to the partnership greater knowledge of particular subjects or skill areas. A special education teacher may have more knowledge about adapting curricula and methodologies to meet individual needs. The "marriage" of these two strengths may provide a more positive and productive learning environment for all children (Working Forum on Inclusive Schools, 1994).

Case Studies and Questions to Consider

STUDENT: JESSICA HOPE

SCHOOL: LOVING ELEMENTARY

CURRENT PLACEMENT: REGULAR FIFTH GRADE/RESOURCE ROOM

AGE: 12 YEARS, 3 MONTHS

Family Structure and Home Environment

Jessica lives in an apartment with her mother, Carol Hope, who is forty-seven years old. She is divorced from Jessica's father, Jesse Hope, who is a forty-four-year-old carpenter. Ms. Hope describes herself as a homemaker but explains that during the school year, she works as a baby-sitter. Ms. Hope says that another important activity for her for the past few years has been assisting Jessica daily with her physical therapy exercises. She feels that these activities have been very valuable to Jessica in coping with her disability. Jessica's cerebral palsy has been described as being at a moderate level. She walks with the aid of braces and crutches. She has full use of her upper extremities. Jessica speaks with a slight speech impairment.

Although Jessica has several older siblings and stepsiblings, only her sister, Carla, lives with her and Ms. Hope. Carla is eleven. Ms. Hope reports that the two girls are very close in their relationship.

Parental Perception of Child's Developmental Progress and Needs

Jessica has been receiving resource services for several years. Ms. Hope is very pleased with Jessica's progress in school. She feels that the resource room help that Jessica has been receiving has been very good for her. Ms. Hope says that she knows Jessica looks forward to going to school, and that she gets along well with the other students.

Ms. Hope says that she is proud of Jessica's accomplishments both in and outside of school. She says that her daughter has come a long way from being a five-year-old who could not walk and had difficulty with even the most basic communication. She expresses gratitude to all who have helped Jessica grow from the need for a full-time special class to the point that she only needs resource help.

The major area where Ms. Hope feels that Jessica continues to need particular help is in self-confidence and assertiveness. Ms. Hope feels that, even given her age, Jessica is too passive.

Ms. Hope wants her daughter to grow up to be able to take care of herself—to be an independent person. She hopes Jessica will learn to stand up for her own rights. Ms. Hope says that what pleases her most about her daughter is her overall personality. She remarked on Jessica's pleasant manner and positive approach to other people.

Additional Considerations

Jessica Hope lives in a family that is doing its best to use its resources to support her in a positive way. Her mother is proud of the progress Jessica is making in school. She seems to be willing to do everything she can to promote Jessica's further development.

Jessica's resource room teacher feels that Jessica's continuing learning needs are actually the result of a slow start in school because of her physical disability. She thinks that this has also been compounded by the lack of social interaction that Jessica experienced in school earlier because of her special class placement. Jessica will be going to middle school next year, and her resource room teacher feels that she is ready for complete inclusion with no special services. Jessica's regular class teacher, however, is not sure that Jessica is ready to be totally independent of special services.

Questions

1. What can be done to further explore the question of the nature of Jessica's school program for next year?
2. What can be done during the summer to help Jessica prepare for the transition to middle school?
3. What can be done at the middle school to further promote Jessica's social development?

STUDENT: JAMIE JOYCE

SCHOOL: PROJECT INFANT

CURRENT PLACEMENT: EARLY INTERVENTION SPECIAL EDUCATION

AGE: 3 YEARS, 1 MONTH

Family Structure and Home Environment

Jamie and his family have benefited from the services of Project Infant for the past two years. His parents are looking forward to having Jamie involved in Project Toddler, a preschool special education class, this year. Jamie has cerebral palsy. He has a specially designed wheelchair that aids not only his mobility, but also his posture and positioning. At home, Jamie is alert and happy.

Jamie lives with his parents, Charles and Catherine Joyce. Dr. Joyce is thirty-six years old and is a psychologist in private practice. Ms. Joyce is thirty-two years old and is an occupational therapist. Presently, she is devoting most of her time and energy to her family. Jamie has two sisters, Samantha and Jill. Samantha is six years old and will be in first grade this year. Jill is four and will be going to nursery school five mornings a week this fall. The Joyce family lives in a pleasant and orderly home. A visitor in their home would observe a loving and healthy environment.

Parental Perception of the Student's School Program

Ms. Joyce speaks with pleasure and pride of the progress that Jamie has been making. In addition to his participation in Project Infant, he has been receiving physical therapy on a regular basis. Ms. Joyce noted that Jamie is making gains in his ability to sit independently, and his production of sound is improving qualitatively and quantitatively.

Jamie's mother believes that his greatest strength is his determination. She describes him as a child who will labor diligently to reach (literally and figuratively) for things. There was a tone of respect in her voice as she described her child in this way.

Ms. Joyce believes that Jamie's greatest need is the continued development of his muscle tone and strength. She hopes and believes that her son's motor development will proceed until he will eventually be able to walk.

Additional Considerations

Jamie's parents are looking forward to his being served by Project Toddler. They are confident he will benefit greatly from this involvement. They have no question that it is the right placement for him.

Questions

1. What are some ways that Jamie might be included in activities with children who do not have disabilities?
2. What additional services during the next few years might help to prepare Jamie for the most inclusive school environment possible?
3. Are there ways that Jamie's sisters might become more involved in their brother's development?

References

Anderson, J., J. Hinojosa, G. Bedell, and M. Kaplan. "Occupational Therapy for Children with Perinatal HIV Infection." *American Journal of Occupational Therapy, 44,* 1990: 249–255.

Batshaw, M. L., and Y. M. Perret. *Children with Handicaps: A Medical Primer,* 3d ed. Baltimore, MD: Paul H. Brookes, 1992.

Best, S., J. Carpignano, B. Sirvis, and J. Bigge. "Psychosocial Aspects of Physical Disability." In J. L. Bigge (Ed.), *Teaching Individuals with Physical and Multiple Disabilities,* 3d ed. New York: Merrill, Macmillan, 1991: 102–131.

Bigge, J. L. (Ed.) *Teaching Individuals with Physical and Multiple Disabilities.* 3d ed. New York: Merrill, Macmillan, 1991.

Brotherson, M., C. Cook, R. Cunconan-Lahr, and M. Wehmeyer. "Policy Supporting Self-Determination in the Environments of Children with Disabilities." *Education and Training in Mental Retardation and Developmental Disabilities, 30,* 1995: 3–14.

Centers for Disease Control. *Guidelines for Serving Children with Acquired Immune Deficiency Syndrome (AIDS).* Atlanta, GA: Centers for Disease Control, 1985.

Cohen, E. *Designing Groupwork.* New York: Teachers College Press, 1986.

Federal Register. 34 C.F.R., Chap. III, Sec. 300.7, 309.7, 1990.

Freeman, J. M., and E. Vining. "Is Surgery the Answer for Childhood Epilepsy?" *Contemporary Pediatrics, 5,* 1990: 88–95.

Harvey, D., and A. Greenway. "The Self-Concept of Physically Handicapped Children and Their Non-Handicapped Siblings: An Empirical Investigation." *Journal of Child Psychology and Psychiatry, 25,* 1984: 273–284.

Heinemann, A., and F. Shontz. "Adjustment Following Disability: Representative Case Studies." *Rehabilitation Counseling Bulletin, 28*(1), 1984: 3–14.

Janney, R., M. Snell, M. Beers, and M. Raynes. "Integrating Students with Moderate and Severe Disabilities into General Education Classes." *Exceptional Children, 61,* 1995: 425–439.

Jones, M., and L. Carlier. "Creating Inclusionary Opportunities for Learners with Multiple Disabilities: A Team Teaching Approach." *Teaching Exceptional Children, 27*(3), 1995: 23–27.

Kirk, S., J. Gallagher, and N. Anastasiow. *Educating Exceptional Children,* 7th ed. Boston: Houghton Mifflin, 1993.

Kobrin, E. R. *Issues and Answers: A Guide for Parents of Teens and Young Adults with Epilepsy.* Landover, MD: Epilepsy Foundation of America, 1991.

McCoy, K. *Teaching Special Learners in the General Education Classrooms.* Denver: Love, 1995.

Mira, M. P., B. J. Tucker, and J. S. Tyler. *Traumatic Brain Injury in Children and Adolescents.* Austin, TX: Pro-Ed, 1992.

Mirenda, P., and J. Iacono. "Communication Options for Persons with Severe and Profound Disabilities: State of the Art and Future Directions." *Journal of the Association for Persons with Severe Handicaps, 15,* 1990: 3–21.

National Information Center for Children and Youth with Disabilities. *Spina Bifida Fact Sheet Number 12* (FS12). Washington, DC: National Information Center for Children and Youth with Disabilities, 1993.

O'Connell, D. G., R. Barnhart, and L. Park. "Muscular Endurance and Wheelchair Propulsion in Children with Cerebral Palsy and Myelomeningocele." *Archives of Physical Medicine and Rehabilitation, 73,* 1992: 709–711.

Office of Special Education Programs. *Sixteenth Annual Report to Congress on the Implementation of the Individuals with Disabilities Education Act.* Washington, DC: U.S. Department of Education, 1994.

———. *Seventeenth Annual Report to Congress on the Implementation of the Individuals with Disabilities Education Act.* Washington, DC: U.S. Department of Education, 1995.

Putnam, J. *Cooperative Learning and Strategies for Inclusion: Celebrating Diversity in the Classroom.* Baltimore, MD: Paul H. Brookes, 1993.

Slavin, R. E. "Cooperative Learning and the Cooperative School." *Educational Leadership, 45,* 1987: 7–13.

Strully, R., and C. Strully. "Friendships as an Educational Goal." In S. Stainback, W. Stainback, and M. Forest (Eds.), *Educating All Students in the Mainstream of General Education.* Baltimore, MD: Brookes, 1989: 59–68.

Unsworth, L. "Meeting Individual Needs Through Flexible Within-Class Grouping of Pupils." *Reading Teacher, 38,* 1984: 298–304.

U.S. Department of Education. "Rules and Regulations." *Federal Register, 58*(145), July 30, 1993: 40961–40973.

U.S. Department of Health and Human Services. *Understanding AIDS.* Rockville, MD: Centers for Disease Control, 1988.

White, S. "Common Drug Therapy of Childhood Seizure Disorders." *Babynetworks, III,* 1995: 7.

Working Forum on Inclusive Schools. *Creating Schools for All Our Students: What 12 Schools Have to Say.* Reston, VA: Council for Exceptional Children, 1994.

Wright, B. A. *Physical Disability: A Psychosocial Approach.* New York: Harper & Row, 1983.

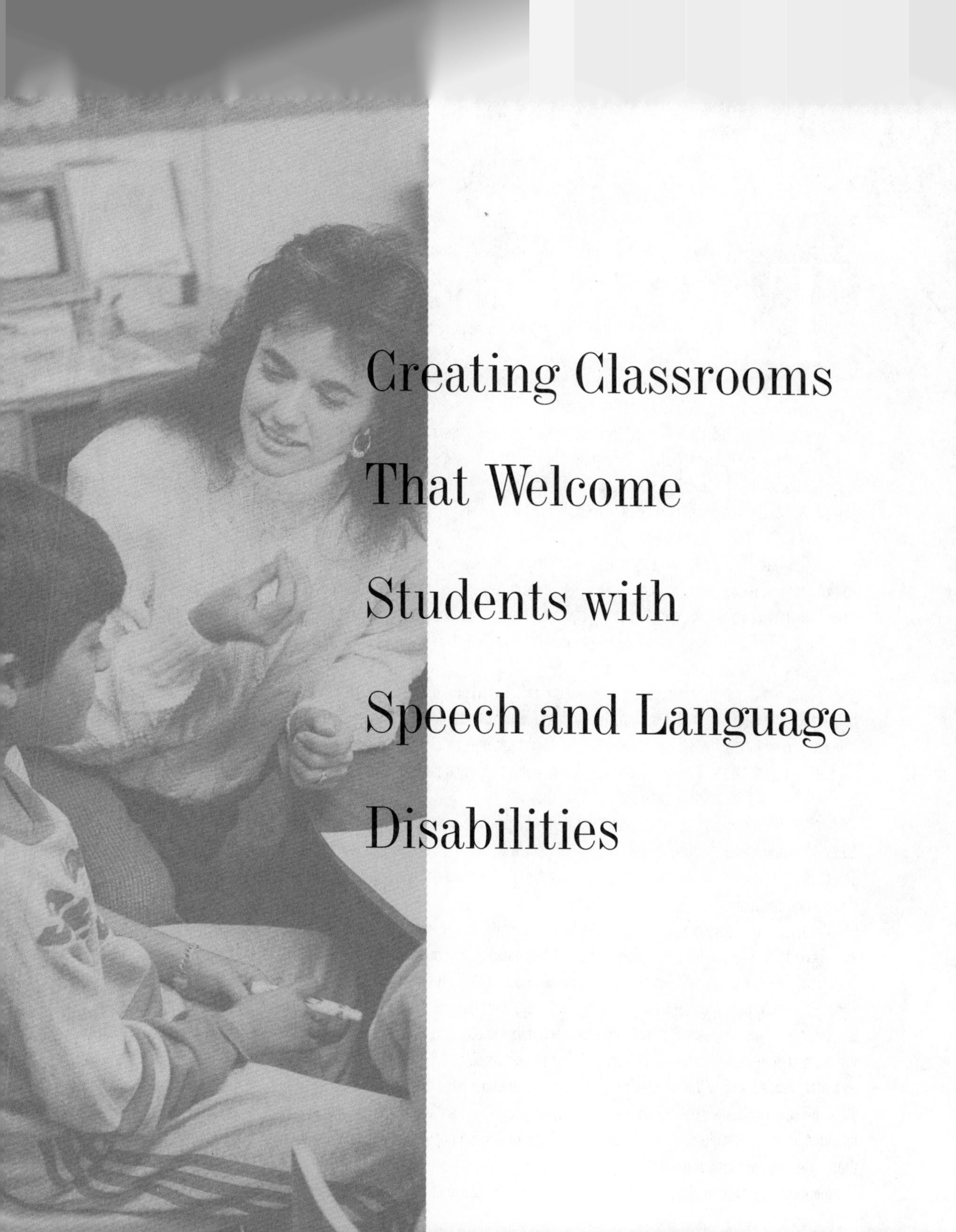

Creating Classrooms That Welcome Students with Speech and Language Disabilities

Learning to Be a Jamaican: Lessons in Patois

The inauguration of President Kennedy, his inspiring speeches, and his youthful leadership are memories that have been vivid in my mind since I was an adolescent. Although some of the dreams of social reform of those years have clearly failed us and some of the hopes of that time have become tarnished, I still cherish the energy and optimism that John Kennedy brought to our country. Although some of the people and events of those years have ebbed and waned in their influence in my personal and professional life, one of the ideals of those days became central to my identity.

In a sense, my adult awareness of the relationship between politics, leadership, and social issues began with the Kennedy presidency, but it all seemed threatened by his sudden and meaningless assassination. Watching the casket-bearing caisson, the lone prancing horse, little John John's salute, and the procession of mourners in the streets brought to my mind questions of whether, indeed, the dreams would die with the dreamer. The dreams were crystallized anew, however, with the campaign of his brother Robert. Listening to Bobby Kennedy's speeches of commitment and resolve convinced me that they could be kept alive.

The year after Bobby's murder and the assassination of Martin Luther King, Jr., my wife Joyce and I decided to be part of the dream that remained alive. We joined the Peace Corps. This had been a goal for both of us that began in high school when we listened to John Kennedy's description of a "moral equivalent of war." We continued to want to be part of that effort, and after we finished college and married, we submitted our Peace Corps applications with visions of being called to serve in Africa or South America.

When the call came, however, it was to an unexpected part of the world. We were invited to enter Peace Corps training for two years of service in Jamaica. All that I knew of Jamaica when the invitation came was rum, the limbo, and, vaguely, a new kind of music called reggae. My stereotypic images of the country were simply those of a would-be Caribbean tourist. Soon, however, I learned of a Jamaica that most people, even those who have visited its tourist beaches, have not heard of or seen.

The Jamaica I discovered as I read the Peace Corps literature was a Third World nation struggling to feed, clothe, house, and educate its people. It was a nation of people with a sense of cultural pride but little else. Economically, it was one of the poorest nations in the Western Hemisphere. It was a country striving to define itself out of the vestiges of slavery and colonialism.

Joyce and I joined the Peace Corps in June 1969. It was an exciting experience for us as we left everything we were accustomed to and flew to California for our initial orientation and training. We were soon caught up in the energy of becoming part of a group of about a hundred people who, for varied reasons, shared our dream of the Peace Corps. We were a diverse group. Most of us were young, but there were several people in their forties and fifties. There were even a few retirees. There seemed to be only two common denominators in our group. First, we all seemed to have a sense of the hope of somehow making a "difference." But there was something else—we also seemed to have a sense of adventure that blended well with that idealism. As we came to know each other, that blend became even more apparent. We were not self-sacrificing martyrs. We were concerned people, but we were also individuals who enjoyed new experiences, new people, and new ideas. When I looked back later on those people who did not survive the training, and some of those who did not make it through the entire two years, I found that in a number of cases part of the blend was missing. The idealism and commitment to service were there, but the sense of adventure that helps sustain a person through such commitments was missing. I think that the same may be true for teaching. It requires a belief in and commitment to ideals. Teachers, however, must be sustained in their work by a sense of adventure and risk-taking. It takes both for a career as daring and demanding as that of an educator.

Each day of training brought new insights and adventures to us. One morning we were taken to the Mexican border at Tijuana, given a map of places to find, given a dollar, and told to be back at the border by seven o'clock. We were placed in an urban ghetto for several weeks to be given the experience of being a minority in an unwelcoming environment. We were scolded by Black Panther intellectuals who questioned our motivations as "do-gooders." They challenged us to stay at home and do something about the racism in our own neighborhoods and the poverty in our own country. We were examined and tested in detail for psychological and medical problems that might interfere with being able to serve in a positive role for two years in a country so much different from our own. We were immunized, even for diseases that had never been detected in the hemisphere, let alone in Jamaica. We were exposed to new diets, a new history, and a new way of thinking about our own competencies. We were also cautioned not to expect to accomplish major transformations. "Small gains" seemed to be the prevailing message from those who did their best to prepare us for our lives as volunteers.

Just as Joyce and I were gaining confidence in our abilities to complete the training and serve successfully as volunteers, we were thrown an unexpected curve. A decision was made that I should go to Jamaica early, and that she would follow with most of the other volunteers in three weeks. My assignment was to be working with teachers on better understanding child development and teaching children with special needs. It was decided that I could best benefit from the remaining weeks of training by being in Jamaica and learning about the schools, families, and culture of the community where I would be living. Joyce would be working with preschool teachers. She was involved in an excellent training program in California in preschool education in developing countries, so she would remain there. She would join me when she and the other volunteers had completed that training.

We were disappointed but understood the reason for the separation. I left one evening with a few other volunteers who were also being sent to Jamaica early, and we arrived in Kingston the following evening. It was the day of the first moon landing. I listened to the words of Neil Armstrong as I sat on the veranda of the home of a Jamaican Ministry of Education official. She explained to me that many of the "country folks" in Jamaica did not believe that Americans were really landing on the moon. The night before, she had heard a fisherman say that Americans couldn't be landing on the moon because the moon was in Jamaica that evening: "Look bov your head, mon. It right there. You see any Americans?"

The next morning I was on my way to meet lots of "country folks." I was taken to the village where we would live for the next two years. I was excited, and a little intimidated, when I was dropped off at the home of a teacher who had agreed to give me room and board until I could find a place for Joyce and me to live. I was immediately made to feel a part of the family, however, and was instructed on how to eat akee and saltfish, curried goat, and boiled green bananas. I was also given a lesson in the proper way to drink white rum (straight, chased with water).

After breakfast on my first morning in the village, I walked around my new neighborhood. People were friendly, although I am certain that most of them thought that I was a tourist who had strayed from the usual tourist haunts. Eventually, I reached the market at the center of town. People were gathered around the edges of a large open area selling fish, vegetables, fruits, and an assortment of clothing and household items. I enjoyed looking at the items that people had spread on the ground in front of them. Again, I was mistaken for a tourist several times and offered special deals on trinkets. I finally gave in to one very persistent woman who said that I needed a hat to "put shade pon you."

Actually, I liked the straw hat a lot and thought it gave me a distinctly nontourist look. It was the kind of hat I had seen a number of Jamaican men wearing. I soon learned, however, that it was not convincing.

After putting on my new hat, I started walking across the open area of the market square. As I did, I heard a strong, clear voice calling out, "Why are you here? This is not your place; this is not your place. Why are you here?" I saw immediately that it was the voice of a man with a long beard and dreadlocks. He was a Rastafarian of about fifty. He carried a long staff, and he had a cloth bag slung over one shoulder. Again he called out, "This is not your place," and this time it was obvious that he was yelling to me. I continued to walk across the square and tried to ignore his calls. I noticed, however, that activity had stopped in the market and people were watching me. I wanted to disappear. I decided, however, that since this was my first day in the place that would be my home for two years, I had better respond to the man. I thought I should try to understand what he was saying to me. I walked over to him, attempting to hide my fear, and asked if he were talking to me.

The man's eyes were clear and piercing. He seemed to look straight through me and then explained, "This is not your place. This is not a place for tourists. You belong somewhere else. This is a market for Jamaican people."

Rastafarians are keenly aware of the psychology and sociology of slavery and colonialism that continues to keep people in bondage even after they have been politically emancipated. They were among the earliest of the people who promoted black pride and a sense of connectedness to their African cultural and religious roots. They have expressed a sense of dignity in separating themselves from what they think has tainted the lives of people of African descent. As this man was telling me, he thought that I didn't belong in his village, that it was not good for me to be there.

I paused for a moment and then responded to him that I was not a tourist. "I have come here to live for a while," I said. "I am a Peace Corps volunteer." The man seemed to ponder my comment for a few moments. He also seemed to be studying my face again with his piercing eyes. I would later learn that he understood very well the mission of the Peace Corps. I would learn, in fact, that his understanding of the government, history, and politics of the United States was quite astute. But after a few more moments he asked quite simply, "What is your mission here with the Peace Corps?"

During our training, we had examined this question repeatedly. What am I trying to do? For Jamaicans? For myself? For my own country? Why am I doing this? Ideals? Adventure? Escape? Some of these questions raced through my mind as I formulated my response to his question, but none of them seemed to matter at the moment. I replied, "I have come here to be a teacher." Immediately he asked, "Who will you teach, Teacher?" I explained that I would be working with Jamaican teachers and that I would also be teaching Jamaican children.

The question that came next from the man in dreadlocks has remained fixed in my memory for over twenty-five years. He again looked me directly in the eyes and asked, "What will you teach them, Teacher—how to be Americans? We need our children to be strong Jamaicans. Can you teach them that?"

I was stunned by the question, and I had no answer for it. I muttered something about teaching reading and writing and other skills, but my response was not satisfying even to me. We talked a little longer, the circle of people around us who had been listening to our conversation dispersed, and we parted ways for the day. For weeks, however, I was haunted by his question and sought for myself the answer to it. What would I teach the children other than reading and writing? What did I know that I could teach them that would help them be strong Jamaicans?

During my years in Jamaica, I revisited that question many times and found many different answers. During that time, I also found a friend in the Rastafarian who had called to me with questions about why I was in his village. He was known by everyone in the village as Tennie. He was also known to many as a wild man who could spend the better part of any day lecturing loudly to the people in the market about his most recent political, religious, or economic concern. I came to understand that he enjoyed debating issues with anyone who took him seriously and that he was actually very open to the ideas of others. He was, in fact, one of the most intellectually active and insightful people whom I have ever met. He was also passionately concerned about his country.

As I became more acclimated to the culture and language of Jamaica, I found that I could follow more easily the conversations in the market and along the roads that were incomprehensible to me when I first arrived. The official language of Jamaica is English. It is the official language of instruction in the schools, and all government and business is conducted in English. The language spoken as the most common social and personal means of expression, however, is Patois (pronounced PAT-wah). Patois is a blend of English, a number of African dialects, and many words and expressions of uniquely Jamaican origin. There is no written form of Patois, so the only way to learn it is to be immersed in it.

Even though my work with teachers and children was in English, I heard them speaking Patois on the playground and at other informal moments. I heard Patois as I traveled the roads between schools, and I heard it in the market. I also heard Patois at the little store (a "shop," to Jamaicans) where I sometimes stopped for hard bread and cheese and something cold to drink on my way home at the end of the day. It was in that little shop that I decided that I would make my first public try at speaking Patois.

One afternoon as I was sitting in the shop eating my bread and cheese and sipping my ginger beer, a child I had worked with that day in her school entered with her mother. She did not see me at first, but when she did, I greeted her with "Whapon" and a few other words in Patois. Immediately, her mother took her by the hand and fled from the shop. The owner, Mr. Peachel, looked at me in disbelief and said, "Forgive me, Teacher, but I must tell you that you insulted that mother and her child." I asked if I had said something the wrong way, with the wrong inflection perhaps, that had made my Patois expression of greeting come out insulting. "No, Teacher, they understood you. But you must not speak Patois to the children. You are a Teacher, and you are an American. The mother thought you were speaking down to her child as if she couldn't understand English." I understood then that my use of Patois with the child was as unnatural as if I had attempted to use an African-American dialect to a child and mother in the United States.

I eventually came to use Patois in my personal relationships. As I came to know fishermen who beached their boats and mended their nets near our home, Patois became a natural part of our conversations. Late-night conversations with my Jamaican educator friends were often facilitated by good Jamaican rum and filled with Patois expressions. In fact, those friends delighted in my use of these expressions and my increasing understanding of the Jamaican "inside jokes" that came to me with time. They would sometimes remark that I was "becoming a Jamaican."

I believe that in some ways I did become a Jamaican and still am. The drawing that hangs on my office wall of a Jamaican woman and her infant (a Jamaican madonna) is one of my most treasured possessions. Tennie also thought I had become a Jamaican, and we both knew that we had become friends. I have a large photograph of him that he reluctantly consented to when another Jamaican friend asked to take his picture. I treasure it also.

During the time we were in the Peace Corps, we missed the spectacle of Woodstock and the tragedy of Kent State. We returned to the United States in 1971 to a country that had changed dramatically. We had also undergone a transformation.

In addition to becoming a little bit of a Jamaican during those years, I think that I also learned a great deal about teaching that has been central to my life as an educator. I learned that I wasn't there to teach the children to become Americans. I learned that I was there to teach them what I could that would enable them to have choices in their lives. I was there to teach them to understand as much as possible about their history and circumstances so that they could make their own decisions about where they wanted to go and what they wanted to become. I was there to help teach them the joy and excitement of learning. In answer to Tennie's question, I hope that in this sense I helped a few of them become stronger Jamaicans.

Speech Differences and Disorders

The American Speech-Language-Hearing Association (ASHA) defines a *speech disorder* as "an impairment of the articulation of speech sounds, fluency, and/or voice" (American Speech-Language-Hearing Association, 1993). In other words, a speech disorder is a problem in the expression of spoken messages. In contrast, ASHA defines a *language disorder* as "impaired comprehension and/or use of spoken, written, and/or other symbol systems" (American Speech-Language-Hearing Association, 1993). A language disorder, according to this definition, may be a problem with the use of words or poor grammar. It may also be a problem in understanding the speech of others. In addition, it may involve written communication.

Speech, then, is the ability to express one's thoughts by speech sounds, while language is defined as communication that may use a system of vocal sounds, the use of written symbols, and the use of signs or gestures. Language, therefore, is a larger and more complex category than speech.

The focus of this chapter will be on disabilities in the expression and/or comprehension of speech. In that sense, it will include both speech and language disorders. It will not, however, include disorders in written communication. These are addressed in Chapter 2, on learning disabilities.

SPEECH AND LANGUAGE DIFFERENCES

Speech is a very individual process. The way a person speaks is a part of her or his identity. During the course of our physical, psychological, and social development, we acquire unique patterns of speech that are manifestations of family, cultural, and physical influences. Each of us speaks with accents, dialects, and idiosyncrasies that reflect these influences. A visitor to Brooklyn, New York, from Beaufort, South Carolina, may be immediately recognized by a vendor as "not being from Flatbush" by the way he orders his hot dog. A visitor to Beaufort from Brooklyn may be obvious in the "low country" of South Carolina by the way he orders a soft drink. Neither of these visitors, however, has a speech disorder. Every language has a variety of forms. These dialects result from demographic and social influences. The English spoken in the United States, for example, includes dialects that have been described as African-American, Appalachian, Southern, and Hispanic.

Speech is considered disordered only when it has characteristics that genuinely interfere with communication and create discomfort for the speaker and the listener. One rule of thumb for considering whether a person has a speech disorder rather than a speech difference is that the line between difference and disorder is crossed when the listener consistently focuses on how things are said rather than what is said. When that line is crossed, speech communication has truly become impaired.

In addition to interfering with communication, a speech disorder may also:

- Create a learning problem for the person,
- Result in a vocational and economic disadvantage,
- Interfere with interpersonal relationships, or
- Cause harm to the person's psychological well-being.

THE PROCESS OF SPEECH

The process of producing speech is a complex one. It involves many parts of the body (see

Figure 6.1). Given the complexity of this process, it is not surprising that there are a number of things that can go wrong. The complexity of this process is also a reason why speech patterns are so unique to individuals and why we consider our own speech to be an important aspect of our personalities.

Speech develops rapidly during the first five years of life. The acquisition of the basic elements of speech comes easily to most children. Box 6.1 lists some of the milestones of speech development that are usually achieved during these early years of life.

The raw power of speech is breath. The lungs and diaphragm move exhaled breath up to the larynx, where sound will be produced. Anything that interferes with breathing, therefore, can cause problems with speech. Most people have had the experience of trying to speak with a bad cough. Being interrupted by a cough spasm can be particularly frustrating in the context of making a presentation or even trying to talk over the telephone. Fortunately, this is only a temporary inconvenience. People who have chronic lung problems, however, may also experience speech disabilities. A person with emphysema, for example, may avoid situations that require speech, especially with strangers, because of the labored speech that is caused by their chronic shortness of breath.

When exhaled breath reaches the *larynx*, this raw material of speech is converted into sound by the vibration of the vocal cords. It is

FIGURE 6.1

The Mechanisms of Speech

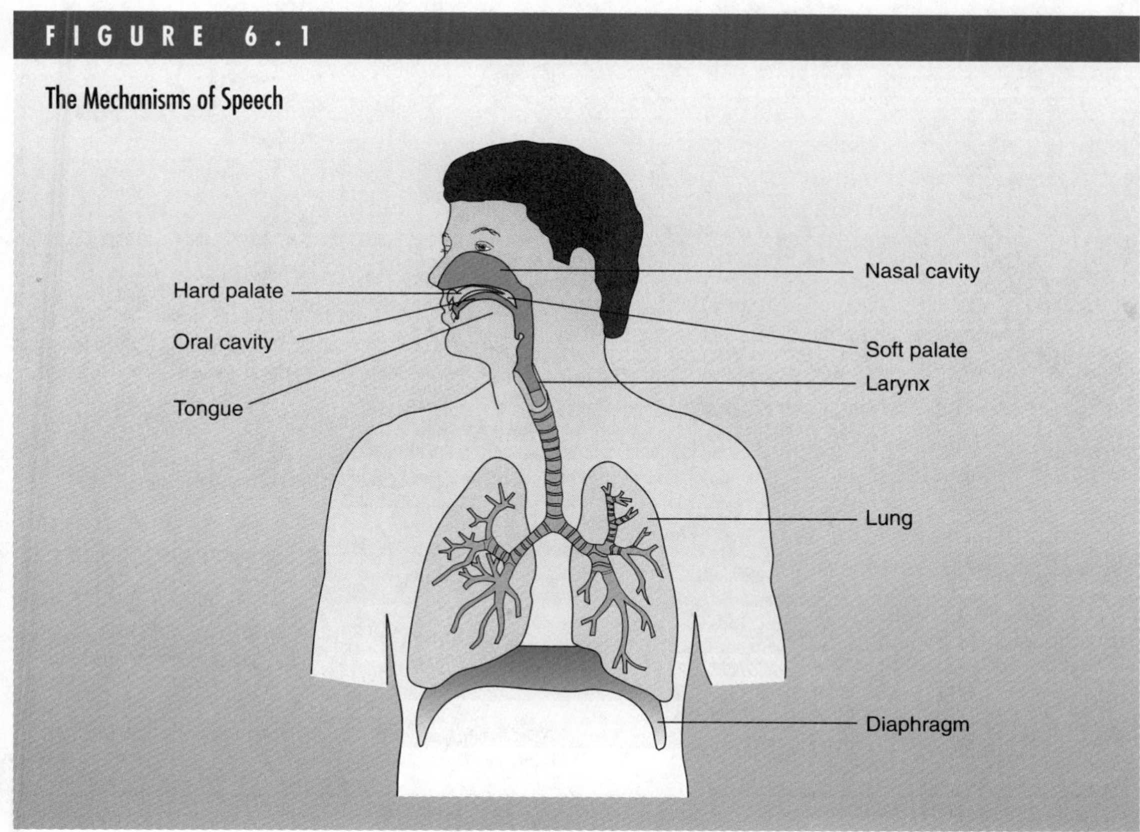

in the larynx that breath becomes voice. When someone has the experience of "losing their voice," the vocal folds are not functioning and the person must speak with breath. Having laryngitis is an inconvenience, and without a voice we feel that we are not, in fact, ourselves. Chronic loss of voice can be an even greater threat to a person's self-concept. Cancer of the larynx and its surgical removal can create problems both in communication and in a

BOX 6.1

Typical Speech and Language Development

First Year

- Crying.
- Different types of crying communicate different feelings and needs (for instance, a hungry cry, an angry cry, a fearful cry).
- Coos develop into babbling sounds.
- Voice inflection develops as the baby is able to control her/his voice.
- The baby may respond to and repeat some words (for example, "mama," "dada").

Second Year

- Articulation attempts are characterized by substitutions, omissions, and other developmentally normal errors ("tar" for *car*, "mi" for *milk*, and so on).
- The child repeats words that are said by others but without comprehension.
- The child may be able to form short sentences (for example, "go tar" or "want mi").
- The child understands many more words than she/he is able to say.

Third Year

- The child talks in full sentences.
- The child engages in meaningful conversations with others.
- The child pronounces most vowel sounds correctly but may still have difficulty with consonant sounds.

Fourth Year

- The child may speak rapidly and talk a lot.
- Repetitions and hesitations in speech are normal (for example, "b-b-breakfast," "l-l-lunch"). This should not be considered stuttering.
- The child understands and appreciates more abstract concepts (for example, honesty, bravery, a promise) and enjoys stories that use abstractions.

Fifth Year

- The child can change her/his speech to be better understood (for instance, understands that talking to a younger child may require accommodations).
- The child can memorize poems and songs, and enjoys doing so.
- The child may still have normal difficulty with the articulation of certain consonant sounds and blends. These difficulties should not be considered articulation disorders.

After Age Five

- After age five, most children have acquired most of the elements of adult speech.
- Some articulation sounds, however, may not be completely mastered until age seven or eight.
- The speech of kindergartners and first graders shows the influence of the family and cultural environment in terms of accent and dialects.

Adapted from W. Heward and M. Orlansky. *Exceptional Children: An Introductory Survey of Special Education.* New York: Macmillan, 1992, pp. 238–240.

person's sense of self. Support groups have proven to be very helpful to persons facing the psychological impact of the permanent loss of their voices. Even though electronic devices or pharyngeal speech (that is, controlled burping) may provide a replacement voice, the effect of losing one's natural voice is not easily dismissed.

The articulation of the voice produced in the larynx takes place in the *oral cavity*. The tongue, teeth, gums, and palate work together to produce the sounds that are put together to make words. The vowels, consonants, and blends that constitute words are articulated in the oral cavity as the final product of the speech process that originated in the lungs.

In another sense, however, the oral cavity is not the end point of the process of speech. The sense of hearing is integral to the learning and monitoring of speech. Problems in hearing can cause delayed speech in children and can result in deterioration in the speech of adults who acquire hearing problems.

The brain is also central to the process of speech. Since speech is such a heavily learned skill, any problem in the brain that interferes with learning may also interfere with speech. The motor areas of the brain also function to control the movements of the various parts of the body that are responsible for speech production. It is not surprising then that speech disorders are often associated with mental retardation and cerebral palsy.

QUALITIES OF SPEECH

The unique and individual character of each of our voices is the result of a number of interacting factors. The thickness and elasticity of the vocal folds (also called the vocal cords) determines the pitch of the voice. As the vocal folds change during childhood and adolescence, the pitch of the voice changes. This process of change is particularly evident for boys during puberty when the changes cause the voice to crack and oscillate. As adults, males tend to have thicker and less elastic vocal folds. Their voices, therefore, tend to have a lower pitch because the folds vibrate more slowly than those of females.

There are two voice resonance chambers. Both the oral chamber (mouth cavity) and the nasal chamber (nasal cavity) contribute to the resonance of the voice. When there is too much nasality (hypernasality) or not enough nasality (denasality) in the voice, the voice sounds distorted. There is a flap attached to the back of the roof of the mouth. If the flap is open, nasal sounds are produced. If it is closed, nonnasal sounds are produced. If the flap is blocked closed (as sometimes happens with a head cold), the voice may sound flat. When there is too much nasality, the voice may actually sound like the person is speaking through the nose (Rice and Schuele, 1995).

The intensity (loudness) of the voice is a function of the pressure of the air coming through the vocal folds. Just as some people have higher-pitched voices than others, some have more intense voices than others. Of course, all people have a range of voice intensities that may be used in varying social situations.

Major Categories of Disorders in Speech and Language

SPEECH AND LANGUAGE DISORDERS are most common among young children. The prevalence of these disorders decreases markedly during adolescence and early adulthood. Speech and language disorders constitute the second-largest category of exceptionality among children. Only the category of learning disabilities is larger. During the 1992–93 school year, more than a million students were classified as having speech and language disorders (Office of Special Education Programs, 1994).

TABLE 6.1

Students with Speech or Language Impairments, Number and Placement Percentages: School Year 1992–93

Number	998,049
Regular Class	81.8%
Resource Room	10.7%
Separate Class	6.0%
Separate School	1.4%
Residential Facility	0.1%
Homebound/Hospital Setting	0.1%

Source: Office of Special Education Programs. *Seventeenth Annual Report to Congress on the Implementation of the Individuals with Disabilities Education Act.* Washington, DC: U.S. Department of Education, 1995, pp. 11, 17.
Note: Numbers do not add up to 100% due to rounding.

TABLE 6.2

Students with Speech or Language Impairments, Basis for Leaving School: School Year 1991–92

	Number	Percent
Received Diploma	3,562	43.9
Certificate (no high school diploma awarded)	596	7.3
Reached Maximum Age for Attendance	87	1.1
Dropped Out	1,633	20.1
Status Unknown	2,230	27.5

Source: Office of Special Education Programs. *Sixteenth Annual Report to Congress on the Implementation of the Individuals with Disabilities Education Act.* Washington, DC: U.S. Department of Education, 1994, p. 19.
Note: Numbers do not add up to 100% due to rounding.

Table 6.1 shows that most children with speech and language disorders are in regular classrooms. Most of these students are removed from their classrooms only for brief periods for speech therapy. The fact that the prevalence of speech disorders decreases as students get older is probably a function of the effectiveness of therapy and the effect of maturation. Students who have persistent speech and language disabilities, however, may encounter even greater difficulties when they reach secondary school. Table 6.2 shows that the graduation rates for these students is low.

Given the potential effectiveness of early intervention for students with speech and language disorders, it is important that teachers know what to look for in students who may need speech therapy. The importance of noticing potential speech disorders, however, must be balanced against the necessity of caution in not inaccurately identifying a child's speech *difference* as a *defect.*

The American Speech-Language-Hearing Association has suggested four guidelines for distinguishing between a speech difference and a speech disorder:

- Is the individual's speech and/or language so different from others of the same age, gender, or ethnic group that it attracts unfavorable attention?
- Is the individual's speech and/or language difficult to understand?
- Does the individual appear to have difficulty understanding the speech of others?
- Does the person avoid communicating with others because the person is self-conscious about speech, hearing, and/or language ability? (ASHA, 1993)

When these questions are asked and the answers are affirmative, the following types of speech and language disorders may be recognized.

ARTICULATION DISORDERS

The most common speech and language disabilities are articulation disorders. These disorders are problems in the production of the sounds that make up words. There are four types of articulation disorders: substitution, omission, addition, and distortion.

Substitution is one of the most common types of articulation disorder. This occurs when the person encounters a word sound that is difficult or impossible to produce. A sound that can be produced more easily is substituted. A common substitution for the *r* sound, for example, is the *w* sound. The result is that the word *red* becomes "wed" or *truck* becomes "twuck."

Another common articulation disorder is *omission*. This occurs when the person leaves out a word sound that is difficult or impossible to produce. Examples of omission are "ook" for *look* and "fi" for *five*.

A third form of articulation disorder is *addition*. This occurs when sounds are added to words that may be difficult to control or articulate precisely. Examples of addition are "bananana" for *banana* and "spaghegetti" for *spaghetti*.

Distortion is a fourth type of articulation disorder. When sounds are distorted, a sound such as the sibilant sound of a lisp is attached to a word. An example is a person who produces the word *sleep* with a lisp attached to the initial sound of the word, making it "s(lisp)eep."

When an elementary school student's speech is filled with articulation errors, he or she may suffer the negative effects of a speech disorder that have been mentioned previously. Other children may tease the child about the "baby talk" he or she uses. Teachers and other children may have genuine difficulty understanding the child. The child may have feelings of low self-esteem because of the "babyish" quality of her or his speech.

It is important to remember that, although articulation disorders are serious speech problems for children of elementary school age and older, articulation errors are common and developmentally normal in younger children. The ability to produce sounds develops in a sequence. When young children encounter speech sounds that they are not developmentally ready to produce, it is normal for them to use substitutions, omissions, and additions, and to experience distortions. Box 6.2 gives additional examples of the kinds of errors typical of younger children and problematic for older children, adolescents, and adults. Can you identify these examples according to the types of articulation disorders?

Articulation disorders can be the result of many different factors. They may result from mental retardation or brain injury. Hearing impairments may result in poor articulation

BOX 6.2

Examples of Articulation Errors

1. We yove to go to Yeyowstone Park.
2. I like dis game.
3. Did you see the wed fiwe twuck?
4. Oh, ook at the big dog.
5. I am almost seben.
6. I have fi dollars.
7. I like to play on the s(lisp)wing.

Kathy McLaughlin/The Image Works

because the child has been unable to hear adequately and imitate correct articulation. On the other hand, articulation errors may be the product of the child having been exposed to poor models of articulation within the family or community.

Regardless of the cause, it is encouraging that articulation disorders are highly amenable to speech therapy. Identification and treatment, therefore, are critical to early correction of these problems.

FLUENCY DISORDERS

Another important characteristic of speech is its flow or timing. As a person speaks, a cadence and rhythm are created that not only facilitate the expression of words but also add emphasis and color to what is said. At times, however, each of us encounters interruptions in our speech. These breaks in fluency may occur as words or syllables that are repeated for no apparent reason. They may come when we are "stuck" and not able to find the word we want to say. They may come when a mistake has been made in the pronunciation of a word. Regardless of the reason, however, these dysfluencies are a normal part of everyone's speech. They may occur more frequently if a person is under stress (for example, speaking before a large and unfamiliar group of people), but they can occur in even the most relaxed moments.

During speech development, children often go through periods of developmental dysfluency. They may exhibit a halting pattern that includes the repeating of words that are difficult to say and noticeable pauses before attempting such words. In most cases, however, these are normal dysfluencies that are part of the process of developing effective speech.

Stuttering

When dysfluencies dominate even a young child's speech, however, the result may be a speech disorder. The most commonly identified fluency disorder is usually referred to as stuttering. Stuttering may take the form of *repetition.* This form of stuttering is characterized by the repetition of word syllables (for example, W-w-we w-w-went to the p-p-park today). Another form of stuttering is *prolongation.* Prolongation is characterized by the prolonging rather than the repeating of a syllable. It sounds as if the person is stuck within the syllable (for example, W——e w——ent to the p——ark today). The form of stuttering know as *hesitation* occurs when the speaker is unable to get a syllable out. It is a fixation before the sound is produced (for example, ——We ——went to the ——park today). Stuttering may also be accompanied by what have been referred to as *struggle behaviors.* When a person who stutters encounters a dysfluency, he or she may struggle to overcome the repetition, prolongation, or hesitation by grimacing the facial muscles and pursing the lips. Blinking the eyes, moving the hands, and even stamping the feet may be used as devices for trying to get a word out.

The cause of stuttering has long been an unresolved question. The reason may be that there is, in fact, no single cause of this speech disorder (Silverman, 1995). In some cases, heredity may be a factor. There is evidence that children with relatives who stutter are at increased risk for stuttering themselves (Andrews et al., 1991). There is evidence, however, that in other cases stuttering is caused by neurological injury (Andrews, Neilson, and Curlee, 1988). There is also evidence that stuttering may result from emotional factors (Gagnon and Ladouceur, 1992).

There are a number of facts about stuttering that may be important in understanding people who stutter and treating them with sensitivity. Some of these facts are listed in Box 6.3. Most important, however, is to remember that the efforts of people to communicate should be honored. It is not polite or helpful to finish what a person who stutters is trying to say. When a block in speech is encountered by a person with this disorder, the listener should respect the challenge that the person is encountering. Giving the person time to finish what they are saying is both courteous and helpful.

Cluttering

Another type of fluency disorder is known as *cluttering*. This disorder involves speech that is so rapid that it is very disorganized and results in the jumbling of words and the confusion of ideas. Words and phrases run together in a manner that may make the speaker's attempt at communication unintelligible to the listener.

LANGUAGE DISORDERS

Language disorders exist when children have problems in the development and use of language, not just in the production of speech. In some cases, children are slow to develop the language skills that others their age have already acquired. They may be significantly behind, for example, in achieving the language milestones included in Box 6.1. In other cases, children may acquire the speech skills presented in Box 6.1 with the exception of those that involve comprehension. In other words, they may develop the mechanisms of speech without the comprehension skills that make speech meaningful.

BOX 6.3

Some Things That Are Known About Stuttering

1. People who stutter do not usually do so while singing.
2. People who stutter do not usually stutter when speaking in unison (for example, saying the Pledge of Allegiance), while speaking in synchronization with a rhythmic beat (for example, speaking to the beat of a metronome), when alone, or when cursing.
3. People who stutter are more likely to stutter on the same words.
4. Stress appears to lead to an increase in stuttering.
5. Most people who stutter during childhood will not stutter as adults.
6. More males than females stutter.

Language disorders in young children are often referred to as *delayed speech*. Delayed speech is associated with other developmental immaturities in children and may be accompanied by delays in emotional and cognitive development. These delays may be the result of mental retardation, emotional disabilities, autism, or brain injuries. In some cases, however, delayed speech may occur in the absence of other disabilities.

Aphasia is another type of language disorder. It has two forms. *Developmental aphasia* is the term used to describe the complete absence of language development that is sometimes characteristic of severe autism. *Acquired aphasia* is the loss of language abilities due to brain injury. Brain injuries from accidents and from infectious diseases like encephalitis are the most common causes of acquired aphasia in children and adolescents (Holland, Swindell, and Reinmuth, 1990; Kaplan, 1996). Children and adolescents may recover completely or partially from aphasia. The likelihood of recovering is a function of many factors, including age at injury, degree of injury, and the opportunity for training and therapy.

CLEFT PALATE

There are *organic disorders* that may interfere with speech. Any disorder of the muscles, nerves, teeth, or bones that are used in speech can cause an impairment to speech. Organic disorders can result from injuries, diseases, or congenital malformations (Batshaw, Perret, and Bleile, 1992).

Two of the most common organic disorders are cleft palate and cleft lip. The prevalence of cleft palate and/or cleft lip is about 1 in 750 to 1,000 Caucasian births. The prevalence is lower for people of Asian and African descent. Clefts occur more often in males than in females (Hallahan and Kauffman, 1994; McWilliams, 1986). Clefts usually result from genetic factors but may be caused by injury to the embryo.

Cleft palate is caused by the incomplete fusion of the roof of the mouth during fetal development. This lack of fusion leaves an opening from the mouth into the nasal area. The result is hypernasality in speech and other problems (for example, infants with open palates have difficulty nursing, and the opening promotes infection). Cleft lips are incompletely fused, and the insensitive term *harelip* that has described this condition refers to the perceived similarity to the split lips of rabbits.

Cleft palates and lips may be reconstructed surgically. Through a series of procedures, a child's appearance and mouth structure may be corrected. In some cases, an obturator (an artificial palate) may be placed over the opening in the roof of the mouth. Surgery, the use of an obturator, and speech therapy may provide the child with normal speech by the time he or she begins school.

Robert Finken/The Picture Cube

Ways of Helping Students with Speech and Language Disorders Succeed in Inclusive Classrooms

ALL SPEECH AND LANGUAGE DISORDERS are potentially isolating for the people who have them. Problems in communication can become serious barriers in the social and educational life of students. It is essential, therefore, to find the best ways of facilitating success in inclusive classrooms for these students.

The first rule of thumb for teachers in helping students with speech and language disorders is to create an environment that encourages the communication efforts of all students. Box 6.4 presents a few guidelines for promoting an encouraging communication environment. Some other suggestions for helping all students with speech and language disabilities are:

- Remember to talk with each child each day about something positive. Often students with disabilities are talked *to* about problems more than they are talked *with* about the good things they have done or are interested in.
- Find ways of encouraging positive discussions between students. Praise students who communicate with each other in positive ways.
- Model sensitivity to the speech efforts of others. Give students the time they need to formulate answers to questions. Do not hurry students who are trying to express themselves.

These guidelines can be summarized into three general principles. These principles for the classroom teacher for helping students with disabilities in speech are: 1) provide a good speech model, 2) improve the student's self-esteem, and 3) create a good speech environment (LaBlance, 1994). More specific suggestions for achieving these goals have been provided by Swan. These include:

- Give the student your undivided attention when speaking with her or him.
- Provide a relaxed and unstressful classroom atmosphere.

BOX 6.4

Encouraging Students in Speech and Language Skills

Teachers can facilitate and encourage the positive development of children's speech and language by:

- Being good speech models by speaking clearly and enthusiastically.
- Listening with sensitivity and interest to what children say.
- Teaching standard English speech by example rather than by correction (for example, Child: *"Them boys all has Braves caps."* Teacher: *"Yes, all of those boys do have Braves caps."*
- Creating a classroom atmosphere that allows children to feel secure in asking questions and participating in discussions.

- Encourage all students to use polite speaking manners.
- Create a sensitivity in all students to the challenges of disorders of speech and language.
- Promote and reward successful experiences in speaking for all students (Swan, 1993).

PROFESSIONAL COLLABORATION

Close collaboration between the classroom teacher and the speech therapist is essential to the classroom success of students with speech and language disorders. Most students with these disabilities have traditionally been in regular classrooms and have left those classrooms periodically for therapy. There has often been little in the way of collaboration between the teacher and the therapist. In some cases, the teacher has even been unaware of the type of therapy the student receives, the goals of therapy, and the connection between the therapy and the student's academic program.

Spencer Grant/Photo Researchers, Inc.

There are a number of models of collaboration that may help create a closer working relationship between the teacher and the therapist. These models offer an alternative to the traditional provision of speech therapy away from the student's classroom, teacher, and peers. These models are:

- *The Therapist as Teacher*: In this model, the therapist works as a classroom teacher in a self-contained classroom. Children in this classroom receive intensive therapy and instruction that help prepare them for a regular classroom. Collaboration takes the form of communication between the therapist/teacher and other teachers in preparation for more inclusive placements of the children receiving intensive classroom therapy.
- *The Therapist as Team Teacher*: In this model, the therapist becomes a team teacher. In collaboration with the classroom teacher, the objectives and goals for the student are identified. Strategies for instruction and therapy are implemented jointly.
- *The Therapist as Classroom-Based Interventionist*: In this model, the therapist provides traditional individual or small-group speech therapy. Different, in this model, however, is that the therapy is provided in the classroom. This allows the possibility of the therapist having greater familiarity with the student's classroom activities and needs. It also affords the opportunity for the teacher to become more informed about the therapy that is being provided.
- *The Therapist as Classroom Consultant*: In this model, the therapist serves as a consultant to the teacher. Regular meetings with the teacher allow the therapist the opportunity to collaborate with the teacher on the implementation of therapeutic strategies and to relate these activities to the overall school program of the student.
- *The Therapist as Staff and Program Developer*: In this model, the therapist provides training to teachers and other school personnel. This training allows the therapist's expertise to be shared and magnified. With some students, this results in a more therapeutic environment for the correction of their speech and language disorders (Miller, 1989; Turnbull et al., 1995).

Greater professional collaboration is a goal that is central to the creation of more inclusive classrooms. As the distance between the efforts of the teacher and those of the therapist is reduced, changes occur in classrooms. It has been noted that collaboration helps to eliminate the labels and the stigma associated with speech disorders, fosters higher self-esteem in students who have these disorders, and promotes greater academic success for them (Denton and Foley, 1994; Green, 1994).

COLLABORATION WITH PARENTS

Parents can be very effective collaborators in the effort to promote greater success for children with speech and language disorders in inclusive classrooms. It has been found, for example, that monthly meetings with parents can increase the efficacy of school treatment programs for speech disorders (Berkowitz, 1994). These meetings may serve to inform parents of the progress that their children are making. They can also allow teachers and therapists to update parents on changes in their children's academic and speech programs.

Parents may also be able to carry the child's school program into the home. If they are aware of the goals and strategies of their children's speech and academic programs, they may be able to reinforce at home what is being done at school. If a student is being helped with an articulation problem at school, for example, the parents may be able to monitor and reinforce the transfer from school to home of therapeutic changes in the student's speech. Parents may also be asked to use materials at home that will provide extra practice with the skills that are being worked on at school (Fitzgerald and Karnes, 1987).

An important consideration in involving parents in the improvement of a child's speech and language skills is that the experience should be rewarding for all. Parents should not be asked to work with their children on their most difficult tasks. This may lead to frustration for both the parent and the child. Instead, parents should be asked to work with their children on skills that they are beginning to experience success with. This allows parents to see that progress is being made and to feel that they are sharing in the successes of their children.

PEER COLLABORATION

The reaction of a student's peers to her or his speech or language disorder helps to form that student's perception of the atmosphere of the classroom. If the student's class peers understand the nature of the student's disability and the importance of encouraging their fellow student, a "safe" environment for communication may be created. If the student fears the ridicule and rejection of her or his peers, the class environment will be perceived as "dangerous" for communication efforts.

Classroom discussions about speech and language disorders may be effective for informing and sensitizing students to the communication disabilities of their classmates. These discussions may include the student or students in the class who have difficulties in speech or language. Having the student with

LAIMA DRUSKIS/STOCK BOSTON

a disability talk about her or his disorder may also open the way for other students to help as the student is attempting to improve her or his communication abilities.

The importance of the teacher as a good speech model has already been discussed. Peers may also serve as models. Increasing their awareness that they can help by talking with their peer with a speech or language disability can give them a sense of being part of a team that is helping a friend. Being a peer model should be presented to classmates as a way of helping without correcting or drawing negative attention to their classmate's disorder. Surrounding the student with speech or language disorders with understanding, sensitive, and positive peer models may be one of the most effective classroom interventions.

COMMUNICATION AND BEHAVIOR

It has been found that more than half of the students who have speech or language disorders also experience problems with their classroom behaviors. It is understandable that the frustrations of having difficulty in communicating can lead to personal and social conflicts. The behavioral difficulties most often associated with speech and language disorders are:

- Inappropriate motor activity,
- Withdrawal,
- Stubbornness and inflexibility, and
- Distractibility and impulsivity (Laughton and Hasenstab, 1986).

These problems in behavior may emerge as an expression of the emotions that students have difficulty verbalizing. They may also result from difficulties that students with speech or language disabilities experience in understanding other people. As teachers, peers, and parents work with these students to help them improve their communication and academic skills, however, their personal and social abilities may also improve.

Communication takes many forms. There are, of course, nonverbal forms of communication. Speech and language, however, are central to the way that people come to understand the world and the people around them. They are also critical to the acquisition of the knowledge and skills that have become so necessary to productive and independent adult life. Helping students with these disabilities succeed in school is an important aspect of creating more inclusive schools for all children.

Case Studies and Questions to Consider

STUDENT: LU HYE

SCHOOL: LINKING ELEMENTARY

CURRENT PLACEMENT: REGULAR THIRD GRADE

AGE: 9 YEARS, 8 MONTHS

Family Structure and Home Environment

Lu lives in a pleasant home. He lives with his parents, Tim and Sue Hye. Mr. Hye is a mechanic at Kmart, and Ms. Hye works as a kitchen helper at a local Asian restaurant. Mr. Hye is forty-seven years old. Ms. Hye is forty-five.

In addition to his parents, Lu also lives with two sisters and a brother. His sisters Cung and Chu are fourteen and sixteen, respectively. His brother Minh is twelve. Mr. and Ms. Hye report that all three of these children are doing well in school. Lu also has two older sisters and an older brother who are now living away from home. Jennifer (who is twenty-four years old) has a seven-year-old daughter and works at the same restaurant as Ms. Hye. Lu's sister Quan (twenty years old) and brother Bin (nineteen) are both students at State University.

Mr. and Ms. Hye provide an orderly, warm, and supportive home for Lu. They furnish books, toys, and activities to encourage his educational development, and they also invest their time and energy toward this end. Lu's older brothers and sisters also seem to be helpful to him in this respect.

Parental Perception of Student's Developmental Progress and Needs

Mr. and Ms. Hye are pleased with the overall developmental progress that Lu has made since he has been receiving speech services. They speak with obvious gratitude of his speech therapist. They say that "she is a good teacher, and she is also like a mother to Lu." Their only statement concerning Lu's future educational programming was that they hope that he will continue to do as well.

Of foremost concern to them is the increased stuttering that Lu has experienced recently. They are upset by the greater frequency and intensity of his difficulties in speech. Mr. Hye particularly is frustrated that Lu's therapy does not seem to be working. Mr. Hye wishes that he had a Vietnamese physician to discuss these matters with in his own language. This family is under a great deal of stress concerning Lu's speech problem.

Mr. and Ms. Hye speak with pride of their perception that Lu has many friends at school. They cite as an example of his developing social skills the fact that he now makes telephone calls to his friends after school.

Mr. and Ms. Hye would like to see Lu take more responsibility at home for taking care of his room and caring for his own clothing. They do not, however, see this as a major problem area. They feel that this responsibility will emerge as Lu grows older.

Additional Considerations

Lu's parents are most pleased with his loving and affectionate temperament. Their hope for him in the future is that he will grow up to be a healthy adult who will be able to communicate effectively with other people. Most of all at this point, they hope he will be free from stuttering. Lu Hye lives in a very positive and accepting family environment. His parents are happy and proud of the progress he has made. They seem to be equally committed to doing everything they can to promote his further development.

Questions

1. Do you think Lu's speech difficulties might stem from language or cultural barriers?
2. As his teacher, what would you do to help Lu's parents understand his difficulties?
3. What role could Lu's college-age siblings play in helping him through his speech difficulties?

STUDENT: JOHNNY HELPER

SCHOOL: SUNNY MIDDLE SCHOOL

CURRENT PLACEMENT: SPECIAL EDUCATION CLASS

AGE: 12 YEARS, 3 MONTHS

Family Structure and Home Environment

Johnny lives with his parents, Sonny Helper and Mildred Helper. Mr. and Ms. Helper are both former residents of the Training Center for Developmental Disabilities. They were residents there from childhood. Both of them were diagnosed as having mental retardation and in need of a limited level of support. They were discharged in the 1980s. Mr. Helper is fifty years old and is not currently employed. Ms. Helper is thirty-five years old and is also unemployed. The Helper family lives in a clean and well-organized apartment in a public housing complex. They are supported by Social Security and Aid to Families with Dependent Children benefits.

Mr. and Ms. Helper report that, other than having tubes placed in his ears because of repeated ear infections, Johnny has not required any special medical attention during his childhood. They describe him as being a child who is easy to live with.

Parental Perception of Student's Developmental Progress and Needs

Mr. and Ms. Helper feel that, in general, Johnny functions well socially within their home. He has begun to help them around the apartment with the cleaning and cooking, and they are proud to see him doing new things. They recognize, however, that he experiences less social success outside their home. They cite a recent incident of Johnny's being teased on the school bus. Children teased him, saying his parents are "retards" and that he "talks like a retard." They know that he was hurt by the teasing and that he had no idea of how to handle it. They are also unsure of how to handle it.

Additional Considerations

Mr. and Ms. Helper feel that Johnny is benefiting from his school program. To quote Mr. Helper, "We think he is making good progress." The thing that Johnny's parents would most like to see changed about him is his sometimes negative attitude. They comment that sometimes he is grouchy and hard to work with. They emphasize that they praise him whenever he does his work or tries hard.

The comments from Johnny's teacher, however, portray a different set of challenges. His teacher reports that, although Johnny has been diagnosed as having mental retardation that requires a special class in school, it is her opinion that Johnny has normal intellectual potential. She feels that it is the limited social stimulation and academic support that he has received at home that has resulted in his developmental delays. She believes that this is particularly true of his poor speech articulation. She emphasizes, however, that she is not implying that the Helpers are not good parents. She says, rather, that they often do things for Johnny that he should be learning to do for himself, such as personal hygiene care and skills for greater social independence. She feels that, although he receives some speech therapy at present, if he had more intensive therapy for his articulation disorder and the proper classroom support, he could benefit from being in a regular classroom.

Questions

1. What can be done to help Johnny experience more inclusiveness in his school and actualize more of his academic and social potential?
2. What things could be done to assist the Helpers in their concern to do the best they can for their child?
3. What can be done to address the problem of Johnny being teased by other children?

References

American Speech-Language-Hearing Association. "Definitions of Communication Disorders and Variations." *ASHA, 35* (supp. 10), 1993: 40–41.

Andrews, G., A. Morris-Yates, P. Howie, and N. Martin. "Genetic Factors in Stuttering Confirmed." *Archives of General Psychiatry, 48,* 1991: 1034–1035.

Andrews, G., M. Neilson, and R. Curlee. "Stuttering." *Journal of the American Medical Association, 260,* 1988: 1445.

Batshaw, M. L., Y. M. Perret, and K. Bleile. "Language and Communication: Development and Disorders." In M. L. Batshaw and Y. M. Perret (Eds.), *Children with Disabilities: A Medical Primer,* 3d ed. Baltimore, MD: Brookes, 1992: 351–364.

Berkowitz, M. "A Non-Traditional Fluency Program Developed for the Public School Setting." *Language, Speech, and Hearing Services in Schools, 25,* 1994: 94–99.

Denton, M., and D. J. Foley. "The Marriage of Special and Regular Education Through Inclusion." *Teaching and Change, 1,* 1994: 349–368.

Fitzgerald, M., and D. Karnes. "A Parent-Implemented Model for At-Risk and Developmentally Delayed Preschool Children." *Topics in Language Disorders* 7(3), 1987: 31–46.

Gagnon, M., and R. Ladouceur. "Behavioral Treatment of Child Stutterers: Replication and Extension." *Behavior Therapy, 23,* 1992: 113–129.

Green, R. "Speech Time Is All the Time." *Teaching Exceptional Children, 27,* 1994: 60–61.

Hallahan, D., and J. Kauffman. *Exceptional Children: Introduction to Special Education.* Needham Heights, MA: Allyn and Bacon, 1994.

Heward, W., and M. Orlansky. *Exceptional Children: An Introductory Survey of Special Education.* New York: Macmillan, 1992.

Holland, A. L., C. S. Swindell, and O. M. Reinmuth. "Aphasia and Related Adult Disorders." In G. A. Shames and E. H. Wiig (Eds.), *Human Communication Disorders,* 3d ed. Columbus, OH: Merrill, 1990: 424–462.

Kaplan, P. *Pathways for Exceptional Children: School, Home and Culture.* St. Paul, MN: West, 1996.

LaBlance, G. R. "Stuttering: The Role of the Classroom Teacher." *Teaching Exceptional Children, 26,* 1994: 10–12.

Laughton, J., and M. Hasenstab. *The Language Process.* Rockville, MD: Aspen, 1986.

McWilliams, B. J. "Cleft Palate." In G. H. Shames and E. H. Wiig (Eds.), *Human Communication Disorders,* 2d ed. Columbus, OH: Macmillan, 1986: 445–482.

Miller, L. "Classroom-Based Language Intervention." *Language, Speech, and Hearing Services in Schools, 20,* 1989: 153–169.

Office of Special Education Programs. *Sixteenth Annual Report to Congress on the Implementation of the Individuals with Disabilities Education Act.* Washington, DC: U.S. Department of Education, 1994.

———. *Seventeenth Annual Report to Congress on the Implementation of the Individuals with Disabilities Education Act.* Washington, DC: U.S. Department of Education, 1995.

Rice, M., and C. Shuele. "Speech and Language Impairments." In E. Meyen and T. Skirtic (Eds.), *Special Education and Student Disabilities: An Introduction.* Denver: Love, 1995.

Silverman, F. H. *Speech, Language, and Hearing Disorders.* Boston: Allyn and Bacon, 1995.

Swan, A. M. "Helping Children Who Stutter: What Teachers Need to Know." *Childhood Education, 69,* 1993: 138–141.

Turnbull, A., H. R. Turnbull, M. Shank, and D. Leal. *Exceptional Lives: Special Education in Today's Schools.* Englewood Cliffs, NJ: Prentice Hall, 1995.

Creating Classrooms That Welcome Students with Visual Impairments

Annie Sullivan Macy: An Educational Biography

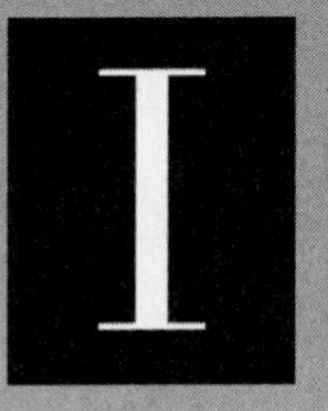

Introduction

Toward the end of her life, Annie Sullivan Macy began to receive extensive recognition for her work and accomplishments with Helen Keller. In 1931 both she and Miss Keller were granted honorary degrees from Temple University, in 1933 they were made honorary fellows of the Educational Institute of Scotland, and in 1936 the Roosevelt Memorial Foundation awarded them its medals for "cooperative achievement of heroic character and far reaching significance" (Hoxie, 1971, p. 482). Since her death, Mrs. Macy's story has been retold in a number of books and in a Broadway play and film, *The Miracle Worker.*

Annie's story, however, has usually been the story of her teaching of Helen Keller and the close relationship that lasted throughout their lives. The result is a vivid and detailed account of Helen's education. From the dramatic episode of the revelation that a pattern of finger movements in her hand carried the meaning "water," to her graduation, cum laude, from Radcliffe, we know how and from what sources Helen was educated. Very little attention has been focused, however, on the sources of Annie Sullivan Macy's own education. What experiences, institutions, and influences shaped and channeled her life? What prepared her to become, as Helen called her, "Teacher"? What is her educational biography?

Feeding Hills

In the early 1860s Alice and Thomas Sullivan left Ireland and joined the swelling tide of immigrants then coming to America. This tide was precipitated by the Great Famine of 1847. Alice was two years old when the famine came; Thomas was perhaps slightly older. They had both been weaned on stories of starvation, cholera, and other horrors. Neither had been to school, neither could read or write, and neither had any training or skills. The money that brought them to America was sent by Thomas' older brother, John, who was working on a farm outside of a village known as Feeding Hills near Springfield, Massachusetts.

Shortly after their arrival, Thomas found work on a farm near Feeding Hills. He and Alice found quarters in a shabby old house with several other Irish families. On April 4, 1866, their first child was born. The infant girl was christened Joanna, but she was to be known as Annie.

Annie was born into what might best be described as the Irish ghetto of Feeding Hills. Held in low esteem by the New England Puritans, Irish Catholics were segregated both socially and economically. They were only tolerated by the established New Englander as a source of "cheap, ignorant labour. Anything else was impertinence" (Braddy, 1933, p. 3). This contempt as well as their poverty served to isolate the Irish.

Although Annie's father could not read to her, he did tell her stories. Apparently, this usually occurred when he was drunk enough to be free of his worries. He told her of the fairy folk and "little people" of his native Limerick, Ireland. He quoted Gaelic poetry, sang songs—all Irish.

The Sullivan family continued to grow. After Annie came Ellen, Jimmy, and Mary. With the addition of each new child, the economic burden of support became more difficult for Thomas to bear. To compound their problems, there came to them a scourge of accidents and diseases. As the result of a fall against a stove, Alice Sullivan was never able to walk again without crutches. Adding to this tragedy, Alice was also stricken with tuberculosis. Then it seemed to be the children's turns to suffer tragedy. Ellen suffered a terrible fever and died when she was five years old. Jimmy was disabled by a tubercular hip. Annie developed a destructive granular inflammation of her eyes, trachoma.

Annie's trachoma was troubling and confusing to the family. When the itching first began and granules appeared on her eyes, they tried a home remedy, washing them with geranium water. Although Thomas sought the help of two physicians, he was only given a salve to help ease Annie's discomfort. The poverty of the Irish did not allow for the more extensive medical care that was available to the wealthy. In desperation Thomas sought sanctuary in Irish folklore. He promised to take Annie back home to Ireland when she was older. There he would wash her eyes in water from the River Shannon. Annie's father told her that "a single drop of water from the River Shannon would cure her eyes, it was that holy" (Davidson, 1965, p. 21). This was a promise that could never be kept.

Courtesy of the American Foundation for the Blind, Helen Keller Archives.

Helen Keller and Annie Sullivan

As Annie's vision grew worse, so did her behavior. She became subject to temper tantrums with other children and with her mother and father. She became known in the community as a difficult and unmanageable child. Refusing to yield to her father's discipline efforts, Annie never cried when spanked.

The circle of poverty and illness that the Sullivans had come to know so well soon literally destroyed them as a family. Annie's eyes grew worse; her brother, Jimmy, became more disabled with tuberculosis; Mrs. Sullivan became more ill; Mr. Sullivan increased his drinking. Finally, tuberculosis conquered and Alice Sullivan died. The family fell apart.

Sullivan relatives felt that they must intercede on behalf of the children. How could they leave three motherless children with a father who was alcoholic? Aunt Ellen Sullivan volunteered to take both Jimmy and Mary. But because of her eyes and temper tantrums, Annie was not wanted. Finally cousins John and Statia Sullivan agreed to take this troubling girl into their home.

These arrangements were doomed to failure. Jimmy's tubercular hip grew worse, and his medicine was expensive. Annie remained an unmanageable child. The relatives came to feel that they had done all they could for the children.

On February 22, 1876, Annie and Jimmy found themselves in a carriage headed for Springfield where, they had been told, they would take a train ride. They had no idea that their destination was to be the state poorhouse in Tewksbury, Massachusetts.

At the close of Annie's family life in Feeding Hills, she had never been to school (she was almost ten), could not read, had never been read to, and hardly knew of children who did attend school. Her education had consisted of her father's tales of Irish folklore, Irish songs, and Gaelic poetry. In addition to fantasies of the "little people," she had learned the realities of poverty, disease, and death.

Tewksbury

There were no nurses and little medicine in the Massachusetts State Infirmary. It was a place for people who had nowhere else to go. Some of the inmates were emotionally disturbed, some were alcoholics, but most were simply old and poor. They all shared the common bond of being unwanted and forgotten people. Annie and Jimmy joined their ranks.

The children spent the first night in a small enclosure at the end of the women's ward. This enclosure, though they did not know it at the time, was the "dead house"—the morgue, into which corpses were wheeled to await burial (Braddy, 1933, p. 19).

The environment at Tewksbury was in many ways similar to what Annie had known all of her life. The ward was filled with older women who were disabled, diseased, and dying, but most of them were Irish like the women she had known in Feeding Hills.

Annie didn't like most of the older women at Tewksbury, and most of them didn't care for the children. Annie was still subject to temper tantrums and was often rude to the women. But in the ward were two ladies who became Annie's friends. One was a blind woman who told her stories. The other was Maggie Carroll.

Maggie was so disabled with arthritis that she had to be strapped to a wooden frame for support. From years of being constricted, her flesh was riddled with ulcerous bedsores. She could not move without help and could not hold anything in her drawn and knotted hands. However, Maggie could read, and a rack had been made for her on which her books could rest.

Maggie introduced Annie to her books. Annie turned the pages for Maggie, and Annie, who was classified at the infirmary as "virtually blind," depended on Maggie's eyes (Braddy, 1933, p. 18). This was her first exposure to reading. Through the months, Maggie read book after book to Annie and Jimmy. Her books were nearly all concerned with the lives of the saints. After reading aloud to the children, she would talk with them about God.

It was Annie's other friend, the blind woman, who first told her that there were schools for children with blindness. The blind woman also explained to Annie that people who were blind could learn to read raised letters with their fingertips—Braille. This knowledge would later determine the course of Annie's life.

Jimmy's tubercular condition worsened quickly in the institution. It became more difficult for him to leave his bed, and Annie even had to help him with dressing. In May 1876 Jimmy died. Annie reacted to his death with prolonged grieving. Her grief often manifested itself in angry outbursts at the other residents of her ward. Even though she had the old blind woman and Maggie Carroll as friends, Annie felt alone and captured at Tewksbury. She wanted to escape, but she had nowhere to go.

A glimmer of hope came into Annie's life when Father Barbara, a Jesuit priest who was assigned to Tewksbury to hold Mass and hear confession, took a special interest in her. Apparently he felt a great deal of compassion for this little girl who had been forced to share institutional life with chronically ill and aged people. He knew that her eyes were very weak now—that she could see almost nothing. He decided to try to help her regain her eyesight.

Father Barbara arranged, through a friend, for Annie to be taken to the hospital of Soeurs de la Charité in Lowell, Massachusetts. While in the hospital, Annie had three surgeries. Each operation resulted in a disappointment; the surgeons were unable to improve her vision.

Her stay at the hospital, however, was not an unpleasant one. The hospital Sisters with their fresh white bonnets were a delight to Annie. She was allowed to help with the folding of the laundry and, when she had recovered from surgery, went with the Sisters on their errands of mercy, carrying baskets of food to the poor. It was on one of these trips that the home of Ben Butler was pointed out to her. Butler was "one of the first advocates in this country of the ten-hour working day for factory employees," as opposed to the fourteen or fifteen hours that were usual (Braddy, 1933, p. 33). He was a strong opponent of literacy requirements for voting and holding office. He was a staunch advocate for Irish immigrants. After seeing his house, Annie's imagination was sparked. She urged the Sisters and others in the hospital to tell her more stories of Ben Butler. He became her first hero, "a knight in shining armor." Later in her life, she continued to admire and support Butler and other radical Democrats.

After a few months, Annie, over her objections, was returned to Tewksbury. The doctors at the hospital felt they had done all they could for her and there was no other place to send her. Annie was absolutely miserable. She had but one aim—to escape the degradation of the Tewksbury institution.

The months went by, then the years—1878 and 1879. Annie was almost totally blind and was no closer to her aim of escape. It seemed to her that she would never return to the outside world. Then in 1880 the outside world came to the institution.

The Massachusetts State Board of Charities came to Tewksbury to investigate conditions there. This investigation was apparently in response to rumors of horrible conditions in the institution. There had been investigations before, and the residents did not expect anything to change as a result of this visit. Annie, however, did expect change.

Maggie Carroll told Annie that the chairman of the board was a man named Frank B. Sanborn. This was a man who could make a difference in Annie's life. Sanborn was a friend of Dr. Samuel Gridley Howe, Ralph Waldo Emerson, and Henry David Thoreau. He was a man of compassion and influence.

On the day of the visit, Annie followed the group from ward to ward. She listened to the sounds of their voices and footsteps, practicing to herself speeches she would make to them when the opportunity came. Just before the tour was to end, she "hurled herself into their midst without knowing which was he, crying 'Mr. Sanborn, Mr. Sanborn, I want to go to school!'" (Davidson, 1965, p. 48). Sanborn inquired about the child: what was wrong with her and how long she had been at Tewksbury. A few of the others asked questions. Then they left.

In a few days, however, Annie received word that she was to leave Tewksbury for the Perkins Institution near Boston. When she left, she carried with her the educative experiences of Tewksbury. These included the influence of significant other people such as the older woman who was blind who had first told her that children who were blind could learn to read, and being read to by Maggie Carroll. Surely, also, conditions in the institution had taught Annie to survive in the presence of constant disease, suffering, and death.

Perkins

Annie was fourteen when she arrived at Perkins. She could not read, write, or do basic arithmetic. She knew practically nothing about English, geography, or history. She had to start at the very beginning. She was placed in a roomful of six-year-olds. To the other children, and to herself, Annie appeared to be large, clumsy, and foolish. She was soon given the nickname "Big Annie."

Annie went through periods of acting out against the teasing provocation of the other children. She was rebellious toward her teachers, often coming close to being expelled from the school. But she did learn.

Gradually, Annie came to be an accepted part of the Perkins community. Not completely, however, since she was still a charity pupil. This caused a special problem. What was to be done with her during the summers while the school was closed?

The first summer was spent with one of the other girls. The father of this girl was a Spiritualist who came to breakfast each morning with stories of women who had paid him spiritual visits during the night. This "tormented his wife (for which purpose it was no doubt intended) and incidentally everyone else in the household. Annie spent an extremely harassed and unrestful vacation" (Braddy, 1933, p. 76).

The next summer was a much happier one for Annie. A man at Perkins found a job for her doing light housework in a Boston rooming house. Annie became well acquainted with one of the boarders, a young man named Clark. He often talked with her, read to her from newspapers, and became interested in her eyes. On his suggestion, she was taken to the Carney Catholic Hospital. There a young surgeon named Bradford examined her eyes and had her come to the Massachusetts Eye and Ear Infirmary for further examinations and treatment.

Over a period of a year, Dr. Bradford performed two operations on Annie's eyes and gave her other treatments. When the course of his medical intervention was completed, a new world had opened up for the girl. Annie Sullivan could see! Her eyes were not perfect. Everything was blurred, and would remain so all her life. Still, the sixteen-year-old girl could see.

Perkins Institution was a school for the blind. Annie was no longer blind, but she returned to Perkins from the hospital and nothing was ever said. It appears that the rules were stretched to accommodate the girl who had nowhere else to go.

Because of the raised Roman type then in use at Perkins, Annie found reading with her eyes easy to learn. Later in life she could not recall having learned to read with her eyes; it seemed to come so easily. She devoured every newspaper and book that she could find with her new eyes. Even when she wrote or read Braille, she no longer did it with her fingers—she read it with her eyes.

The teachers soon found Annie's eyes to be useful to them; many of the teachers were blind themselves. Annie carried messages and ran errands. It was discovered that she worked well with the younger children, and she was soon taking them on excursions into Boston. Annie was even trusted to teach a few classes.

With her newfound happiness, however, Annie apparently never forgot her earlier experiences of blindness, poverty, and loneliness. This may be the reason she became so interested in Laura Bridgman.

Laura had spent more than forty of her fifty years at Perkins. She was deaf, blind, and mute. Dr. Samuel Gridley Howe, the founder of Perkins, brought Laura there when she was eight years old. He adapted the manual alphabet in such a way as to communicate with her through the sense of touch. He spelled words into her hands. Dr. Howe was able to teach Laura isolated words, but very few connections between words. He also had difficulty in teaching her abstractions such as "love," "friendship," and other relational concepts.

Dr. Howe was dead now, and Laura was growing old. All of the students at Perkins were taught to communicate with Laura, but most were too busy to spend much time with her. Annie, however, spent time each day talking into Laura's hands. She became very skilled in communicating in this way.

The students at Perkins were often visited by wealthy and socially prominent people. They were also frequent houseguests in the homes of Dr. Howe's daughters and other influential Bostonians. Annie was no exception. She was exposed to the "best" of culture, ideas, and political philosophy. Her early experiences, however, seem to have inculcated in Annie a philosophy that would not yield to these new influences. As a former classmate wrote in 1927, "As Miss Sullivan was a homeless girl, it was no discredit to her that she came to our school from a charitable institution, unkempt and badly clothed. Nor is it strange that, from such surroundings, she came with strong prejudices and a narrow point of view. . . . Politically, Annie was always a radical Democrat with which point of view I had no sympathy" (Braddy, 1933, p. 88).

There were eight graduates of Perkins in 1886, four of them boys. Annie Sullivan was valedictorian. The governor of the state and other notables were present at the graduation exercises. An excerpt from Annie's address to the gathering may be indicative of the cumulative effect of her education at this point in her life: "Self-culture is a benefit, not only to the individual, but also to mankind. Every man who improves himself is aiding the progress of society, and everyone who stands still holds it back" (Davidson, 1965, p. 78).

Helen

Following graduation, Annie went to Cape Cod for a vacation with her housemother from Perkins. Her summer, however, was less than carefree. For the first time in six years, Annie had no place to go. She had received no job offers. She had considered everything from working as a dishwasher in Boston to selling books from door to door. Her options seemed very limited.

Then in late August came a letter from Mr. Anagnos, the director of Perkins:

> Dear Annie,
>
> Please read the enclosed letter carefully, and let me know at your earliest convenience whether you would be disposed to consider favorably an offer of a position in the family of Mr. Keller, as governess to his little deaf-mute and blind daughter. . . .
>
> I remain, dear Annie, with kind remembrance to Mrs. Hopkins.
>
> Sincerely, your friend
> M. Anagnos
> (Braddy, 1933, p. 81)

The story of Annie's acceptance of the position and the results of her work with Helen Keller are well known. Not four months after Helen understood the meaning of the manually spelled word *water*, she could write almost as well as Laura Bridgman. She was soon writing letters in Braille to the girls at Perkins. In the spring of 1904, Helen graduated cum laude from Radcliffe College. She was to become world famous as a writer and lecturer.

In a sense, Helen Keller's educational biography became a part of Annie Sullivan Macy's own biography. Annie accompanied Helen to all of her classes at Radcliffe, spelled the lectures into Helen's hands, and spent as much as five or six hours a day reading course assignments to her.

The two women traveled and lectured widely. Annie served as interpreter for Helen, always receptively, often expressively. Annie acted as a mediator of much of what Helen Keller learned and what others learned from Helen Keller.

Many people, including Helen Keller, have speculated as to what Annie Sullivan Macy might have accomplished under other circumstances. What if her early life had been different? Suppose she had been more fortunate in social, physical, and educational endowments? What might she have done if she had not dedicated her life to Helen Keller? The fact is, however, that through her experiences she developed the sensibilities, temperament, and talents that allowed for her success as the teacher of a person like Helen Keller.

In spite of all her talents and strengths, life was never easy or fully satisfying for Annie. She lacked confidence in herself throughout her life. She experienced an unsuccessful marriage to John Albert Macy, a Harvard instructor who worked with Helen on her autobiography. Her vision, which worsened later in her life, was a burden she could neither accept nor surmount. Perhaps only her devotion to Helen Keller gave Annie Sullivan Macy the self-discipline she need for her accomplishments.

The example that Annie and Helen provide for the "miracles" that are possible for eager students and dedicated teachers is unique. They are both truly heroic figures whose lives have much to teach us about the potentials of students with special needs and the power of caring educators.

Students with Visual Impairments: Causes and Characteristics

At some time in childhood, almost all of us played "blindman's bluff" or "pin the tail on the donkey." We have awakened in the middle of the night and groped to find our bearings in a darkened room. These experiences give us a temporary awareness of what it is like to be without vision. In addition to the problem of physically finding our way around without vision, the experience of being blindfolded during a game makes real for us the social difficulties generated by being unable to see. Others laugh at our movements and mistakes, and we are unable to determine what it is that we have done that is humorous. A temporary feeling of isolation may be a part of the experience of the game.

Many people rank the fear of blindness near the top of the list of their greatest fears. This personal fear may be expressed by avoidance of or discomfort with people who are blind. Literature is filled with instances where blindness is portrayed as a punishment for sins or depravity. Sometimes, as in the case of Oedipus, it is a self-imposed penalty for personally unacceptable acts.

As Lowenfeld (1975) pointed out, attitudes toward people with visual impairments have historically evolved from very negative forms of separation (annihilation) and perhaps more positive but equally separative views (veneration for possessing unusual spiritual qualities, for example), to "humane" attempts at protection by isolation, and finally to movements toward integration of persons with visual impairments into society. While the movement toward full integration of people with visual disabilities into society has certainly begun, the realization of this goal is far from complete. The aims of this chapter will be to present information that provides a basic understanding of the process of vision, to provide knowledge of impairments to vision and their educational implications, and to explore the role that teachers and other professionals may have in assisting students with visual impairments to have the fullest lives possible.

THE PROCESS OF VISION

The human eye is an intricate anatomical structure (see Figure 7.1). It operates something like a camera for the brain. Problems in vision can best be understood by briefly reviewing the structure and function of the eye. The parts of the eye can be divided into four groups according to function. These are protective, refractive, orientational, and receptive structures.

Protective Structures

Those structures that serve primarily a protective function for the eye include the bony socket within the skull that houses the eyeball, the eyelashes, eyebrows, eyelids, and tear ducts. The *conjunctiva* is a thin membrane that lines the interior surface of the eyelid. The *sclera* is the tough outer covering of the eyeball. It is the sclera that gives the eye its white color. The *choroid* is an internal layer of tissue that is rich in blood vessels. It provides nourishment to the eye.

Refractive Structures

The refractive structures of the eye function to focus light on the retina. The *cornea* refracts light back through the *aqueous humor,* a chamber filled with fluid that maintains constant pressure behind the cornea. Before reaching the *lens,* the amount of incoming light is regulated by the *iris* (the colored area of the

FIGURE 7.1

Basic Anatomy of the Eye

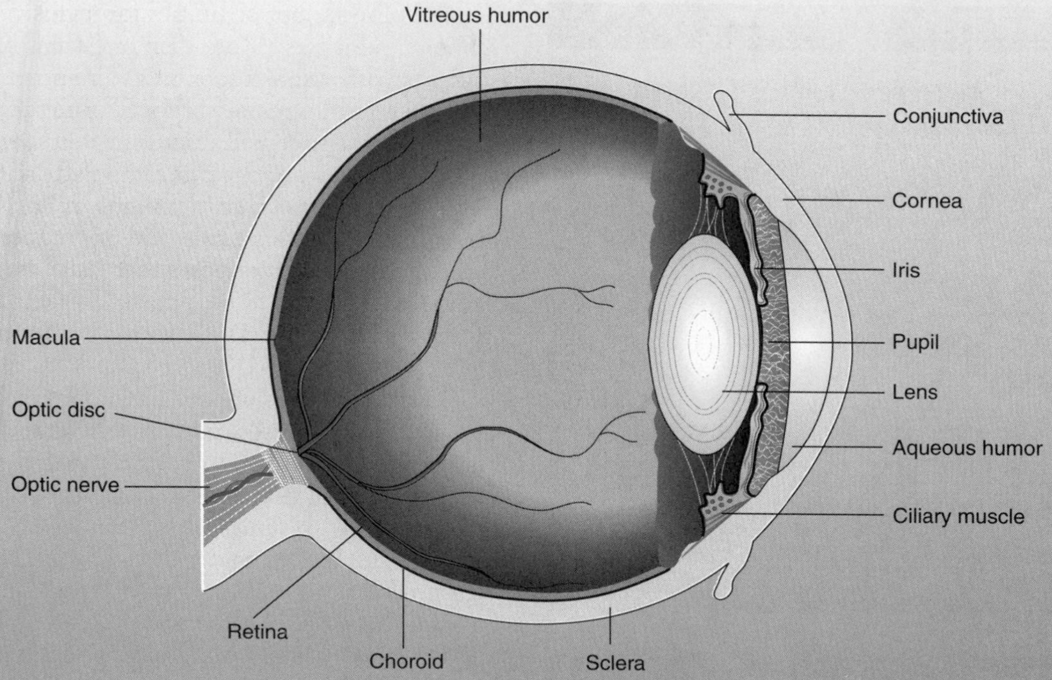

eye). Depending on how large the opening (pupil) at the center of the iris is, differential amounts of light strike the lens. The lens focuses the light back through the *vitreous humor* and onto the *retina.*

Orientational Structures

The orientational structures are six muscles that are connected to the outside of the eyeball. These muscles function to turn the eyes up and down, left and right. They also serve to keep the two eyes in proper alignment with each other.

Receptive Structures

The first of the receptive structures is the *retina.* The retina contains *rod cells* for black-and-white vision and *cone cells* for color vision. When the light that has been refracted by other structures in the eye strikes the retina, neural energy is generated by an electrochemical process. The *optic nerve* fibers pick up and transmit these impulses to the *occipital lobe* of the brain, where this visual information is processed and interpreted.

INCIDENCE, TYPES, AND CAUSES OF VISUAL IMPAIRMENT

Incidence

Because of our ability to correct most vision problems, the number of children who are disabled by impairments to vision is relatively low. During the 1992–93 school year, 23,544 students in the United States were identified as having visual impairments (see Table 7.1). This number constitutes less than one-half of 1 percent of the school population in the United States.

TABLE 7.1

Students with Visual Impairments, Number and Placement Percentages:* School Year 1992–93

Number	23,544
Regular Class	45.5%
Resource Room	21.1%
Separate Class	18.0%
Separate School	5.6%
Residential Facility	9.4%
Homebound/Hospital Setting	0.5%

*Placement figures are from the 1991–92 school year.
Source: Office of Special Education Programs. *Seventeenth Annual Report to Congress on the Implementation of the Individuals with Disabilities Education Act.* Washington, DC: U.S. Department of Education, 1995, pp. 11, 17.

TABLE 7.2

Students with Visual Impairments, Basis for Leaving School: School Year 1992–93

	Number	Percent
Received Diploma	879	60.7
Certificate (no high school diploma awarded)	172	11.9
Reached Maximum Age for Attendance	55	3.8
Dropped Out	166	11.5
Status Unknown	177	12.2

Source: Office of Special Education Programs. *Sixteenth Annual Report to Congress on the Implementation of the Individuals with Disabilities Education Act.* Washington, DC: U.S. Department of Education, 1994, p. 19.
Note: Numbers do not add up to 100% due to rounding.

Table 7.1 also demonstrates, however, that students with visual impairments are in need of more opportunities for inclusive school experiences. More than one-third of all students with visual disabilities were served in separate classes, separate schools, or residential facilities. As we will discuss in this chapter, some of this segregation can be attributed to the need for specialized training in Braille, other communication skills, and orientation and mobility. Still, it appears that visual impairments continue to be a major obstacle to the involvement of many students in the full life of public schools.

The significance of providing more inclusive services for these students is illustrated by the information in Table 7.2. During the 1992–93 school year, only 60.7 percent of the students with visual impairments who left school in the United States did so by graduating from high school. Another 11.9 percent finished their school careers with a certificate of attendance or other nondiploma document. More than 27 percent of students with visual disabilities either reached the maximum age for school attendance, and therefore became ineligible to return, dropped out of school, or were of unknown status. These figures demonstrate a real need for creating schools that welcome students with visual impairments and promote their educational success.

Refractive Errors

The most common of all visual impairments are *refractive errors.* Although refractive errors can be serious enough to cause major disabilities for the affected individuals, they are usually correctable with ordinary glasses or contact lenses. In fact, most refractive errors are corrected by these means so that the person's vision is within normal limits. If we did not have the long history of optics technology that we do, a large percentage of our population would have significant disabilities as a result of refractive errors.

These errors result from irregularities in the shape of the eyeball. Figure 7.2 shows that *myopia* (nearsightedness) results from the eyeball being too long. The refracted image comes into focus in front of the retina instead of on it. This occurs when objects at a distance are focused upon. Vision for near objects is not impaired. This condition is corrected through the use of concave lenses. Myopic people will often be noticed holding objects close to their eyes in an attempt to see them clearly. *Hyperopia* (farsightedness) occurs when the eyeball is too short. The refracted image is targeted for a point of focus beyond the retina. While far vision is not impaired, vision for near objects is reduced. This condition is correctable with convex lenses. Another refractive error, *astigmatism*, is caused by an irregularity in the curvature of the cornea or lens. This results in overall blurred vision. This is corrected by lenses that are ground in such a way as to compensate for the irregularity.

FIGURE 7.2

The Shape of the Eyeball in Nearsightedness and Farsightedness

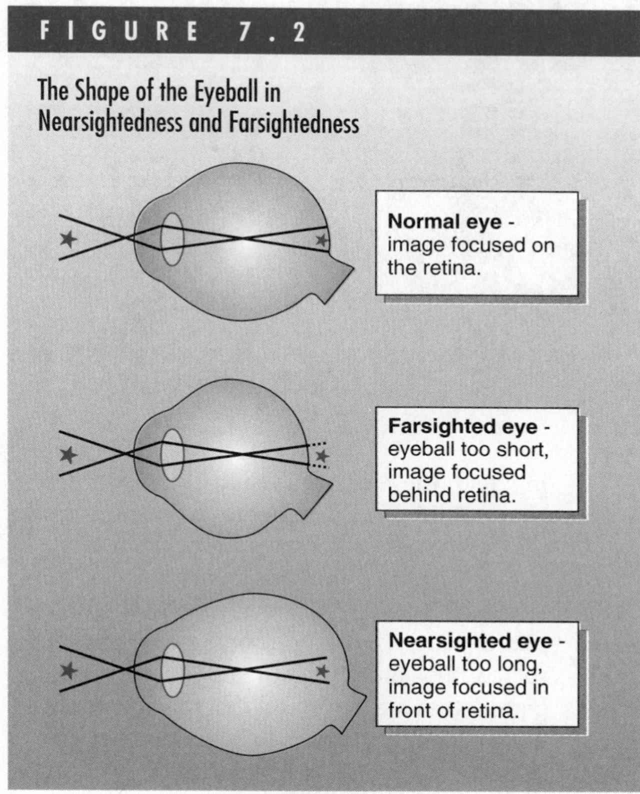

Muscle Disorders

There are several muscle disorders that can result in vision problems. *Strabismus* (unfortunately sometimes called "crossed eyes") is caused by a lack of coordination of the external muscles of the eyes. As a result, the two eyes do not work together; they do not focus or move in a coordinated manner. This condition may be a chronic or temporary problem. Strabismus is often corrected through surgery. *Nystagmus* is a condition in which the eyes move involuntarily in rapid, jerky spasms. Although nystagmus may occur in anyone as a result of fatigue or stress, it is sometimes indicative of brain injury or other chronic medical problems. *Amblyopia* (often referred to as "lazy eye") is an inefficiency of vision due to a lack of proper muscle balance between the two eyes. It is treated through the use of specially prescribed glasses and/or by periodically placing a patch over the stronger eye to force the use of the weaker one. *Heterophoria* is a difficulty in the fusion of the images from each of the two eyes into a single image. This results from a tendency of the eyes to stray slightly from their normal position in fixating on certain points. The condition is sometimes treated by training exercises.

Retinal Disorders

There are conditions that directly involve the retina and result in serious loss of vision. *Retinitis pigmentosa* is a hereditary disorder

Culver Pictures, Inc.

in which the retina gradually deteriorates or atrophies. As this degeneration progresses, the range of vision becomes progressively more narrow (this is commonly referred to as "tunnel vision" or "keyhole vision"). Although the deterioration may stop short of complete destruction of the retina, the effects of retinitis pigmentosa are profound. Night vision may be particularly difficult for persons with this disorder. *Retinopathy of prematurity* is a condition that was previously known as "retrolental fibroplasia." It has long been attributed to overexposure to oxygen in incubators. Premature or very ill newborns exposed to high concentrations of oxygen are at increased risk for the development of scar tissue in the eyes. As growth of the eyes occurs, this scar tissue can pull the retina away from its blood supply. Blindness or less severe vision loss may result. Although the connection between retinopathy of prematurity and excessive oxygen exposure is currently being questioned, there is no question that it is a cause of serious visual impairment (Finkelstein, 1989). *Diabetic retinopathy* is the loss of vision due to hemorrhaging of small blood vessels in the eye of people with diabetes. The hemorrhages cause clouding of the vitreous humor and reduced blood supply to the retina. Because of the increased life expectancy among people with diabetes, the incidence of diabetic retinopathy is also increasing. It is one of the leading causes of blindness among older people. Repair of broken blood vessels with lasers is often possible.

Other Disorders

A *cataract* is a condition in which the lens becomes opaque and light is blocked from entering the eye. Cataracts may be caused by injury, heredity, or disease factors. While usually thought of as a disorder of adulthood, cataracts do sometimes occur in children. Recent advances in surgical techniques and the development of implantable synthetic lenses have made cataracts a much more correctable problem. *Glaucoma* is a condition of excessively high pressure within the eyeball. This increased pressure is due to an obstruction of the circulation of fluid through the eye. If detected early, glaucoma can be controlled by medication. If not detected and treated, it can cause blindness.

In addition to those already mentioned, there are many other diseases and conditions that may result in visual impairment. These include syphilis, tumors, infectious diseases, albinism, and accidental injuries.

This listing of causes of visual impairment is not complete or comprehensive. The purpose of this overview is to provide a basic understanding of causes through which to view the needs of students with visual impairments.

IDENTIFYING VISUAL IMPAIRMENTS

Screening

Most vision screening is based on the use of the Snellen chart. This chart is designed to measure distant, central visual acuity. It does not measure near vision or peripheral vision. Actually there are two charts. For children and adults who are literate, there is a standard letter chart (see Figure 7.3). The person being tested simply calls out the letters in each row. For younger children or for testing persons who are not literate, the symbol chart is used. The response to testing in this case is to point in the direction each "E" is facing (see Figure 7.4). The testing distance is marked at 20 feet from the chart. Each eye is tested independently. The rows of different-size letters or symbols were standardized according to what people with normal vision were able to see at various distances. If, for example, a person standing 20 feet from the chart can see only the line that most people can see standing 80 feet away, vision in that eye

FIGURE 7.3

The Snellen Alphabet Chart

E 1

F P 2

T O Z 3

L P E D 4

P E C F D 5

E D F C Z P 6

F E L O P Z D 7

D E F P O T E C 8

L E F O D P C T 9

F D P L T C E O 10

P E Z O L C F T D 11

Source: National Society for the Prevention of Blindness.

FIGURE 7.4

The Snellen Symbol Chart

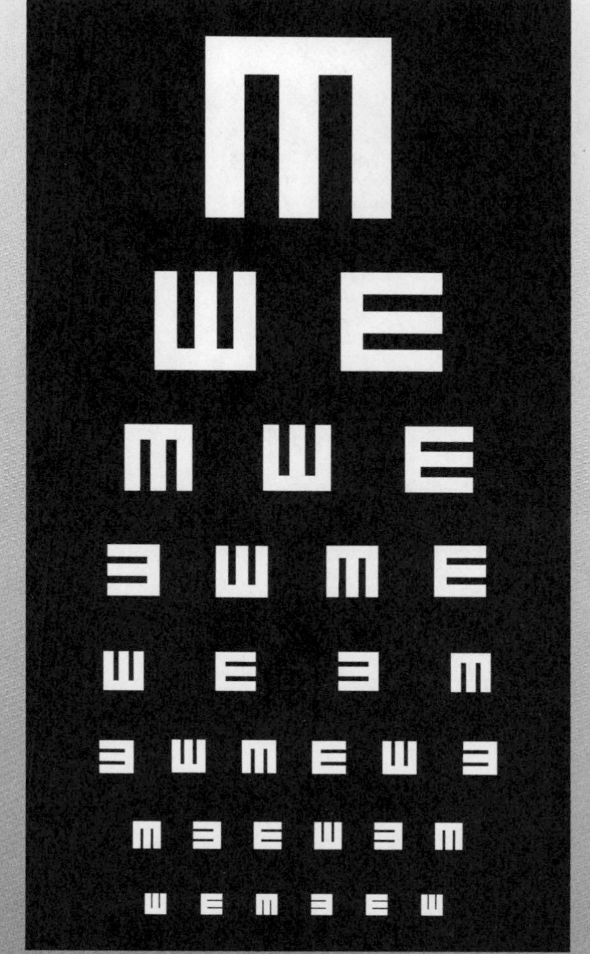

Source: National Society for the Prevention of Blindness.

would be recorded as 20/80. It is possible for visual acuity to differ greatly in the two eyes. A person might have 20/100 vision in one eye (the person can see only the line at 20 feet that most people see standing 100 feet away) and 20/20 vision in the other (normal vision).

Even though the Snellen charts are the most commonly used screening technique, there are limitations to their use. As mentioned previously, they do not measure near vision; therefore, hyperopia might not be detected. Problems in peripheral vision—for example, the early stages of retinitis pigmentosa—may also go unnoticed using this technique. Use of the Snellen charts can be invaluable for screening purposes but cannot provide the detailed information an ophthalmological assessment can yield.

BOX 7.1

Signs of Possible Eye Problems

The following signs should be considered as indications that parents should be advised that an eye examination for their child may be appropriate:

Student's Behavior

- Rubs eyes excessively
- Shuts or covers one eye, tilts head, or holds head forward
- Has difficulty in reading or in other close work
- Blinks excessively
- Holds books close to eyes
- Is unable to see distant things clearly
- Squints or frowns excessively
- Is irritable when required to do close work or work from the board

Student's Appearance

- Eyes appear out of alignment with each other
- Red-rimmed, encrusted, or swollen eyelids
- Inflamed or watery eyes
- Frequent stys

Student's Complaints

- "My eyes itch, burn, or feel scratchy."
- "I cannot see well."
- "I feel dizzy," "my head aches," or "I feel nauseous when I do eye work."
- "I have blurred or double vision."

Ophthalmological Examination

In addition to testing for visual acuity, an *ophthalmologist,* a physician specializing in the diagnosis and treatment of disorders of the eye, can perform a direct examination of the structures and functioning of the eye itself. By use of an *ophthalmoscope* and other instruments the interior parts of the eye can be examined.

Although eye screening procedures are a great help in identifying people who may have vision problems and an ophthalmological examination can provide detailed diagnostic information and treatment implications, it is most important that parents and teachers be sensitive to signs of potential vision problems in children. Box 7.1 presents a list of "danger signals" for eye problems that both parents and teachers should be aware of. These are signs that may be indicative of vision disorders in children.

DEFINITIONS AND CLASSIFICATIONS OF IMPAIRMENTS TO VISION

Legal Definitions

Definitions for visual disabilities were first formulated as part of the Aid to the Blind Act

(Goldstein, 1980) and were adopted in the Social Security Act passed by Congress in 1935. These definitions are used to determine eligibility for disability benefits, income tax exemptions, and special services and materials. The definition for *blindness* is as follows:

> Central visual acuity of 20/200 or less in the better eye with corrective glasses or central visual acuity of more than 20/200 if there is a visual field defect in which the peripheral field is contracted to such an extent that the widest diameter of the visual field subtends an angular distance no greater than 20 degrees in the better eye (Koestler, 1976, p. 45).

This definition is based on the measure of visual acuity previously discussed. When a person can only distinguish at 20 feet a letter or symbol that people with normal vision can distinguish at 200 feet, that person is described as having a visual acuity of 20/200 and is considered *legally blind.* The definition also designates those people with 20 degrees of vision or less as legally blind. This refers to situations, such as in retinitis pigmentosa, where visual acuity may remain within normal limits but the field of vision has been so reduced as to constitute a serious disability (see Figure 7.5).

It is important to remember that legal blindness does not always mean that the person has no vision. The residual vision that legally blind persons may have is important for the education and training they receive. This point will be considered more thoroughly later in the chapter.

A second legal category is that of *partially sighted*: "The partially seeing are defined as persons with a visual acuity greater than 20/200 but not greater than 20/70 in the better eye after correction" (National Society for the Prevention of Blindness, 1966, p. 10).

FIGURE 7.5

Illustrations of Field of Vision

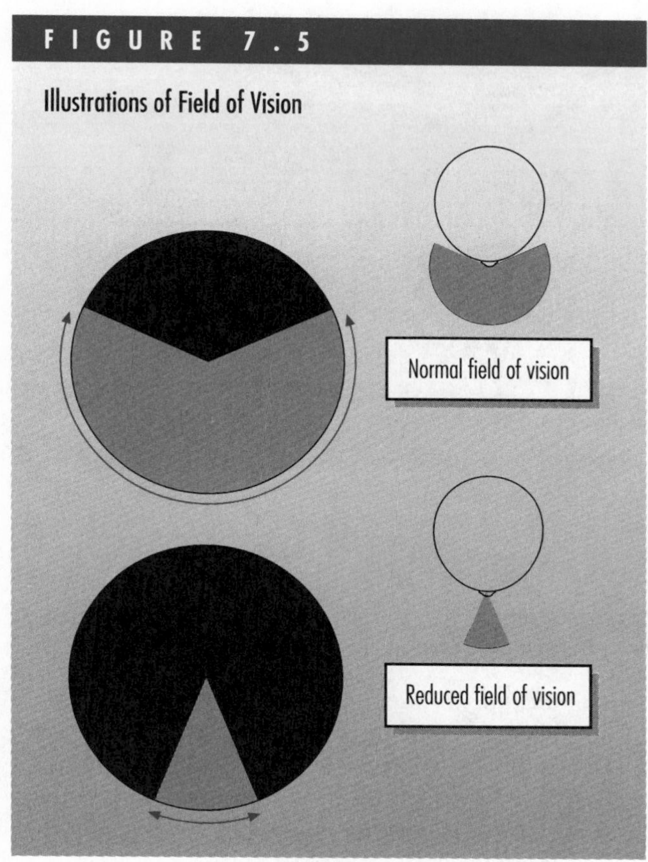

The terms *correction* or *corrective* in these definitions refer to glasses or contact lenses. The determination of a person's legal status in vision is based on what the person can see with the stronger of the two eyes with the most effective lenses available for that person.

Educational Definitions

For the purpose of providing educational services to students with visual impairments, legal definitions are of little use. Educators need to view the needs of these students according to the means through which they can best learn. Appropriate to this need, more functional definitions have been adopted by educators. Public Law 94-142 used the term

SHAFFER PHOTOGRAPHY

visually handicapped to describe students with a "visual impairment which, even with correction, adversely affects a child's educational performance. The term includes both partially seeing and blind children" (*Federal Register*, 1977, 300.5).

According to an educational definition first proposed by Harley (1973), students who are blind are those who have visual impairments so severe that they must be taught to read by the use of Braille. Students who are partially sighted, from this perspective, are those who have enough residual vision so that they can read print either through the use of large print materials or with magnifying devices and special lighting.

More recent definitions have elaborated on the distinction between blind and partially sighted. Caton's educational definition of *blindness* is "Learns through tactile or auditory materials" (1981, p. 219). Corn uses the category of *low vision* to mean: "Severely visually impaired after correction but can increase visual functions" (1983, p. 3). Barraga and Erin describe *limited vision* as "use of vision limited under average circumstances" (1992, p. 23).

In the past, students with visual impairments were often grouped for educational purposes solely according to whether they were classified as blind or partially sighted. These groupings were based entirely on measurements of visual acuity. For several decades, however, educators have recognized that functional vision, the way that a student utilizes vision, is more important than measured visual acuity (Lowenfeld, 1981). Barraga and Erin (1992) have described visual efficiency by use of educational characteristics. Rather than emphasizing the student's measured visual acuity, importance is placed on how well he or she uses the vision that remains. Some students with severe visual impairments are able to use their residual vision very effectively. Other students, with much less serious impairments, do not use their remaining vision up to potential. Placement decisions and educational planning can be much more soundly based on assessments of visual functioning than on measures of visual acuity.

The Educational Needs of Students with Visual Impairments

AT TIMES IN HER OR HIS EDUCATIONAL experience, a child with a visual impairment may have a need that can only be met in a very specialized facility such as a residential school or special day school. Instruction in Braille for some students, for example, might best take place in such a setting. For other students, this instruction might best be provided by a special teacher in a regular public school. For still others, the regular classroom with consultation is most appropriate. The critical point is that the selection of the best facility for meeting the educational needs of a student with a visual impairment should be based on where *this* student's needs at *this* point in her or his development can best be served.

In the past, most visually impaired students were educated in special residential schools. Today most children with impairments to vision are educated in public school programs in their own communities. Some are placed, at least for a while, in self-contained special classes for students with visual impairments. Many more, however, are placed in regular classrooms according to their age and level of academic function. They are provided special education services through resource room teachers or itinerant special education teachers who visit the class and work with students on a regular basis. These teachers also provide consultation and assistance to the student's regular classroom teacher.

In an overall sense, students with visual impairments are more like other students than they are different. They share the same needs, fears, joys, and pains. There are some differences in educational needs, however, that should be kept in mind. Lowenfeld (1975) identified three principles that should guide the process of education for these students.

Concrete Experiences. Since the student's ability to experience the environment through vision is absent or limited, it is important that he or she have the opportunity to relate to the world through the other senses. It is important that the student be presented with objects that can be touched and manipulated. This allows the student to learn about the qualities of shape, size, texture, and orientation that would not otherwise be understood.

Unifying Experiences. People with normal vision experience life as units. When we look around a classroom, for example, we see objects that belong in a classroom (books, chalkboard, desks) and we see relationships (teacher's desk in front, students' desks in rows) that we associate with the "wholeness" of a classroom. In order to achieve this unifying perspective, students with visual impairments often need to be provided with systematic explorations and experiences through their other senses.

Learning by Doing. Obviously a student with a visual impairment will find it difficult or will be unable to "learn by watching." Activity and involvement, therefore, are crucial in the education of these students. The student must be stimulated to become actively involved in the environment.

Although there is increasing emphasis on including students with visual impairments in regular classrooms and having the same academic goals for them as for other students, there are some additional educational

KAREN PREUSS/THE IMAGE WORKS

goals that often must be included for them. These are skills that are necessary for these students in the areas of communication, learning, and mobility.

BRAILLE READING AND WRITING

According to the educational definition discussed earlier, students are considered to be blind if they cannot, even under special conditions, read print. For these students, skill in reading and writing through Braille is critical for communication and learning. Braille is a system that utilizes raised dots to represent letters, numbers, and other symbols. The system is based on a six-dot cell that is two dots wide and three dots high. Standard English Braille is the accepted form of this system in the United States (see Figure 7.6).

Grade 1 (uncontracted) Braille is the literal spelling out, letter by letter, of each word in the raised dots. This method has been found to be needlessly slow and cumbersome for some Braille readers. Grade 2 Braille was developed in order to shorten many words and, thereby, speed up the process of Braille reading and writing. It consists of 189 contractions and shortened words.

Most students who are blind receive initial instruction in Braille at the first-grade level. It usually takes these students longer to become competent with the Braille system than it takes sighted students to become competent with print. Braille reading is almost always a slower process than print reading. Even those students who become very proficient at Braille read slower than the average reader of print.

In learning Braille, students are instructed to read with the index finger of one hand and to keep place vertically on the page with the other. They are encouraged to read with a smooth, continuous horizontal movement and to minimize vertical movements. Light and constant finger pressure is necessary to sense the configuration of the raised dots as the hand moves across them. Advanced readers sometimes use the index fingers of both hands in reading (see Figure 7.7).

Students learn to write Braille by using a *slate and stylus* and the *Perkins Brailler.* When using the slate and stylus, the stylus is pressed

FIGURE 7.6

The Braille Alphabet

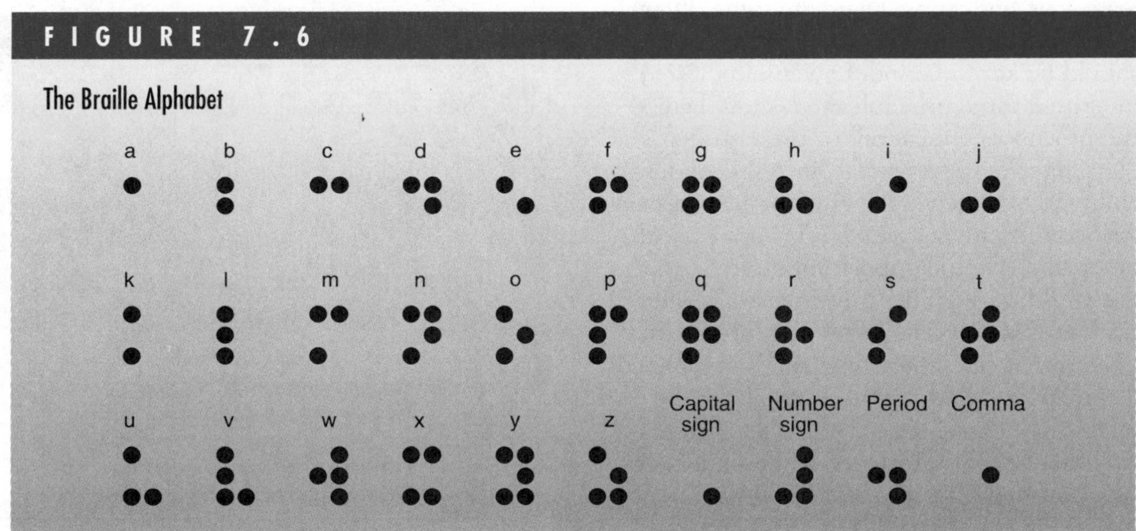

through openings in the slate (see Figure 7.8). Raised dots are thus formed on paper that is placed between the folding halves of the slate. Learning to write using the slate and stylus can be quite difficult since in order for the raised dots to be in the correct configuration for reading, they must be written in reverse order. An easier method for writing Braille is the use of the Perkins Brailler. Much like a typewriter, the Brailler consists of six keys (one for each of the dot positions) and a spacing bar. All possible dot configurations can be formed by depressing the appropriate keys simultaneously.

Many Braille textbooks as well as other educational materials are available from the American Printing House for the Blind. State agencies and volunteer groups also often provide Braille materials and services to students who are blind. In addition, the Library of Congress maintains a large collection of Braille materials that are available through state libraries.

FIGURE 7.7

The Index Fingers Are Commonly Used in Reading Braille

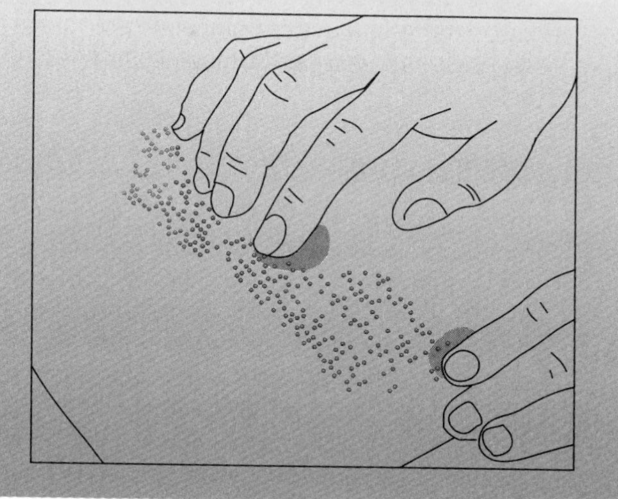

FIGURE 7.8

Slate and Stylus

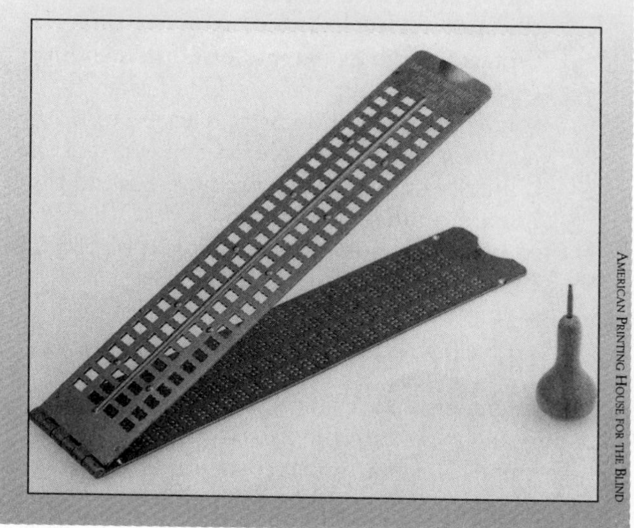

AMERICAN PRINTING HOUSE FOR THE BLIND

KEYBOARDING

The use of a standard keyboard is a skill that allows a person who is blind to communicate in written form with other individuals. It can be a critical factor in a student's ability to function in a classroom with a sighted teacher and classmates. Students who are blind are usually taught to use a keyboard as early as is appropriate for the individual. Keyboarding is then utilized as the primary response mode for tests, homework, and other schoolwork where Braille is not appropriate. The only handwriting skill that is stressed for these students is the ability to form a signature.

CALCULATION AIDS

In math the abacus has long been an important aid for people who are blind. By manipulation of the beads of the abacus, the basic math operations can be performed and the results made available in a tactile form. More commonly used today is a small electronic calculator that presents both entries and results in voice form. This allows the person who is blind to monitor the correctness of entries as well as receive the results of the calculations in a usable manner. It also allows for greater ease in performing higher-level calculations.

THE OPTACON

The Optical-to-Tactile Converter (Optacon) was developed by the Electronic Laboratory of Stanford University. This machine, the size of a small tape recorder, converts printed material into patterns of vibrations on the user's fingertips. The Optacon consists of a camera with photosensitive elements connected to an array of tactile pins. A letter passing beneath the camera causes a particular pattern of vibrations in the tactile pins corresponding to that particular letter. The user places her or his index finger on the pins and feels different vibrations as the camera moves across letters and words. The camera "sees" an area about the size of a single letter at any one time. The Optacon requires extensive and demanding training. Although this machine has given some persons with blindness access to materials never before possible, its expense and the difficulty of learning its use have limited the number of individuals who use it. Other forms of technology have largely replaced the Optacon as an aid for reading.

THE KURZWEIL READING MACHINE

Engineers and linguists worked for about ten years to develop the Kurzweil Reading Machine. This machine reads a printed book, and the results are produced in voice form. When printed material is placed on a sheet of glass for electronic scanning and the machine is activated by a button, the synthesized voice reads the material aloud. When other buttons are pressed, the endlessly patient voice will repeat a word, a sentence, or a paragraph any number of times, or spell any word requested. As the machine is modified and improved, its cost and size will probably gradually decline. Early floor models sold for $50,000; now, portable units about the size of two large briefcases cost about $20,000 each. Estimates are that further improvements in technology and production will bring costs down dramatically (Barraga and Erin, 1992).

TALKING BOOKS

Talking books have become standard educational media for people who are blind. The Talking Books Program is sponsored by the Library of Congress. Books and magazines are recorded on disks or cassettes and are distributed to persons with visual impairments free of charge. These books are read by volunteer readers and are heard at the rate of 160–170 words per minute for fiction and about 150 words per minute for nonfiction. On request, a qualified individual may have any textbook recorded.

One drawback in listening to textbooks or other materials is that it is a slower process than normal reading. It usually takes a student who is blind much longer to listen to a chapter than for other students to read it. One solution to this problem has been the development of *compressed speech devices.* These devices eliminate nonessential elements from the recorded speech. This is done without major distortion. This process results in a considerably increased rate of listening.

COMPUTER TECHNOLOGY

Advances in computer technology are having a very positive impact on the education of students with visual impairments. Software is available that produces large print on a monitor and then prints the final copy in standard-size print. This enables students with low vision to produce assignments that can be read and evaluated by regular classroom teachers.

There are also computer systems that will take input in either Braille or print and will produce output in either form. This allows students who are blind to function much more effectively in inclusive classrooms.

Computer hardware and software are also available that allow for the reading aloud of either Braille or print. Technologies such as these are developing rapidly and will certainly continue to open up new educational opportunities for students with visual impairments.

MOBILITY AND ORIENTATION TRAINING

Students with visual impairments often experience restrictions in movement within their environments. In order to be independent at home, in school, and in the community, the student must be able to recognize her or his surroundings and her or his relationship to these surroundings—*orientation*. It is also necessary that the student be able to move safely and effectively within these environments—*mobility*. Training in these skills can, and should, begin at home as parents help the child develop techniques that are unique to their child and their home. Formal mobility and orientation training, however, should begin as soon as the student is enrolled in a school program. Among the techniques and options available are the following.

Use of a Sighted Human Guide

A sighted human guide is often a great help in crowded areas, on strange terrain, or in unfamiliar buildings. Through a very simple technique, a guide can provide information to a person who is blind concerning changes in position, changes in direction, or needed changes in pace. The person with a visual impairment should grasp the inside of the arm of the guide just above the elbow. With just a light grasp and by walking about a half step behind the guide, the person with the visual disability can easily detect changes in position, direction, and gait. This technique allows for easy and natural movement of the two people even in very congested conditions. The guide should never grasp the other person from the back or attempt to "push" her or him along. In addition to being embarrassing for the individual with a visual impairment, it can easily result in this person becoming a "battering ram" for obstacles that the other person may not notice.

Guide Dogs

Although the use of guide dogs seems to spark a great deal of interest in the general public, they are actually used by only a small percentage of people with visual impairments. Larger breeds of "work" dogs are usually selected to be trained as guides. At birth, the puppies are placed in volunteer homes until they are approximately a year old. They are then trained by professional guide dog instructors for three to four months. The dog and the "master" are trained together for an additional month. Dogs are trained to follow those instructions of the master except where following those instructions would place the visually impaired person in danger. By law, guide dogs are permitted in public places.

Guide dogs have practically no value for children. The dogs walk too fast for children and are often too large for them to handle. They also require care that a child may not be capable of providing.

The Hoover Cane

The most commonly used aid to mobility for persons with visual impairments is the *Hoover cane*. The systematic use of this long cane was developed by Dr. Richard Hoover in his work with World War II veterans who had been blinded. Contrary to the impression that many people have that the cane is used as a random probe for obstacles, the cane is used in a very methodical fashion for independent travel. The person with blindness moves the cane in a wide arc in front of her or him while at the same time moving the cane in a probing pattern. When the cane is at the right side of the arc, the left foot is brought forward, and vice versa. By use of this procedure, the person is always stepping into an area that has been determined to be obstacle-free by the sweep of the cane. The vertical motion of the cane is used as an indicator of changes in the terrain (curbs or stairs, for example). The cane technique is a part of most programs of mobility training for students who are blind.

Electronic Aids to Mobility

Several electronic aids to mobility have been developed. The *Russel Pathsounder* is worn around the neck and produces a warning signal when objects are in the pathway of the person. The *Mowat sensor* is a handheld device that sends out a beam of ultrasonic energy. When the beam strikes objects, a signal relays a message to a receiver. The receiver emits sounds that the person can interpret in terms of the nature of the object and how far away it is. This same radar principle has also been used in building a similar device, the *sonic guide*, into the frames of glasses.

SELF-HELP AND DAILY LIVING SKILLS

Skills such as dressing, bathing, grooming, table manners, and basic etiquette are of critical importance in the lives of people with visual impairments. These students do not have the same opportunity to observe and imitate behaviors in the way that other children do. As a result, it is often necessary that they receive direct and systematic instruction in these skills. Step-by-step instructions have been developed for teaching these skills and for helping persons with visual impairments make necessary adaptations in these and other areas of their lives.

Ways of Helping Students with Visual Impairments Succeed in Inclusive Settings

WITH THE GROWING COMMITMENT to placing students with visual impairments into inclusive school settings, more classroom teachers are exploring ways to meet the special needs of these students. Working with a student with a visual impairment for the first time can create questions and concerns for even the most experienced and dedicated teacher. The cardinal principle for those teachers finding themselves in this situation should be to remember, as was previously stated, that sighted students and students with visual impairments have more similarities than differences. They have the same basic needs. Usually any fears or negative feelings that a teacher may have about working with these students will gradually disappear as he or she becomes familiar with the student's characteristics and capabilities.

The overall objectives in the education of students with visual disabilities are much the same as those for any other student (see Box 7.2). The key to teaching these students in the general classroom seems to be an appropriate blend of sensitivity to modifications that may be necessary to optimize learning and the encouragement of self-reliance and independence. It is also important to remember that these students are not a homogeneous group but are individuals who share only the reality of reduced vision or blindness. Some suggestions that may be helpful to a classroom teacher who is working with a student with a visual impairment for the first time are offered in Box 7.3.

USE OF RESIDUAL VISION

Students who have partial sight should be encouraged and instructed in how best to make use of their residual vision. A central academic goal for these students may be to enable them to read print. Since the degree of loss of vision varies greatly among those students who are considered partially sighted, the individual needs of each must be carefully assessed in developing appropriate teaching strategies and selecting instructional aids. The most common techniques used to facilitate the reading of print, however, are control of illumination, changes in the size of print, and the use of magnification.

Control of Illumination

Proper illumination can be critical for the success of a student with a visual impairment in the classroom. Both the intensity and type of lighting must be taken into consideration. Some students will actually see better when the intensity of light is decreased. Others may need special lamps at their desks. Glare can be a major problem and can be reduced by adjustable desktops, special shields, and careful seating arrangements. Writing paper should be used that does not have a slick or shiny surface. Students should be seated and positioned so that shadows and light from windows do not interfere with their vision.

BOX 7.2

General Education Objectives for Students with Visual Impairments

1. To understand each student in terms of visual and intellectual potential and needs, and to plan his or her adapted curriculum according to this understanding.
2. To provide a general academic program closely related to that of other students.
3. To teach adaptive skills and their application—the use of large-type materials when necessary, the use of the tape recorder, the use of magnifiers where helpful, and the use of the typewriter (and/or Brailler) as a communicative device.
4. To teach listening skills.
5. To develop visual perception to the extent of each student's potential.
6. To develop independent study skills, utilizing auditory devices as much as possible, and encouraging perseverance, originality, curiosity, creativity, and ingenuity.
7. To encourage adequate social adjustment of the student within the regular classroom.
8. To develop self-discipline appropriate to age and to grade-range expectations.
9. To encourage the student's own acceptance of his or her visual limitation, but to teach the efficient use of residual vision.
10. To fully utilize each student's individual potential in terms of intelligence, special talents, and abilities, with consideration for visual limits.
11. To prepare each student insofar as possible and as quickly as possible, to function efficiently in a regular classroom environment.
12. To give guidance, encouragement, and counsel in the direction of higher education, occupational training, and job placement, giving serious thought to the student's individual potential and her or his ultimate contribution to society.

Adapted from V. Bishop. *Teaching the Visually Limited Child.* Springfield, IL: Charles C. Thomas, 1971.

Use of Large Print

Materials that are produced in large print can be very helpful to students with impaired vision. The most popular size is 18 point type (see Figure 7.9). Much larger print, however, is available for students who require it. Large print is also an advantage for many older adults who, because of deterioration of vision due to the aging process (presbyopia), are unable to read smaller print effectively. Several newspapers and magazines are available in large print. The American Printing House for the Blind and several other publishers produce educational materials in large print.

BOX 7.3

Tips for the Classroom Teacher: Getting Started with a Student with a Visual Impairment

- Give the child a "tour" of the classroom. Make sure he or she is familiar with the basic classroom arrangement. Be sure to inform him or her when changes are made in the location of furniture or equipment.
- Find out what kind of aids the child uses (for example, magnifier, typewriter, or tape recorder), how they operate, and how they are maintained.
- Be as specific as possible with verbal directions. Check with the child frequently at first to make sure you have been clear.
- Acquaint the other children in the class with the nature of this child's disability. He or she may want to demonstrate how to use Braille, a cane, or a magnifying aid. This may be a good "ice-breaker." It all depends on this particular child's personality.
- Encourage the child to be as independent as possible in all appropriate activities.
- Don't be overprotective.
- Use a "buddy" system in activities where needed.
- Don't use praise too lavishly. Don't draw attention to the fact that the child is able to do something that all the other children do every day.
- Don't hesitate to seek help or information from other professionals when you need it.

FIGURE 7.9

Example of 18 Point Type

18 point type is this large

Magnification

Optical magnification aids are helpful to many students with visual disabilities. Special glasses and handheld magnifiers are often used to enlarge regular print. A telescopic device is sometimes used to aid these students in reading from the chalkboard. A closed-circuit television system is available that displays an enlargement of regular print onto a TV screen for viewing.

Students with partial sight are often unaware of just how much use they can make of the vision they have. Teachers need to be sensitive to the fact that through training and assistance these students can learn to optimize their visual function in the classroom.

In the past the attitudes of people with normal vision have often prohibited persons with visual impairments from being as independent and as much a part of society as they might have been. Social attitudes toward people with limitations to vision are still much in need of improvement. The social climate today, however, seems to offer the greatest opportunity yet for full participation in society for people with blindness and partial sight. The work of teachers who understand the needs and potentials of these students will help make this opportunity a reality.

Case Studies and Questions to Consider

PUPIL: JON JOVEN
SCHOOL: CLEARLY ELEMENTARY
CURRENT PLACEMENT: SECOND GRADE
AGE: 8 YEARS, 10 MONTHS

Family Structure and Home Environment

Jon lives with his mother, Pamela Joven, in a rented house. Ms. Joven, who is thirty-six years old, is the manager of the deli at a fitness center. Jon also lives with his sister, Kim, who is sixteen years old and is a tenth grader. Ms. Joven, who earned a GED certificate, has also found it necessary to take a second job in order to meet the financial demands of her family. She works evenings each week at the fitness center performing maintenance activities.

Jon's father, Buddy Joven, is thirty years old and, until recently, worked as a carpenter. Mr. Joven is now incarcerated. His wife explained that he will probably not be released for three and a half years. Mr. Joven's conviction and incarceration have had a profound negative effect on Jon. Ms. Joven explained that Jon and his father have always had a strong and positive relationship. She described her husband's approach to Jon as one of patience, understanding, and encouragement. Ms. Joven said that things began to change when Mr. Joven started having serious substance abuse problems. This change in his father's behavior was upsetting to Jon. His father's incarceration was devastating to him. Ms. Joven said that Jon is seeing a counselor regularly. This has helped, but the loss of his father's presence is still a major event in Jon's life.

Parental Perception of Child's Developmental Progress and Needs

Jon was recently diagnosed by an ophthalmologist as having retinitis pigmentosa. He has apparently been losing his peripheral vision gradually since he was an infant. The condition had gone undetected, even through school vision screenings, because he could read the charts perfectly. Even though he was not aware that his sight was different from others, he has less than 25 percent of the normal range of vision. He has only 40 degrees of vision in each eye, and this has interfered with his ability to learn to read and otherwise succeed in school. His vision is particularly poor under low illumination conditions. His vision is likely to continue to deteriorate. The ophthalmologist expects that Jon will become legally blind before he finishes high school.

Although the last few months have been particularly difficult for Jon, his school problems predate these recent events. Ms. Joven said that Jon has had problems since kindergarten. She reports having been confused ever since Jon started school as to the nature of his problems. She said that at various times she has viewed his academic and social troubles as being due to hyperactivity, processing problems, dyslexia, and low self-esteem. She has experienced frustration at the lack of a clear cause of her son's problems in school.

Ms. Joven said that some of Jon's classmates have now become aware of his visual impairment. He has apparently become very sensitive to this and is embarrassed when it is mentioned. Ms. Joven said that his vision has become a symbol to Jon that something is wrong with him, that he is "handicapped." She said that he has also started to blame things on his vision. On several occasions, he has apparently attributed a simple mistake or personal problem to his retinitis pigmentosa.

Ms. Joven feels that Jon's lack of satisfactory academic progress has made school difficult and deflating for him. He is unable to do his work adequately, and he feels like a failure. This relates to a second important factor in considering Jon's behavior. Jon is a perfectionist. Unless he is able to do things perfectly, he perceives himself to be a total failure. He finds it very difficult to accept small increments of success. The greater his perception that he has failed, the more demanding of perfection he becomes of himself and, consequently, the greater the chances of feeling he has failed again.

Additional Comments

Ms. Joven feels that Jon has come to need the reassurance of the security of their relationship. They have always been close, but he expresses an even greater need for her now. She said he becomes anxious at the prospect of doing anything that requires him to be away from her for any length of time.

Ms. Joven describes Jon as an affectionate and caring child. She hopes that he can overcome his academic problems, the tyranny of feeling that he must do things perfectly or not at all, and his sensitivity about his visual impairment.

Questions

1. As a teacher, do you think Jon's father's incarceration should be something that you discuss with him?
2. How could the realities of Jon's retinitis pigmentosa be discussed with him in relation to his work in school? Should it be discussed with the other children in the class? How?
3. How could you go about better understanding Jon's visual impairment and finding ways of helping him function most successfully in your class?

STUDENT: LINDA HAP

SCHOOL: HOPEFUL HIGH SCHOOL

CURRENT PLACEMENT: SPECIAL EDUCATION CLASS

AGE: 17 YEARS, 1 MONTH

Family Structure and Home Environment

Linda lives with her mother, Delores Hap, and her father, Ronnie Hap. Ms. Hap is forty years old and is employed as a salesclerk at Kmart. Mr. Hap is forty-two years old and is currently unemployed. He formerly managed a restaurant. Linda also lives with her sister, Lucky, who is eighteen. Lucky graduated from Hopeful High School this year and will be attending Upward College this fall. Linda, her parents, and Lucky live in a house in a modest residential area. Beginning in late August, Lucky will be living in a dormitory at Upward College.

Parental Perception of the Student's School Program

Linda has been diagnosed as having mental retardation at a level that requires that she be given more social support than most people of her age. She also has mild cerebral palsy, which causes her to have a somewhat awkward gait and to have poor fine motor coordination in her hands. Associated with her cerebral palsy, Linda has strabismus. The condition has been corrected as much as possible. She wears very strong glasses, but her vision is very impaired. Ms. Hap believes that her daughter has been making marked progress in school. She thinks that Linda's placement in the class for students with multiple disabilities at Hopeful High has been most positive for her. In Ms. Hap's opinion, both the curriculum and the teacher are meeting Linda's needs in a very efficacious way.

Ms. Hap also feels that the Ritalin Linda is taking is helping her function better in school. She commented that she noticed an almost immediate change in her daughter's ability to attend to her work when she began to take the medication. Ms. Hap feels that, in general, given her disabilities and developmental level, Linda is functioning well in both the personal and social realms of her life.

Ms. Hap commented several times on the effect that Linda's new medication has had on her behavior. She said that since her daughter has been taking Ritalin, she is generally more pleasant to everyone. She said that just prior to when the drug was prescribed to Linda, there had been instances when Linda's tantrums and impulsive behavior had become very problematic for her family.

Additional Considerations

Ms. Hap is now beginning to explore the options that will be open to Linda in a few years when she makes the transition from school to adult life. Ms. Hap has already talked with local vocational rehabilitation personnel and is beginning to gather information on programs such as those available at the Progressive Rehabilitation Center and at Sunrise Sheltered Industries. Ms. Hap hopes that Linda will eventually be able to live at least semi-independently and have a job that will be meaningful to her.

Linda's teacher feels that Linda has been somewhat overprotected and indulged at home. She believes that Linda's sister Lucky, in particular, has been overly protective of Linda. She hopes now that Lucky will be graduating and leaving home, Linda may become more independent. Linda has been reluctant to venture very far from her special education classroom at Hopeful High. She has also been resistant to try new activities.

Questions

1. What are some things that might be tried at Hopeful High to expand Linda's involvement and make her school experience more inclusive?
2. What are some things that might be tried to begin to prepare Linda for the transition from school to her community?
3. What are some ways that the Hap family can be involved in these changes?

References

Barraga, N., and J. Erin. *Visual Handicaps and Learning,* 3d ed. Austin, TX: Pro-Ed, 1992.

Bishop, V. *Teaching the Visually Limited Child.* Springfield, IL: Charles C. Thomas, 1971.

Braddy, N. *Anne Sullivan Macy: The Story Behind Helen Keller.* Garden City, NY: Doubleday, Doran, 1933.

Caton, H. R. "Visual Impairments." In A. E. Blackhurst and W. H. Berdine (Eds.), *An Introduction to Special Education.* Boston: Little, Brown, 1981: 217–232.

Corn, A. "Visual Function: A Model for Individuals with Low Vision." *Journal of Visual Impairment and Blindness, 77,* 1983: 373–377.

Davidson, M. *Helen Keller's Teacher.* New York: Four Winds Press, 1965.

Federal Register. 42(163), 1977: 42659–42688.

Finkelstein, D. *Blindness and Disorders of the Eye.* Baltimore, MD: National Federation for the Blind, 1989.

Goldstein, H. *The Demography of Blindness Throughout the World.* New York: American Foundation for the Blind, 1980.

Harley, R. K. "Children with Visual Disabilities." In L. Dunn (Ed.), *Exceptional Children in the Schools.* New York: Holt, Rinehart, and Winston, 1973: 330–354.

Hoxie, E. F. "Anne Sullivan Macy." *Notable American Women,* Vol. 2. Cambridge, MA: Belknap Press, 1971: 481–483.

Koestler, F. *The Unseen Minority: A Social History of Blindness in the United States.* New York: David McKay, 1976.

Lowenfeld, B. *The Changing Status of the Blind.* Springfield, IL: Charles C. Thomas, 1975.

———. *Berthold Lowenfeld on Blindness and Blind People.* New York: American Foundation for the Blind, 1981.

National Society for the Prevention of Blindness. *Estimated Statistics on Blindness and Vision Problems.* New York: National Society for the Prevention of Blindness, 1966.

Office of Special Education Programs. *Sixteenth Annual Report to Congress on the Implementation of the Individuals with Disabilities Education Act.* Washington, DC: U.S. Department of Education, 1994.

———. *Seventeenth Annual Report to Congress on the Implementation of the Individuals with Disabilities Education Act.* Washington, DC: U.S. Department of Education, 1995.

Creating Classrooms That Welcome Students with Hearing Impairments

Helen Keller: The Voice of the Miracle

On a very cold March afternoon some years ago, I made my way back to my hotel room from the Library of Congress in Washington, D.C. The wind and low temperature did not bother me. I had made a discovery that day that had my adrenaline output at a peak. While working on another project in the Manuscript Division, I had happened upon a reference to letters from and about Helen Keller in the Alexander Graham Bell Collection. I started looking through these papers and was soon enthralled with them. Here were letters actually written by people like Annie Sullivan Macy and Alexander Graham Bell to, and concerning, Helen. These letters, I believe, present a unique and important view of Helen and some of her life experiences.

I share these letters here with the same enthusiasm as when I first shared them with my colleague, Dr. Burton Blatt. Burt read the letters, just as he approached most things, with vigor and depth of feeling. He wrote an article, using some of the letters, which appeared shortly after his death (Blatt, 1985). It is with Burt Blatt in mind that I share what follows.

Helen Keller was born in Tuscumbia, Alabama, in 1880. Her father, Arthur H. Keller, was a Confederate Civil War veteran and published a small weekly newspaper. Her mother, Kate Adams, was much younger than her father and was originally from Memphis. She was related to the famous and influential Adams family of New England.

At nineteen months of age, Helen was stricken with a severe, acute illness that left her deaf and blind. As a result, she was unable to develop spoken language. Her handicaps created in Helen great turmoil and resulted in her being a very difficult child for the Kellers to manage.

When Helen was six, her parents brought her to see Alexander Graham Bell. He was known for his interest in the education of children with deafness, and they hoped he would be able to advise them on what to do for Helen and where to seek help. He suggested they contact the Perkins Institution near Boston. They did, and soon the director recommended to them a recent graduate, Annie Sullivan, as a teacher for Helen.

On November 29, 1889, Captain Arthur Keller wrote to Alexander Graham Bell:

> My Dear Sir:
>
> Remembering how very kind you were to my little deaf, dumb, and blind girl whilst we were in Washington last winter, and how much interest you expressed in her behalf, it affords me great pleasure to report that her progress in learning is phenomenal and the report of it almost staggers one's credulity who has not seen it.
>
> In March last I secured the services of Miss Annie Sullivan, a graduate of the Perkins Institution in Boston, who was educated whilst blind, and had her sight restored last year by an operation. In a month the little girl [Helen] learned to spell about four hundred words and in no less than three months could write a letter unaided by anyone. In six weeks she mastered the "Braille" [French] System which is a cipher for the blind enabling them to read what they have written. She has also mastered addition, multiplication, and subtraction and is progressing finely with Geography.
>
> Miss Sullivan has sent Prof. Anagnos a short sketch of her life and her progress in her studies which will shortly appear in the Annual Report of the Perkins Institution.

I send you a picture of Helen and her teacher and also a specimen of her writing believing you will be glad to hear again from the dear little treasure.

With high regard
I am very truly yours
A. H. Keller

There was soon much publicity concerning the accomplishments of Helen and Annie. They were internationally known in a very short time. In 1888 Helen became a pupil at Perkins. Most of her instruction was done by Annie Sullivan. In Boston, of course, they became even more of a focus of public attention than they had been in Tuscumbia.

Among the letters in the Bell Collection at the Library of Congress was the handwritten transcript of a conversation between Helen and Alexander Graham Bell. This conversation may have taken place as a part of a public demonstration. In any case, it is a remarkable example of the thoughts of a nine-year-old girl who—just two years before—had been almost totally isolated from the world around her.

Conversation Between Mr. Bell and Helen A. Keller at the Perkins Institution in South Boston on May 7, 1890

Do you know what a cloud is?

Rain.

What is rain?

Moisture.

Where does rain come from?

From the ocean.

From the ocean! How?

It falls down.

How does it come from the ocean?

It rises up.

What makes it rise up?

The waves—sun and waves.

Have you been upon the ocean?

Yes, I went in a steamboat to Plymouth. The ocean is very large and deep.

What did you think about the wind?

I think the wind is not as gentle as the breeze. . . .

Here is a hard question. What is thought?

When we make a mistake, we say I thought it was right.

Are you thinking now?

I am trying to think. Sometimes we are thinking about something in our heads.

Is thought in your head?

Yes.

Where is your thought?

(Helen illustrated by describing the outline of her face and head and then said, "Mind.") My head is full of mind. . . .

Helen and Annie remained at Perkins for six years. They then moved to New York so that Helen could attend the Wright-Humason School. This was a school that had been established to teach oral language to deaf children. The goal of this move seems to have been to improve Helen's speech. The living expenses for Helen and Annie, and for Helen's tuition, were paid by a sugar millionaire, John Spaulding. Her attendance at the school was not enthusiastically endorsed by Bell, who had other ideas of what would be best for Helen. In a letter of July 20, 1894, he expressed his opinions on the best educational arrangements for Helen.

Dear Major Keller:

I must apologize for not writing to you before this regarding Helen, but I did not wish to make any suggestion until I had an opportunity of talking with Helen herself and with Miss Sullivan. . . .

I doubt the advisability of sending her to a school for the deaf, for she is already further advanced than any of our pupils. She would be at just as much disadvantage in a school for the deaf or the blind as she would be in any ordinary school, for she needs a special interpreter. Why not send her to whatever may be the best private school for hearing and seeing young ladies? . . .

Alexander Graham Bell

Even though Bell did not support the idea of Helen going to a school for deaf children, once the decision was made he continued to be a source of encouragement and support. Helen had a close relationship with Mrs. Bell and with the Bell children. Writing to Mrs. Bell on December 2, 1895, from New York, Helen described her progress in school:

My dear Mrs. Bell:

I have just discovered that Teacher has written to you, and, as I have a little leisure, I think I will write you a letter. I have thought of you and dear Mr. Bell very often during the many months which have sped away since we last saw each other. . . . I am studying French myself this year, and I enjoy it very much. I expect to have a French teacher soon, and then I shall learn to speak French as well as read it. I study German too, and find it interesting. It reminds me of a proud oak tree with tender mistletoe twining round it. Besides French and German I study Physical Geography, Arithmetic, voice-training and lip-reading; so you see what a busy little girl I am! Sometimes I feel quite overwhelmed when I think what a vast mine of knowledge this world of ours is! It almost seems as if its weight would crush me: but when I remember the great men whose minds have gone down into the dark depths of the mind, and brought back to us the precious gems of truth which we call science, I begin to think our minds are as vast as the world, and I feel encouraged. Physical Geography is one of my favorite studies now. . . . Arithmetic and I have never been very good friends, as you probably know; but I am getting to like it better and better as I go on. My enemies in lip-reading and voice-training are still assaulting me quite furiously, and I have to be very vigilant in order to keep them away from my fortress; but I am not at all shaken in my resolution to conquer them, knowing that a brave heart and patient perseverance will triumph in the end. . . .

I hope you and Mr. Bell are quite well and happy. How is his flying-machine getting on? Can he fly yet? Please give my dear love to him and your daughters.

Lovingly your little friend,
Helen Keller

In 1896, Dr. Bell's original advice concerning Helen's education was heeded. That fall she was enrolled in the Cambridge School for Young Ladies to prepare for Radcliffe College. Again, financial support as well as friendship came from Bell. In a September 3 letter, she expresses appreciation and shares a personal sorrow with him.

My dear Mr. Bell,

Mr. Warner has forwarded your check for four hundred dollars to Teacher, and I am going to acknowledge it myself because I want to thank you for your great kindness to me.

I would like to write you a nice, long letter, and tell you all about our vacation by the seaside, and our plans for next year; but my heart is too full of sadness to dwell upon the happiness the summer has brought me, or upon the bright prospects which await me in Cambridge. My father is dead. He died last Saturday at my home in Tuscumbia, and I was not there. My own dear, loving father. Oh, dear friend, how shall I ever bear it! It seems as if a great, dark cloud had fallen upon my life that would always keep out the brightness of everything. How strange it is. I never knew how dearly I loved my father until I realized that I had lost him. I think we do not know the depth of love in our hearts until some dreadful sorrow reveals it to us, and then we realize a little of what God's love must be like.

Please give my love to Mrs. Bell, and Elsie and Daisy. Teacher sends her love to you all.

Lovingly your friend,
Helen

The Cambridge School was headed by Arthur Gilman. After only nine months of study there, Helen passed the first set of tests that were required for admission to Radcliffe. Annie felt that Helen could complete all of the remaining tests within a two-year period. Gilman opposed this as a too-demanding schedule. This became the starting point of a schism and power struggle between him and Annie that resulted in Helen and Annie leaving the Cambridge School. They moved to a friend's farm in Wrentham, Massachusetts, and Helen worked with a private tutor during the next two years.

During this period, Helen wrote to Bell concerning her progress and, in one letter, expressed delight that he had bothered to learn Braille so that she could read his letters without an interpreter.

March 9, 1900
My dear Mr. Bell:

I was perfectly delighted to receive your letter and to be able to read it myself. It seemed almost as if you clasped my hand in yours and spoke to me in the old, dear way. A letter always seems more truly my own when I can run my fingers over it, and quickly enter into the thoughts and feelings of my friends without an interpreter, even though the interpreter be the dearest and sweetest in the world. It was very kind of you to learn those queer little hieroglyphics and write to me yourself; and nothing but hard work has prevented me from sending a more prompt reply. O yes, I could read every word you wrote; indeed, I did not find a single mistake in the Braille, and I trust since your "first attempt" was such a wonderful success, I shall receive many such "attempts." . . .

I need not tell you that my dear teacher is ever at my side, ready to encourage and help me in my work. The only drawback to our complete happiness is her eyes. They trouble her constantly, and I cannot help worrying about them. . . .

Affectionately your friend,
Helen Keller

Helen entered Radcliffe in September 1900. She was accompanied to every class by Annie, who spelled the lectures into her hands. While still a student, she wrote her autobiography, *The Story of My Life*. After she and Annie had started on the book, they ran into some difficulty completing it in a manner that was satisfying to them. To complete the writing, they turned to John Albert Macy, a young Harvard professor, for help. *The Story of My Life* was published in 1902. It was well received by the public and has become a classic. After reading the book, Alexander Graham Bell wrote to John Macy, praising the book and commenting particularly on some of the correspondence it included that illuminated Annie's approach to teaching Helen. The letter, dated April 2, 1903, also contained a suggestion that would further serve to highlight the importance of Annie's instructional techniques.

Dear Mr. Macy:

I have read with the greatest interest, *The Story of My Life*, by Helen Keller. The book is a most valuable contribution to our literature; it will be read by all with interest, and the material is so carefully and wisely arranged that it will undoubtedly exert a profound influence upon the education of the deaf. The world, I think, is to be congratulated that Helen and Miss Sullivan have been able to secure an editor who has compiled his material with such intelligence and judgement as you have done. Congratulations upon your success.

You have made a great find in Miss Sullivan's letters to Mrs. Hopkins. . . . They are of the greatest importance as giving a contemporaneous account of the earlier stages of Helen's education. They reveal the fact that had long been suspected, that Helen's remarkable achievements were as much due to the genius of her teacher, as to her own brilliant mind. They show that she was guided all along by the principles of the greatest importance in the education of the deaf—that she did have a method, and the results have shown that her method was a true one. . . .

Yours very sincerely,
Alexander Graham Bell

In 1904 Helen graduated from Radcliffe cum laude. She and Annie settled down in Wrentham, where Helen's writing continued with John Macy's assistance. Throughout her life, Helen continued to write. In addition, she became a strong advocate and activist for the rights of people with disabilities. This work eventually broadened. She became a vocal supporter of women's suffrage, a pacifist, and a social reformer. Helen's influence was felt nationally and internationally for more than half a century. She often acknowledged the influence of Annie, not only for opening up the pathways to communication for her, but also for the influence that Annie had on her thinking about the world. She also paid tribute to John Macy, whom, although his marriage to Annie ended in permanent separation, continued to influence her views on life. There were many others who were important in the development of her "vision," and Helen was quick to recognize herself as a product of the contributions of others. Perhaps the most fitting close to this section are the words of tribute that Helen sent to Alexander Graham Bell in a letter of July 5, 1918.

. . . Even before Teacher came, you held out a warm hand to me in the dark. Indeed, it was through you that she came to me. How vividly it all comes back! How plainly I see the vanquished little child, and the young girl God sent to liberate her! Untrained, alone, almost blind, she journeyed swiftly to me. I still feel her strong, tender, quivering touch, her kisses upon my face. Sometimes I feel that in that supreme moment she thought me into being. Certainly she forestalled and defeated a cruel fate. O the waking rapture! O the shining joy of feet approaching light, of eager, inquisitive hands grasping knowledge! My fingers still glow with the feel of the first word that opened its golden heart to me. How everything seemed to think, to live! Shall I, in all the years of eternity, forget the torrent of wonders that rushed upon me out of the darkness and silence? And you are part of that wonder, that joy! I have not forgotten how you followed step by step my teacher's efforts to free my mind, my life, my heart from the tyranny of circumstance. From the first you understood the stupendous task of the young teacher. You were quick to realize her ability, her tireless energy, enthusiasm, and originality. I love you for the generous way in which you have always upheld her work . . . when I made up my mind to learn to speak, you cheered us on with a faith that outran our own. How closely I felt your sympathy and forwardlooking faith in me when I fought my way through college! Again and again you said to me, "Helen, let no sense of limitations hold you back. You can do anything you think you can. Remember that many will be brave in your courage." You have always shown a father's joy in my success and a father's tenderness when things have not gone right. . . . As Praxiteles animated stone, so you have quickened dumb lips with living speech. You have poured the sweet waters of language into the deserts where the ears hear not, and you have given might to man's thought, so that on audacious wings of sound it pours over land and sea at his bidding. . . .

With dear love from us both, I am,
Affectionately your friend,
Helen Keller

Hearing Impairments: Causes and Characteristics

HEARING LOSS: THE OVERLOOKED DISABILITY

Most of us have a tendency to take for granted our sensory modalities. We engage in the processes of seeing, hearing, smelling, tasting, and touching with no more reflection than we normally place on the act of breathing, on a heartbeat, or on an eye blink. Total or partial loss of function in any of these senses, however, creates unique, complex, and unexpected problems for any person. Loss of vision or hearing usually constitute more serious problems than losses of the other senses, for these two senses are so critical to our overall human function. In Chapter 7, we examined the impact of impairments of vision. This chapter will be devoted to an exploration of the nature of hearing disorders and the implications for creating inclusive school environments for students with these disorders.

Many of us can recall childhood musings about whether we would (if we had to make the choice) rather be blind or deaf. For most of us, the response was, "I'd rather be deaf." This choice was based on the idea that living in a world of silence would be much less devastating than living in a world of darkness.

It is difficult for those of us with unimpaired hearing to comprehend what living with a hearing loss is like. We can simulate for ourselves what it is like to be without vision by groping in a dark room, playing "blindman's bluff," or simply closing our eyes. But we find it much more difficult to appreciate what it is like to have a loss of hearing. Our hearing is always at work—even during sleep. Perhaps because of the constant, and often subtle, presence of the hearing sense, we find it easier to overlook how important it is to us.

In some respects, the loss of hearing may result in more serious educational disabilities than loss of vision. The acquisition and use of symbolic language is usually more difficult for a child with a hearing impairment than for a child with a visual impairment. The earliest evidence of learning in infants is often through their response to the sound of their mother's voice. First through hearing, then through primitive interpretation, and finally through imitation, children acquire speech. In school, the verbal symbols that have been learned are translated into written symbols, and the processes of reading and writing begin. The child who does not hear or who does not hear adequately is likely to have difficulty with these and other developmental tasks. In fact, the child with impaired hearing is likely to encounter significant obstacles in most areas of personal, social, and academic development. It is of critical importance that all teachers understand these obstacles and that they are prepared to assist students with hearing impairments in overcoming or compensating for them.

DISABILITIES IN HEARING: LOW INCIDENCE, HIGH IMPACT

Hearing loss is often referred to, like vision loss, as a "low-incidence" category of disability. This is certainly correct according to the number of students identified as having these disabilities under IDEA. In contrast to the hundreds of thousands of students identified as having learning disabilities, mental retardation, and emotional disabilities, there were fewer than 61,000 students identified in the 1992–93 school year as having hearing impairments (see Table 8.1).

Further examination of the information contained in Table 8.1, however, reveals that students with hearing impairments present a very real challenge for inclusive schooling.

More than 50 percent of the students with hearing impairments were served in separate classes, schools, or residential facilities. While some of this separation can be explained by the need for special communication training, the number of students with hearing impairments that could be included more fully in regular classes appears to be large.

The importance of providing the best special services *and* increased opportunities for inclusion in total school programs is illustrated by the information in Table 8.2. During the 1992–93 school year, only 55.8 percent of students with hearing impairments who left school received a high school diploma. Another 17.3 percent completed their school careers with only a certificate of attendance or comparable documentation of having participated in a special (nondiploma) program. More than 26% of students with learning impairments either reached the maximum age for school attendance and were no longer allowed to attend, dropped out of high school, or were not in school but of unknown status. These figures portray a very real need to reach students with hearing disabilities in ways that will more adequately promote their success in schools.

TABLE 8.1

Students with Hearing Impairments, Number and Placement Percentages: School Year 1992–93

Number	60,616
Regular Class	29.5%
Resource Room	19.7%
Separate Class	28.1%
Separate School	8.3%
Residential Facility	14.0%
Homebound/Hospital Setting	0.4%

Source: Office of Special Education Programs. *Seventeenth Annual Report to Congress on the Implementation of the Individuals with Disabilities Education Act.* Washington, DC: U.S. Department of Education, 1995, pp. 11, 17.

TABLE 8.2

Students with Hearing Impairments, Basis for Leaving School: School Year 1992–93

	Number	Percent
Received Diploma	1,900	55.8
Certificate (no high school diploma awarded)	587	17.3
Reached Maximum Age for Attendance	69	2.0
Dropped Out	444	13.0
Status Unknown	403	11.8

Source: Office of Special Education Programs. *Sixteenth Annual Report to Congress on the Implementation of the Individuals with Disabilities Education Act.* Washington, DC: U.S. Department of Education, 1994, p. 19.
Note: Numbers do not add up to 100% due to rounding.

THE COMPLEX PROCESS OF HEARING

The process of hearing is a complex and intriguing one. In order to understand hearing losses and the effect of these losses on children, it is important to have a basic understanding of this process. Hearing is the end result of several transformations of the energy of sound as it travels through the hearing mechanism.

The Outer Ear

The outer ear consists of the pinna and the ear canal. The pinna is the external portion of the ear (see Figure 8.1). It functions as a funnel for "capturing" sound waves in the environment. These sound waves are channeled into the ear canal for transmission to the tympanic membrane. The canal serves two purposes. First, it amplifies sound as it is conducted to

FIGURE 8.1

Basic Anatomy of the Ear

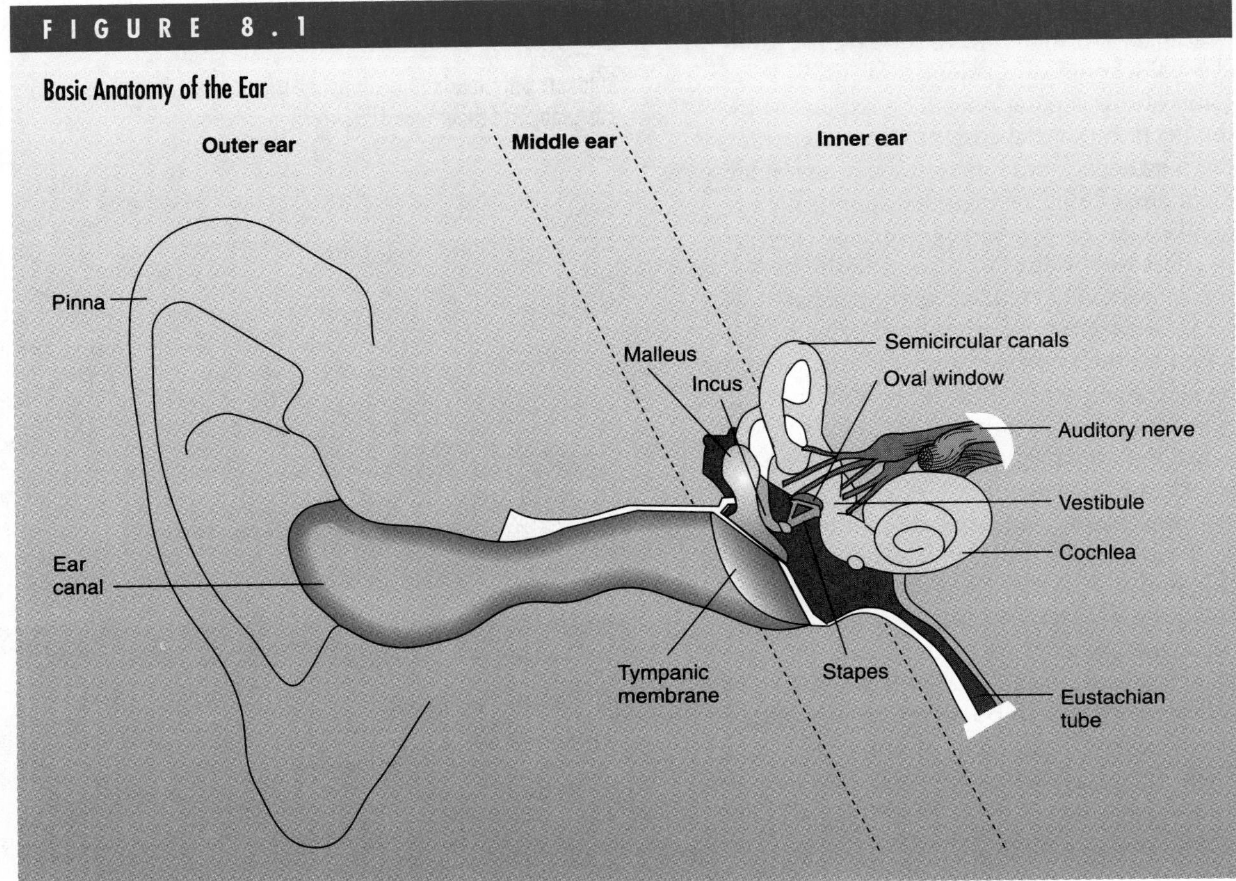

the tympanic membrane (eardrum). Second, the canal is lined with cerumen (earwax) and hair, which serve a protective function for the more internal parts of the ear.

The Middle Ear

The tympanic membrane separates the outer and middle ear. Vibrations are set up on this membrane by sound waves passing from the ear canal. Connected to the tympanic membrane and extending across the cavity of the middle ear are the three smallest bones in the human body, known collectively as the ossicles. The first of the ossicles, the malleus (hammer), is connected directly to the tympanic membrane. Changes in the pressure exerted on the tympanic membrane cause vibrations of the malleus. The malleus in turn sets up vibrations in the incus (anvil), and finally these vibrations are transmitted to the third ossicle, the stapes (stirrup). The vibrations are further amplified by each successive ossicle. The stapes is connected to the oval window, a membrane that separates the middle and inner ear. The oval window is the next link in the transmission of the vibrations that have been conducted and amplified by the ossicles.

The middle ear is connected to the nose and throat by the Eustachian tube. This connection allows air from the external atmosphere to enter the middle ear. Chewing, swallowing, and yawning cause this connecting tube to open at its lower end. Air can enter through this opening and equalize the pressure on both sides of the tympanic membrane. This equalization of pressure is essential for the normal functioning of the ear.

The Inner Ear

The inner ear is the point at which hearing is converted into a neurological function. It consists of two sections, the vestibule and the cochlea. The entire inner ear is filled with fluid. Fluid waves are transmitted from the vestibule to the cochlea. The cochlea is lined with thousands of hair cells with a nerve ending at the base of each. As waves of fluid ripple through the cochlea, the hair cells are stimulated and electrical impulses are created in the basal nerve endings. These impulses are then conducted by the auditory nerve to the appropriate receptive areas of the brain.

It should be noted that the inner ear serves a second important function. Located within the vestibule section of the inner ear are three semicircular canals (see Figure 8.1). These canals are sensitive to changes in body position, direction of body movement, and rate of movement. By transmitting information to the brain regarding movement and position of the body, the semicircular canals are responsible for maintaining body balance.

DEFINITION AND CLASSIFICATION OF HEARING IMPAIRMENTS

In defining hearing disorders from the viewpoint of educational needs, it is important to consider both the severity of the loss and the age of the person when the loss occurs. The severity of the loss is obviously important in terms of the utilization of whatever residual hearing the person may have. The age of onset of the hearing loss is a critical consideration, however, due to its relationship to language development. If the loss is prelingual, occurring before a child has acquired oral language, the effect of the loss is usually more disabling than if the loss is experienced after oral language has developed, a postlingual loss. The later in development the hearing loss occurs, the greater the chance that the child has already acquired significant linguistic and conceptual skills.

The term *hearing impairment* is used to describe both people who are "deaf" and those who are "hard of hearing." According to the definitions developed for PL 94-142:

> "Hard of hearing" is a hearing impairment, whether permanent or fluctuating, which adversely affects a child's educational performance but which is not included under the definition of "deaf" in this section.
>
> "Deaf" means a hearing impairment which is so severe that the child is impaired in processing linguistic information through hearing, with or without amplification, which adversely affects educational performance (*Federal Register*, 1977, p. 42478).

INTENSITY AND FREQUENCY: THE DIMENSIONS OF SOUND

The decibel is a unit used for the measurement of the loudness or intensity of sound. Decibel measures are used as indicators of the range of intensity of sound that an individual is able to perceive. The range of human hearing normally encompasses intensities from 0 to 130 decibels. Sounds lower than 1 decibel are not usually heard at all, and sounds louder than 130 decibels are painful. Figure 8.2 illustrates the decibel level of some common sounds and the corresponding levels of hearing loss. One approach to the classification of hearing losses is to determine the intensity

FIGURE 8.2

Decibel Levels of Common Sounds and Corresponding Levels of Hearing Loss

Sound	Decibels	Hearing Loss
Jet taking off	120	Profound Hearing Loss
Thunder		
Rock band	110	
	100	
Food processor	95	Severe Hearing Loss
Lawn mower	90	
Traffic noises		
	80	
	70	Moderate Hearing Loss
Normal speech		
	60	
	50	
Quiet restaurant sounds		Mild Hearing Loss
Empty house sounds	40	
Keyboard sounds		
	30	
Rustling leaves		Slight Hearing Loss
	20	
Whispered voice		
Sound of normal breathing	10	
	0	

level of sound below which a person does not hear. The following categories are based on those of the International Standards Organization. Decibel losses refer to the level of hearing in the best unaided ear averaged across speech frequencies (Paul and Quigley, 1990).

Slight Hearing Loss

Students with slight difficulty in hearing have losses of between 27 and 40 decibels. They may have difficulty in hearing faint or distant speech. Although they do not necessarily experience difficulty in school, consideration should be given to favorable seating. These students may benefit from hearing aids. Speech therapy may be needed to foster speech development and correct faulty patterns that have developed.

Mild Hearing Loss

Students with mild difficulty in hearing have losses of between 41 and 55 decibels. They have difficulty in hearing conversation unless it is within a distance of three to five feet and is face to face. They may miss as much as 50 percent of class discussions if modifications are not made. These students need the amplification that hearing aids may provide. Speech development and maintenance are much more difficult for these students than for those with slight losses. Articulation problems are common, and speech therapy is usually required.

Moderate Hearing Loss

Students with moderate difficulty in hearing have losses of between 56 and 70 decibels. They have difficulty in understanding conversation unless it is loud. They have serious disabilities in the development and/or maintenance of language skills. They may need the help of a resource teacher. Hearing aids, auditory training, lipreading instruction, and speech services may be needed.

Severe Hearing Loss

Students with severe difficulty in hearing have losses of between 71 and 90 decibels. They may hear loud voices only if very near the ear. Even with the amplification provided by a hearing aid, they have serious difficulty in hearing speech sounds adequately or accurately. Special services are absolutely essential to minimize the effect of the disability on overall growth and development.

Profound Hearing Loss

Students with profound difficulty in hearing have losses of 91 decibels or more. They may hear some very loud sounds but generally are aware only of vibrations. In general, they rely on vision rather than hearing as the primary avenue for communication. They have a critical need for extensive special services in order to develop language skills and alternate forms of communication.

The second major dimension of sound is frequency. Sound, as discussed earlier, travels in waves. The closer together these waves occur, the shorter the wavelength. The shorter the wavelength of a particular sound, the greater the rapidity of the stimulation of the various mechanisms of the ear. The frequency (pitch) of sounds is measured in cycles per second, or hertz units (Hz). From the top of one wave of sound to the top of the next is a single cycle (see Figure 8.3). This dimension of sound is important in determining which sounds we are capable of hearing and our perception of any given sound. The more rapid the frequency (the shorter the wavelength), the higher the perceived pitch of the sound. The human ear is responsive to sounds over a wide range of frequencies from a low of approximately 20 Hz to a high of around 20,000 Hz. Sounds below and above this range are abundant but are simply not heard by human beings. The classic example of the existence of sound beyond the human range of hearing is the dog whistle, which is silent to humans but obviously elicits a response from pets.

Hearing impairments sometimes involve only particular frequencies of sound. As part of the normal developmental process, there is a tendency with increasing age toward diminished ability to hear high-frequency sounds. Because various areas within the cochlea are responsive to different frequencies of sound, it is possible for damage within the inner ear to result in a hearing loss for particular sounds while hearing for other frequencies remains intact. The loss of ability to hear sounds at any frequency may have a significant impact on an individual's functioning, but the inability to hear sounds between the frequencies of 500 and 2,000 Hz has a particularly profound influence on the ability to understand speech.

FIGURE 8.3

The Interaction of Intensity and Frequency of Sound

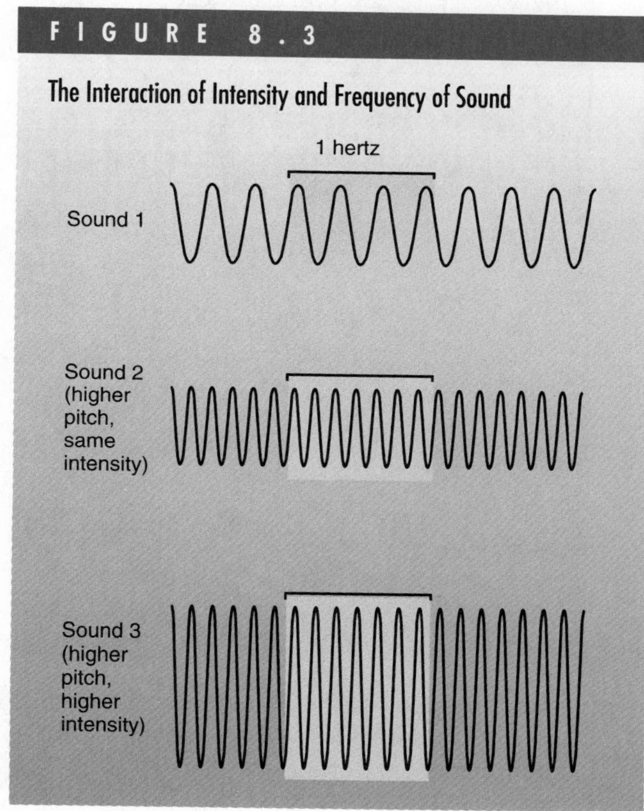

CLASSIFICATION ACCORDING TO THE ANATOMICAL LOCATION OF THE HEARING LOSS

Another important consideration in understanding the nature of an individual's hearing loss is the specific part of the ear that is not

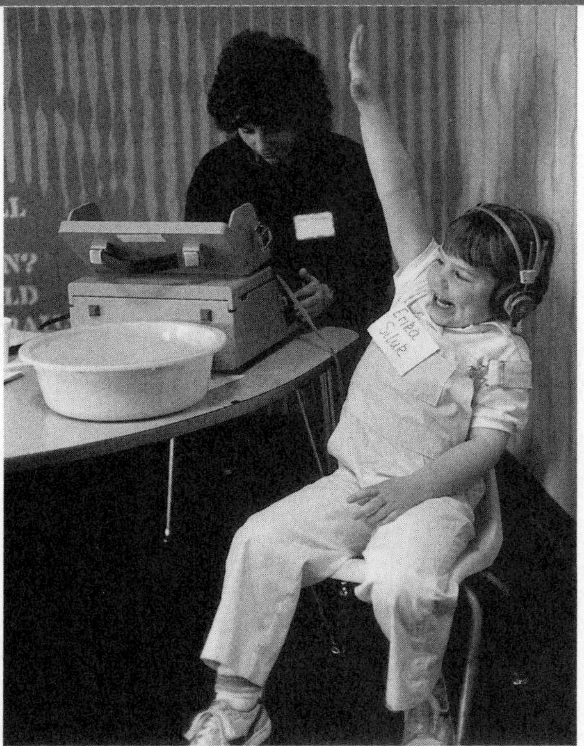

Michael Siluk/The Image Works

functioning properly. Classification according to the location of loss, when combined with information concerning the degree of loss (intensity) and the range of loss (frequency), can provide a comprehensive description of an individual's hearing disability. Classification of hearing losses according to anatomical location includes conductive, sensorineural, and mixed.

Conductive Hearing Loss

A conductive hearing loss is caused by interference in the conduction of sound from the ear canal to the inner ear. Because of a problem in either the outer or middle ear, the intensity of sound reaching the inner ear is diminished. This breakdown in conduction of sound may occur for any number of reasons. A blockage of the ear canal will interfere with the transmission of sound. Objects lodged in the canal (beans, beads, or nuts, for example) and excessive wax buildup are common problems. A torn or immobilized tympanic membrane will not vibrate sufficiently to conduct sound. Conditions that reduce the ability of the ossicles to vibrate will significantly reduce the amount of sound conducted to the inner ear. Fortunately, many conductive hearing losses can be corrected medically or surgically, particularly if detected early. If not treated, a permanent loss may result.

Sensorineural Hearing Loss

A sensorineural hearing loss is caused by damage to either the inner ear or the auditory nerve. These losses may be complete or partial and, as mentioned earlier, may involve only certain frequencies. Sensorineural losses are often the result of destruction of receptors in the inner ear. When this occurs, hearing of those frequencies for which the destroyed receptors were responsible is lost.

Mixed Hearing Loss

In some cases, hearing loss may occur as a consequence of both impairment in the conduction of sound and sensorineural damage. The resulting disability is characterized as a mixed loss.

MEASUREMENT OF HEARING

Many tests have been devised over the years in the attempt to measure hearing losses. Several of these techniques were developed prior to the development of the present level of sophistication in audiology (the science of detecting and remediating hearing impairments). These tests involved the use of tuning forks, noisemakers, whispers, ticking watches, and bells. These measures, of course, provided only crude assessments of whether a hearing impairment existed and the nature of that impairment. Audiologists today employ mea-

FIGURE 8.4

Blank Audiogram with Degree of Loss Ranges Indicated

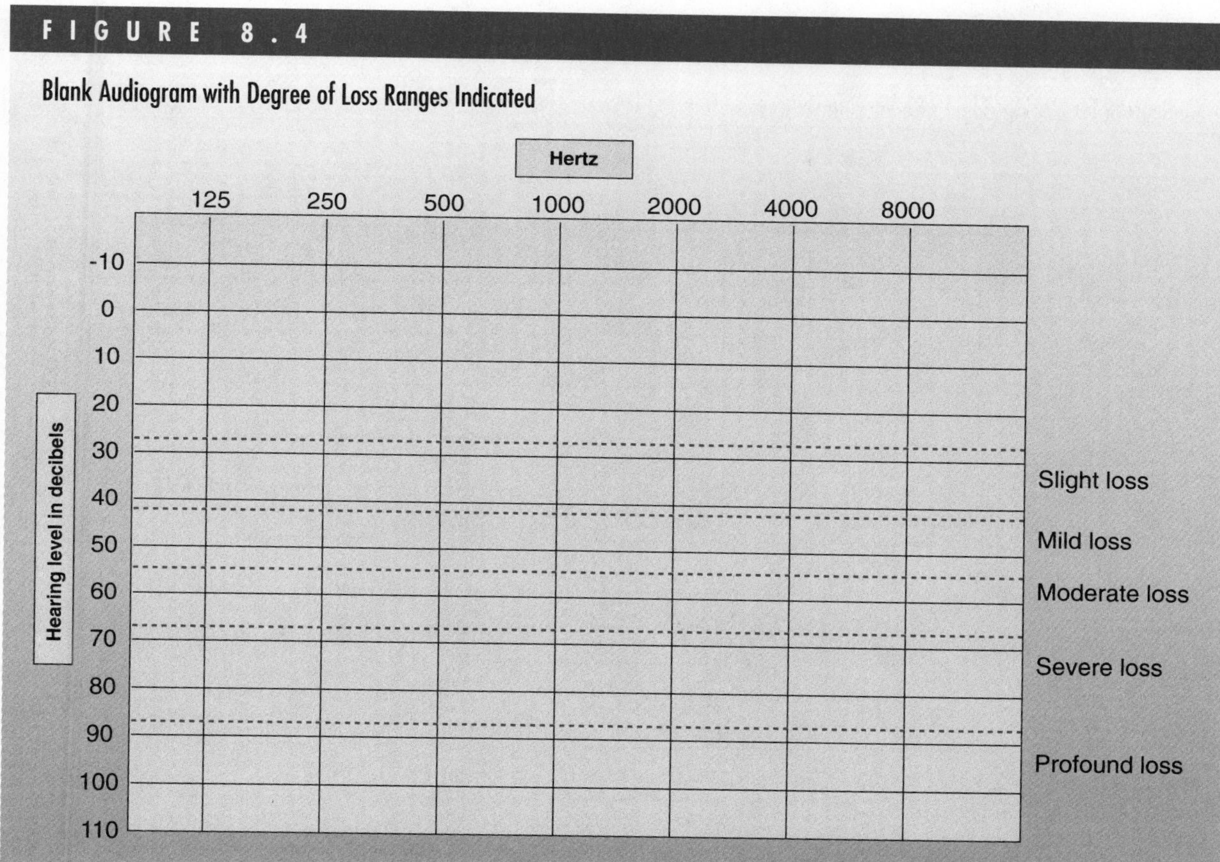

surement techniques that are more accurate and that yield much more useful information.

Pure-Tone Audiometry

The most commonly used device for hearing assessment is the pure-tone audiometer. The audiometer is used to present tones of varying frequencies and intensities across the range of human hearing. It produces tones ranging from a low of 125 Hz to a high of 8,000 Hz. The tone at each frequency may be presented at volumes ranging up to 110 decibels. The examiner tests each ear separately, and responses are recorded on a graph known as an audiogram (see Figure 8.4). Through earphones, the audiologist presents each tone and gradually raises the decibel level of that tone until the person being tested indicates either verbally, by a hand signal, or by pressing a button that the tone has been heard. The person's ability to hear the tones at each frequency is then plotted on the audiogram.

Figure 8.5 is an audiogram of a child who shows hearing loss in both ears. Mark consistently demonstrates slightly better hearing in the right ear. The higher the frequency of sound, the greater the difficulty he has in hearing it. The moderate hearing loss within the speech range (500–2,000 Hz) would be of particular importance in educational

FIGURE 8.5

Audiogram for Mark, A Child with Varying Degrees of Hearing Loss

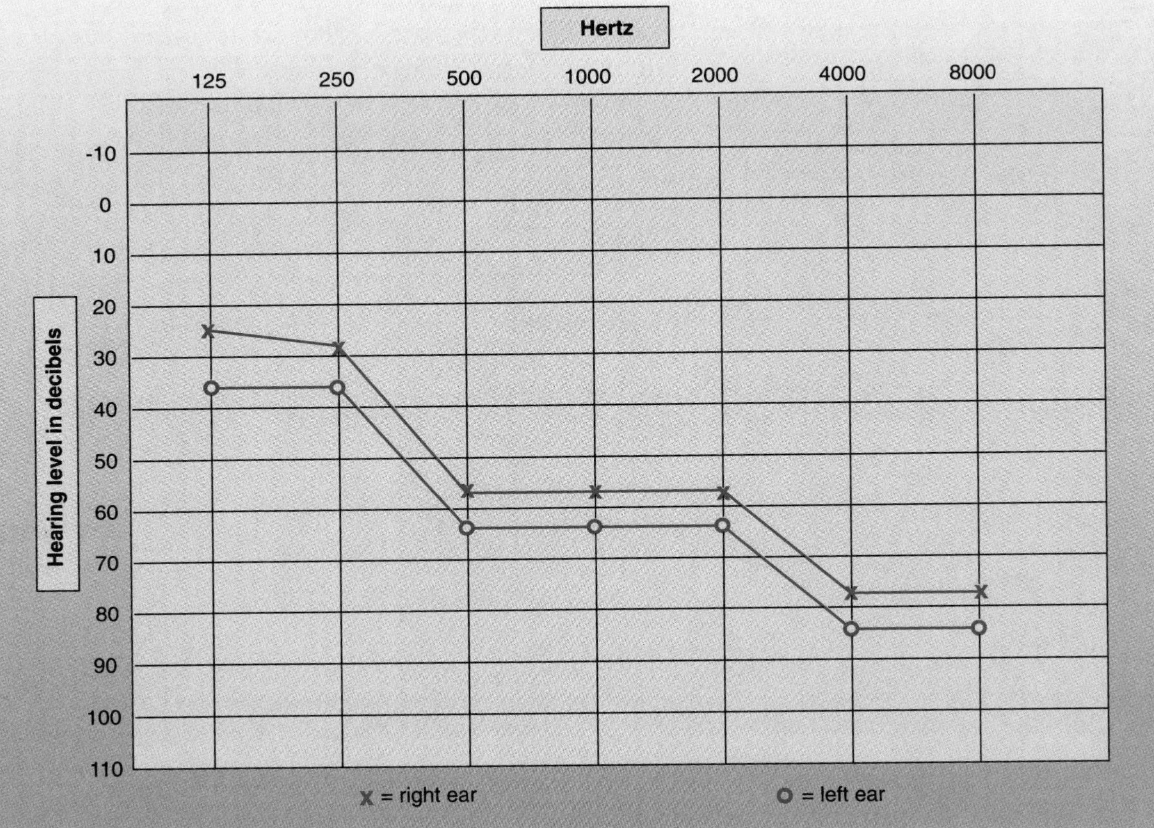

planning for him. The severe loss of hearing at the higher frequency levels could cause difficulty for Mark in perceiving danger signals in the environment (sirens and fire alarms, for example). He may find lower-pitched male voices easier to hear than higher-pitched female voices. Mark probably has difficulty following conversations. With special assistance and modifications, functioning effectively in a general classroom should be possible for him.

Speech Audiometry

In addition to testing the ability to hear pure tones, it is important to assess a person's ability to hear and understand meaningful speech. The speech reception threshold (SRT) is determined by presenting spondaic words (words with two syllables of equal stress). The lowest decibel level at which the person being tested can hear and repeat 50 percent of the words is considered his or her threshold. Again, each ear is tested separately. A second measure that is often used in speech audiometry is speech discrimination. This test assesses the person's ability to differentiate between individual speech sounds. Speech audiometry is especially significant from an educational viewpoint since it provides direct information about the actual level of functioning of the individual in relation to spoken language.

Audiometric Measures for Hard-to-Test Students

The procedures for hearing assessment that have been described thus far cannot be used with infants, very young children, and other hard-to-test individuals such as severely/profoundly mentally retarded persons. When the person being examined is unable to comprehend and follow instructions and/or is unable to voluntarily indicate that a tone or word has been heard, alternative measures must be utilized.

Simmons (1977) described techniques that can be utilized in assessing the hearing ability of hard-to-test children. One method is to systematically observe an infant or child's movements in response to environmental sounds. A more exacting technique, however, is the use of conditioning. The child, for example, is exposed to a light that flashes each time a tone is presented. After repeated pairing of the flashing light and tone, the tone is presented without the light. If the child turns toward the light when the tone alone is presented, it is assumed that the child has hearing for that frequency and intensity of sound.

Although there are a number of other techniques that have been developed for hard-to-test children and adults, one procedure is particularly intriguing. The Crib-O-Gram consists of a motion-sensitive device that is attached to the infant's crib, a continuous strip of paper that records movement, timing equipment, and a speaker. The baby's movements in response to sounds are recorded. Assessment of the child's ability to hear a given sound is based on changes in activity level as that sound is presented. Simmons (1977) indicates that the test is most accurate when administered while the baby is sleeping, and that if the sound is responded to within two seconds, the chances are better than 99 to 1 that the baby has heard that sound.

Evoked-response audiometry is a hearing test that measures brain responses to sound using the electroencephalogram (EEG). All sounds evoke electrical activity in the brain. EEG measurement of this activity thus allows for the detection of hearing impairments without a voluntary response from the person being tested.

Every person is, of course, unique in hearing abilities. The cautions discussed earlier in this book concerning intelligence tests also apply to audiometric measures. Effectiveness or deficits of hearing cannot be assessed by looking at the results of audiometric tests alone. Some students with very low levels of hearing are able, with appropriate help, to function quite well. Others with less loss of hearing are more severely impaired in their function. Each student must be viewed individually within the context of her or his home, school, and community.

CAUSES OF HEARING LOSS

There are both genetic and environmental/experiential causes of hearing losses. These factors may have an impact on hearing during the prenatal, perinatal, or postnatal periods.

Genetic Factors

Genetically linked hearing losses may be transmitted by parents to their children either by recessive genes (the parents have normal hearing) or by dominant genes (one or both parents have a genetically based hearing loss).

More than two hundred forms of genetically caused deafness have been identified (National Information Center on Deafness, 1989). Genetic factors most often result in sensorineural hearing losses. In a smaller number of cases, however, genetic influences may cause malformations of the bones of the middle ear, thereby resulting in a conductive loss (Northern and Downs, 1974).

Environmental/Experiential Factors

Premature Birth. Children who are born prematurely seem to be at increased risk for hearing loss. As has been discussed in previous chapters, prematurity is also a factor in other disabilities. Hearing loss due to prematurity may therefore accompany these other conditions.

Viral Infections. Rubella (German measles) is a viral infection often associated with hearing loss. When a woman is infected with rubella during the first trimester of pregnancy, the effect can be deafness in the developing fetus. At one time, maternal rubella was the leading cause of deafness among students enrolled in educational programs in the United States. A vaccine has been developed that prevents rubella. As women of childbearing age have become more aware of the dangers of rubella and the availability of the vaccine and screening programs have increased, the incidence of hearing loss due to this virus has been largely eliminated (Crocker and Nelson, 1983).

Among other viruses that may cause hearing losses are infectious meningitis, encephalitis, mumps, and influenza.

Blood Incompatibility. Hearing loss may occur when a woman with Rh negative blood is carrying a fetus with Rh positive blood. By administering a drug called Rho Gam, it is now possible to prevent antibodies from forming in the mother's system that would otherwise attack the developing organs of hearing in the fetus.

Otitis Media. A buildup of fluid in the middle ear may occur when the Eustachian tube becomes blocked due to infection or other factors. This is a very common problem in young children. The condition is often accompanied by ear pain, but not always. Chronic otitis media may do permanent damage to the ear, resulting in hearing loss. The condition requires medical treatment. In some cases, a myringotomy is required. This procedure involves the placement of tubes in the child's ears to promote drainage of the fluid. Parents and teachers need to be sensitive to the early detection and treatment of otitis media.

Other Causes. There are a number of lower-incidence causes of hearing loss. Certain drugs, particularly those of the mycin group (streptomycin, neomycin, and others) can cause permanent hearing losses. Otosclerosis, a disease of the bones of the middle ear, can cause a conductive hearing loss. Concussion, birth complications, and other "slings and arrows" of growth and development can result in varying degrees of loss in hearing. Of particular importance in our increasingly loud world is the effect of noise on hearing. It has become evident in recent years that many people suffer significant hearing loss due to exposure to excessive noise levels. This is as much a danger at a rock concert as in a factory.

FIGURE 8.6

Basic Structure of a Hearing Aid

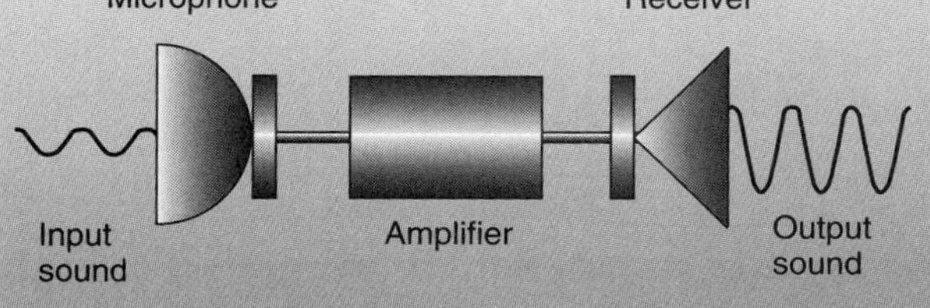

The Educational Needs of Students with Hearing Impairments

AIDS TO HEARING

Children with hearing impairments frequently use hearing aids. It is important, therefore, that teachers and other professionals have a basic understanding of how hearing aids work and how they must be maintained.

A hearing aid is essentially a miniature loudspeaker system. It is composed of three parts: a microphone for picking up sound, an amplifier for increasing the volume of sound, and a receiver for delivering the intensified sound to the ear. These basic components are illustrated in Figure 8.6. The power source for the systems is usually a battery.

A hearing aid, then, is simply a system for amplifying sounds reaching the ear. We have all had the experience of cupping a hand around an ear to amplify the sound available to us. The earliest hearing aids, such as ear trumpets, were simply an elaboration of this means of *mechanical* amplification. Today there are a variety of hearing aids, but all depend on *electrical* amplification of sound. The *conventional* or *body type* hearing aid is the largest and most powerful type (see Figure 8.7). The microphone, amplifier, and battery are contained in a case that is worn on the chest. The amplified sound is conveyed through a wire to the receiver. The receiver is connected to the ear by an earmold that is fashioned, much like a dental impression, to fit the individual configuration of the wearer's outer ear. Other common models include hearing aids built into the *frames of glasses*, the *behind-the-ear* type, and the *all-in-the-ear* model. Many people with hearing impairments prefer these models because they are less noticeable. They may also be more comfortable to wear than

FIGURE 8.7

Conventional or Body Type Hearing Aid

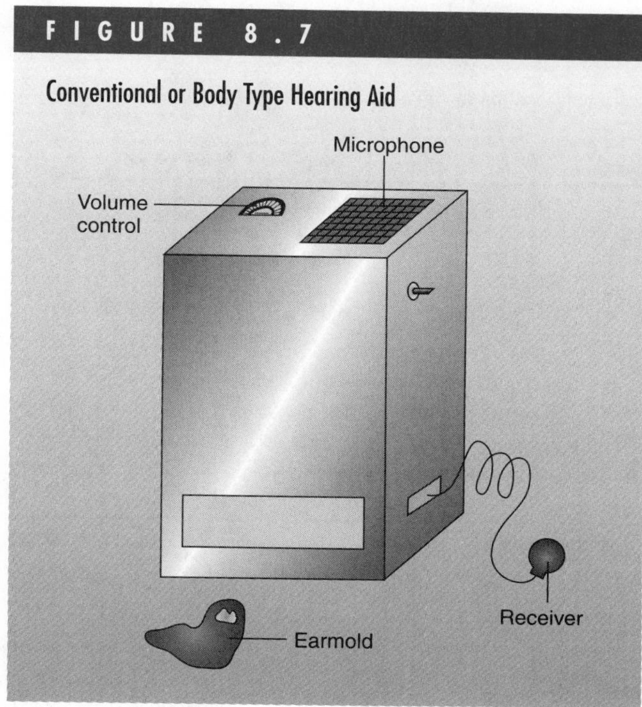

the body type hearing aid. It must be noted, however, that these instruments do not have as much potential power for amplification as the body type aids. These models, therefore, are not suitable for many people with hearing impairments.

Another amplification system used by students with hearing losses is the *frequency modulated system*. This is a wireless system that transmits the teacher's voice through a microphone worn by the teacher directly to a receiver worn by the student. The frequency modulated signal is more intense and clear than the amplification provided by an individual hearing aid.

A *cochlear implant* is a device that is surgically implanted in the inner ear. Sounds picked up by an external microphone are transmitted directly to an electrode in the cochlea. The electrode stimulates electrical impulses in the auditory nerve. The cochlear

TABLE 8.3

Troubleshooting for Hearing Aid Problems

Problem	*Possible Causes*
• High-frequency feedback or whistling noise	• Defective earmold or poorly fitted earmold • Volume set too high
• Crackling noise	• Corrosion on battery terminals • Defective cord
• Poor amplification	• Earmold clogged • Defective battery • Improper placement of battery

BOX 8.1

Basic Hearing Aid Care

Earmold

- Keep it clean and free of wax buildup.
- Wash it in lukewarm water at regular intervals.

Battery

- Remove from aid when not in use.
- Make sure battery terminals are free of corrosion.
- Make a note of how long a battery usually lasts so that you can anticipate when replacement will be needed.

Cord

- Keep it as untangled as possible.
- Avoid jerking the cord.

Overall Hearing Aid

- The aid should not be exposed to water.
- Changing batteries and other handling of the aid should be done at a desk or table to avoid damage from dropping.
- The aid should be tested each morning before use.

implant does not amplify sounds. It bypasses the outer ear and middle ear and, in a sense, creates sound directly in the inner ear. Cochlear implants, therefore, may be particularly useful to people who are unable to use amplification because of the nature of their hearing loss.

A hearing aid should always be fitted by an audiologist, who can select the most appropriate device on the basis of an audiological examination. It should not be assumed that the use of a hearing aid results in normal hearing. Aids do make sounds louder, even unwanted and distracting sounds. The sounds are different, however, from sounds perceived through normal hearing. Perhaps the closest that persons with normal hearing can come to understanding what reliance on a hearing aid is like is to imagine hearing all sound through a telephone receiver.

HEARING AIDS IN THE CLASSROOM: HOW TEACHERS CAN HELP

When a hearing aid is not functioning properly, parents should be encouraged to call on their audiologist to check the instrument. The same is true when the student seems to have chronic problems in the appropriate use of the aid. There are, however, some common trouble areas that a teacher can check. Suggestions for basic troubleshooting are listed in Table 8.3. Teachers can also encourage the child in the proper care of her or his hearing aid. A few basic points for the maintenance of a hearing aid are provided in Box 8.1.

A teacher who for the first time is faced with having a student who uses a hearing aid in class may become, understandably, concerned about how best to assist this student. The points listed below may provide a few helpful guidelines.

1. Remember that the hearing aid does not replace normal hearing. It only makes sound louder, even unwanted and distracting sounds. You may have to help the student learn to avoid or ignore these "amplified" distractions.
2. Unless there have been special instructions, the student should wear the aid at all times.
3. Where the student is seated is an important factor. Try to seat the student where hearing is optimal and distractions are minimal. Although it may be difficult, try to achieve the best seating arrangement without isolating or bringing undue attention to the student.
4. Other students in the class will be curious about the hearing aid. A good way to satisfy the curiosity and "break the ice" may be to have the student demonstrate how the aid works to the class.
5. Discuss with the student and her or his parents arrangements for keeping extra batteries at school.
6. Try to view this student from the same perspective as you do a student who wears glasses as an aid to vision. Remember that your reaction to the student will influence the reaction of the other students in the class.

ALTERNATE MODES OF COMMUNICATION

A primary educational concern for hearing-impaired students and their teachers is the development of communication skills. When the hearing component of human communication is absent or disturbed, the entire communication process is disrupted. In some cases, this disruption is so great that alternate means of communication must be employed. Educators must sometimes find specialized ways of communicating with these students so that the entire educational process can begin. They must also find ways of teaching these students to communicate with other people. There are three basic approaches to teaching alternate means of communication to hearing-impaired students who are unable to develop and/or use standard means of communication. These approaches are the *manual* method, the *oral* method, and the *total communication* method.

FIGURE 8.8

Examples of Signs Used in American Sign Language

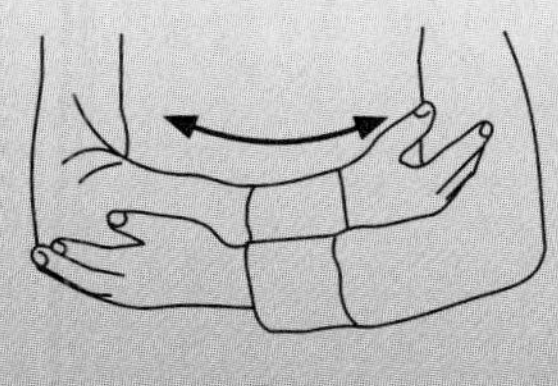
Baby

Bed

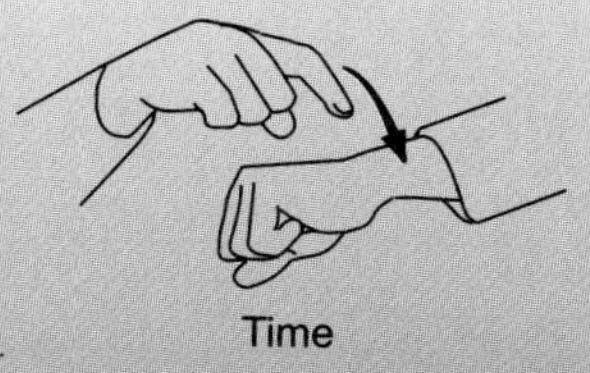
Time

The Manual Method

The manual method of communication has two basic components. The first is *sign language*. A standard set of signs known as *American Sign Language* (ASL) is used to represent words or concepts. There is often a literal relationship between the position of the hand

FIGURE 8.9

The Manual Alphabet

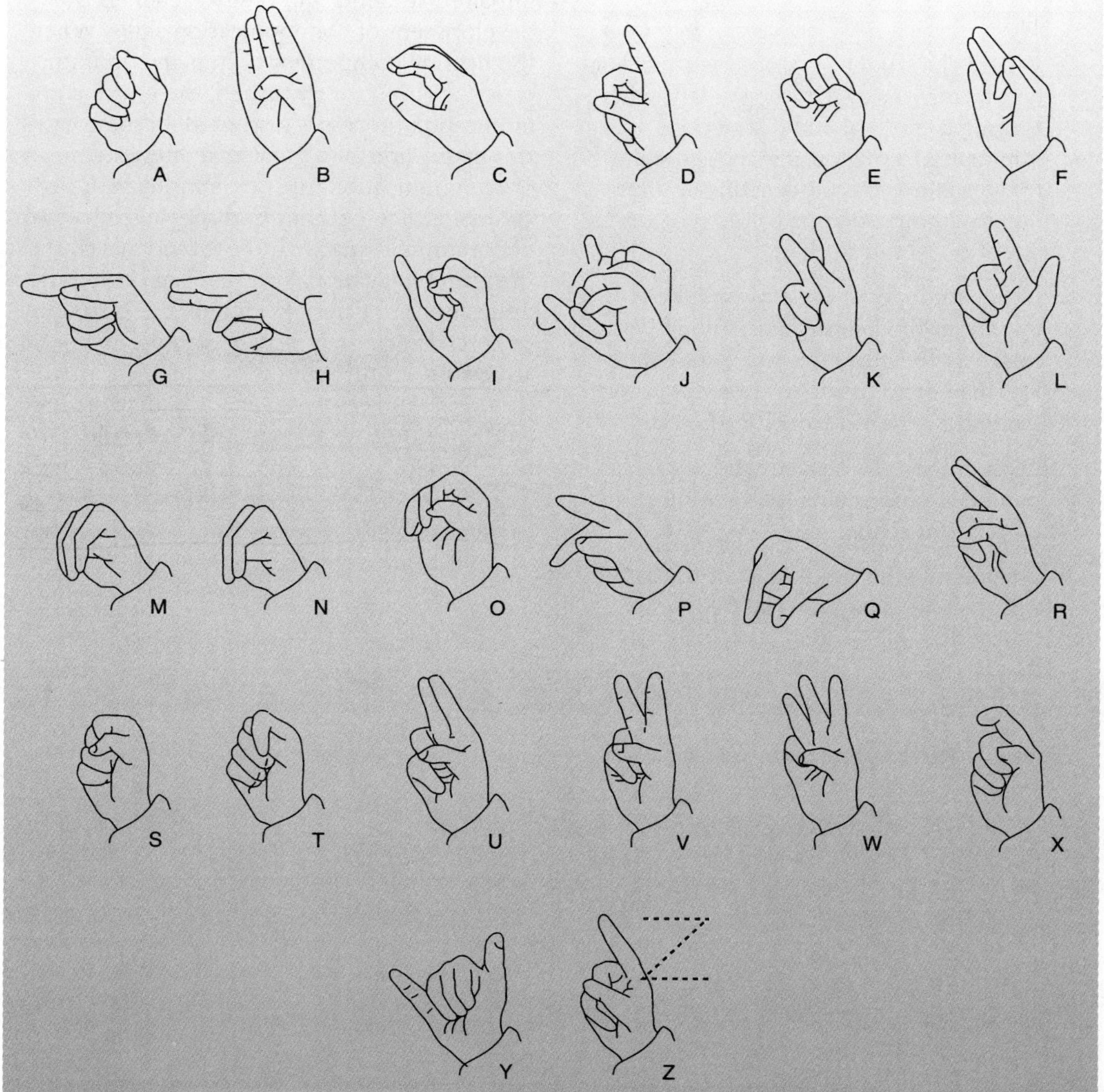

and the word it represents (see Figure 8.8). Sign language is unambiguous in that most signs are distinct and do not look like signs for other words. ASL does not conform to the grammatical structure of English. Attempts have been made, however, to increase the total vocabulary of signs and to make the grammatical structure of signing more consistent with that of English (Bornstein, 1982). ASL, however, continues to be the most widely used system of sign language.

The second component of the manual method is *finger spelling*. Finger spelling is achieved by use of the manual alphabet (see Figure 8.9). Hand positions are designated for each letter of the English alphabet. Finger spelling usually serves as a supplement to sign language. If there is no sign for a word, it is spelled out. Finger spelling will commonly be used for proper names and when a person is not sure of the sign for a particular word. The amount of finger spelling versus signing that a person uses will vary with the age, intelligence, and other characteristics of the individual.

The Oral Method

The oral approach emphasizes the development of speech and speechreading. Those special educators who advocate a strict oral approach feel that reliance on signing and finger spelling leads to the exclusion of people who are deaf from the rest of society. They argue that since only other individuals who are deaf and a few interested persons can use and understand manual communication, people who are taught those techniques as their primary means of communication are doomed to live fairly restricted and isolated lives. In programs for students who are deaf that adhere strictly to an oral approach, students are discouraged from using manual communication of any kind.

BOX 8.2

Some Characteristics of the Speech of Profoundly Deaf Individuals

- Speech may be more "breathy."
- Speech may be slow and labored.
- Vowel sounds may be longer.
- Speech may lack rhythm.
- Monotone speech is common.
- Correct pronunciation of consonants and combinations of consonants may be difficult.

Adapted from D. C. Dale. *Deaf Children at Home and at School.* London: University of London Press, 1972.

BOX 8.3

Basic Considerations in Teaching Children Who Use Speechreading

- The teacher should speak a little slower than usual.
- The teacher should emphasize the most important words.
- There must be adequate light on the teacher's face.
- The teacher should be about six feet from the child. Standing too close causes problems.
- The teacher should be at face level with the child.

The oral method focuses on the use of whatever residual hearing the student may have through the help of hearing aids and special training. Emphasis is placed on increased sensitivity to sound and improved discrimination between sounds. The student is also trained in how to use and monitor her or his voice in speech. Teaching speech to students who are deaf is a very difficult task for both students and teachers. Box 8.2 lists some characteristics of the speech of profoundly deaf individuals. Those teachers who advocate this approach, however, feel that the effort results in a person who is much more independent and socially integrated.

Speechreading (commonly called lipreading) is the utilization of visual cues to assist in understanding the speech of another person. Students are trained to watch the movement of the lips and the positions of the teeth and tongue in order to discern what is being said. They are also taught to read cues such as facial expressions that will facilitate their understanding of what is being said (see Box 8.3).

Critics of the oral approach feel that very few students who are deaf can actually learn to speak in a way that is intelligible and truly functional. They also charge that speechreading is not an adequate language technique to meet the receptive language needs of deaf persons. They point out that 40 to 60 percent of all speech sounds in English are homophonous—the formation of the lips in producing these sounds is identical to that in other sounds. It has also been argued that oral techniques are more stress-producing than manual techniques. Menchel (1988) reports that there are a number of variables (such as lighting, position of the speaker's head, and rapid speech) that make effective speechreading problematic. Babbidge (1965) reported that most adults who are deaf prefer to use manual techniques.

The Total Communication Method

An attempt was made by the Maryland School for the Deaf in 1969 to resolve the methodological and theoretical differences between the oral and manual approaches. The concept of *total communication* was introduced. The following definition was offered for this approach to teaching hearing-impaired children:

> By total communication is meant the right of every deaf child to learn to use all forms of communication in order that he (or she) may have the full opportunity to develop language competence at the earliest age possible. This implies the introduction of a reliable receptive expressive symbol system in the preschool years between the ages of one and five. Total communication includes the full spectrum of language modes; child-devised gesture, formal sign language, speech, speechreading, fingerspelling, reading and writing. With total communication every deaf child has the opportunity to develop every remnant of residual hearing by aids and/or high fidelity group amplification systems (Denton, 1970, p. 3).

Total communication has gained a great deal of acceptance in recent years among educators of children with hearing impairments. It is likely that this acceptance of a wide variety of teaching strategies will continue as educators attempt to meet the needs of children with hearing disabilities more comprehensively and in more inclusive settings.

PSYCHOLOGICAL AND SOCIAL ASPECTS OF EDUCATING STUDENTS WITH HEARING DISABILITIES

While students with hearing impairments demonstrate the same wide variability in personal and social characteristics that would be found in any group of individuals, they do seem to be more subject to a number of developmental, emotional, and social difficulties than children with unimpaired hearing. A basic theme in these difficulties seems to be one of psychological and social isolation. In reviewing studies of the personality characteristics of children with deafness, Meadow (1984) has found that the social isolation experienced by these children often manifests itself in rigidity, impulsiveness, and related behaviors that give the appearance of disregard or insensitivity of other people. Added to their fundamental difficulties in communication, these traits may constitute major obstacles to the establishment of satisfactory interpersonal relationships for young people with hearing impairments. Research has shown, in fact, that loneliness is a challenge that is confronted and coped with by even the most successful adolescents with deafness (Charlson, Strong, and Gold, 1992).

The difficulty that individuals with hearing impairments have as children and adolescents in establishing and maintaining relationships with people with normal hearing probably contributes significantly to the tendency for adults with hearing impairments to congregate in what could be termed "colonies of deafness." More than two decades ago, Furth remarked that of "all physical disabilities, deafness is the only one that makes its members part of a natural community. Therefore, although we do not find blind or crippled subgroups in society, we are justified in referring to a deaf community as a societal subgroup" (Furth, 1973, p. 1). Harlan Lane (1992) has argued that deafness is, in fact, a cultural attribute, not a disability. Lane, and others who advocate on behalf of a culture of deafness, feel that the education of students with deafness should be approached like that of other students with multicultural and bilingual needs.

The Commission on Education of the Deaf was established in 1987. It reported in 1988 on the findings of its study. The commission concluded that nationwide the educational system had failed to recognize that American Sign Language is a legitimate language and that the deaf culture is a real culture. The commission emphasized that:

> Almost unrecognized is the legitimate status of American Sign Language (ASL) as a full-fledged native minority language to which all of the provisions of the Bilingual Education Act should apply. Also too seldom recognized is the need for a deaf child to have other deaf children as part of his or her peer group, and to be exposed to deaf adults (Commission on Education of the Deaf, 1988, p. 9).

Even some of the technology that has been developed to enhance hearing has been criticized as an assault on the cultural integrity of people who are deaf. Cochlear implants, for example, have been questioned in terms of the necessary general anesthesia, protracted surgery, severe structural damage to the middle ear and inner ear, and extended rehabilitation required. In addition, the lack of data on the long-term risks and actual benefits has been criticized (Lane, 1993).

The legitimacy of people with deafness as a cultural group is portrayed poignantly by Lane in his description of the need for broader recognition of this status.

> There is increasingly the well-founded view in America, as around the globe, that the deaf communities of the world are linguistic and cultural minorities. Logic and morality demand that where there are laws or mores protecting such minorities, they extend to the deaf community. In America, this recognition of the status of the deaf community, fueled by the civil rights movement, is leading to greater acceptance of deaf people. The interests of the deaf child and his parents may best be served by accepting that he is a deaf person, with an elaborate cultural and linguistic heritage that can enrich his parents' life as it will his own. We should heed the advice of the deaf teenager who, when reprimanded by her mother for not wearing the processor of her cochlear prosthesis, hurled back

bitterly: "I'm deaf. Let me be deaf" (Lane, 1992, p. 238).

As students with impairments to hearing progress through the years of elementary schooling, the tendency to avoid interaction with their hearing peers seems to increase. There is research, however, that suggests that when these students are integrated into preschool programs with normally hearing students and are given extensive language training, they are less likely to become social isolates (Kennedy and Bruininks, 1974). This underscores the important role that classroom teachers can play in the social and personal development of students with hearing impairments. Recognizing that the need for special services will be dependent upon the nature and extent of an individual student's hearing loss, teachers who welcome the presence of these students in their classrooms, appreciate their cultural and language differences, and encourage their full involvement in class activities may well be the deciding influence between a life of social restriction or one of personal options and greater freedom.

HIGHER EDUCATION FOR STUDENTS WITH HEARING DISABILITIES

For many young people with hearing impairments, a college education is a viable option. Gallaudet College in Washington, D.C., was created by Congress in 1954 to provide higher education opportunities for individuals with hearing impairments. Of course, many, if not most, people with disabilities in hearing who are interested in undergraduate or graduate training attend colleges and universities other than Gallaudet. Often this is possible with only minor modifications and/or adaptations. Technical training programs are available at the National Technical Institute for the Deaf in Rochester, New York. Obviously, the likelihood that a person with a hearing impairment will succeed in a college, graduate, or technical program will vary, as with any other person. All of the relevant characteristics of the individual, other than hearing, must be taken into account along with the characteristics of the educational institution, in planning for advanced training or education.

OTHER CONSIDERATIONS

Technical developments are resulting in the opportunity for persons with hearing impairments to experience far greater communication opportunities than they have had in the past. The TTY (teletypewriter) system is enabling persons who formerly could not use a telephone to do so. The system allows typed messages to be sent over the telephone system. Messages appear on a printout screen. Inability to use the telephone has long been an occupational and social barrier to persons with deafness. This has changed as the TTY has come into more widespread use.

Captioned television news is now widely available in the United States. The older technique used for transmitting these programs was called the *open method.* The national news, for example, was taped daily and captions were added. The program was then rebroadcast over public television at a later time. The newer technique now in operation is the *closed method.* Captions are added to programs as they are broadcast but only appear on the screens of sets that have been adapted with a decoder. The decoder picks up signals that result in the captions appearing on line 21 of the television screen. This system has the advantage of not transmitting the captions to those who do not need them. Most television programs are now captioned in this manner, and many televisions are manufactured with the decoder included. A library of captioned films for the deaf is also maintained by the

U.S. Department of Education. These films are available for loan at no cost other than return postage.

Most people have heard of "seeing-eye" dogs, which are used by some blind persons. Fewer people are aware, however, that "hearing-ear" dogs are trained for use by persons who are deaf. These dogs can be trained for a variety of purposes. Common uses include making their owners aware of doorbell and alarm clock sounds, and emergency sounds like sirens. They have also been trained to alert parents who are deaf to a baby's cry.

A recent development in computer technology may prove to be a real benefit to students with hearing impairments who are learning American Sign Language, and to teachers who teach these students. A CD-ROM version of the *American Sign Language Concise Dictionary* is now available. It includes video clips of how to make over two thousand signs. By typing in a word or phrase, a demonstration is produced on the computer monitor that shows exactly how to make the appropriate sign. The dictionary also gives background information on each sign. This tool might be used as a valuable aid to teachers who are working for the inclusion of students who use ASL (Langberg, 1994).

Ways of Helping Students with Hearing Impairments Succeed in Inclusive Classrooms

THE ULTIMATE GOAL OF EDUCATION for students with hearing impairments is to provide them with skills that will allow them to participate as fully as possible in all facets of life. Part of this goal may be to return a child to or retain a child in a regular classroom. Some teachers will have a child with a profound hearing loss as a student. Many more teachers, however, will have children with some degree of hearing loss in their classrooms. The following suggestions are offered for teachers who find that they have children with this special need in their classrooms:

1. Try to provide preferential seating for the child in the front of the room away from vibrations from heating duct fans and air-conditioning units. Avoid placing the child in a "heavy traffic" area of the room where a lot of noise is likely to be generated.
2. Give the child as many opportunities to speak in class as you do other children.
3. Try rephrasing a question or statement if the child does not seem to understand.
4. Stress the importance of clear enunciation to all children in the class.
5. Remember that a child with a hearing impairment may become fatigued more quickly than other children. This child is working harder at hearing and understanding.

HARVEY FINKLE/IMPACT VISUALS

6. Check the child's facial expression to be sure you have made contact before speaking to her or him.
7. Consider using a buddy system. A hearing buddy could be a great help to this child in activities that are heavily dependent on hearing.

Another important consideration for teachers, particularly those teaching younger children, is recognizing hearing losses that have thus far gone undetected. Often children with mild hearing losses go for years without those losses being recognized for what they are. These children may be accused of being inattentive and uncooperative by teachers and parents. While their academic achievement suffers because of the hearing loss, it may be attributed to anything from laziness to mental retardation. Some signs that might alert a classroom teacher to the possibility that a child may have a hearing loss are:

1. Lack of attention to conversations around her or him.
2. Frequent earaches and other ear complaints.
3. Tendency to be withdrawn.
4. Ignoring verbal directions.
5. Frequent confusion or misinterpretation.
6. Reading and language arts difficulties.
7. Eyes often fixed on the teacher's face.
8. Lack of interest in music activities.
9. Difficulty with speech sounds.
10. Dizzy spells or "ringing" in the ears.
11. Head turning or "cocking" when listening.

Students who rely on speechreading as at least part of their means for receptive speech ("hearing others") may require the best view possible of your mouth and facial muscles. They depend heavily on "seeing" what you are saying. The following guidelines may be important to remember when teaching a class of children with at least one member with a special hearing need:

- Do not roam around the room while talking to the class.
- Try to stand where adequate light is on your face.
- Make sure there is not a glare (for example, from a window) in the eyes of the student with a hearing impairment.
- Try to keep your hands away from your face while talking.
- Be sure to face the class while explaining material from the chalkboard.
- A mustache makes speechreading difficult.
- Do not use excessive "mouthing." Try to speak naturally.

The inclusion of students with severe or profound hearing losses in regular classrooms has been a controversial issue in recent years. Leah Hager Cohen has pointed out that even when a child who is deaf is provided with an interpreter, translations of teacher instructions and student exchanges may be problematic for that child. Many words, phrases, and idioms simply cannot be translated literally from American Sign Language to English. This may place the child who is deaf at a very real educational disadvantage.

Cohen also points out that students with deafness need others in their classrooms whom they can communicate with freely without the encumbrances of the difficulties of lipreading or paper and pencil messages.

She argues that simply placing students with deafness in classrooms and assuming that they will benefit may in fact result in more harm to them than good (*Inclusive Education Programs,* 1994b).

An approach for addressing this concern has been developed by three secondary schools in Burbank, California. This model uses a "co-enrollment" strategy. Classes with students who are deaf are reduced in enrollment. These classes have ratios of students with deafness to hearing students that vary with the age of the children. Preschool and kindergarten programs have a higher ratio of children with hearing losses. This ratio is based on the reasoning that younger children with deafness need more contact with their nonhearing peers for communication, social, and self-concept purposes. The Burbank Co-Enrollment Schools also apply the following principles in providing inclusive classrooms for students who are deaf:

- a total communication philosophy
- providing role models who are deaf
- a bilingual/bicultural emphasis
- family sign language classes provided once a week to parents
- bilingual teacher pay (a $2,000 stipend) to teachers who demonstrate competence in sign language (*Inclusive Education Programs,* 1994a, pp. 5–6).

The goal of this chapter has been to help teachers or those who otherwise serve children to become aware of the meaning and consequences of hearing loss. It has also been written in an attempt to increase your sensitivity to the possible implications of hearing loss among children in schools.

Hearing loss is often not understood. Loss of hearing is not accompanied by outward, easily recognized characteristics. A person with a hearing impairment can pass other people on the street without their knowing that this person has a disability. At other times, a hearing loss may be mistaken for an emotional disorder or for mental retardation. Some people argue that hearing loss (particularly deafness) is not a disability at all but a cultural difference.

The impact of a hearing loss on a particular individual's life, however, may be minimal or devastating. Much depends on the kind of understanding, educational assistance, and social acceptance that the individual receives.

Case Studies and Questions to Consider

STUDENT: WAYNE WRENN

SCHOOL: HOPEFUL ELEMENTARY

CURRENT PLACEMENT: SPECIAL EDUCATION CLASS

AGE: 9 YEARS, 10 MONTHS

Family Structure and Home Environment

Wayne lives with his parents, Jim and Sheila Wrenn. Mr. Wrenn is thirty-two years old and is employed as a sales representative for Worldwide Roofing. Ms. Wrenn is thirty-three years old and is employed as a quality control technician for Electronics Systems Inc. For the past several months, however, she has been on disability leave from her work following back surgery. Wayne also lives with his brother, Duncan, who is twenty-two months old. The Wrenn family lives in a pleasant and attractive house in the Pine Ridge Farms subdivision. The Wrenn home provides a warm and caring atmosphere in support of Wayne's development.

Parental Perceptions of the Student's School Program

Wayne is classified as having a moderate hearing loss. He also has cerebral palsy, which has resulted in loss of motion in his legs and restricted movement in his arms and hands. Wayne is in a wheelchair.

In general, Wayne's parents feel that he is making considerable progress in his behavioral and communication skills in his special class. They describe Wayne as a child who is becoming more pleasant to live with and is growing in his ability to relate to other people. They have also noted frequent expressions of affection from Wayne toward his little brother, Duncan. They are observing that Duncan's speech development seems to be stimulating Wayne to use more words, phrases, and sentences. The Wrenns are optimistic over the progress their son is making in self-help skills, such as dressing, and believe he will continue to advance in these abilities with the instruction he is receiving in school. He is presently enrolled for the third year in his special education class at Hopeful Elementary. Previously, he was served through the Project Infant and Project Toddler programs.

Mr. and Ms. Wrenn are pleased with Wayne's school placement and program. They believe that the various elements of his special education program and the related services he receives have done much to promote his growth and development. They want to do everything they can to reinforce and complement the efforts of his teachers and therapists.

Additional Considerations

The most important goal that Wayne's parents have for him is that he reach the highest level of independence possible. When asked what they would change about their son if they could, they responded that they would like to see him able to learn more easily and quickly. Given the realities of his disabilities, however, they wish only to support him in his own unique pace and pattern of development.

Wayne's teachers and therapists also believe that he is in the best possible placement given his disabilities. They do not believe that he could otherwise be provided with the extensive individual instruction, speech therapy, physical therapy, and occupational therapy that he requires.

Questions

1. Are there ways that Wayne's school experience could become more inclusive? How?
2. Given the good progress that he is making, how might you initiate a discussion with his parents and teachers of the need for more inclusion?
3. Are there ways that Wayne's involvement in more inclusive activities could be beneficial to other children in the school?

STUDENT: APRIL SHOWERS

SCHOOL: OPEN GATE ELEMENTARY

CURRENT PLACEMENT: SPECIAL EDUCATION CLASS

AGE: 6 YEARS, 3 MONTHS

Family Structure and Home Environment

April lives with her mother, Linda Showers. Ms. Showers is forty-one years old and works in an accounting position at Limited Enterprises. Ms. Showers is divorced from April's father, Grant Showers. According to Ms. Showers, April's father has not been a presence in April's life for a number of years. April and her mother live in a rented house.

Parental Perception of the Student's School Program

April is receiving special services for her hearing impairment and associated learning needs in a self-contained special class. Ms. Showers is very pleased with April's school progress. She feels that the program has been appropriate for her daughter and has done much to promote her development in academic and communication skills. She is particularly positive when she speaks of April's teacher, Mr. Lonnie Dove. She feels that Mr. Dove has made a personal and professional investment in April that is admirable.

Ms. Showers commented that she and April's school are in agreement that her daughter should be placed in a regular class for some first-grade subjects next year. She feels that April is ready for this challenge, and that it will be a positive addition to her school program.

In general, Ms. Showers thinks that her daughter's social and personal behavior is comparable to that of other six-year-old girls. She does not believe that there are any major areas of adaptive deficiency in April's life. On the contrary, she emphasized that April is very independent and has not allowed her hearing impairment to hold her back in any sphere of her life.

Additional Considerations

Ms. Showers' long-range goal for her daughter is that she grow up to be a happy and productive adult. She is sure that this will be true and is confident that April can do anything in life that she wants. In response to a question about changes she would wish for April's life, she emphatically stated that she would not change anything about April. She said, "She is just so beautiful. I wouldn't want April to be different in any way."

Ms. Showers and Mr. Dove are concerned that the first-grade teachers at Open Gate Elementary may not be as receptive to April's presence in their classes as they would wish. Some of these teachers have commented that they would not know how to meet April's special needs. One of the teachers, for example, commented that she has trouble understanding April's speech and she wouldn't know how to help April take care of her hearing aids.

Questions

1. How can Ms. Showers and Mr. Dove help the first- grade teachers become more open to April's inclusion in their classrooms?
2. Up to this point, April has always been in a special class. What things might be helpful in preparing her for inclusion in regular classes?
3. What are some things that could be done to help the children in the regular first-grade classes understand April and enjoy her as a friend?

References

Alexander Graham Bell Collection, Manuscript Division, Library of Congress, Washington, DC.

Babbidge, H. D. *Education of the Deaf.* Washington, DC: U.S. Department of Health, Education, and Welfare, 1965.

Blatt, B. "Friendly Letter on the Correspondence of Helen Keller, Anne Sullivan, and Alexander Graham Bell." *Exceptional Children, 51,* 1985: 405–409.

Bornstein, H. "Towards a Theory of Use for Signed English: From Birth Through Adulthood." *American Annals of the Deaf, 27,* 1982: 26–31.

Charlson, E., M. Strong, and R. Gold. "How Successful Deaf Teenagers Experience and Cope with Isolation." *American Annals of the Deaf, 137*(3), 1992: 261–270.

Commission on Education of the Deaf. *Toward Equality.* A Report to the President and the Congress of the United States. Washington, DC: U.S. Government Printing Office, 1988.

Crocker, A., and R. Nelson. "Mental Retardation." In M. Levine, W. Carey, A. Crocker, and R. Gross (Eds.), *Developmental-Behavioral Pediatrics.* Philadelphia: Saunders, 1983: 156–168.

Dale, D. C. *Deaf Children at Home and at School.* London: University of London Press, 1972.

Denton, D. M. *Total Communication.* Fredrick, MD: Maryland School for the Deaf, 1970.

Federal Register. Washington, DC: U.S. Government Printing Office, 1977: 42478–42479.

Furth, H. G. *Deafness and Learning: A Psychological Approach.* Belmont, CA: Wadsworth, 1973.

Inclusive Education Programs: Advice on Elementary Students with Disabilities in Regular Settings. "California District Includes Deaf Students in Regular Classes." *1*(12) December 1994a.

———. "Train Go Sorry: Are Educators Missing the Boat with Deaf Students?" *1*(4), April 1994b.

Kennedy, P., and R. H. Bruininks. "Social Status of Hearing Impaired Children in Regular Classrooms." *Exceptional Children, 40,* 1974: 336–344.

Lane, H. *The Mask of Benevolence: Disabling the Deaf Community.* New York: Knopf, 1992.

———. "The Medicalization of Cultural Deafness in Historical Perspective." In R. Fisher and H. Lane, *Looking Back: A Reader on the History of Deaf Communities and Their Sign Languages.* Hamburg, Germany: Signum Press, 1993.

Langberg, M. "CD Speaks Fluently with Signs." *The State.* Columbia, SC: Knight-Ridder Newspapers, December 25, 1994: B3.

Meadow, K. P. "Social Adjustment of Preschool Children: Deaf and Hearing, with and Without Other Handicaps." *Topics in Early Childhood Special Education, 3,* 1984: 27–40.

Menchel, R. S. "Personal Experience with Speechreading." *Volta Review, 90*(5), 1988: 3–15.

National Information Center on Deafness. *Deafness: A Factsheet.* Washington, DC: National Information Center on Deafness, Gallaudet University, 1989.

Northern, J. L., and M. P. Downs. *Hearing in Children.* Baltimore, MD: Williams and Wilkins, 1974.

Office of Special Education Programs. *Sixteenth Annual Report to Congress on the Implementation of the Individuals with Disabilities Education Act.* Washington, DC: U.S. Department of Education, 1994.

———. *Seventeenth Annual Report to Congress on the Implementation of the Individuals with Disabilities Education Act.* Washington, DC: U.S. Department of Education, 1995.

Paul, P., and S. Quigley. *Education and Deafness.* White Plains, NY: Longman, 1990.

Simmons, F. B. "Automated Screening Test for Newborns: The Crib-O-Gram." In B. F. Jaffe (Ed.), *Hearing Loss in Children.* Baltimore, MD: University Park Press, 1977: 95–111.

Creating Classrooms That Welcome Students with Special Gifts and Talents

A Proud Moment: The Day Allison Became a Gifted Samaritan

"What are you going to do about it?" In 1987 my daughter, Allison, asked me that question. We were on vacation in New York City. My wife, Joyce, and I had looked forward for a long time to introducing our three children to the city. We had lived there while studying and working at Columbia University, and we had many treasured memories that we wanted to revisit and share with our children, Link, Allison, and Sallie.

In the decade since we had lived in the city, however, New York had been faced with greater challenges than ever before. Changes in federal policies and programs had manifested themselves most visibly among the urban poor. There were many more homeless, confused, and disenfranchised people on the streets of New York than we had ever seen before. My children had learned the term *street people* as an abstraction. Now, as we walked the streets of the city, they connected that term with the real people they saw sleeping on the pavement, rummaging through garbage, or walking about disoriented and clearly impoverished.

Allison, who was seven, was particularly moved by what she saw, and asked if I thought that one man, who looked alarmingly dirty, ill, and exhausted, would die. I answered that unless something happened, unless he got help soon, he probably would. That was when she asked what I have come to call "Allison's question": "Daddy, what are you going to do about it?"

Joyce and I, like most parents, have tried to teach our children to do the "right thing" in relation to other people. Again, like most other parents, we try to teach our children by example, modeling that other people must be treated with care and respect. At least we hope that we have provided this example. Therefore, I took Allison's question as a positive sign: She had come to expect her parents to try to help people who need it. At seven, however, she also believed that her mother and I had the ability to do whatever needed to be done to help others. She believed we could always "make things better."

On that street in New York, however, I was inarticulate in answering Allison's question. As I stumbled and stammered my way around her concern, the best I could do was talk with her about not being able to help everyone in need. I talked about how our contributions to church and charities help people like the man she was so concerned about. Allison was not satisfied with this answer. I was also immediately embarrassed to have offered it to my child. The moment passed, but my discomfort did not.

In the story of the Good Samaritan, the two men who passed by the sufferer without helping him crossed to the other side of the road when they saw him. Not only would they not help, they avoided being near the suffering man. These men were probably not unfeeling and inhumane. They simply did not want to risk becoming involved. Perhaps they were family men with responsibilities to others that they felt took precedence. Maybe they were afraid of being tricked and finding themselves victims of attack and robbery. They may have been wary of becoming involved with someone who would require more and more of them. And so, they walked to the other side of the road to avoid even seeing the hurting man whom they felt they could not help.

Months passed before I spoke with Allison again about her question. Finally, I was able to talk with her about the limits to what one person can do in helping others. In addition, recalling the parable of the Good Samaritan, I explained to

Allison that, though her mother and I could not help everyone who needed help, we did care. I promised her that, though seeing a need one cannot meet is painful, we will always see others and their needs, and care about them. I explained that what is most important is that we not walk to the other side of the road, that we not avoid seeing the needs of others even when we can't meet them immediately. We talked, and I believe she understood what I was trying to say.

The philosopher Judith Jarvis Thomson, in discussing the murder of Kitty Genovese decades ago in New York City, revisited the story of the Good Samaritan. Kitty Genovese was murdered by being repeatedly and brutally attacked, while thirty-eight people watched from their apartments and did nothing to help her. Thomson said that a Good Samaritan would have rushed out, risking death in an attempt to help. Such a person, she said, would be not just *good* but a *Splendid Samaritan*! In fact, however, not one of the thirty-eight witnesses even picked up a telephone to call the police, an action that would have caused them no danger. Calling the police, Thomson said, would have been the act of a *Minimally Decent Samaritan.* Thomson's observation has made an important impact on my view of many of our contemporary social problems. What we need to make a decent society is not a few Splendid Samaritans but millions of Minimally Decent Samaritans. We all need to strive for greater decency in the ways that we treat each other.

Two years after our New York trip, while visiting Allison's elementary school, I was again confronted with her question and, this time, with her insight on that question. She was nearing the end of the third grade, and I was on a mission not previously unexperienced. I was bringing a forgotten lunch bag to school.

As I entered the hallway, her teacher Ms. Vaughan was closing her classroom door behind her. She seemed a little more surprised to see me than usual, and she hesitated for a moment as she took the lunch bag. She explained that she had something important to tell me.

The afternoon before had apparently been very traumatic for some of the children in Allison's class. The announcement of the selection of children for the gifted program had been made. Only one child from her class made the list. The elementary gifted program in this system included a pull-out program for the fourth and fifth grade. Students selected for the program spent these years at the "GO" Center. They rejoined their peers at middle school two years later. Ms. Vaughan explained, as she took the brown bag from me, that Allison had been her clear choice for the "GO" program. A boy in the class, however, had higher test scores and, on that basis, had been picked by the Selection Committee. She was most apologetic and uneasy until I explained that it was not a big deal for us. In fact, had Allison been selected I was doubtful that we would have wanted her to leave her peers and the school she loved so much even for two years of accelerated and enriched programming. We were pleased with the education Allison was receiving, and I didn't think we would have traded it for something so different.

Ms. Vaughan smiled and said she had something special to share with me. That morning two girls in the class had been quite upset. One felt that her parents were terribly disappointed that she was not selected for the gifted program. Both the mother and the father were highly competitive and high-achieving people. Their daughter felt she had let them down by not being "number one." The other girl was also afraid that she had disappointed her parents. She had an older brother who had been selected for the program several years earlier.

Ms. Vaughan had found both girls being comforted by Allison. Allison was assuring them that not being selected for the program was no disaster. She had also consoled them by saying, "It is more important that we will all be together next year. I would rather be a Samaritan than be in the GO program. Good Samaritans stick together and help each other. We are really Good Samaritans. My Dad says it is better to be a Good Samaritan than to be rich or famous."

Ms. Vaughan explained to me that the comforting that Allison had offered the other girls had worked. They both seemed to be feeling better. I explained to the teacher that I couldn't be prouder of my daughter. Allison had shared a rare and precious gift.

I read an excellent book not long ago by William F. May called *The Patient's Ordeal.* In his introduction to the book, May describes an exchange that T. S. Eliot had with a college student. Eliot had given a lecture on some serious problem in American life. During the question-and-answer period following the lecture, the student asked urgently, "Mr. Eliot, what are we going to do about the problem you have discussed?" Eliot replied to the student, "You have asked the wrong question. You must understand that we face two types of problems in life. One kind of problem provokes the question, 'What are we going to do about it?' The other kind poses the subtler question, 'How do we behave toward it?'"

It seems clear to me that the first kind of problem can be solved with direct, sometimes simple, and immediate action. The immediate relief that a doctor or dentist can give a patient is an example of this kind of problem resolution. The second kind of problem is a greater challenge. This is a problem that has no direct, simple, or immediate solution. What do you do for a dying friend or family member? Do you avoid the person because you cannot cure his or her suffering or prevent the inevitable? Abiding by your friend or relative in such a situation requires a different approach to the problem: You must see it as a factor to be lived with as part of an enduring relationship.

When I initially tried to respond to Allison's question of "What are you going to do about it?" I sought a fast and clean solution to the problem of the protection and well-being of another human being. I understand now that he needed more than a "quick fix" to his problems: He needed a sense of connectedness to his culture that would endure. I suspect that this is the greatest need of many of our fellow human beings. The simple problems that can be fixed quickly are not the ones that drain us. Having people who will endure with us is one of the greatest of our human needs. It is a gift of great value. Schools that promote this kind of caring are helping to educate truly gifted students.

Students with Special Gifts and Talents: Definition and Identification

GIFTEDNESS: AN HISTORICAL CONTEXT

The history of education for students classified as gifted and talented has been a history, at least until recently, of special education for a privileged few. Children identified as gifted were usually those who clearly showed outstanding abilities and who were also provided with exceptional opportunities to further develop their gifts. Children who were thought of as "prodigies" or "geniuses" were, therefore, identified by their already apparent and unusual talents. A child who could speak five languages by the age of eight or who had read all of the Greek and Roman classics by that age might be identified as a genius. A child who could compose symphonies or who had devised new mathematical formulas while still needing help with dressing might be considered a prodigy. It is important to note that such children were likely to live in environments that gave them rich opportunities to develop these attributes, and that those same environments were likely to continue to be supportive of their further development after these unusual abilities were recognized. Children growing up in environments that did not provide the opportunities and encouragement needed for the development of their potential gifts, however, were not likely to achieve the levels of performance in intellectual and creative pursuits that their more fortunate peers would realize.

There are, of course, notable exceptions to the early recognition of outstanding abilities. Albert Einstein's scientific genius was not recognized until he had reached adulthood. Winston Churchill did not show early signs of his genius for leadership. Einstein and Churchill were both, in fact, considered to be backward and problematic as children.

There are also historical exceptions to the practice of relying on already apparent talents for the identification of children as gifted and the provision to them of special educational opportunities. For nearly two thousand years, educators in China have recognized that some children with outstanding potential may not achieve that potential without the appropriate nurturance. As early as 500 B.C., Confucius argued that education should be available to children of all social classes and that the education of each child, including those with unusual talents or abilities, should be designed to foster the potential of individual children (Tsuin-Chen, 1961).

EDUCATION FOR STUDENTS WITH GIFTEDNESS

In the United States, special educational provisions for children considered to be gifted were first offered in St. Louis in 1867. The public schools there created a system of flexible promotion for these children that allowed them to progress according to their abilities without being held back by a rigid grade system. By the 1920s, most school systems in the larger metropolitan areas of the United States had some form of gifted education program. These were often developed with the encouragement of parents or civic organizations. In Cleveland, Ohio, for example, a group of concerned women promoted the creation of classes for gifted children in 1922. They were encouraged in this effort by the psychologist H. H. Goddard. Another psychologist, Leta Hollingworth, initiated gifted education programs in the schools of New York City during the 1930s. Hollingworth developed enrichment activities for children identified as gifted that encouraged their potential for what she believed was their greatest gift, original thinking. She also advocated the provision of counseling services for children with gifts and talents, emphasizing that they needed emotional education as well as intellectual enrichment.

In 1957 the Russian satellite Sputnik was launched into space. To many Americans, this event was a sign of the emerging scientific superiority of the Russians. It was also considered by many to be a symbol of the inferiority of American education in the sciences and in math. This event also created increased interest in programs for students identified as gifted and talented. Accelerated study and ability grouping became common in American schools. More advanced study, particularly in math and science, was emphasized in high schools. This "startle response" approach to education for students with special gifts and talents has reoccurred in subsequent decades and has often come as a response to concerns about declining quality in public education.

DEFINING GIFTEDNESS

There are varying definitions of giftedness. The most widely used definition, however, is the one included in the Education Consolidation and Improvement Act. That definition describes giftedness in a comprehensive manner that recognizes that students may be gifted in a variety of skills and abilities. The federal definition says that gifted students are those

> who give evidence of high performance capability in areas such as intellectual, creative, artistic, leadership capacity, or specific academic fields, and who require services or activities not ordinarily provided by the school in order to fully develop such capabilities (*PL 97-35*, Education Consolidation and Improvement Act, sec. 582, 1981).

There are several aspects to this definition that are important to highlight. First, it recognizes that there are a number of ways that a student may be gifted. It includes leadership, creative pursuits, and the performing and visual arts as legitimate areas of giftedness even if they are not accompanied by high general academic ability. Second, by using the term *capabilities*, it acknowledges that some students may have the potential for gifted performance but that the potential may not be realized unless it is nurtured and encouraged. Third, it emphasizes that the educational nurturing and encouragement that these students require to realize their potentials is genuinely an issue of their having "special needs" just as surely as does a student with a learning disability or some other exceptionality. These aspects of the federal definition are quite different from earlier conceptions of giftedness.

THE TERMAN STUDY

Lewis Terman conducted a famous long-term study of giftedness that contributed greatly to the knowledge base concerning the characteristics of individuals with giftedness. From 1925 through 1959, five volumes of reports on more than 1,500 people who were selected as children for study were published under Terman's authorship. The reports, entitled *Genetic Studies of Genius*, described these individuals from childhood through midlife. After Terman's death, his colleagues continued to follow the lives of these people. Most are now retired, about half are now dead, and researchers continue to report on those who are still alive (Friedman et al., 1995).

Terman used only one criterion for the selection of the children who became the subjects of his study—high IQ. All of the children selected had scores on the Stanford-Binet Intelligence Scale that placed them in the upper 1 percent of the population (most had IQs of 140 or more). After being selected for the study, each subject was assessed for physical and social development, academic achievement, and personality traits. Over the decades that followed, the physical, social, and professional development of the "Termites" (as they nicknamed themselves) was traced.

Terman's findings exploded some of the myths about giftedness that were pervasive at the time he initiated his research. One was that of "early ripe, early rot." This myth held that early intellectual maturation resulted in an early decline or "burnout" of abilities in adulthood. Another was that very high abilities create a vulnerability for mental illness—"genius and insanity go hand in hand." Conventional opinions at that time also held that children who were gifted tended to be frail and introverted. Contrary to these stereotypes, Terman found that his research subjects were physically, socially, and psychologically healthy—above average, in fact, in all of these domains. He also found that, as expected, they tended to be outstanding achievers in school. Over the decades, the Termites as a group continued to be high achievers in their educational and vocational pursuits.

Although Terman's gifted subjects tended to be high achievers, the title he selected for his studies, *Genetic Studies of Genius*, has proven to be a misnomer. There are no names in his list of subjects that would be widely recognized as the names of geniuses. There are no Picassos or Einsteins, no Madame Curies or Helen Kellers in the study. There are no Nobel or Pulitzer Prize winners among the Termites (Kassan et al., 1993). Two names that might be commonly recognized from the list of subjects are Ancel Keys and Jess Oppenheimer. Keys, a physiologist, developed the military rations first used in World War II—named K rations in his honor—and was central to the discovery of the role of high cholesterol in coronary disease. Oppenheimer was the creator, head writer, and producer of *I Love Lucy* (Shurkin, 1992).

ELIZABETH CREWS/STOCK BOSTON

GIFTEDNESS: BROADENING DEFINITIONS

The fact that there are no geniuses among Terman's subjects is made even more striking by the fact that two of the children who were screened out of his study because their IQs were not high enough did become Nobel Prize winners (physicists William Shockley and Luis Alvarez). This also points to the likely reason that there were no Einsteins or

Curies in Terman's sample: He relied entirely on intelligence test scores for his selection. This, of course, reflected his belief that intelligence was truly what the tests were measuring, that the tests were accurate and valid measures of giftedness (Shurkin, 1992).

Over the decades since Terman defined giftedness as a unitary trait, subject to measurement by an intelligence test, the conception of what it means to be gifted has broadened (see Box 9.1). This broadening of the idea of giftedness has followed the move toward more complex conceptions of how intelligence itself functions. Gardner, for example, conceives of "intelligences" rather than intelligence. The "intelligences" he describes include:

1. *Linguistic* (verbal) intelligence includes verbal comprehension, syntax, semantics, and written and oral expression and understanding.
2. *Logical-mathematical* intelligence includes inductive and deductive reasoning and computational abilities.
3. *Spatial* intelligence is the capacity to represent and manipulate spatial configurations.
4. *Musical* intelligence includes such abilities as pitch discrimination; sensitivity to rhythm; the ability to hear and perform themes in music; and music composition.
5. *Bodily-kinesthetic* intelligence is the ability to use all or part of one's body to perform a task or fashion a product.
6. *Interpersonal* intelligence is the ability to understand the actions and motivations of others and to act sensibly and productively based on that knowledge.
7. *Intrapersonal* intelligence refers to a person's understanding of self, that is, one's own cognitive strengths and weaknesses, feelings and emotions (Ramos-Ford and Gardner, 1991).

BOX 9.1

Defining Giftedness: Points to Remember

- There are different kinds of intelligence.
- Creativity and motivation are as important as high ability in defining giftedness.
- Giftedness must be developed and nurtured. It will not "emerge against all odds."
- Intelligence tests are not necessarily the most accurate measure and are usually not adequate for identifying giftedness.

Another approach to broadening the conception of giftedness was developed by Gagné. Separating and redefining the terms *gifts* and *talents,* Gagné draws a distinction between ability and performance. *Ability,* in this context, is an intellectual, creative, social, or sensorimotor gift or aptitude that the individual is endowed with from birth. *Performance,* according to Gagné, is the actual use of the ability; this expression of the ability is called a *talent.* The likelihood that an ability will be expressed as a talent is influenced by the personality traits of the individual and the influence of the person's family, school, and other environmental variables. Talents may be academic, technical, artistic, interpersonal, or athletic (Gagné, 1991). An important implication of this conception of gifts and talents is that a student may be gifted (the ability is present) yet not talented (the ability is not used; the student's performance, therefore, is not commensurate with her or his ability). This is a critical consideration in comprehending the importance of education that will truly facilitate the development of potential in students who are gifted.

RENZULLI'S DEFINITION

Joseph Renzulli has made a valuable contribution to the understanding of students with special needs through his comprehensive definition of giftedness (see Figure 9.1). According to Renzulli, giftedness

> reflects an interaction among three basic clusters of human traits—these clusters being above average (but not necessarily high) general and/or specific ability, high levels of task commitment (motivation), and high levels of creativity. Gifted and talented children are those possessing or capable of developing this composite set of traits and applying them to any potentially valuable area of human performance (Renzulli and Reis, 1991).

Renzulli's conception of giftedness is based on his study of the characteristics of highly productive and creative people. His findings led him to develop a definition that emphasizes the interaction between ability, creativity, and commitment. Renzulli believes that when these factors converge in an individual, the result is a person who is "truly gifted" in the sense that exceptional performance and significant contributions to society are likely. It should be noted that Renzulli does not believe that a student must have high ratings in all three categories in order to be considered for gifted education services. In fact, it may be the student who has high ability, but needs help in developing creativity or commitment, who most needs special attention. Likewise, a student may be very creative but need help in achievement and motivation.

FIGURE 9.1

Renzulli's Conception of Giftedness

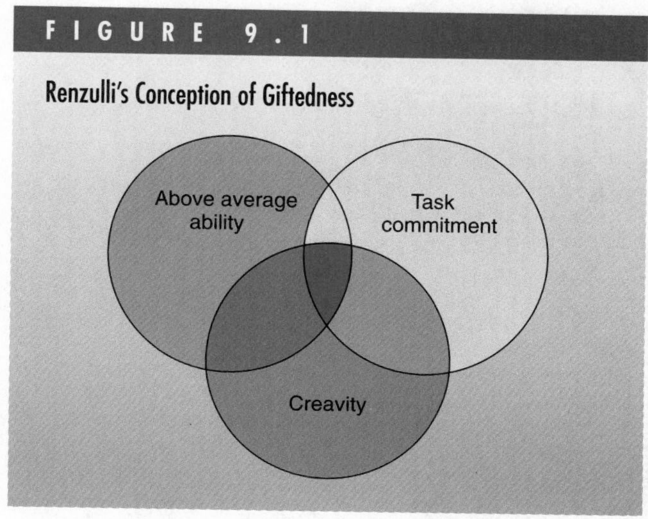

GIFTEDNESS: IDENTIFICATION MEASURES

Intelligence tests are still used extensively in the identification of students who are gifted. It is widely recognized that a high IQ, by definition, implies a capacity for rapid and effective acquisition of information, particularly in academic settings (Kassan et al., 1993). There are well-known problems, however, with the use of both intelligence and achievement tests for this purpose. Standardized tests may be biased against children from a language background other than English. They may also not be fair measures of the abilities of children from minority backgrounds and those who have been denied learning opportunities because of socioeconomic factors (Baldwin, 1991). A multifaceted approach to the identification of giftedness is necessary if these biases are to be reduced. Box 9.2 provides a list of the types of identification measures that may be used. Most school systems use some combination of these measures. Whatever the combination of measures, however, the goal should be to allow all children

BOX 9.2

Identifying Giftedness: A Variety of Measures

- *Intelligence Tests*
  Individual Intelligence Tests (for example, the Wechsler Intelligence Scales for Children).
  Group Intelligence Tests (for example, SRA Primary Mental Abilities Tests).
- *Achievement Tests* (for example, the Iowa Tests of Basic Skills and the Stanford Achievement Tests).
- *Teacher Nomination* (one of the most common procedures for identifying giftedness; the danger of bias toward children who engage in teacher-pleasing practices is evident).
- *Creativity Measures* (for example, the Torrance Tests of Creative Thinking).
- *Parent Nominations* (care must be exercised in using parent nomination—our children are our "gifts," but they may not all be "gifted").
- *Peer Nominations* (this technique can be very effective if students understand that it is not a popularity contest but a real effort to identify the best students in math, reading, and other subjects).
- *Self-Nomination* (this can take the form of having students write an essay on their interests and strengths).

the opportunity to show their talents and potential talents so that these may be encouraged and cultivated in the classroom.

STUDENTS WHO ARE GIFTED: HOW MANY?

As would be expected with the variation that exists in the ways that children are identified as having giftedness, there is considerable variance in the number of children who are identified. Schools that rely heavily on IQ scores for identifying students may use a score of 125 or 130 as the cutoff point for qualifying for gifted programs. This tends to result in a 2 to 3 percent figure for the number of students qualifying (Webb, Meckstroth, and Tolan, 1982). This approach reflects a clear perception of exclusivity about the nature of giftedness and the number of students who should be served. A different opinion concerning the nature of giftedness and the number of students to be served is held by Renzulli and Reis. They believe that the pool of students with giftedness should include 15 to 20 percent of the school population (Renzulli and Reis, 1991). According to Reis, however, a much lower figure is closer to the reality of the actual numbers of students being served as gifted. Reis reports that 4.5 percent of the student population of the United States receives these services (Reis, 1989).

Although definitions differ and the number of children identified as being gifted varies, all teachers have children in their classrooms who have gifts and talents that need to be recognized and nurtured. Whether or not these students are officially identified, they deserve an education that is appropriate for their abilities and needs. It is the responsibility of all teachers to recognize and work effectively with the gifts of all students.

The Special Educational Needs of Students Identified as Gifted and Talented

THE MAJORITY OF CHILDREN WITH giftedness spend most of their school days in general classrooms. Even when they are involved in special programs, most of their instruction takes place in a general classroom. A study of the most common types of special services provided to students who are gifted in the United States has shown that these are all structured around general classroom placements. These services are: part-time special classes, enrichment programs and activities, independent studies, resource rooms, and itinerant or consulting teachers (Cox, Daniel, and Boston, 1985). Although each of these alternatives for providing special help and opportunities to students with giftedness is important, the fact remains that for students participating in these alternatives, most of their education is still the product of their experiences in general classrooms. Nothing is more important, therefore, than the general classroom teacher being understanding of their needs and being willing to work with them in creative ways. As with the education of all students, the education of students with gifts and talents is, indeed, a responsibility and privilege of the entire school community.

DOMAINS OF GIFTEDNESS

Clark (1988) has described five domains of characteristics of students with giftedness. These domains are: the cognitive, the affective, the physical, the intuitive, and the societal. The *cognitive domain* includes the kind of high-ability skills described earlier in Renzulli's conception of giftedness. Students who are gifted are fast learners and excellent retainers of information. They may also be quick to see the relationships between the things that they learn in different contexts. The cognitive also includes, however, the persistence and motivation that Renzulli describes as high task commitment.

The *affective domain,* according to Clark, is a tendency toward emotional depth and sensitivity to the feelings of others. Also included in this domain is the tendency toward advanced levels of moral judgment.

In the *physical domain,* Clark observes that students who are gifted may show an unusual discrepancy between their physical and intellectual development. They may also demonstrate a low tolerance for the difference between their own standards for themselves and their physical inability to meet these standards.

The *intuitive domain* relates to creative ability. Again, similar to Renzulli's definition, Clark finds that students who are gifted may demonstrate unusual creative capacities in any area of endeavor.

In the *societal domain,* students who are gifted may show a strong desire to fulfill their personal potentials while also making a positive social contribution. They may apply advanced intellectual abilities toward the solution of the problems of their cultural environment.

GIFTEDNESS: INTERACTING FACTORS

David Feldman has conducted longitudinal and extensive research on a sample of six children who were described as "prodigies"

JEAN-CLAUDE LEJEUNE/STOCK BOSTON

(Feldman, 1980, 1986). As a result of his qualitative research, Feldman has described characteristics that may be found (to some degree at least) in many of the children identified as being gifted in American schools. The characteristics that Feldman found illustrate that giftedness is a result of interacting factors, some of which are *intrinsic* to the individual (an inherited capacity) and others that are the result of a *favorable environment.* According to Feldman, the subjects of his study:

- possessed extraordinary native ability;
- were born into families that recognized, valued, and fostered that ability;
- received instruction from master teachers who possessed superior knowledge of a domain and its history, and who imparted that knowledge in ways that engaged interest and sustained a commitment to learn; and
- showed strong inner-directedness and a passionate commitment to their field;

Ansell Horn/Impact Visuals

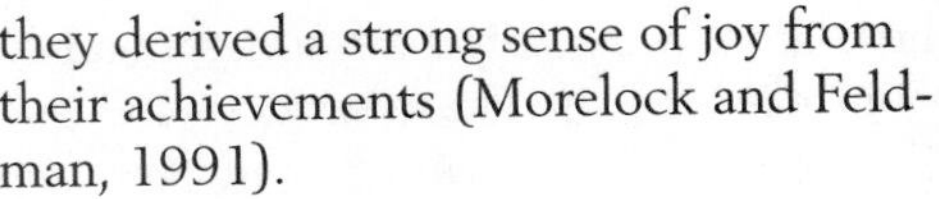
they derived a strong sense of joy from their achievements (Morelock and Feldman, 1991).

STRENGTHS AS VULNERABILITIES

The very strengths that students who are gifted possess may become weaknesses in their interactions with teachers and other students. This is particularly true if these strengths are not channeled in an appropriate manner. Some of the less than positive attributes that have been noted that may be characteristic of these students are:

- A tendency to dominate class discussions.
- An impatience to proceed to the next level of a subject or task.
- A resistance to rules, regulations, and standard procedures.
- A tendency to get "off the subject" in class discussions.
- A tendency to become bored by repetitive exercises.
- Frequent shifts of attention and interest.
- A tendency to insist on knowing the logic behind required tasks and activities (Heward and Orlansky, 1992, p. 461).

EDUCATIONAL OPTIONS: REPLACEMENTS AND SUPPLEMENTS

The educational options available for students with special gifts and talents have been categorized as either *replacement* or *supplementary* options. Replacement options for students who are gifted are offered as a replacement for general classroom activities. Supplementary options are programs or activities that are provided to these students outside of the general school program. Replacement options include:

- Enrichment or accelerated activities in the general classroom.
- Part-time special classes.
- Full-time special classes.
- Full-time special schools.
- Special residential schools.

Supplementary options include:

- Concurrent enrollment in high school and college.
- Advanced classes offered during non-school time periods by colleges/universities or community agencies.
- Internships and mentoring programs (Milgram and Goldring, 1991).

Schwartz has noted that the most appropriate educational program for an individual with giftedness may include some combination of replacement and supplementary options. Regardless of the options employed, however, the most appropriate school program for a student who is gifted must address the following facets of learning: the appropriate rate of learning for this student, the appropriate level of difficulty of the material presented to the student for learning, the amount and quality of what the student is to learn, and the promotion of self-direction in the student (Schwartz, 1994, p. 83). These are, of course, considerations that are important in the education of all students.

STUDENTS WHO ARE GIFTED: HOW DIFFERENT ARE THEY?

The following comments were made as responses to questions about being gifted. They were made by adults who as children were enrolled in Hunter College Elementary School, a school for children who had been identified as being gifted.

- I didn't consider myself gifted, except for the fact that we were consistently told that we were (Male, age 50).
- I was very confused by the word, gifted. . . . It's a euphemism, and to some extent was meant to be euphemistic, not to be completely understandable to children. They were very concerned about us getting swelled heads. I remember saying, "I don't have a lot of gifts" (Male, age 50).
- I don't think of the term [gifted] as relevant to life. There are smarter people out there than I am. I'm aware of that. But I don't feel superior in any way to anybody else. I'm aware I can see things. . . . I think of myself as being quicker than other people, not smarter than other people (Female, age 49) (Kassan et al., 1993, p. 37).

These comments indicate that these individuals did not or do not think of themselves as being very different from other people. They also bring into question the separation of students from the general classroom and/or school on the basis of being gifted. They bring into question the appropriateness of segregated education. A part of the school reform movement in the United States in recent years has focused on the question of segregated education for students identified as being gifted. It has even questioned the value of the term *gifted* itself (Gallagher, 1992). Others believe there is a philosophical tension between providing the best possible education for "promising" students and the improvement of education for "at-risk" students, and this is creating a crisis in the field of gifted education (Renzulli and Reis, 1991). Still other observers believe that inclusive schools can be created that will meet the goals of both equity for all students and excellence in the education of all (Stevens, 1992).

Ways of Helping Students with Special Gifts and Talents Succeed in Inclusive Classrooms

SNOW (1992), AN ADVOCATE FOR inclusive education, has made the following observations about the concept of giftedness:

> The culture of inclusion begins in the affirmation that all human beings are gifted. This statement sounds strange to many ears because our traditional world reserved the adjective *gifted* for only a chosen few whose talents and abilities, usually in very circumscribed ways, impress, enlighten, entertain or serve the rest of us. The inclusion culture views giftedness much differently. We affirm that giftedness is actually a common human trait, one that is fundamental to our capacity to be creatures of community. Gifts are whatever we are, whatever we do or whatever we have that allows us to create opportunities for ourselves and others to interact and do things together—interactions that are meaningful between at least two people (Snow, 1992, p. 109).

THE DEBATE: INCLUSIVE OR EXCLUSIVE?

The debate over how inclusive or exclusive education for students who are gifted should be involves a number of issues. Critics of segregated education for these students make the following points:

- An essential feature of inclusive schools is a sense of community. This sense of community is disrupted when students are pulled out for special services.
- The message that "if you are different, you have to leave" may challenge a student's sense of a secure place in the classroom.
- Having some children selected out for a gifted program can create a climate of alienation and distrust among students.
- Having students come and go to gifted programs may create disruptions in the flow of the classroom day and may make it more difficult for the teacher to create a sense of cohesiveness in the class.
- Taking children away from the general classroom to meet their needs as students who are gifted may dilute the teacher's sense of competence in teaching to a diverse group. Teachers may come to see themselves as less responsible for the education of all of the children in their classrooms (Sapon-Shevin, 1995).

Sapon-Shevin describes inclusive school communities as being those in which all students feel they belong, and no one is excluded on the basis of any particular characteristic. In these communities, teachers acknowledge and celebrate the individual differences of their students. In this kind of environment, honesty among students and teachers about strengths, weaknesses, skills, and needs becomes a foundation for trust and a sense of belongingness. A sense of interconnectedness is achieved as all individuals in this type of school community work together, share resources, help

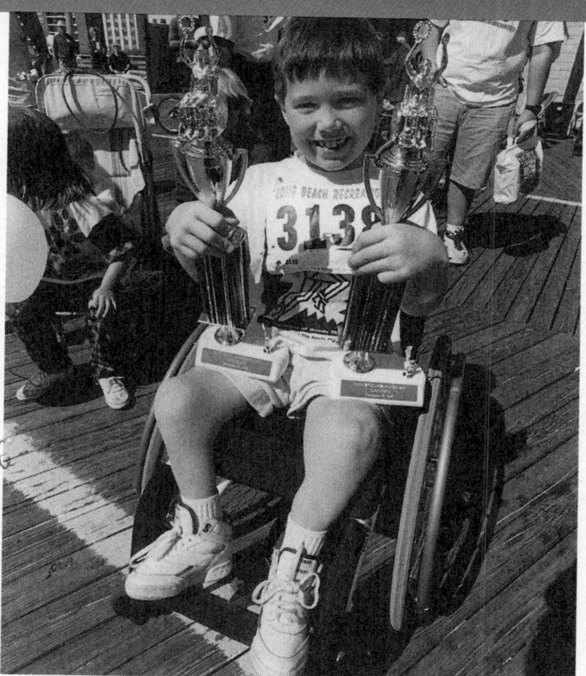
Kirk Condyles/Impact Visuals

those in need, and communicate their own needs openly (Sapon-Shevin, 1994).

Critics of inclusive approaches to the education of students who are gifted have presented arguments for the importance of separate programs designed to meet the needs of these students:

- Special programs for students who are gifted have been established *because* their needs have not been met in general classrooms.
- Classroom conditions such as class size, lack of teacher training, and competing demands on teachers make it difficult for teachers to adapt instruction for students who are gifted.
- Research indicates that teachers are more likely to make instructional modifications for struggling learners than for advanced learners.
- Although there is a great deal of discussion of achieving both equity and excellence in classrooms, at-risk learners continue to be a higher priority than advanced learners in access to the services they require.
- Results of inclusion programs are far from unanimously positive (Tomlinson, 1995).

GIFTED EDUCATION: INTEGRATION AND SERVICES

Although students with giftedness are not eligible for the protections and assurances of the Individuals with Disabilities Education Act, it is clear that they do have special educational needs. It is also reasonable to apply the basic tenets of IDEA to their needs. Two of the most basic tenets of that legislation are, as discussed in Chapter 1, the assurance that students will be educated in the most integrated setting that will meet their educational needs, and that a full array of educational placements and services will be available for those students who need them in order to meet their educational goals. Students who are gifted require these same assurances. Some may need services that require them to leave the general classroom at times during their school careers. The objective for most of these students should be, however, to meet their needs in inclusive school environments. The primary reasons for this objective are the same as those that have been discussed earlier concerning students with disabilities.

THE CLASSROOM TEACHER AT THE CENTER

The general classroom teacher is the central figure in the education of almost all children. This is the person who is essentially charged with dealing with the diverse needs and characteristics of most students. Other teachers may serve as consultants, team-teaching members, and resource personnel, but it is usually the classroom teacher who must coordinate these efforts. The efforts of classroom teachers not only promote the individual successes of each student but also promote in their students the skills and sensitivities that they need to be members of a heterogeneous society.

GIFTED STUDENT, GIFTED TEACHER

Must a teacher be gifted to effectively teach students who are gifted? Does a teacher have to be brighter and more creative in all areas than all of her or his students? If the answer to these questions were yes, then teachers would have to constantly be on the defensive to guard against being "shown up" by students. Teaching would be a continual struggle to maintain a superior posture in every way in regards to students. Fortunately, this is far from the truth about teaching in general and the teaching of students who are gifted in particular. Students with giftedness, like other students, when asked to describe an excellent teacher, will often respond with three descriptors:

- A great teacher is a person who loves to teach (loving the work of being a teacher).

- A great teacher is a person who loves what they teach (loving to share knowledge).

- A great teacher loves who they teach (genuinely caring about students).

The comments that can be elicited by asking students about bad teaching usually show an absence of these same three qualities.

In his book *Hard Times,* Charles Dickens created a school environment and an educator entirely lacking in these qualities. The character, Thomas Gradgrind, insists on a class setting that is "a plain, bare, monotonous vault of a schoolroom," and his philosophy of education is clear from the first paragraph of the novel:

> Now, what I want is, Facts. Teach these boys and girls nothing but Facts. Facts alone are wanted in life. Plant nothing else, and root out everything else. You can only form the minds of reasoning animals upon Facts: nothing else will ever be of any service to them. This is the principle on which I bring up my own children, and this is the principle on which I bring up these children. Stick to Facts, sir! (Dickens, 1868, p. 1)

In sharp contrast to this view of education and the role of an educator is a response that Albert Einstein wrote to a request from the National Council of Supervisors of Elementary Science that describes his perception of the role of the teacher:

> The most important thing for a teacher to impart to the children is not information and knowledge but rather a longing for information and knowledge and a respect for . . . values, be they of an artistic, scientific, or moral kind. To impart knowledge where a playful joy in thinking and curiosity over the facts and results of a school subject have not previously been awakened is directly harmful, for such teaching produces in the pupil a feeling of disgust just as eating when one has lost appetite produces a dislike for food. If, on the other hand, a lively interest once has been successfully stimulated, it will prove active beyond school and will increase the spiritual powers throughout life (Einstein, 1934).

WORKING WITH STUDENTS WHO ARE GIFTED: PROMOTING GROWTH

A few of the characteristics that help teachers work most effectively with students who are gifted are listed in Box 9.3. It must be emphasized, however, that the most important qualities of excellent teachers are those that are genuinely devoted to the growth of each student. As with all children, students with giftedness require compassion and understanding on the part of their teachers. Students who are gifted are likely to encounter problems in their school life just as students with disabilities encounter difficulties. The problems may be different, but they are just as real and require the same kinds of encouragement and support. Parke (1989) has provided four guidelines that may help teachers provide the kinds of help these students need.

BOX 9.3

Teacher Characteristics that Promote the Success of Students with Giftedness

- Intellectual openness.
- A joy for learning and for the learning of others.
- The security of feeling good about a student knowing more about a subject than the teacher.
- Appreciation for unconventional ideas and unusual solutions to problems.
- The ability to let students explore topics that are not a part of the planned curriculum.
- The willingness to allow students to progress at their own rate.

1. *Accept each student as someone having distinct capabilities.* In any classroom, there will be different kinds and degrees of student ability. Teachers who acknowledge this make a great contribution to students who are gifted. "Programs for these students must be considered within the context of appropriate programs for all students" in the classroom.
2. *Create "student-centered classrooms."* Students' needs ought to guide the decision-making process in the classroom. Students can and should be included as team members at the very center of this process, empowering them to be responsible participants in their own education.
3. *Design instructional models that respect the unique contributions of each student.* Use instructional methods that permit each student to participate in the education process at his or her own level of competence. Multiple methods for learning "accommodate the many ability levels within the classroom without designating who the slow and rapid learners are." These multiple approaches allow students to learn according to their own styles and at their maximum ability.
4. *Keep in mind that "gifted students are not 'better'; they are just 'different' in their abilities, needs, and interests."* Refrain from making value judgments of any student's ability. Avoid putting any student on a pedestal as an example for others to imitate. "They are students with their own needs and problems who require the same compassion and care as the other students in the class." Although they may have different needs, their needs are no less important than the needs of other students (Parke, 1989, pp. 14–15).

DIFFERENTIATION IN THE CLASSROOM

Differentiation within the curriculum of the classroom is an important strategy in promoting the success of students who are gifted. Differentiation is necessary because of three important characteristics of these students: 1) They often have interests that differ from those of other students, 2) They often have the ability to learn new information more rapidly than other students, and 3) They often have the ability and time to go into greater depth in the subjects that they study (Piirto, 1994).

The differentiation that is required for teaching students with giftedness must occur in several ways:

- *Differentiation as a Function of Interest*: Students who are gifted may be interested in the abstractions, concepts, and underlying themes rather than just the factual information concerning a subject. They should be allowed and encouraged to explore these interests.
- *Differentiation in the Rate of Learning*: Many students who are gifted are rapid, "one-shot" learners of factual information. These students should be allowed to move ahead at their own pace. It is not necessary for these students to engage in much repetition and practice to acquire basic information.
- *Differentiation in Depth*: Because the basic facts of subjects may be acquired very rapidly by students who are gifted, they may be encouraged to explore topics in greater depth.
- *Differentiation Through Independent and Guided Study*: The differentiations described above may be accomplished, at least in part, by allowing students who are gifted to explore their interests in greater depth and at their own pace through independent study that is guided by the teacher and/or a classroom consultant. The results of the student's independent study may also result in an enriched learning experience for other children through the sharing of findings (Piirto, 1994).

The kinds of differentiation just described can occur best in a classroom that is student-centered. Some of the characteristics of a student-centered classroom are described in Box 9.4. It is also important to emphasize that teachers must be prepared for and supported in their efforts to differentiate the curriculum for the benefit of students who are gifted. The stereotype of the classroom as a place where one teacher meets all of the needs of the entire class of students single-handedly must change. Team teaching, collaboration, and consultation must become commonplace in

BOX 9.4

A Student-Centered Learning Environment

- Each student is a partner in curricular decision making. Each student is allowed to participate in the scheduling of activities and may pick options for developing skills.
- Groupings for individual, small group, and whole group learning are facilitated. The teacher may move from group to group, to individual work, and to whole group activities during the day.
- It is expected that there will be a reasonable level of activity and noise. Students who are actively engaged in learning are not expected to be silent and stationary at all times.
- Individual plans are developed and executed for all students. These plans (similar to IEPs) are based on the abilities, achievements, and interests of the students.

Based on B. V. Parke. *Gifted Students in Regular Classrooms.* Needham Heights, MA: Allyn and Bacon, 1989, pp. 65–67.

schools. Classrooms must be viewed as places where students work together and actively participate in each other's education. Classrooms must be seen as places of cooperation rather than competition for all students (Sapon-Shevin, 1995).

FEMALE STUDENTS AND GIFTEDNESS

Although there have been dramatic changes in social attitudes toward the education of girls and women in the United States during the twentieth century, there are still problems of gender equity to be overcome. One of these is in the area of giftedness. A more subtle form of the educational philosophy expressed by Rousseau in the eighteenth century may still be influencing attitudes toward females and educational excellence. In his classic exposition on education, Rousseau addressed his ideal of the education of women:

> The good constitution of children initially depends on that of their mothers. The first education of men depends on the care of women. Men's morals, their passions, their tastes, their pleasures, their very happiness also depend on women. Thus the whole education of women ought to relate to men. To please men, to be useful to them, to make herself loved and honored by them, to raise them when young, to care for them when grown, to counsel them, to console them, to make their lives agreeable and sweet—these are the duties of women at all times, and they ought to be taught from childhood (Rousseau, 1979, p. 365).

Females are not represented in the gifted population at the level that would be expected. Callahan (1991) has identified a number of factors that may contribute to this underrepresentation. These include lower parental expectations for girls than for boys, the effect of stereotypes of male and female characteristics and roles, bias in educational practices, and the promotion of dependence rather than independence among girls. Silverman (1986a) has found, however, that when females have the opportunity to develop the beliefs, values and expectations that are encouraged in high-achieving males, they reach the same level of excellence. Silverman (1986b, 1988) also offers suggestions for providing greater educational opportunities for girls who are gifted. She recommends:

- Hold high expectations for the educational achievement of girls.
- Act on the belief in the logical and mathematical abilities of girls.
- Provide both boys and girls with positive female role models.
- Actively recruit girls for advanced placement in math and science.
- Encourage a wider range of interests and talents in girls.
- Pay greater attention to the use of nonsexist language in texts, class communication, and language in general.
- Provide support groups for girls.
- Encourage greater independence in girls.

STUDENTS WITH DISABILITIES AND GIFTEDNESS

Children who have disabilities and are also gifted are at a high risk for not being recognized for their talents. A student who has a hearing disability may have difficulty communicating her or his true abilities. The same may by true of a student with visual impairment or cerebral palsy. Students with learning disabilities may have difficulty demonstrating their true capabilities because of problems with writing or reading. Whitmore and Maker (1985) have estimated that there may be more than 150,000 students who have both disabilities and giftedness. Along with the need for improved recognition of girls, minority students, and students with socioeconomic disadvantages who are gifted, students with disabilities need to be viewed with care and sensitivity to the nurturance of their full potential.

EXCELLENCE AND EQUITY REVISITED

Durden and Tangherlini (1993) have observed that there has long been a debate in the United States over whether education should serve the overall needs of society or promote the achievement of excellence for the individual. They cite the famous debate between W. E. B. Du Bois and Booker T. Washington. While Washington promoted education as a means for millions of African-Americans to achieve economic independence, Du Bois argued for academic excellence for the "talented tenth" who would provide the leadership needed for greater equality and advancement.

There are proponents today of equity on the one hand and excellence on the other. The answer to the search for both, however, may lie in classrooms that welcome the strengths and needs of all children. Classrooms that are inclusive of students with giftedness and that teach them about their place among all other children may promote both excellence and equity.

Case Studies and Questions to Consider

STUDENT: MICHELLE KNEADLY

SCHOOL: HOPEFUL ELEMENTARY

CURRENT PLACEMENT: GENERAL CLASS/FOURTH GRADE

AGE: 9 YEARS, 6 MONTHS

Family Structure and Home Environment

Michelle lives in an apartment in a low-income housing project. She lives with her mother, Jacqueline Kneadly, who is twenty-six years old. Ms. Kneadly is a single parent and reports that she has no current information concerning Michelle's father. Ms. Kneadly is a graduate of Hopeful High School. She reported that, at present, she does not work outside her home.

Michelle also lives with her younger brother, Tony Ray Kneadly. Tony is two years old. Ms. Kneadly says that she has noted some jealous feelings on Michelle's part toward Tony. Ms. Kneadly feels that she has seen some dramatic changes in Michelle's home and school behavior since Tony was born.

Parental Perception of the Student's School Program

Michelle is now in the fourth grade but is doing poorly according to the grades she is earning.

Ms. Kneadly says that she has been concerned with Michelle's difficulties in school. Things seem to get worse each year. Ms. Kneadly has difficulty understanding Michelle's school problems. She has been told that her daughter has a high IQ, and every year she scores at the top of her class on the achievement tests that her school gives.

Michelle's mother feels that her daughter would benefit from more small group and individual instruction. She describes Michelle as having a short attention span. Ms. Kneadly says that she thinks that school has become frustrating for Michelle and that her daughter would benefit from some special attention and instruction. Ms. Kneadly also commented that she knew another child in their apartment building who had made progress after being "put in LD." She thinks this might help Michelle.

Although Ms. Kneadly thinks that Michelle has a high level of intelligence relative to other children of her age, she is not sure Michelle feels very good about herself and that this may be related to her poor performance in school.

Additional Comments

Ms. Kneadly says that she hopes her daughter will graduate from high school. She says after that, Michelle would have to decide for herself about college—"that should be her choice." She said that Michelle talks about wanting to be a teacher when she grows up. Ms. Kneadly said that she is most pleased with Michelle when she is able to settle down and do the work she is supposed to do in school. She wishes that happened more often.

Questions

1. Ms. Kneadly is suggesting that Michelle might have learning disabilities. What would you say to her on this issue?
2. What are the most important questions you would want to ask Michelle's teacher about her classroom behavior and work?
3. Are there factors in Michelle's life that particularly put her at risk for not having her "gifts" recognized? Do you think that it is likely that Michelle herself recognizes them?

STUDENT: BOBBY BETTS

SCHOOL: HOPEFUL HIGH SCHOOL

CURRENT PLACEMENT: NINTH GRADE

AGE: 14 YEARS, 8 MONTHS

Family Structure and Home Environment

Bobby lives with his parents, Harry and Susan Betts. Mr. Betts is thirty-seven years old and works as a factory manager. Ms. Betts is thirty-four years old and is employed as the registrar at Hopeful Valley Community College. Bobby also lives with his sister, Lisa, who is eleven years old. The Betts family lives in a house in an upper-middle-class residential development.

Parental Perception of the Student's School Program

Bobby has been having difficulty adjusting to being a student at Hopeful High School. Earlier in the year, he told his mother that he didn't have anyone to walk around school with, and she feels that this represented the loneliness he was feeling at his new school. Ms. Betts also said that Bobby has been having some strong feelings about being involved in the advanced classes there. She stated very frankly, "he doesn't want to be in the gifted track." She feels he is troubled by being in the program both because of social embarrassment and because it reminds him of an identity he would like to escape. She says that in elementary and middle school he was embarrassed to be thought of as a "brain."

Both Mr. and Ms. Betts are proud that Bobby has been on the honor roll on every report card received this year. They are concerned, however, that their son seems so unhappy and lonely. They have very mixed feelings about Bobby's continuing in the gifted track. They feel he needs the academic challenge of the track, but they are worried about his social and per-sonal feelings.

Additional Comments

The Betts have one goal for Bobby—that he continue to grow as a person and find the role that is best for him in life. They commented that for a long time they had hoped he would become an attorney. They no longer believe that this is consistent with his personality and talents. They now want him to find what will make him happy.

Questions

1. What further questions would you want to ask Mr. and Ms. Betts about Bobby's school program?
2. What questions would you want to ask Bobby about his feelings about being in the gifted track?
3. What would you want to discuss with Bobby's teachers that might help to improve the situation for him at Hopeful High School?

References

Baldwin, A. Y. "Gifted Black Adolescents: Beyond Racism to Pride." In M. Bireley and J. Genshaft (Eds.), *Understanding the Gifted Adolescent: Educational, Developmental, and Multicultural Issues.* New York: Teachers College Press, 1991: 231–239.

Callahan, C. M. "An Update on Gifted Females." *Journal for the Education of the Gifted, 14,* 1991: 284–311.

Clark, B. *Growing Up Gifted: Developing the Potential of Children at Home and at School.* 3d ed. Columbus, OH: Merrill, 1988.

Cox, J., N. Daniel, and B. A. Boston. *Educating Able Learners: Programs and Promising Practices.* Austin, TX: University of Texas Press, 1985.

Dickens, C. *Hard Times.* London: Chapman and Hall, 1868.

Durden, W. G., and A. E. Tangherlini. *Smart Kids: How Academic Talents Are Developed and Nurtured in America.* Kirkland, WA: Hogrefe and Huber, 1993: 1–9.

Einstein, A. "To National Council of Supervisors of Elementary Science," Einstein Papers, Princeton University, July 3, 1934.

Feldman, D. H. *Beyond Universals in Cognitive Development.* Norwood, NJ: Ablex, 1980.

———. *Nature's Gambit: Child Prodigies and the Development of Human Potential.* New York: Basics, 1986.

Friedman, H. S., J. S. Tucker, J. E. Schwartz, C. Tomlinson-Keasey, L. R. Martin, D. L. Wingard, and M. H. Criqui. "Psychosocial and Behavioral Predictors of Longevity: The Aging and Death of 'Termites.'" *American Psychologist, 50,* 1995: 69–78.

Gagné, F. "Toward a Differentiated Model of Giftedness and Talent." In N. Colangelo and G. A. Davis (Eds.), *Handbook of Gifted Education.* Needham Heights, MA: Allyn and Bacon, 1991: 65–80.

Gallagher, J. J. "Gifted Students and Educational Reform." In Ohio State Department of Education, *Challenges in Gifted Education: Developing Potential and Investing in Knowledge for the 21st Century.* Columbus, OH: State Department of Education, 1992: 21–27.

Heward, W., and M. Orlansky. *Exceptional Children: An Introductory Survey of Special Education.* New York: Macmillan, 1992.

Kassan, L., R. Subotnik, E. Summers, and A. Wassar. *Genius Revisited: High IQ Children Grown Up.* Norwood, NJ: Ablex, 1993.

May, W. F. *The Patient's Ordeal.* Bloomington, IN: University Press, 1991.

Milgram, R. M., and E. B. Goldring. "Special Education Options for Gifted and Talented Learners." In R. M. Milgram (Ed.), *Counseling Gifted and Talented Children: A Guide for Teachers, Counselors, and Parents.* Norwood, NJ: Ablex, 1991: 23–36.

Morelock, M. J., and D. H. Feldman. "Extreme Precocity." In N. Colangelo and G. A. Davis (Eds.), *Handbook of Gifted Education.* Needham Heights, MA: Allyn and Bacon, 1991: 347–364.

Parke, B. V. *Gifted Students in Regular Classrooms.* Needham Heights, MA: Allyn and Bacon, 1989.

Piirto, J. *Talented Children and Adults: Their Development and Education.* New York: Macmillan College Publishing, 1994.

PL 97-35, Education Consolidation and Improvement Act, sec. 582, 1981.

Ramos-Ford, V., and H. Gardner. "Giftedness from a Multiple Intelligence Perspective." In N. Colangelo and G. A. Davis (Eds.), *Handbook of Gifted Education.* Needham Heights, MA: Allyn and Bacon, 1991: 55–64.

Reis, S. M. "Reflections on Policy Affecting the Education of Gifted and Talented Students: Past and Future Perspectives." *American Psychologist, 44,* 1989: 399–408.

Renzulli, J. S., and S. M. Reis. "The Reform Movement and the Quiet Crisis in Gifted Education." *Gifted Child Quarterly, 35,* 1991: 26–35.

Rousseau, J. J. *Emile, or On Education.* New York: Basic Books, 1979. First published 1762.

Sapon-Shevin, M. *Playing Favorites: Gifted Education and the Disruption of Community.* Albany, NY: State University of New York Press, 1994.

———. "Why Gifted Students Belong in Inclusive Schools." *Educational Leadership, 52,* 1995: 64–67.

Schwartz, L. L. *Why Give "Gifts" to the Gifted?: Investing in a National Resource.* Thousand Oaks, CA: Corwin Press, 1994.

Shurkin, J. N. *Terman's Kids: The Groundbreaking Study of How the Gifted Grow Up.* Boston: Little, Brown, 1992.

Silverman, L. K. "Parenting Young Gifted Children." *Journal of Children in Contemporary Society, 187,* 1986a: 73–87.

———. "What Happens to the Gifted Girls?" In C. J. Maker (Ed.), *Critical Issues in Gifted Education: Defensible Programs for the Gifted.* Rockville, MD: Aspen, 1986b.

———. "Gifted and Talented." In E. L. Meyen and T. M. Skirtic (Eds.), *Exceptional Children and Youth.* 3d ed. Denver: Love, 1988: 281–283.

Snow, J. A. "Giftedness." In J. Pierpoint, M. Forest, and J. Snow (Eds.), *The Inclusion Papers: Strategies to Make Inclusion Work.* Toronto: Inclusion Press, 1992: 97–111.

Stevens, M. "School Reform and Restructuring: Relationship to Gifted Education." In Ohio State Department of Education, *Challenges in Gifted Education: Developing Potential and Investing in Knowledge for the 21st Century.* Columbus, OH: State Department of Education, 1992: 37–46.

Tom**linson, C. A.** "Gifted Learners Too: A Possible Dream?" *Educational Leadership, 52,* 1995: 68–70.

Tsuin-Chen, O. "Some Facts and Ideas About Talent and Genius in Chinese History." In G. Z. F. Bereday and J. A. Lauwerys (Eds.), *Concepts of Excellence in Education: The Yearbook of Education.* New York: Harcourt, Brace, and World, 1961: 392–401.

Webb, J. T., E. A. Meckstroth, and S. S. Tolan. *Guiding the Gifted Child: A Practical Source for Parents and Teachers.* Dayton, OH: Psychological Press, 1982.

Whitmore, J., and J. Maker. *Intellectual Giftedness in Disabled Persons.* Rockville, MD: Aspen Systems, 1985.

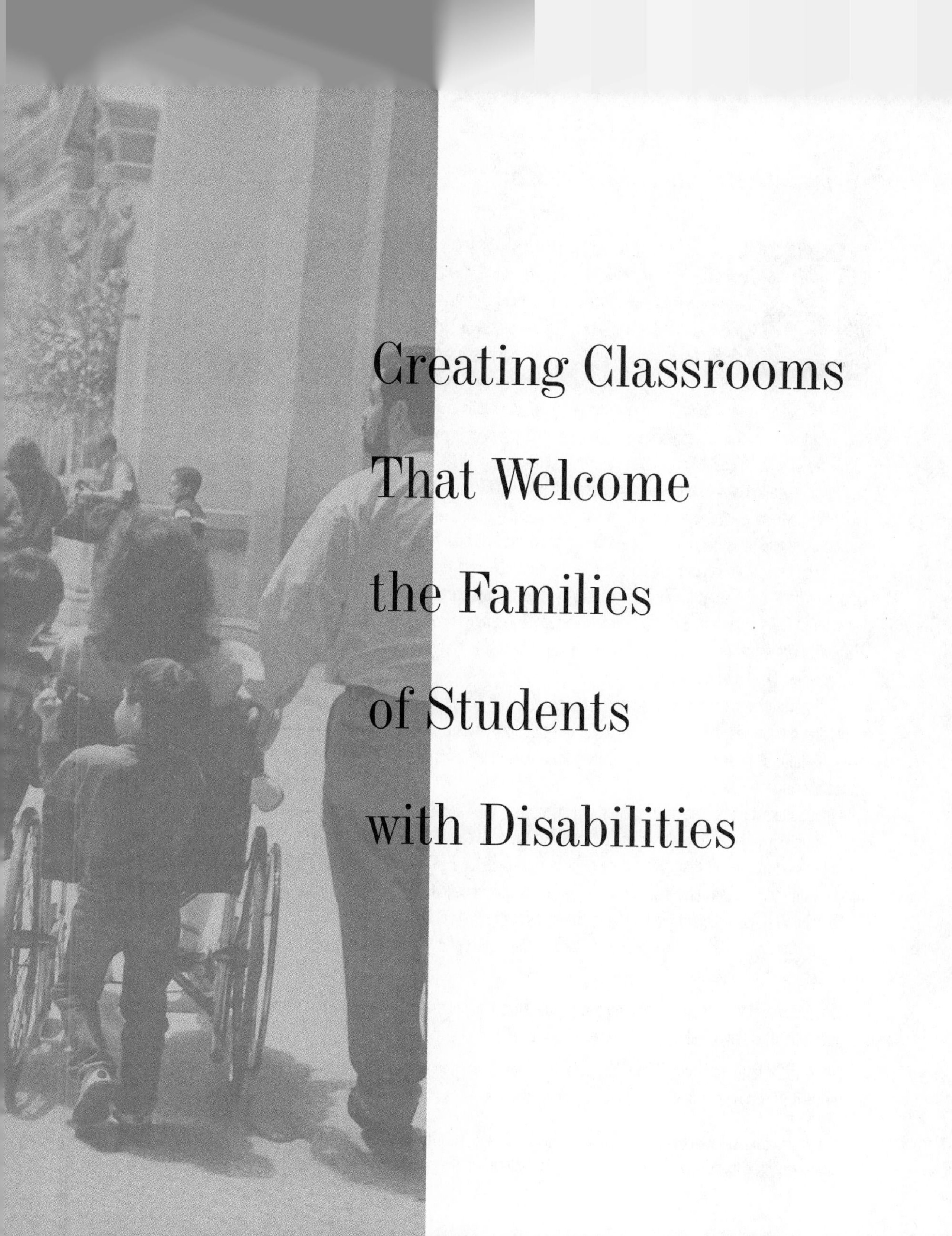

Creating Classrooms That Welcome the Families of Students with Disabilities

Pearl Buck and the Child Who Never Grew: Letters to Emma

Pearl S. Buck first captured the attention of the American public when her book, *East Wind, West Wind*, was published in 1930. In this novel, she portrayed the conflicts created by cultural change in China. She wrote the book with the authority of personal experience and actual observation. Pearl Buck grew up in China as the daughter of missionaries. In 1931, *The Good Earth*, a novel of Chinese peasant life, brought her increased fame. For that book, she won a Pulitzer Prize. For over forty years, Pearl Buck continued to be a prolific and respected writer. In 1938 she was awarded the Nobel Prize for literature.

In addition to her literary accomplishments, Ms. Buck was known for her humanitarian commitments. She worked diligently to foster racial tolerance and to promote the welfare of immigrants in the United States. She was a dedicated advocate for disadvantaged Asian people, particularly children. In 1941 she created the East and West Association. The goal of that organization was to promote greater harmony and understanding among people of different cultural backgrounds. In 1949 she founded Welcome House, an adoption agency for Asian-American children. She and Richard Walsh, her second husband and publisher, raised a large family of adopted children of diverse racial and ethnic origins.

Far less known about Pearl Buck is that her only biological child, Carol, had severe mental retardation. Although Carol was born in the early 1920s, Ms. Buck was reluctant to discuss her daughter publicly for many years. She finally told her story of Carol in an article in the *Ladies Home Journal* in May 1950. It was published that same year in book form as *The Child Who Never Grew*. Proceeds from both the book and the article went to the Vineland Training School in New Jersey, where Carol was a resident.

I have often quoted excerpts from *The Child Who Never Grew* in discussions with my students about the impact of disabilities on families. The beauty and candor of Pearl Buck's words in that little book are remarkable. Her observations and reflections allow people who are preparing to work with students with disabilities to have a glimpse of the emotional and intellectual turmoil that parents encounter in redefining their lives and the lives of their children with disabilities. It was with great interest and excitement, then, that I discovered that Pearl Buck had corresponded extensively concerning Carol with Emma White, her former classmate at Randolph-Macon Women's College in Lynchburg, Virginia. Upon examining those letters, I found that they told a story of pain, friendship, and growth. There is much to be learned from them about people with special needs and their families. The letters span a period from 1924 through 1963. They are all contained in the Pearl Buck Collection at the Randolph-Macon Women's College (Buck, 1924–1963).

In *The Child Who Never Grew*, Pearl speaks in retrospect of a time early in Carol's life when she was hoping to find a cure for her child's condition.

> One famous gland specialist gave me considerable hope and undertook a year-long treatment with dosages with gland medicine. It did my child no good (Buck, 1950, p. 20).

A 1924 letter to Emma White, however, illustrates how strongly Pearl's wish for a cure was coloring her perception of her child. This is a wish that must be felt by many parents.

> Things are going well with us. Carol is improving remarkably well and is trying to say everything. She is beginning to make up. We have every hope that she will be perfectly normal. Evidently it was the gland medicine she needed.

Two subsequent letters indicate that Pearl's hope for Carol's "normality" became tempered and, at last, faded.

May 7, 1927

Carol continues to develop steadily if not rapidly. We just take her as she is from day to day and enjoy and love her. She is a sweet child in many ways and easy to dwell on.

January 4, 1929

Carol progresses steadily at her own rate. She talks a good deal now and has developed a great deal since you last saw her but of course she is as she is. . . . Sometimes I can scarcely bear to look at the other children her age and see what might have been.

By 1930, Pearl had placed Carol at the Vineland Training School and had returned to Asia. Emma White continued to have an interest in her friend's daughter and sent Carol cards and presents. That year, Pearl wrote to Emma asking that she help her in monitoring Carol's well-being.

May 26, 1930

Your letter came the other day and I was so pleased to get it. You must not deny me the pleasure of writing a little note for Carol: it is one of the few things I can do for her now and my heart just rushes out to anyone who thinks of her. But you are one of the faithful ones and I love you for your fine loyalty and want you to know that you are dearer to me than any friend I have and like my own sister.

Emma if I send you money could you go to see Carol once or twice a year? . . . I don't want you to have any expense—I know you can't—but if you will tell me if you could spare the time I will furnish the money gladly. I trust your eyes and I want your opinion on her from time to time. Let me know if you could get away.

Emma accepted this responsibility. She journeyed at regular intervals to New Jersey from her Virginia home to check on Carol's welfare and progress. In 1931 Pearl began to make mention to Emma of the significance of her emerging literary success to Carol's future. It is clear that Carol's well-being was central to her financial aspirations.

March 1931

Success means much to me—most to me—because it is the beginning of the sum that still looms vast—of Carol's life annuity. If the success had come earlier, or if my life had been different as regards Carol, I think I would have been wildly thrilled. As it is, nothing means overwhelmingly much to me, since the fundamental inevitable for me must remain inevitable. But I have learned to accept that now, at least, and to be quietly grateful for any success which will mean removal of fear for Carol's protection and care. I shall be glad if you can see Carol this summer. I haven't the faintest idea what the trip will cost. I will send a $100 just as quickly now as I can get a gold draft from the bank. When you go stay at a private boarding house just across the street diagonally from the gates of the training school. It is cheap and clean. It is kept by a widow—really her home, but she has rooms and lodging.

May 2, 1931

I don't know yet how much money it will bring in—not enough still perhaps for Carol's life. How long a life can stretch ahead into the years! I wish I could know she would not outlive me—on the hope that we shall know each other beyond this life, how glorious a thing to know I shall see my precious child as I have never seen her here! But I only hope. I can't tell you what it means to me to have someone like you on which I can depend as on no one else, to do something regularly for her. So many promise and yet no one except you has kept on doing it. I do think faithfulness is the rarest quality in the world and one that is the most enduring.

Pearl and Emma corresponded frequently during 1931. Emma was obviously very supportive of Pearl in helping her to deal with her anxiety over being separated from her daughter and reassuring her about Carol's treatment at Vineland. One letter also contained Pearl's reaction to a question from Emma about discussing Carol publicly.

June 18, 1931

This morning your wonderful letter came from Vineland and I have read it aloud . . . and then have sat here for the last hour reading and rereading it and extracting from it everything I possibly could. It is exactly the sort of letter I hoped you would write and while parts of it bring me face to face again with the bitterest thing in my life—that Carol will never improve—still I have learned to face it pretty steadfastly on the whole. And your letter is so sane, so wise that it is the best I have had about her and next to my own eyes. . . .

I have just finished a letter to Dr. Johnstone [the superintendent of Vineland for many years] telling him your judgment on the school—how favorable it is, how this situation gratifies me . . . I am so glad you approved the choice of the school. I think we did the best we could under the circumstances. Your impression of the attendants in the cottage was my own.

Emma my dear I think I can't bear for you to mention Carol. Indeed I do not understand a publisher wanting such information about me—or information of any sort. At John Daly's request and to save myself from misinformation, I wrote a short sketch of my life. But I could not and cannot mention Carol. It's not a shame at all but something private and sacred, as sorrow must be. I am sore to the touch there and I cannot endure even too much of sympathy. Silence is best and far easiest for me. I suppose this is because I am not resigned and never can be. I endure it because I must but I am not resigned. So make no mention of her and so spare me. . . . Someday I shall write a novel which is to be literally a study in sorrow, and what it may do to a person.

By the latter part of 1931, Pearl seems to have become confident that she could make permanent provisions for Carol.

November 13, 1931

I am afraid I am beginning to measure all my friends by what they do for Carol—not money spent, but just remembering her and if they pass by Vineland, as many do often, stopping in and seeing her and writing me. I hope I can make a return someday to you.

When I come back next year I want to make all financial arrangements for Carol's lifetime, if we still feel Vineland is the place for her, as I suppose we will unless something new develops, then I shall feel safe about the child. *The Good Earth* has gone into translations now in German, French, Dutch, Spanish, Danish, Norwegian and Chinese pending, and I think there will be enough for all I want to do for Carol.

In August 1932, she described the arrangements she had made while visiting at Vineland.

August 15, 1932

Thank you so much for your letter which reached me at Vineland. By the way it is better not to address letters there to me, since it seems necessary for Carol's protection that it is not known that she is there. This is by Dr. Johnstone's request. You would be shocked if you knew how many idle curiosities there are about her, and how much trouble it is to keep her shielded. It is better not to tell people about her or where she is.

We have made life provisions for Carol there now. I have given money for the building and the upkeep of a cottage, to be called Carol's Cottage and she will have a room in it, and a bath and the porch. There will be a well-equipped playground with it, and a wading pool. I have made it as perfect as I could.

Carol seems well and happy and I am confirmed in my opinion of the spirit of the school. I believe and hope we have done the best for her.

Over the next several years, Pearl visited Carol frequently on her return trips from Asia. She usually arranged for an extended stay at Vineland. She wrote Emma often, reporting that she was pleased with the way that things had worked out for Carol there.

In 1935 Pearl divorced John Lossing Buck, and married Richard Walsh. They settled in a home in Bucks County, Pennsylvania. Her visits with Carol now became more frequent, and she regularly shared her impressions of her daughter's life with Emma.

November 3, 1938

Carol was home for a visit and better than she has ever been.

September 16, 1944

Carol was home for a visit for a while this summer, and we went to see her not long ago. She grows more quiet as she grows older, and while she does not improve markedly in mental development, she seems improved in other ways.

Carol is as usual and seems well. I have not been able to see her for the last few weeks because I have been away to Martha's Vineyard to escape hayfever (and did escape it) and now there is a ban on visitors to the school because of infantile paralysis.

December 1945

I see Carol regularly of course. She grows quieter as she gets older, otherwise is the same. We have her come home for a while every summer during the berry season, which she enjoys.

Perhaps the most intriguing letter within the collection of correspondence between Pearl and Emma was one written more than thirty-five years after Carol's birth. Contact between Pearl and Emma had become less frequent. Apparently in response to an inquiry concerning Carol's health or survival, Pearl wrote to Emma, giving an account of how well her daughter was doing and sharing the news that she had finally discovered what had caused Carol's retardation. Although Pearl's description of phenylketonuria (PKU) is not entirely consistent with our present understanding of the condition, it is sobering to consider the impact that this revelation must have had on her. She lived through a period when medical science moved from an almost complete lack of knowledge concerning PKU, to the possibility for detection and control. Simply knowing what caused Carol's disability may have brought some solace to Pearl.

August 6, 1959

First of all, let me say that Carol is very much alive and in fact is unusually well. The eczema which plagues her life seems to have abated for some reason. While we are speaking of her, I must tell you that we have at last discovered what makes her condition.

> She has phenylketonuria. This is an inherited inability to absorb essential proteins. Its presence is discovered through the urine. It is not present in my side of the family, for we have all had tests made. Her father has a brother who is affected. He has two normal children, and I suppose there must be a recessive gene somewhere in my side so that the result is something like RH factor. Carol seemed entirely normal at birth and for several months thereafter. This is usual in such a case, for the doctors say that the mother's elements protect the child for the first months after birth. In Carol's case, I noticed changes about the sixth month, or rather, my mother did. If the cause had been discovered in time, she would have been given injections and concentrated proteins and would have grown up entirely normal, although the injections would have had to be continued throughout her life. But after a year, it is too late. Doctors are now trying to get hospitals to make these tests on babies after the first few months in order to prevent brain damage.

Emma and Pearl continued to correspond with each other. Emma also continued to write to Vineland, not only cards to Carol, but letters to the employees who were responsible for her care. It seems that the staff kept her informed and even called upon her when there were problems. She was truly a devoted friend to both Pearl and Carol.

Pearl's letters to Emma strike me as markers on her journey toward a deeper acceptance of her daughter's life condition. Perhaps the most convincing evidence of her growing acceptance was the public statement she made in her account of Carol's life, *The Child Who Never Grew*. Her letters to Emma help us understand how she reached the point where she could write:

> So what I would say to parents is something I have learned through the years and it took me long to learn it, and I am still learning. . . . Be proud of your child, accept him as he is and do not heed the words and stares of those who know no better. This child has a meaning for you and for all children. You will find a joy you cannot now suspect in fulfilling his life for and with him. Lift up your head and go your appointed way. I speak as one who knows (Buck, 1950, p. 59).

Families in Change: New Roles, New Configurations

THERE HAS BEEN MUCH DISCOURAGing news concerning families in the United States in recent years. The effects on the family structure of divorce, substance abuse, poverty, violence, teen parenthood, and other social forces have been widely discussed. According to the Children's Defense Fund:

- A baby is born into poverty in the United States every 30 seconds.
- A baby is born in the United States every 59 seconds to a teen mother.
- A baby is born every two minutes in the United States to a mother who has had inadequate prenatal care.
- A baby is born every two minutes in the United States who has low birth weight.
- Every two hours a child is murdered in the United States (Children's Defense Fund, 1994).

One observer believes that even more important than the challenges to the American family structure mentioned above is the diminishing value placed on families in our culture. Popenoe (1993) argues that people have simply become less willing to invest time, money, and energy in family life. Reviewing data from the U.S. Census reports of the last thirty years, he cites indicators that families have lost power, practical functions, and authority because people have placed less value on the role of the family in their lives.

Wetzel (1990), however, emphasizes that families are shaped by the larger society and that for many years families have been buffeted by intense social and economic pressures. These forces have led to a diminishing number of children per family, shifting economic roles for family members, and an increase in the variety of definitions of *family*.

CHALLENGES FAMILIES FACE

Whether the sources of the changes in families are viewed as resulting from individual parental actions, societal changes, or some combination of factors, it is clear that these changes have created serious difficulties for many children. Radical changes in economics and demographics in the United States over the last three decades have placed an increasing number of children at risk for not receiving adequate care. These deficiencies have developed from the interactions of changes in the institution of the family and the fact that other social institutions have not responded adequately to these changes (Rosewater, 1989). Some of the most important of these factors are critical for teachers to be aware of in order to understand the home environments in which students live. These include changes in family composition and family work patterns, and the effects of increasing poverty.

FAMILY COMPOSITION

The "ideal" family has been persistently portrayed in the United States as a father, a mother, and their biological children living in harmony with clearly defined roles and relationships. This "Father Knows Best" portrayal has promoted the image for decades that "good" families that raise their children in "healthy" environments are composed of a working father, a mother who is a full-time homemaker, and several children. An analysis of the composition of American families for much of the twentieth century, however, reveals that prior

BARBARA RIES/PHOTO RESEARCHERS

to 1960 up to 34 percent of white children and 60 percent of African-American children lived in homes with only one or neither of their biological parents (Hernandez, 1994). Of course, these figures would include children raised in families with a stepparent and children of adoptive parents. Still, they indicate that the "typical" family of the past was not as typical as has been assumed.

The most dramatic change in families over the past few decades has been in the number of children living in one-parent families. During this period, sharp changes in the number of births to single mothers and rising rates of separation and divorce resulted in substantial increases in the proportion of children living with only one parent (Kitagawa, 1981). Births to unmarried women have increased 500 percent since 1960 (U.S. Department of Health and Human Services, 1990). This fact has also contributed to an increasing and persistent pattern of poverty among American children (Duncan and Rodgers, 1991).

POVERTY

The effects of poverty are felt by an increasing number of Americans (U.S. Bureau of the Census, 1992). These effects are most devastating for children. The following facts were revealed in the 1990 census:

- One of every five children in the United States lived in a family with an income below the federal poverty level.
- Almost thirteen million children lived in poverty. This was an increase of two million over the 1980 census. More than a third of these children lived in families with incomes of less than half the federal poverty level.
- The impact of poverty is greater for children in minority groups.
    - Approximately 44 percent of African-American children lived in poverty in 1990.
    - Over 30 percent of Hispanic children lived in poverty in 1990.
    - About 15 percent of white children lived in poverty in 1990.
- Poverty is more prevalent in one-parent families headed by a mother. Approximately 43 percent of these families lived in poverty in 1990 (National Commission on Children, 1991a).

The risks to physical, social, and psychological development that accompany poverty are well known. Hanson and Carta (1995) have noted that children living in poverty are at greater risk for premature delivery, low birth weight, and lead poisoning. They are also more likely to live in families that are under stress themselves and that may, therefore, be unable to offer the social support that children need in order to thrive.

EMPLOYMENT RESPONSIBILITIES AND DEMANDS

Another social change that has had an impact on families is the work patterns of parents. This change has made a significant difference in the lives of most families, even two-parent families. According to the Children's Defense Fund (1994), nearly two-thirds of all married women with children younger than six years old work outside their homes. When both parents work outside the home, the time and energy demands on those parents are increased. For some families, these demands are also heightened by the number of hours of work required to meet their economic needs. The National Commission on Children reports the following statistics:

- Fifty percent of fathers say they regularly work more than forty hours a week.
- Fifteen percent of mothers say they regularly work more than forty hours a week.
- Over 30 percent of heads of one-parent families (primarily mothers) report that they work more than forty hours a week (National Commission on Children, 1991b).

As the time and energy demands on families increase because of work schedules, the stress that parents encounter in providing adequate care, supervision, and support for their children may become a major challenge in their lives.

FAMILY DIVERSITY

It is critical that educators understand that every family is unique in the way it is organized and the way it attempts to meet the needs of its members. Generalizations about families, the responsibilities of their membership, their economic circumstances, and the demands that they face are of limited value. The diversity found in families is truly a strength that should be appreciated. Winton (1990) has identified the following areas of family diversity that are important for understanding and working with families:

- *Families Vary in Membership*: The "Norman Rockwell" family is now a minority in the United States. Alternative family structures are increasing, and they provide care and support for their members in varying ways.
- *Each Family Fulfills Certain Functions in Unique Ways*: Families find different ways of meeting the physical, economic, social, and emotional needs of their members. Understanding the various ways that families fulfill these needs may increase the appreciation educators have for the unique efforts that families make for the benefit of their members.
- *Families Vary in Needs and Resources*: Families define their needs and the resources they require to meet those needs in varied ways. What one family views as a necessity may be considered unnecessary by another family. Educators need to understand that family values differ and that values often determine what is viewed as a need.
- *Families Define Events in Different Ways*: Different families may react to the same event in very different ways. Just as individuals may be optimists or pessimists, families may interpret the meaning of events in the lives of their children in ways that are characteristic of their history and outlook (Winton, 1990, pp. 509–511).

Families of Children with Disabilities: A Special Challenge

PARENTS OF CHILDREN WITH DISABILITIES often encounter challenges added on to the usual (and substantial) responsibilities assumed by other parents. They are sometimes called upon to invest even more of their time, energy, and resources in the care and development of their children (Darling, 1991).

The birth of an infant or caring for a child with a serious illness can have a profound influence on relationships within a family. The presence of a newborn, for example, can dramatically change the relationship that a young couple has developed prior to becoming parents. A child who becomes ill with a sudden and serious illness may alter, at least for a while, the relationships of the parents to other children in the family. The impact of the birth of a child with a disability (for example, Down's syndrome) or the discovery of a disability in a child (for example, a learning disability) may have an even more powerful impact on a family.

STAGES OF PARENTAL RESPONSE

One of the most common parental reactions to the birth of a child with a disability is shock. Parents may be overwhelmed by the reality that the "expected" child is not the child who was born to them. A similar reaction can be experienced by parents who learn that their child has a disability later in her or his development. Parents may be shocked, for example, to learn that their child has an emotional disability. The shock of knowing that a child has a disability may be manifested in overwhelming feelings of grief, confusion, and anxiety.

Some observers of parental reactions have described a sequence of stages that parents may pass through as they move toward accepting the child they have instead of grieving for the child who was "expected." Beginning with a grief reaction and working toward acceptance of the child and the child's disability, the stages are:

- Shock
- Denial
- Sadness
- Anxiety
- Fear
- Anger
- Adaptation
  (Drotar et al., 1975)

The emotions and behaviors included in this model of the stages of parental response to having a child with a disability may be characteristic of some families. It is important, however, to recognize that not all parents experience every one of these stages of response. The sequence of the response may also vary. As pointed out earlier, families interpret events in different ways, respond to these events in different ways, and use varying resources in response to these events. This is as true for family responses to disabilities as it is for other challenges encountered in the life of a family.

A FAMILY LIFE CYCLE AND DISABILITY

Families progress through a family life cycle. In one sense, a family begins with the relationship of two people. When a couple has children, however, their relationship changes, and the focus of the family is broadened to include the needs of the children. As children grow, their needs change and parental responsibilities change accordingly. Finally, when adult children leave home, the relationship of the couple again changes.

One conception of the family life cycle describes seven points in that cycle:

- Couple
- Birth of Children and Early Childhood-Age Children
- School-Age Children
- Adolescent Children
- Young Adult Children
- Post-Parental Couple
- Aging Parents (Turnbull and Turnbull, 1990)

Each stage of the family life cycle brings its own demands and expectations. Parents are able to bear the responsibilities of the physical demands of caring for an infant because they expect that, when the stage ends, the diapering, sleepless nights, and drooling will also end. Parents who must be constantly vigilant of a young child's safety on the playground or on the street expect that eventually their child will be able to handle traffic and other dangers independent of their vigilance. Parents who endure the emotional storms of their adolescent children expect that this stage too will pass.

Families of children with disabilities may not experience the family life cycle in the same way as other families. Mallory (1986) has suggested that the presence of a child with a disability may cause a disturbance in the synchronization of the family life cycle. In other words, the timing of changes in parental roles and responsibilities may not be the same as in other families. The parents of a child with a severe disability may never reach the point in the timing of their family life cycle when diapering, feeding, and dressing are no long necessary. The parents of a child with autism may never feel confident that their adult child can live safely without support and supervision. The parents of a child with emotional or learning disabilities may need to provide help and encouragement to that child long after parents of other children the same age have experienced a relaxation of their parental responsibilities.

THE SPECIAL FAMILY: STRENGTHS AND POSITIVE OUTCOMES

Parents of children with disabilities experience greater stress than do parents of children without disabilities (Mahoney et al., 1992). The disturbances caused by a family life cycle that is out of synchronization may contribute substantially to this stress. In general, however, parents of children with disabilities find the resources they need to manage this stress (Dyson, 1991). Most professionals who have worked with children with disabilities, in

Linda Eber/Impact Visuals

SHAFFER PHOTOGRAPHY

fact, have stories of families that have been extraordinary in managing their special responsibilities. Some families actually appear to be stronger and happier because of their exceptional circumstances.

One such story was written by Christopher De Vinck. In his book, *The Power of the Powerless: A Brother's Legacy of Love*, he describes his experience of growing up in a large family with his brother Oliver, who was born with a disability.

> I grew up in the house where my brother was on his back in his bed for thirty-two years, in the same corner of his room, under the same window, beside the same yellow walls. He was blind, mute. His legs were twisted. He didn't have the strength to lift his head. . . .
>
> Oliver was born with severe brain damage which left him and his body in a permanent state of helplessness (De Vinck, 1988, p. 9).

De Vinck goes on, however, to explain that, although Oliver was helpless in one sense, he was powerful in another.

> Oliver still remains the most helpless human being I ever met, and yet he was one of the most powerful human beings I ever met.
>
> As a teacher, I spend many hours preparing my lessons, hoping that I can influence my students in small significant ways. Thousands of books are printed each year with the hope that the authors can move people to action. We all labor at the task of raising our children, teaching them values, hoping something "gets through" to them after all our efforts.
>
> Oliver could do absolutely nothing except breathe, sleep, eat and yet he was responsible for action, courage, insight.
>
> For me, to have been brought up in a house where a tragedy was turned into a joy, explains to a great degree why I am the type of husband, father, writer and teacher I have become (De Vinck, 1989, p. 12).

De Vinck goes on to describe the way that his entire family shared the responsibility for Oliver's care. All the children in the family helped with Oliver's daily needs, including feeding him. De Vinck also describes the impact that had on their lives.

> When I was a child I was afraid of the dark and shared a room with my younger brother. Our room was separated from Oliver's room by a single wall. Five inches of wood and plaster divided us from each other during the night. We breathed the same night air as Oliver . . . and slowly, without our knowing, Oliver created a certain power around us which changed

our lives. I cannot explain Oliver's influence except to say that the powerless in our world do hold great power. The weak do confound the mighty (De Vinck, 1989, pp. 13–14).

FAMILY RISKS

Even though many families respond with strength and cohesiveness to the needs of a child with a disability, there are risks to those families that educators need to understand. The following vulnerabilities are important to consider when attempting to understand the challenges families may have as they become aware that their children have special needs:

- *Experiences of Isolation*: Parents may feel that there is no one who understands what they are facing as a family with a child with a disability. A mother and father who have an infant with Down's syndrome, for example, may not know anyone else with a child with this condition. The support and encouragement that family and friends normally provide to new parents may not be forthcoming when the child has a disability.
- *Feelings of Loneliness*: Parents may feel loneliness associated with their isolation. They may be less socially active than before the birth of a child with a disability or the discovery of a disability. Parents of children with learning disabilities, for example, may feel left out and lonely when friends and family discuss the academic success and other accomplishments of their children.
- *Feelings of Confusion and Desperation*: Parents may feel confused about the causes of their children's disabilities and what they can do to best promote their children's development. They may be confused by the professional jargon used to describe their children's disabilities and needs. The parents of a child with cerebral palsy, for example, may feel that no one will give them an understandable reason for their child's disability. They may also feel that the professionals they encounter do not really try to help them understand what they can expect for their child in terms of an eventual level of independent living.

Supporting Families of Children with Disabilities as Active Members of the School Community

PARENTAL ATTITUDES TOWARD INclusive classrooms vary. This would be true, of course, of parents facing any important issue or decision concerning their children. Some parents of students with disabilities are strong advocates for inclusive classrooms. Others are skeptical about the creation of more inclusive schools. This skepticism is often based on fear that the movement toward inclusion will result in abandonment of the special services that their children need to optimize their chances of success in school and in life.

Many parents of students without disabilities also have strong feelings about the movement toward creating inclusive classrooms. Some of these parents feel that the inclusion of students with disabilities in regular classrooms will detract from the instruction their children receive. Other parents feel that greater diversity in classrooms has a positive influence on all of the students in these classrooms. The following statement from a parent who "volunteered" his twenty-month-old daughter for an inclusive preschool program illustrates the latter perspective:

> When I was young, a handicapped boy named Ralph lived down the street. Though he was ten years older than I, he liked to play with me and my friends. We loved Ralph, but our parents forbade us to play with him. Their severe demeanors communicated the message that we weren't to ask why. It wasn't until I was an adult, studying psychology in a university, that I understood Ralph's problems. Because my daughter's first school friends are special ones, she may understand handicapped persons in a way that I couldn't. Perhaps some day she can help her own friends understand children like Ralph. . . .
>
> Do I have second thoughts about placing my daughter in a classroom with handicapped children? I observe Kara each day and yes, I do. I feel grateful that she is having such a priceless experience. And I feel sorry that every child can't have the same opportunity (Giordana, 1982, p. 26).

LYDIA GANS/IMPACT VISUALS

This statement reflects a consistent argument made in support of the positive effects of inclusive classrooms for those students who do not have disabilities. Stainback and Stainback have emphasized the important role that inclusive classrooms can play in teaching students to work and play together. They also stress that such classrooms give students the opportunity to learn to "affirm and enjoy the beauties and inherent value of individual differences" (Stainback and Stainback, 1985, p. 10). Galant and Hanline quote parents who believe that the experiences of their children in inclusive classrooms have been positive in these regards.

> One parent shares her daughter's experiences: "She has become much more sensitive to others' limitations and needs. This sensitivity has caused her to look beyond her immediate self." And another parent states: "My daughter often talks about the children with special needs as if she is proud that she knows them" (Galant and Hanline, 1993, p. 295).

Some parents of students with disabilities speak out with misgivings about the movement toward more inclusive classrooms. They generally do so because they are concerned that greater inclusion may be accompanied by an abandonment of the commitment to the appropriate education promised their children under IDEA. The Learning Disabilities Association of America (LDA), for example, has spoken out vigorously against what has been called *full inclusion.* The interpretation given to this term and other related issues were discussed in Chapter 1. However, it is important to understand LDA's position and the concern that underlies it. The LDA is an organization of parents, professionals, and persons with learning disabilities. In a position statement on inclusion, the LDA stated:

> The Learning Disabilities Association of America does not support "full inclusion" or any policies that mandate the same placement, instruction, or treatment for ALL students with learning disabilities. Many students with learning disabilities benefit from being served in the regular classroom. However, the regular education classroom is not the appropriate placement for a number of students with learning disabilities who may need alternative instructional environments, teaching strategies, and/or materials that cannot or will not be provided within the context of a regular classroom placement.
>
> LDA believes that decisions regarding educational placement of students with disabilities must be based on the needs of each individual student rather than administrative convenience or budgetary considerations and must be the results of a cooperative effort involving the educators, parents, and the student when appropriate (Learning Disabilities Association of America, 1993, p. 594).

The statement goes on to describe the mandates under IDEA for:

- A free and appropriate public education in the least restrictive environment appropriate for the student's specific learning needs;
- A team-approved Individualized Educational Program (IEP);
- A placement decision made on an individual basis; and
- A continuum of alternative placements to meet the needs of students with disabilities.

The concerns of the LDA about what it perceives to be the call for full inclusion are summarized by this statement:

> LDA believes that the placement of ALL children with disabilities in the regular classroom is as great a violation of IDEA as is the placement of ALL children in separate classrooms on the basis of their type of disability (Learning Disabilities Association of America, 1993, p. 594).

Similar statements have also been issued by the Council for Learning Disabilities (1993) and the National Joint Committee on Learning Disabilities (1993). All of these statements focus on the concern that placement options and the full array of services needed by students with disabilities will be abandoned as general classrooms become more inclusive. As discussed in Chapter 1, however, such an abandonment would be a clear violation of the basic tenets of IDEA. Responsible efforts for the creation of more inclusive classrooms are based on the commitment to best serve the educational needs of students with disabilities. It is recognized that there will always be a need for the full continuum of placements and services for students who need them in order to achieve their individual potentials. Parents and educators must share this commitment.

PARENTS AND PROFESSIONALS: THE CRITICAL PARTNERSHIP

Parents of children with disabilities who have actually participated in inclusive classroom settings tend to have very favorable opinions about these classrooms (Miller et al., 1992). On the other hand, parents of students who are being reintegrated into general classrooms after having been served in special education programs are sometimes reluctant to have

BOX 10.1

Reasons Why Students with Disabilities Belong in Their Neighborhood Elementary School: A Parental Perspective

1. Families become a part of the "mini-community" that lives around and attends the neighborhood elementary school. In parenting a child with a disability, most families strive to make life "as normal as possible." Attending school with brothers and sisters is a "normal childhood experience."
2. Our children have developed real friendships with classmates at the neighborhood schools. They are invited to birthday parties, and called on the telephone. Friends come over to the house to play with our kids.
3. Students have made good academic gains while attending neighborhood schools.
4. These students feel positively about themselves and their abilities.
5. Simple adaptations in school programs promote physical adaptations such as improving print accessibility through enlarging reading or worksheets on the copy machine; allowing students to use the computer for written work; or adapting the amount of practice required.
6. Our kids have shown us that they learn best when trying to learn what their friends are learning.
7. Our children will always be interdependent on others for a decent quality of life. The ratio of typical students to students with significant disabilities mirrors that in the world at large. Our children are learning valuable lessons and gaining practice in how to "be a person with disabilities and succeed in the real world," and their classmates are learning lessons in helping others and being a part of a community.
8. Our kids are able to learn. They have the same needs for learning as any other students in their class.
9. A forced change of schools, based solely upon a child's disability, is discriminatory. A move could cause much harm to our children's self-esteem, causing learning difficulty.

Adapted from A. Q. Robinson and G. A. Robinson. "Integration—Don't Take It for Granted." *Exceptional Parent, 21*(6), 1991, p. 71.

their children in those classrooms. Their reluctance seems to be based on their appreciation of the caring attitudes of special education teachers rather than on issues of academic performance in special versus general education (Green and Shinn, 1993).

Parents want their children to be part of caring school communities. This fact is central to the purpose for creating more inclusive classrooms that are truly caring communities for all of their citizens. Robinson and Robinson (1991) have discussed the reasons that parents of students with disabilities want their children to be in the same schools and classrooms as their friends and siblings. Some of these reasons are summarized in Box 10.1.

A review of these reasons for parental support of inclusive schools reveals that most of them are related to social and personal development of their children. These factors, of course, also help promote academic growth. Parents can, and should, be active participants in the caring community of an inclusive classroom.

In order to encourage parents to become more active partners with educators in inclusive classrooms, it is important that parents believe that professionals understand the needs of "special families." Parents of students with special needs have often been bombarded with negative information about their children. They have been told *what's wrong* with their children. They have been told what their children need to do and what they as parents *need to do*. These parents need to hear *what's right* about their children. They also may be greatly encouraged by someone who recognizes that they have *needs* rather than hearing again what they *need to do*. Box 10.2 lists a few of the things parents have indicated were most helpful to them when said by a professional. A good rule of thumb for parent conferences and other parent-professional conversations may be to never let a parent go without saying something *positive* about their child. It is also good to remember to say something positive about the things the parent is doing for the child.

Kroth and Otteni (1983) have emphasized that parents of children with special needs bring both needs and strengths to their partnerships with schools. Parents usually know their own children best. They should be encouraged to collaborate and contribute in every way to the development, implementation, and evaluation of their child's educational program. Students move through educational systems, and their relationships with teachers change. The role of the family in a child's education, however, is a continuing commitment.

BOX 10.2

What Is the Most Helpful Thing A Professional Ever Said to You?: Parental Responses

- "It's not your fault!"
- "What do you need for yourself?"
- "I value your input."
- "Under the circumstances, you are doing the best you can do. Frankly, I don't know what I would do or how I would be able to carry on."
- "I agree with you."
- "Your son has made progress and I know he can do more, so we will continue to work with him."
- "I don't know. I can't tell you what's wrong with your child or what caused the problem."
- "There is a lot of love in your family."
- "You know, it's okay to take care of yourself too."
- "I don't know. I have to give that serious thought."
- "Believe in your instincts. You're the expert on your child."
- "You're being too hard on yourself."

Adapted from B. Stubbee. "Having Our Say." *Focal Point,* 4(2), 1990, p. 9.

CREATING A "PARENT-FRIENDLY" ENVIRONMENT

Waggoner and Wilgosh (1990) found that parents of children with disabilities describe some teachers as helpful, supportive, and flexible. They describe others as uncooperative, inflexible, and uninformed about disabilities. Overall, the positive qualities were attributed to teachers who were perceived to be making an effort to understand the needs of their children, to be accepting of the disabilities of their children, and to be communicating well with the parents.

Family-oriented teachers and schools can be very effective in helping to create inclusive classrooms that welcome the involvement of parents.

Dunst et al. (1991) classified human service programs and their family orientations in the following ways:

- *Professionally Centered*: This approach emphasizes the professional as the expert and the family as the consumer of this expertise.
- *Family-Allied*: In this approach, the family is enlisted to carry out the interventions that professionals prescribe for it.
- *Family-Focused*: In this approach, families also assist in choosing among the goals and strategies that professionals develop for them.
- *Family-Centered*: This approach emphasizes that professionals work for families

BOX 10.3

Developing "Parent-Friendly" Schools

- Create a school climate that's open, helpful, and friendly.
- Communicate clearly and frequently with parents about school policies and programs and about their children's progress.
- Treat parents as coworkers in the educational process.
- Encourage parents, formally and informally, to comment on school policies and to share in some of the decision making.
- Get every family involved, not simply those most easily reached.
- Make sure that the principal and other school administrators actively express and promote the philosophy of partnership with all families.
- Encourage volunteer participation from parents and other members of the community.

Adapted from School Improvement Council Assistance. "Creating 'Parent Friendly' Schools." *SICA News*. Columbia, SC: School Improvement Council Assistance, Fall 1995.

and work for them in ways that truly support and strengthen the family.

Trivette et al. (1995) have found that the family-centered approach is the most promising model for working with parents of young children with disabilities. Coupled with help-giving practices such as active listening by helpgivers, helpgiver honesty, trustworthiness, and other practices that encourage collaboration, this model may be an effective way of facilitating greater participation in inclusive classrooms. Box 10.3 presents some suggestions for helping to create more family-centered, "parent-friendly" schools.

PARENTS AS ADVOCATES

The concept of inclusion involves some basic underlying assumptions. Some of these assumptions are listed in Box 10.4. The philosophy of inclusion assumes that all people have equal and inherent value, and that they should be included in society and schools without regard to their differences. Families have an important advocacy role in helping to ensure this right for their members. Educators need to be aware of, and in some cases join with, the various advocacy roles that families assume. Alper, Schloss, and Schloss have described the following types of advocacy that family members may be involved with:

- *Self-Advocacy*: Families may teach children with disabilities to speak and act on their own behalf to improve the quality of their lives in schools and society.
- *Social Support Advocacy*: Families may work in the community to improve attitudes and change specific conditions that have an impact on the lives of their children with disabilities.
- *Interpersonal Advocacy*: Families may intervene with the providers of services to their children with disabilities (for example, through parent-teacher conferences and IEP meetings).
- *Legal Advocacy*: Families may intervene legally to be certain that the state and federal protections and rights of their children with disabilities are honored (Alper, Schloss, and Schloss, 1995).

Parents who become advocates for inclusive classrooms for their children can be the strongest voices for greater diversity in schools. They should be encouraged to become involved in every aspect of the life of the school. They should also be kept informed of changes in the school that may have an effect on the inclusiveness of their children's school life. Robinson and Robinson (1991) have discussed some of the changes in schools that may warrant a parent's attention in terms of possible impact on the inclusiveness of a child's experience in those schools (see Box 10.5).

THE FAMILY: OTHER CONSIDERATIONS

Families are diverse and complex social institutions. There are family facets and variables that are too numerous to discuss in this text. A few other aspects of families, however, deserve the consideration of educators as they work with these families toward the creation of more inclusive classrooms and schools.

Siblings of Children with Disabilities

Brothers and sisters may play an important role in the life of a person with a disability. They may serve at various times and in varied ways as advocates, models, and tutors for their siblings. They may also be called upon by parents to assume caregiver roles that other children may not be expected to assume.

McLoughlin and Senn (1994) have pointed out that siblings of children with disabilities may also have special needs. They may need, for example, information about their sibling's disabilities. They may need emotional support and encouragement from parents and professionals. They may also need training in the best ways they can help their brothers and sisters in academics, communication, or self-care skills.

Grandparents of Children with Disabilities

The most recent census figures show that approximately three million children in the United States live in their grandparents' homes. Almost 900,000 of them live with grandparents without the presence of a parent (Smolowe and Ludtke, 1990). Grandparents, then, are caregivers for many of the children in our schools. Teachers of children with disabilities are likely to encounter grandparents who are the primary caregivers and advocates, and who need to be treated with the same consideration as parents. They may also fulfill the same role in classroom collaboration that have been described for parents (Bell and Smith, 1996).

Grandparents may also serve an important supportive role for parents who are the primary caregivers for children with disabilities. Sherrill (1994) has discussed the important kinds of support that a grandparent may provide the parents of a child with special needs:

> We are learning the role grandparents can play in this situation. Certainly, support of the child's parents is first. Since children with disabilities often require more services from the medical field than nondisabled

BOX 10.4

Exclusion and Inclusion: Underlying Assumptions

Among the underlying assumptions for exclusion are:

- We are not all equal in capacity or value.
- It is not feasible to give equal opportunities to all people.
- We must identify and train an "elite" who will care for "the rest."
- All will benefit from the "trickle-down" from the accomplishments of the "elite."

Among the underlying assumptions for inclusion are:

- We are all equal in value, and we all have unique capacities.
- All people can learn.
- All people have the potential to make contributions.
- All people deserve the opportunity to make a contribution.
- The criterion for inclusion is not intellectual ability, physical or emotional condition, race, gender, or language—it is simply being human.

Adapted from A. Condeluci. *Interdependence: The Route to Community.* 2d ed. Winter Park, FL: GR Press, 1995, p. 201.

BOX 10.5

Changes That May Have an Impact on the Inclusive Education of a Student with a Disability

Changes in School Administration: Principals, special education directors, and superintendents create the overall attitude and atmosphere for inclusion. When changes in these positions occur, parents should determine the views of new administrators on inclusion.

Changes in School Budget: Tight economic times and budget reductions can influence the placements of students with special needs. Parents need to be aware of the impact of changes in school budgets on practices concerning students with disabilities.

Changes in School Level: As students with disabilities move from elementary to middle schools and from middle schools to high schools, the types of placements available to them may change. Parents should understand and influence the options available for their children before these transitions occur.

Changes in Grade: Teachers at some grade levels may be more or less open to and knowledgeable about inclusive practices. Parents should be active in the selection of the classrooms to which their children are "promoted."

Teacher Changes: Teachers vary in their attitudes toward and skills for creating inclusive classroom environments. Parents need to be aware of and involved in the choice of teachers for children with special needs. They also need to be involved when teacher assignments change during a school year due to illness, pregnancy, or other factors.

Adapted from A. Q. Robinson and G. A. Robinson. "Integration—Don't Take It for Granted." *Exceptional Parent, 21*(6), 1991, p. 74.

children, grandparents can often provide some financial assistance. They can also provide the emotional support and love their children have come to know and trust. And they can show their children that they love and accept their grandchild.

Finally, grandparents need to give their children time to work through the grief in their own private lives.

In addition, grandparents and other family members must learn how to treat a child with a disability. Most important, they must treat that child just as they would any other grandchild, giving him or her the same amount of attention and gifts as other children in the family. The child with a disability should become "just another member of the family" (Sherrill, 1994, p. 12).

THE EXCEPTIONAL FAMILY

The family with a child with special needs becomes a "special family." Whether it is special because of its needs, its strengths, or both, educators must work with these families to best meet the needs of their exceptional students. Through collaborative efforts and shared understandings, parents and teachers have the best chance of creating more inclusive classrooms.

Case Studies and Questions to Consider

STUDENT: MARTHA CHILD

SCHOOL: NURTURING ELEMENTARY

CURRENT PLACEMENT: REGULAR FIFTH GRADE

AGE: 12 YEARS, 7 MONTHS

Family Structure and Home Environment

Ms. Child is concerned that her daughter is not progressing well in school. She feels that Martha requires special services to enable her to achieve her academic potential.

Ms. Child is a single adoptive parent. She has earned degrees in nursing and in counseling. Presently, she is employed as a substance abuse counselor. She became Martha's mother a little over two years ago. Ms. Child has no information on her daughter's biological parents. Prior to her adoption, Martha lived in Bogotá, Colombia. She had apparently fended for her-self on the streets for some time there. Ms. Child has indicated that when she adopted Martha, she was living in Nebraska. Martha attended school there for only a few weeks. They then moved to their new home in a townhouse in the Washington, D.C., metropolitan area.

Martha is now a resident of the Helping Home, a foster care facility for troubled families. Ms. Child indicates that there were difficulties in their relationship, which made it best for Martha to live in the Helping Home. She also explains that Martha has a fear of abandonment that complicates close relationships for her. She constantly tests relationships in very disturbing ways.

Parental Perception of Developmental Progress and Needs

Martha has been having difficulties in social relations with her classmates. She is also described by her teacher as being very negative and, at times, hostile. Ms. Child asserts her opinion that it is the school, not Martha, that has a problem. She believes that her daughter has not been provided the kind of assistance she needs in order to meet the challenges she faces as an adopted South American child in a mainstream U.S. classroom. When asked for an example of the kind of help she felt Martha should have, she cited instruction in English as a second language.

Ms. Child feels that Martha's self-image suffers as a result of her comparing her academic skills to those of the other fifth graders she encounters each school day. She says that there is no evidence that Martha had any formal schooling while she lived in South America. Accordingly, she feels that Martha has actually done remarkably well in the two years she has been attending American schools. She feels, however, that Martha thinks of herself as being "stupid" relative to the abilities of other children her age.

Additional Considerations

Ms. Child views her daughter's social behavior as being typical of other twelve-year-old girls. The only areas where she feels that Martha may have deficits are those related to self-concept. She added that social skills related to language are more likely problematic for Martha than for the typical child of her age.

The primary goal that Ms. Child has for Martha is that she grow up to be a person with feelings of positive self-worth. She said that what pleases her most about Martha is her seemingly irrepressible will to live and learn.

Questions

1. Should Martha be evaluated for special education services?
2. What other assistance might be helpful for Martha?
3. What kind of help might be beneficial for Ms. Child?

Student: Dustin Luke
School: Hopeful Elementary
Current Placement: Kindergarten
Age: 5 years, 8 months

Family Structure and Home Environment

Dustin lives in a very pleasant home with his parents, James and Debra Luke; his brother Barry, who is ten; and his brother Tim, who is thirteen. Mr. Luke is thirty-four years old and has a management position at the Ironworks Foundry. Ms. Luke is thirty-two years old and is a patient services representative at Hope Valley Hospital. Mr. Luke is a graduate of American Business College. Ms. Luke completed one year of study at the Community College of Hope Valley.

The description that Ms. Luke gives of Dustin's relationships with his brothers is reflective of a typical six-year-old boy with brothers. The boys apparently have the regular misunderstandings and disagreements usual for their ages. Dustin's mother feels, however, that overall, the boys have a positive relationship.

Mr. and Ms. Luke have created a supportive and warm environment for their boys. They not only provide books, toys, and activities that are appropriate for the encouragement of their children's educational development, but they also invest their time and energy toward that end.

Parental Perception of the Student's School Program

Ms. Luke is concerned about Dustin's difficulty in following directions, his problems in understanding his teachers, and his apparent inability to keep up with other students in his class. According to his teachers, Dustin has problems staying on task with his work at school and has experienced significant social difficulties. Ms. Luke reports that it did not come as a great surprise to her when Dustin experienced difficulties in kindergarten. She feels that she has noted developmental differences in him all along due to his prematurity and considerably low birth weight. She feels that his fundamental problem is his short attention span. Ms. Luke believes that Dustin is a very intelligent child but that his poor performance in school is a direct result of his attention deficit. She thinks that one-to-one instruction in the skills that are most difficult for Dustin would be very helpful.

Dustin's mother reports that he has reacted well to the recent news that he will be retained in kindergarten next year. She says that he speaks of having failed kindergarten but that he also talks confidently of doing better next year. Dustin apparently continued to have a positive attitude toward school even as his performance difficulties increased. He appeared to his mother to always leave for school looking forward to the day. Her recollection was that he had missed only four or five days during the school year and that these were due to his chronic problems with asthma.

Dustin's mother refers to him as a "people person." She feels that he has strength in his ability to relate well with other people. She is also pleased with him being a very expressive and affectionate child. She hopes, however, that Dustin will be able to calm down and function better in school in the future.

Additional Comments

Dustin Luke lives in a positive and accepting family environment. His parents are pleased that, in many areas of his life, he is developing as a capable and happy child. Mr. and Ms. Luke are apparently committed to doing everything they can to help him grow in those areas where he needs assistance in order to more fully realize his potential.

Dustin's teacher also feels that he has the potential to do well in his work at school. She describes him as being developmentally young. She says that she often has the impression that he was simply not ready for many of the tasks he encountered in kindergarten. In her opinion, he will be more mature and ready for school next year.

Questions

1. Dustin's parents wonder if he should be placed in a summer program for tutoring to better prepare him for repeating kindergarten. What would be your advice to them?
2. Based on the information available, should Dustin receive any special education services next year?
3. What activities might be helpful in preparing Dustin for repeating kindergarten with a new, and younger, group of children?

References

Alper, S., P. J. Schloss, and C. N. Schloss. "Families of Children with Disabilities in Elementary and Middle School: Advocacy Models and Strategies." *Exceptional Children, 62*(3), 1995: 261–270.

Bell, M. L., and B. R. Smith. "Grandparents as Primary Caregivers: Lesson in Love." *Teaching Exceptional Children, 28*(2), 1996: 18–19.

Buck, P. S. *The Child Who Never Grew.* New York: John Daly, 1950.

———. Letters to Emma White. Pearl Buck Collection, Lipscomb Library. Lynchburg, VA: Randolph-Macon Women's College, 1924–1963.

Children's Defense Fund. *The State of America's Children, 1994.* Washington, DC: Children's Defense Fund, 1994.

Condeluci, A. *Interdependence: The Route to Community.* 2d ed. Winter Park, FL: GR Press, 1995: 201.

Council for Learning Disabilities. "Concerns About the Full Inclusion of Students with Learning Disabilities in Regular Education Classrooms." *Journal of Learning Disabilities, 26*(9), 1993: 595.

Darling, R. "Initial and Continuing Adaptation to the Birth of a Disabled Child." In M. Seligman, Ed., *The Family with a Handicapped Child.* 2d ed. Boston: Allyn and Bacon, 1991: 55–91.

De Vinck, C. *The Power of the Powerless: A Brother's Legacy of Love.* New York: Doubleday, 1988.

Drotar, D., A. Baskiewicz, N. Irwin, J. Kennell, and M. Klaus. "The Adaptation of Parents to the Birth of an Infant with a Congenital Malformation: A Hypothetical Model." *Pediatrics, 56,* 1975: 710–717.

Duncan, G. J., and W. Rodgers. "Has Children's Poverty Become More Persistent?" *American Sociological Review, 56*(4), 1991: 538–550.

Dunst, C. J., C. Johnson, C. M. Trivette, and D. Hamby. "Family-Oriented Early Intervention Policies and Practices: Family Centered or Not?" *Exceptional Children, 58,* 1991: 115–126.

Dyson, L. "Families of Young Children with Handicaps: Parental Stress and Family Functioning." *American Journal on Mental Retardation, 94,* 1991: 250–258.

Galant, K., and M. J. Hanline. "Parental Attitudes Toward Mainstreaming Young Children with Disabilities." *Childhood Education, 69*(5), 1993: 293–297.

Giordana, G. "Would You Place Your Normal Child in a Special Class?" *Teaching Exceptional Children, 15*(2), 1982: 95–96.

Green, S. K., and M. R. Shinn. "Parent Attitudes About Special Education and Reintegration: What Is the Role of Student Outcomes?" *Exceptional Children, 61*(3), 1993: 269–281.

Hanson, M., and J. Carta. "Addressing the Challenges of Families with Multiple Risks." *Exceptional Children, 62*(3), 1995: 201–212.

Hernandez, D. J. "Children's Changing Access to Resources: A Historical Perspective." *Society for Research in Child Development Social Policy Report, 8*(1), 1994: 1–23.

Kitagawa, E. M. "New Life-Styles: Marriage Patterns, Living Arrangements, and Fertility Outside Marriage." *Annals of the American Academy of Political and Social Science, 45,* 1981: 1–27.

Kroth, R., and H. Otteni. "Parent Education Programs that Work: A Model." *Focus on Exceptional Children, 15,* 1983: 1–16.

Learning Disabilities Association of America. "Position Paper on Full Inclusion of All Students with Learning Disabilities in the Regular Classroom." *Journal of Learning Disabilities, 26*(9), 1993: 594.

Mahoney, G., P. O'Sullivan, and C. Robinson. "The Family Environments of Children with Disabilities: Diverse But Not So Different." *Topics in Early Childhood Special Education, 12*(3), 1992: 386–402.

Mallory, B. J. "Interactions Between Community Agencies and Families Over the Life Cycle." In

R. R. Fewell and B. F. Vadasy, Eds., *Families of Handicapped Children: Needs and Supports Across the Life Span.* Austin, TX: Pro-Ed, 1986: 317–356.

McLoughlin, J. A., and C. Senn. "Siblings of Children with Disabilities." In S. Alper, P. J. Schloss, and C. N. Schloss, Eds., *Families of Students with Disabilities: Consultation and Advocacy.* Boston: Allyn and Bacon, 1994: 95–122.

Miller, L. J., P. S. Strain, K. Boyd, S. Hunsicker, J. McKinley, and A. Wu. "Parental Attitudes Toward Integration." *Topics in Early Childhood Special Education, 12*(2), 1992: 230–246.

National Commission on Children. *Beyond Rhetoric: A New American Agenda for Children and Families.* Washington, DC: U.S. Government Printing Office, 1991a.

———. *Speaking of Kids: A National Survey of Children and Parents.* Washington, DC: National Commission on Children, 1991b.

National Joint Committee on Learning Disabilities. "A Reaction to Full Inclusion: A Reaffirmation of the Right of Students with Learning Disabilities to a Continuum of Services." *Journal of Learning Disabilities, 26*(9), 1993: 596.

Popenoe, D. "American Family Decline, 1960–1990: A Review and Appraisal." *Journal of Marriage and the Family, 55*(3), 1993: 527–542.

Robinson, A. Q., and G. A. Robinson. "Integration—Don't Take It for Granted." *Exceptional Parent, 21*(6), 1991: 71, 74.

Rosewater, A. "Child and Family Trends: Beyond the Numbers." *Proceedings of the Academy of Political Science, 37*(2), 1989: 4–19.

School Improvement Council Assistance. "Creating 'Parent Friendly' Schools." *SICA News,* Fall 1995: 1, 4.

Sherrill, D. "A Grandfather's Perspective . . . A Child with a Disability Is Born into Our Family." *CEC Today,* December 1994: 12.

Smolowe, J., and M. Ludtke. "To Grandmother's House We Go." *Time, 136*(20), November 5, 1990: 86–88.

Stainback, S., and W. Stainback. *Integration of Students with Severe Handicaps into Regular Schools.* Reston, VA: Council for Exceptional Children, 1985.

Stubbee, B. "Having Our Say." *Focal Point, 4*(2), 1990: 9.

Trivette, C. M., C. J. Dunst, K. Boyd, and D. W. Hamby. "Family-Oriented Program Models, Helpgiving Practices, and Parental Control Appraisals." *Exceptional Children, 62*(3), 1995: 237–248.

Turnbull, A., and H. R. Turnbull. *Families, Professionals, and Exceptionality: A Special Partnership.* Columbus, OH: Merrill, 1990.

U.S. Bureau of the Census. "Poverty in the United States, 1991." *Current Population Reports.* Series P-60, 181. Washington, DC: U.S. Government Printing Office, 1992.

U.S. Department of Health and Human Services. *National Center for Health Statistics of the United States, 1988. Volume 1: Natality.* Washington, DC: U.S. Government Printing Office, 1990.

Waggoner, K., and L. Wilgosh. "Concerns of Families of Children with Learning Disabilities." *Journal of Learning Disabilities, 223*(2), 1990: 97–98, 113.

Wetzel, J. R. "American Families: 75 Years of Change." *Monthly Labor Review, 113*(3), 1990: 4–13.

Winton, P. "Families of Children with Disabilities." In N. Harry, L. McCormick, and L. Haring, Eds., *Exceptional Children and Youth.* 6th ed. New York: Macmillan, 1990.

Inclusive Schools and the Full Spectrum of Human Diversity

Aunt Celie and the Marble Cake

Race issues continue to create dilemmas for our society and for our schools. At times it seems that racism and racial conflict have increased rather than decreased in recent decades. As evidenced by the publication of *The Bell Curve*, arguments for racial differences in intellect and other human attributes continue to be presented and enveloped in the mantle of science. I offer here a few recollections and reflections on race. They are given in a spirit of concern and hopefulness. They are intended as appeals for the dignity and respect for all people that must characterize American education if it is to achieve its potential.

One of the most vivid memories I have from my childhood is of a trip to Alabama when I was seven. The trip was a visit with my mother's family in Montgomery. It was my second rail pilgrimage from Virginia to Alabama. The first was when my brother Carl was an infant and I was four. I have no recall at all of that visit. The second time, probably because of their *vivid* recollection of having traveled with me as a four-year-old, my parents decided to leave Carl, now that age, at home with relatives. I remember, and relish even now, the excitement of sleeping in the Pullman car and eating in the dining car. Even more exciting was having the conductor acknowledge our special status. We were traveling on a free pass because my father worked as a machinist in the Norfolk and Western Railway Shops. I even had a chance to ride with the engineer for a few precious minutes.

I also remember so clearly changing trains in Birmingham, the colossus of the passenger station there, and riding a new coach the last leg of the trip into Montgomery. A vendor passed through the car selling sandwiches and snacks from a large metal box. The image of the cardboard cone of shelled peanuts my mother bought and shared has remained with me now for more than four decades.

Arriving in Montgomery on the hot summer night was a sleepy blur for me as a seven-year-old. I remember only that my Uncle Ray picked us up in a big, black boat of a car. We made a quick stop at my grandmother's house. It was late, and we soon went on to Uncle Ray's house for something to eat and to bed.

The next morning was devoted to a real visit with my grandmother and a stop at the firehouse where my uncle worked. Wearing his fireman's hat, ringing the bell on the hook and ladder truck, and blowing the siren for just a second—these are the sorts of things that childhood memories are supposed to be made of. That afternoon, however, was to grant me another kind of memory, a memory that would echo through the rest of my life.

My mother had often talked with me about a woman she called Aunt Celie. I knew Celie was an African-American woman who had been very kind to my mother when she was a little girl. I had heard many times descriptions of how Aunt Celie brushed my mother's hair and told her stories of her own childhood. My mother also frequently recounted for me the fact that Celie had been a slave when she was a very young child. Somehow, however, this had not found a special register in my mind and had made no particular impression on me.

That afternoon in Montgomery we went to Aunt Celie's home. My perceptions of her, of my mother, and of human relationships were changed profoundly as a result of that visit. When we drove up to Aunt Celie's house in Uncle Ray's Buick, my mother could not wait to get out of the car. Her feet were barely on the sidewalk when she was met by squeals of laughter and delight from Celie and her daughter, Agnes. Soon my mother was squealing also. There were lots of hugs all around, and repeatedly I heard an ancient, thin voice crying, "My baby, my baby." Before I realized what was happening, I was out of the Buick myself and unexpectedly in the embrace of Aunt Celie. She was the oldest person I had ever touched. She squeezed me to her bony and wrinkled body. She was immaculately groomed, and she wore a starched white apron over her Sunday dress. Aunt Celie smelled of talcum powder, and her bare hands felt like fine leather gloves. Soon Agnes joined in the hugging, and the two of them alternated with choruses of "It's Joyce's boy! It's Baby's boy!" I felt absolutely overwhelmed. I also felt like a celebrity.

Soon we were inside the house. Other people, young and old, male and female, all African-American, moved self-consciously in and out of the living room where we sat with Aunt Celie and Agnes. My impression was that all of these people were being headquartered in the kitchen and that each person was assigned his or her turn to come out and be introduced. There were lots of "Growin' like a weed," "Hasn't changed a bit," and "Law me!" I was stunned by it all. Never before had I been so physically close to so many African-American people. I had just been smothered with embraces from two black women out on the sidewalk, and now I was sitting in their home being introduced to what seemed like an army of other black people appearing from their kitchen.

As I remember it, Agnes had a deep, rich voice, and she was soon insisting that we must all have a "little something" to eat. Almost immediately, it seemed to me, the army of people, now all introduced, were streaming from the kitchen with coffee, cake, and lemonade. The cake was cut in thick slices. It was a marble cake, apparently a special treat prepared for my mother. It was served first to her, then my father, uncle, and grandmother; then Agnes brought a piece of cake, a big piece, for me.

I sat silent, confused and afraid with the cake, plate, napkin, and fork balanced on my lap. It seemed to me that everyone in the room was watching and waiting for me to take a bite of the cake. I could not move. I felt frozen. I knew that I couldn't lift the cake to eat it, and I was frightened that if the plate started to slide off my lap I wouldn't be able to move my hand to stop it. "Take just a bite," "Try a little bit," "Taste Celie's cake," my mother and everyone else in the room seemed to be urging me, cajoling me. I couldn't eat the cake! The moment passed, the embarrassment waned, and the conversation moved on to other things. Later my mother quizzed me about the cake. I couldn't tell her why I wouldn't eat it—I honestly did not know myself. It took many years before I was able to reflect on my memory of that visit with Aunt Celie and decipher what it must have meant in my seven-year-old grasp of people and relationships.

I did not eat the cake because it was made and served by "colored people." I'm sure that is the correct word to use in describing my sense of the people who were trying so hard to be kind and hospitable to me. The people to whom I could not respond were "colored." I'm certain that is the way I was thinking of Aunt Celie, Agnes, and the others that day. My parents did not use the term *colored* in the pejorative way that other more hateful terms are used. While they were certainly products of the Southern culture of their own upbringing, they would not have used the other words with their children. They would not have been part of my vocabulary or of my way of thinking about people. No, I'm sure that *colored* would have been the word in my mind. I had not been taught to hate, but somehow I knew that there were cautions and limits necessary when dealing with "colored" people.

A song from the play *South Pacific* asserts that children must be "carefully taught" to hate and discriminate. I disagree—I think that prejudice is informally caught rather than formally taught. I think that by the time I was seven years old I had caught the belief from my social environment that black people were not to be touched or trusted. I think that I had already learned a sense of race and an ethic of racial separation. I cannot recall ever being taught them, but I know I had learned those lessons.

But what of my mother? Certainly she knew these things, but yet I had seen her allow herself to be embraced like a little girl by Aunt Celie and Agnes. Even more disturbing, she had returned their hugs with enthusiasm and obvious deep affection. She had not only eaten the marble cake, she had tried to persuade me to do the same. It didn't make sense. I was soon relishing my other adventures in Montgomery, however, and remembering with pride having sat behind the wheel of the hook and ladder truck at Uncle Ray's firehouse. The memories of the marble cake and Aunt Celie soon settled several layers below my consciousness.

In 1952, racial segregation in public schools was still the norm by law or practice in most parts of the United States. Racial separation in most areas of social life was an enforced standard. *Brown v. Board of Education* was still only being formulated in Topeka. Freedom rides and lunch counter protests were as yet undreamed expressions of the yearning for civil rights and personal dignity among America's black people. In Montgomery where I rode the streets in my uncle's shiny, black Buick, Rosa Parks was still riding on the back seat of the bus or standing in its crowded aisle while seats at the front remained unfilled. The bus boycott that would occur there in a few years was as yet unthinkable. Martin Luther King, Jr., was an obscure young preacher.

Over the next twenty years and more, my memories of Aunt Celie were called up by events that stimulated once again the puzzling contradiction: Celie loved and was loved deeply by my mother. My mother respected and trusted her. Yet I had learned that the right thing to do was to distance myself from people like her. How could it be that this woman evoked such behavior from my own mother? I recalled Aunt Celie throughout the events of the civil rights movement. I thought of her as I watched news reports of young black men and women being knocked to the ground with fire hoses. I remembered her as I watched black boys and girls being cursed by hate-filled white adults as they entered segregated public schools. I saw her features in the faces of hundreds of elderly black people during my two years in the Peace Corps. Recognizing Aunt Celie's capacity for love and remembering my immature rejection of her have served as a challenge for growth and change throughout much of my life. I am deeply in her debt.

As I mentioned earlier, my mother told Carl and me stories of Aunt Celie before I met her in Montgomery. She also told the stories for years afterward. The stories were always the same. My grandmother ran a small neighborhood grocery in Montgomery. She, my mother, and my uncles lived behind the store. The store had no name. It was "nothing fancy." There was no electricity in the store and no indoor plumbing. They sold bologna, bread, crackers, beans, sugar, and other things that were considered staples at the time. Kerosene lamps were used for lighting, and clothes were washed in a tub with a scrub board. My mother washed clothes in the mornings before going to school and pressed clothes using a charcoal-heated iron at night. She often talked of wearing clothes that other people handed down to her. She explained that "there was a woman who Mama bought candy from for the store who had a girl a little older than me, and she would bring me clothes."

Celie often went to their home behind the store. She brought a wooden box with her to sit on because she refused to sit on their furniture. My mother would sit on the floor; Celie sat on the box, brushed her hair, and told stories of her childhood in slavery. Aunt Celie and her mother were separated when she was very small. They were sold to different slaveholders. Her new "mistress" gave her a little perfume bottle to play with in an effort to comfort her. She stayed with this family as a slave until she was emancipated a few years later. She told my mother that her "mistress" was "good" to her. Aunt Celie treasured the perfume bottle for most of her life. She treasured it, but she treasured my mother more. She gave it to her "baby" as a gift of love.

I always assumed that Aunt Celie was hired by my grandmother to care for my mother. My grandmother raised four children without the help of a husband. I believed that Celie was probably paid to come in during times when my grandmother was most busy with the store. I must admit that there have been times when I have spoken reluctantly of Aunt Celie with other people because I thought her story would sound too much like a "kindly black mammy" tale about the woman who was hired to raise my mother, and what a loyal and loving "servant" she had been. A recent conversation, however, added a new dimension to my understanding of the relationship between Aunt Celie and my mother. Aunt Celie was not hired to care for my mother. She was instead a genuine friend and a kind neighbor who was in no sense employed to care. My grandmother's store was in a "colored" section of Montgomery. Most of her customers were black people. When my grandmother went into the labor of my mother's birth, she went to the back of the store to her bed. She sent one of my uncles for help. The local doctor could not be found, so she asked for Celie whom by then she had known for some time. Celie came and, "before Dr. Bickerstaff could be found," delivered my mother. For the rest of her life, she called my mother her baby or simply "Baby." It was a just claim. She literally brought my mother into the world.

Celie visited often with my mother in her home behind the store. As I said earlier, on these visits she lovingly combed my mother's hair and told her the stories of her life that have remained with my mother to this day. My mother also visited in Celie's home frequently. She remembers that Celie had a stereoscope, the antique forerunner of what some of us knew in childhood as a Viewmaster. She would sit for hours and look at cardboard pictures of dramatic scenes and faraway places. They talked, looked at the pictures through the stereoscope, and ate fresh figs from the tree in Aunt Celie's backyard. These were wonderful times for my mother, and she still becomes radiant when she describes them.

Prejudice is a form of mental illness—I'm convinced of it. Unfortunately, it is often a form of shared mania that results in great hurt to those who are the objects of its madness. Most people with other forms of mental illness are dangerous only to themselves. Prejudice is different. Its primary symptom is hatred of others, and those who are hated are at high risk for being hurt. The irrationality of hatred for others because of their race, nationality, religion, gender, social class, or other characteristic can become all-consuming. That irrationality has proven itself repeatedly to be resistant to all reason and evidence contrary to its poisoned convictions.

Prejudice, however, has often been elevated and dignified by powerful and influential people who have supported it in the name of reason and have advanced it in the name of science. There have been scientific assaults on people because of their social class or racial identity. Laws and practices have been aimed at controlling the lives of people deemed inferior because of race or class. Claims have been made for a scientific basis for those laws and practices. The illness of prejudicial thought can infect the intellect at what we consider its highest levels and in what we think of as its purest forms. Many people in law, medicine, science, and human services have been convinced that they have the right and responsibility to intervene in powerful and intimate ways in the lives of other people for "their own good" and for the protection of society. People have been hurt by what was done to them in the name of scientific, medical, or political necessity.

Our culture is even more socially complex and confusing today than in our past. Confusion and complexity, however, should not seduce us to engage in simple and expedient actions that rob others of their liberty and dignity. Prejudice must be struggled against continually. I don't think that you can simply overcome a "bad case" of it or that you can inoculate a child for life against ever "catching" it. It is all around us, and I believe that the challenge is to examine each day the assumptions that we make about other people and the fears we harbor of people because of the way they look, speak, worship, or otherwise live their lives. Just when you think you have overcome a prejudicial view, you find yourself on one of those dark, lonely streets of life and the complexion of the stranger coming toward you makes a difference in the degree of your discomfort.

In a world filled with negative, and all too often evil, abstractions about people who are different from oneself, I have found comfort and reassurance in concrete human interactions. My relationships with people from diverse cultural and ethnic backgrounds have taught me much about dignity in human life. Some of my most profound lessons about freedom have come from knowing people who have been oppressed because they came from a particular minority group. When I am tempted to allow race to become something negative in my thinking, I remember Aunt Celie. I recall her embracing my mother on the sidewalk as I watched in Montgomery that afternoon in 1952, and I imagine the day years before when she gently bathed a newborn with love.

Several times during the last few years, I have asked my mother about the perfume bottle. I remember seeing it as a child, and the image I have is of a small glass vial with a metal filigree covering. Each time I have asked about it, she has replied evasively that it is "put away somewhere" and that she will try to find it sometime before my next visit. Somehow, the next time I ask it has slipped her mind, and it is just too late or she is too busy to look for it just then. I suspect that the bottle is wrapped carefully in flannel cloth scraps and put in a box that once held Christmas cards. I imagine it has been placed safely under rarely used things in a dresser drawer. I also suspect that it has become too precious to share when the house is filled with activity and grandchildren. I understand. I have memories. That is all that matters.

Creating a School Atmosphere of Multicultural Respect

Marian Wright Edelman is the Executive Director of the Children's Defense Fund. In 1992 she wrote an insightful and inspiring book entitled *The Measure of Our Success: A Letter to My Children and Yours*. Included in her book are the "lessons for life" that she offers to young people. One of those lessons encourages the next generation to remember its roots, its history, and the "shoulders" on which it stands. Edelman explains:

> And pass these roots on to your children and to other children. Young people who do not know where they come from and the struggle it took to get them where they are now will not know where they are going or what to do for anyone besides themselves if and when they finally get somewhere. All Black children need to feel the rightful pride of a great people that produced Harriet Tubman and Sojourner Truth and Frederick Douglass from slavery, and Benjamin Mays and Martin Luther King and Mrs. Fannie Lou Hamer from segregation—people second to none in helping transform America from a theoretical to a more living democracy.
>
> All children need this pride of heritage and sense of history of their own people and of all the people who make up the mosaic of this great nation. African American and Latino and Asian American and Native American children should know about European history and cultures, and white children should know about the histories and cultures of diverse peoples of color with whom they must share a city, a nation and a world. I believe in integration. But that does not mean I become someone else or ignore or deny who I am. I learned the Negro National anthem, "Lift Every Voice and Sing," at the same time I learned "The Star Spangled Banner" and "America the Beautiful" and I love them all. I have raised you, my children, to respect other people's children, not to become their children but to become yourselves at your best. I hope others will raise their children to respect you (Edelman, 1992, pp. 73–74).

Edelman adds to this emphasis on cultural knowledge and respect a call for remembering that human beings, regardless of race, class, gender, or other differences, are more alike than different. She also asks that young people recognize the responsibility that we all share for the well-being of all people in our society.

> Be decent and fair and insist that others be so in your presence. Don't tell, laugh at, or in any way acquiesce to racial, ethnic, religious, or gender jokes or to any practices intended to demean rather than enhance another human being. Walk away from them. Stare them down. Make them unacceptable in your homes, religious congregations, and clubs. Through daily moral consciousness counter the proliferating voices of racial and ethnic and religious division that are gaining respectability over the land, including on college campuses. Let's face up to rather than ignore our growing racial problems, which are America's historical and future Achilles' heel. . . .
>
> Let's not spend time pinning and denying blame rather than healing our divisions. Rabbi Abraham Heschel put it aptly: "We are not all equally guilty but we are all equally responsible" for building a decent and just America (Edelman, 1992, pp. 54–55).

THE MELTING POT

The metaphor of a pot of molten metals was used in the early twentieth century to describe the United States. In 1909 Israel Zangwill in his play, *The Melting-Pot*, portrayed this country as a cauldron in which the languages and traditions of varied immigrant groups were melted down into a common American substance. Zangwill had one of his characters speak of America as a melting pot in religious terms:

> America is God's Crucible, the great Melting-Pot where all the races of Europe are melting and re-forming! . . . Germans and Frenchmen, Irishmen and Englishmen, Jews and Russians—into the Crucible with you all! God is making the American (Zangwill, 1909, p. 37).

This concept, that to become an American means to give up a previous cultural identity, is no longer widely accepted and was probably never an accurate description of the multicultural realities of the United States.

The reality that has been true of the United States for centuries is that it has been a society built on difference and diversity. This country may, in fact, be the most multicultural society in the world. For example, in his book, *Who We Are: A Portrait of America Based on the Latest U.S. Census,* Sam Roberts reports 1990 census data that gives an indication of the language diversity that exists today in America.

> 15 percent of the city's [New York] public school children are not proficient in English and speak a different native language—including 90,000 who speak primarily Spanish, 13,000 who speak Chinese, 7,000 who speak Haitian Creole, 5,000 who speak Russian, 500 who speak Farsi. Of the 230 million Americans over the age of 5, more than one in eight, or nearly 32 million, speak a language other than English at home, a 38 percent increase over 1980. About two in ten of those say they don't speak English very well or at all. In California, 5,478,712 said they speak Spanish at home. In New York, 400,218 speak Italian; in North Dakota, 106 do. Another 117,323 New Yorkers speak mostly Yiddish; so do 12 residents of Alaska. In Massachusetts, 133,373 still speak Portuguese. Nationwide, more than 17 million people speak Spanish at home (Roberts, 1995, p. 68).

Even though the United States has been a multicultural society for generations and has become even more so in recent decades, it has also been a deeply culturally divided society. Kierstead and Wagner (1993) believe, in fact, that the "melting pot" was always a mythical characterization. They point out that Israel Zangwill's play spoke only of the immigrants who were white and from northern Europe. The concept of bringing people together to assimilate the American culture and beliefs ignored the presence of millions of African-American people and growing numbers of Hispanic-Americans. It also ignored the Asian-Americans who had been brought to this country to construct a transcontinental railway system. Kierstead and Wagner observe that rather than as a "melting pot," Americans have lived for centuries as a "tossed salad," a hodgepodge of cultures thrown together but still separate (Kierstead and Wagner, 1993, p. 98).

A CULTURAL TAPESTRY

Is there a better way of portraying the United States than as a melting pot or tossed salad? A third metaphor might be a more positive and productive way of portraying the goal of creating classrooms that are truly inclusive of

Shaffer Photography

students from varying cultural and ethnic backgrounds. That is the metaphor of a tapestry. A society woven of different cultural strands may be stronger and more interesting than a society made of a single fabric. Cultural strands can be woven together in such a manner that each retains its individuality while contributing to the resiliency and beauty of the entire societal fabric. Inclusive classrooms, therefore, strive to bring students together as a compatible and working group while preserving and valuing the unique individual character of each of the students.

A simple rule of thumb that might be helpful to teachers as they attempt to promote more inclusive environments for all of their students is a statement made more than twenty years ago in the book entitled *Cultural Pluralism in Education*:

> No child should have to feel that he must reject his parent's culture to be accepted. Indeed, his chances of adjusting successfully to his school, to his community, and to the larger society are enhanced if he is not encumbered by a feeling of shame and inferiority because he was not born into another family and another culture (Stent, Hazard, and Rivlin, 1973, p. viii).

The impact that negative attitudes about a child's ethnic or cultural heritage can have on the identity of that child is illustrated by a fragment of writing that William Ayers describes:

> Kelyn (and other black children) were sometimes given to calling one another derogatory racial names and I was painfully aware of hurt and rage. Here, for example, is a fragment of writing I found at that time, by eleven-year-old Carolyn Jackson:
>
> *When I ride the train and sit next to a person of the opposite race*
> *I feel like a crow in a robin's nest,*
> *And I feel dirty.*
>
> Carolyn has a powerful interpretation of what it means to be black in America: to be not wanted; to be "dirty"; to be "a crow in a robin's nest." This was what I was teaching *against* (Ayers, 1995, p. 23).

MINORITY STUDENTS IN SPECIAL EDUCATION

According to the most recent census figures, approximately 22 percent of the overall population of the United States can be classified as belonging to a minority group. However, a larger number of school-age children are members of a minority group. That number is 30 percent, and it is expected to reach 36 percent by the year 2000 (Hodgkinson, 1993).

Janesick (1995) has summarized a number of findings concerning minority students and special education. Among her findings are:

- There is a relationship between minority status and the likelihood of receiving certain disability classifications (for example, disproportionate members of minority children are classified as having mild retardation).

- There are inequities in the special education resources available in low-income and high-income schools.
- Being classified as having a disability may have a powerful impact on the school and work careers of students (that is, the stigmatizing effects of classification may limit the student's future opportunities) (Janesick, 1995, pp. 722–725).

The percentage of students in various racial/ethnic groups identified as receiving special education in 1990 is presented in Table 11.1. It should also be noted that minority children are underrepresented in education programs for students who are gifted (Smith, Le Rose, and Clasen, 1991).

The U.S. Department of Education's Office of Civil Rights (OCR) is concerned that minority students are being wrongly placed in special education programs. The OCR has made investigating allegations of abuses against students of diverse backgrounds a priority. It is attempting to determine if the disproportionate number of minority students receiving special education services is caused by factors that violate civil rights laws (Council for Exceptional Children, 1995).

While the incidence of special education placements among minority students is high, minority status itself does not explain this high incidence. Garmezy has found, for example, that when the effects of socioeconomic class are controlled, ethnicity apparently has little or no relationship to emotional or behavioral disorders. The risks that accompany ethnicity appear to be a function of the high levels of poverty in many ethnic groups (Garmezy, 1991).

Hodgkinson has made some important observations about the relationship of minority status and poverty in the schools of America.

> Given that minorities are more likely to be in poverty than whites (most poor kids are white, although black and Hispanic kids have a much higher percentage of their total number poor) and given our look at the future, we might ask how schools are likely to fare. . . . The top 15 percent of America's students are world class on any set of indicators. The "forgotten middle" needs some work, but will graduate from high school and pay taxes. America's lowest 35 percent (in terms of school attainment) is truly awful, due to factors that were present when they first knocked on the kindergarten door. (Factors such as: poverty, out of wedlock birth, teen births, cocaine-addicted at birth, short of food and housing, born premature, are only a few.) (Hodgkinson, 1992, p. 13)

TABLE 11.1

Percentage of Students in Racial/Ethnic Groups Receiving Special Education

Group	Percent
African-American	11.26
Native-American	10.76
White	9.53
Hispanic	8.24
Asian/Pacific Islander	3.26

Note: These percentages include only those students with mental retardation, serious emotional disturbance, specific learning disabilities, and speech impairments. It should also be noted that Hispanic people may be of any race. This may have influenced the percentage figures. Source: Office of Special Education Programs. *Sixteenth Annual Report to Congress on the Implementation of the Individuals with Disabilities Education Act.* Washington, DC: U.S. Department of Education, 1994, p. 201.

POVERTY AND SPECIAL NEEDS

In 1993 more than 23 percent of the children in the United States were living in homes below the poverty line. This was one of the highest child poverty percentages in the "developed" world. As has been pointed out, these children bring risks with them from the day they enter school (Hodgkinson, 1993).

Children born in poverty may be at greater risk for disabilities regardless of other social or ethnic factors for a number of reasons. They begin life weakened, more susceptible to illness, and with neurological problems that will contribute to academic difficulties later in development (Drew, Hardman, and Logan, 1996). In 1992 the Office of Special Education and Rehabilitative Services reported that young people who were actually identified as having disabilities are more likely than students from the general population to come from families that have lower household incomes and that are otherwise characterized by lower socioeconomic status (U.S. Department of Education, 1992).

Creating a School Atmosphere of Gender Equality

RESEARCHERS IN A THREE-YEAR study of fourth-grade, sixth-grade, and eighth-grade classrooms discovered that teachers talk more to male students. Boys were eight times more likely than girls to speak out during discussions without waiting their turns. Teachers tended to accept this behavior. When girls spoke out, however, teachers discouraged and corrected their behavior. They tended to tell these girls to follow the rules and raise their hands (Sadker, Sadker, and Stulberg, 1993).

The boys in the study received more attention than the girls, and they also, the researchers report, received more positive kinds of attention. The attention that boys were given more often took the following forms:

- praise (positive reaction to a student's comment or work);
- criticism (explicit statements that answers are incorrect); . . .
- remediation (helping students to correct or improve responses) . . . [and]
- acceptance [which] is a less specific reaction to student contributions such as a teacher comment like uh-huh or okay (Sadker, Sadker, and Stulberg, 1993, p. 46).

A report issued by the American Association of University Women (1992) indicates that girls not only receive less attention from teachers but that they are also less likely to see themselves represented in the materials they study in school. Many textbooks and other curricular materials still send stereotyped messages about sex roles. In addition, what is left out of books and other curricula may send a negative message to girls. According to Sadker, Sadker, and Steindam (1989), females are likely to be underrepresented in history, literature, math, and science texts. Other research on this issue has revealed that only 1 percent of history text material examined referred to women (American Association of University Women, 1992).

Teachers can create classroom environments that are fair and respectful of children of both genders. Sadker (1994) emphasizes that teachers can find teaching materials that are inclusive of the history, abilities, and contributions of females. There are considerations that teachers should give to how they promote

BOX 11.1

Strategies for Creating a More Gender-Equitable Classroom

- *Increase wait time*: A rapid question-and-answer pace favors males. Allow girls time to respond.
- *Recognize and reward cooperative behavior*. Teachers may spend more time on discipline than on recognition of positive behavior. This may result in more time being spent with boys.
- *Integrate classroom activities by gender*. Organize seating, games, and projects so that boys and girls will learn to work and play together cooperatively.
- *Actively support the self-confidence of girls*: Make a point of encouraging girls to take leadership roles in class projects and other activities that may increase their confidence.

Adapted from M. Sadker, D. Sadker, and L. Stulberg. "Fair and Square? Creating a Nonsexist Classroom." *Instructor, 102*(7), 1993, pp. 67–68.

gender equity in their classrooms. A few of these are represented in Box 11.1. Teachers need to be aware of the role that language has played in stereotyping females. They should try to use and encourage the use of language that is more sensitive to and respectful of the changing roles of females in society. The same is true of the career stereotypes of women that have been pervasive in the United States. Both boys and girls must be exposed to information about careers and models of the career options that are available to them regardless of gender.

WOMEN WITH DISABILITIES

The special impact that disabilities may have on the lives of women was a long neglected issue. In recent years, however, the psychological, social, and economic implications of disabilities for women have been given more attention (Mudrick, 1983). Two important social factors have changed the needs of women with disabilities.

The first of these is the dramatically changed participation of women in the workforce. The income of women has become an increasingly important portion of the income of most families for significant periods of time in the family life cycle. If a disability restricts a woman's ability to work, it may have an impact on both her economic well-being and that of her family.

A second important change has been the increase in female-headed households. This has occurred primarily because of high rates of separation and divorce. Women with disabilities that interfere with their ability to earn a living may be at an increased risk of the devastating effects of marital dissolution (Mudrick, 1983).

These factors point out the importance of making certain that girls with disabilities have every opportunity to develop the academic and vocational skills that will enable them to function as competently and independently as possible in society.

HIV/AIDS: Helping Students Understand, Encouraging Their Sensitivity

AIDS IS AN ACRONYM FOR A DISEASE called acquired immunodeficiency syndrome. The disease impairs the ability of the human body to maintain immunity to other diseases. The person with AIDS is, therefore, susceptible to illnesses that her or his body would ordinarily be able to ward off. It has been discovered that AIDS is caused by HIV, a virus that may infect the person years before AIDS develops from it.

HIV/AIDS is most often thought of as transmitted in adults through sexual intercourse or the use of illegal intravenous drugs. It is possible, however, for infants to be born with the disease because of exposure to the mother's infection during fetal development. Infants may also become infected from the breast milk of an HIV-positive mother. In June 1990 the Centers for Disease Control reported that 1,266 children younger than thirteen years old had died from AIDS (Kaiser, 1990). By 1994 AIDS had been diagnosed in 6,245 children under the age of thirteen years (Centers for Disease Control, 1994). Approximately 10,000 children in the United States are infected with HIV, and the number is growing by nearly 20 percent each year (Altmann, 1995).

The growing number of children with HIV and AIDS presents important questions to schools and educators. The progress of HIV infection and AIDS may be very gradual. A child may not become seriously ill until long after the disease has been diagnosed. There is no known cure and, therefore, the disease does not end. Because of the stigma associated with HIV and AIDS, there are important issues of confidentiality involved. There is also the issue of what constitutes appropriate precautions for the protection of the child and others.

Children with HIV or AIDS do not generally present a danger to other people. The Americans with Disabilities Act protects children with HIV from exclusion from schools (Savage, Mayfield, and Cook, 1993). Turnbull reported that students with AIDS "may be considered disabled under IDEA if the disability causes them to need special education or related services" (Turnbull, 1993, p. 63).

Since it is clear that students with HIV/AIDS have a right to the most inclusive education that is best for them, it is important that teachers be prepared to work with these students in the following ways. First, they need to know the procedures and precautions necessary for the well-being of the student and her or his classroom peers. Teachers of these children should be given information about the student's special needs, medication, protection from exposure to complicating diseases, and the signs of a health crisis that needs immediate attention. They should also be given specific instructions about handling the exposure of other students and themselves to blood or other body fluids. This information should be provided to teachers by the school or school district.

An even more important consideration, however, is how the teacher can reduce the stigma that often is projected onto a student with HIV/AIDS. There is a great deal of misunderstanding about the disease that contributes to this stigma. One study, for example, found that many elementary school students believed that AIDS could be transmitted by contact with a toilet seat or through contact with clothing worn by a person with the disease (Schvaneveldt, Lindaver, and Young, 1990). A major challenge then, is for teachers to help inform students and their parents about the realities of HIV/AIDS.

The educational challenge of HIV/AIDS is twofold. On one hand, teachers need to participate in the important task of educating students about the ways of preventing HIV and AIDS infections. They must cooperate with parents in informing students about the precautions and healthy behaviors that can keep them from contracting the disease. On the other hand, they need to help families educate their children about people with HIV/AIDS in ways that will reduce the unfounded fears and prejudices associated with the disease (Lesar, Gerber, and Semmel, 1995).

Celebrating Human Diversity

NO EASY ANSWERS—THE SCHOOL AS A CARING COMMUNITY

Jared Diamond has provided an important perspective on the ultimate rejection of one group of human beings by another group, otherwise known as genocide or the attempted extermination of an entire people defined by culture or race. He observes that all societies have sanctions against murder and that, for genocide to occur, these sanctions must somehow be suspended. The rationale given for lifting these sanctions includes:

> self-defense, revenge, manifest rights to land, and possessing the correct religion or race or political belief. These are the principles that fan hatred and transform ordinary people into murderers. A further universal feature of genocide is an 'us/them' ethical code that views the victims as lower beings or animals to whom laws of human ethics don't apply. For instance, Nazis regarded Jews as lice; French settlers of Algeria referred to local Moslems as ratons (rats); Boers called Africans bobbejaan (baboons); educated northern Nigerians viewed Ibos as subhuman vermin (Diamond, 1988, p. 8).

Genocide is a terrible topic to discuss but one that brings into focus the ultimate dangers of racial and ethnic prejudice. It is something that we are inclined to attribute to "those awful Nazis." In fact, however, racial and ethnic hatred leading to acts of genocide have occurred repeatedly, even among "nice" people like many of our own ancestors. Although the physical extermination of Native Americans was never accomplished, it came close to being completed by an earlier generation of Americans. It is, in fact, clear that not all of the people who contributed to the Holocaust were psychopaths. Most of the people who ran the gas chambers, operated the crematoriums, and turned their heads and said nothing were "nice" people. How is it that "nice" people can behave in this manner?

The developmental psychologist Erik Erikson attributed the capacity for inhuman acts by decent human beings to what he termed "pseudospeciation." He used this as a description of the process of an "in" group defining an "out" group and deciding that its members are less than human. When it is believed that a group is not really human, the normal standards of human conduct toward them no longer apply. They are less than human and therefore it is not a matter of guilt to treat them accordingly. Erikson explained:

> The term denotes the fact that while man is obviously one species, he appears and continues . . . [to] split up into groups (from tribes to nations, from castes to classes, from religions to ideologies) which provide their members with a firm sense of distinct and superior identity. . . . This demands, however, that each group must invent for itself a place and a moment in the very centre of the universe where and when an especially provident deity caused it to be created superior to all others (Erikson, 1969, p. 431).

And yet there is another facet of pseudospeciation. Although many "nice" people have taken part in it, other people have refused to take part or have actively resisted it on behalf of its victims. Samuel and Pearl Oliner, in their book, *The Altruistic Personality: Rescuers of Jews in Nazi Europe*, describe people who at great risk to themselves and their families helped Jews during the Holocaust. The

Oliners explained the purpose of their study as follows:

> Holocaust technology created a means whereby selected populations could be plucked out from among their neighbors and destroyed. The Holocaust thus points not only to the fragility of Jews but to the precariousness of any group that might have the misfortune of being so arbitrarily designated. If we are to live in a world free from the threat of Holocausts, we will need to create it. If we can understand some of the attributes that distinguish rescuers from others, perhaps we can deliberately cultivate them (Oliner and Oliner, 1988, p. xviii).

The Oliners found that the rescuers were "ordinary" people. Those who hid, cared for, and transported Jews to save them from the Nazi atrocities were farmers, teachers, businesspeople, and factory workers. They were both rich and poor. They were Protestants and Catholics. They were ordinary people unrecognizable as heroes in either personalities or personal histories. What did distinguish them, however, was their connectedness to the other people in their lives, their relationship of care and commitment. According to the Oliners:

> Their involvements with Jews grew out of the ways in which they ordinarily related to other people—their characteristic ways of feeling, their perceptions of who should be obeyed; the rules and examples of conduct they learned from parents, friends, and religious and political associates; and their routine ways of deciding what was wrong and right. They inform us that it is out of the quality of such routine human activities that the human spirit evolves and moral courage is born. They remind us that such courage is not only the province of the independent and the intellectually superior thinkers but that it is available to all through the virtues of connectedness, commitment, and the quality of relationships developed in ordinary human interactions (Oliner and Oliner, 1988, p. 260).

The Oliners found that moral heroism resides in people as an expression of the ways that they come to view and interact with others in everyday life. Heroism is, in this sense, born out of the ordinary and everyday institutions of society. The rescuers learned their sense of connection and commitment from their families, school, and neighbors. It is also apparent from the Oliners' work that the influence of the family had created in many of them a sense of caring that was missing in the nonrescuers. The Oliners emphasize, however, that the teaching of caring and commitment is also a community responsibility. They stress that the school is the single institution outside the family that reaches all children.

THOR SWIFT/IMPACT VISUALS

SHAFFER PHOTOGRAPHY

Schools must, therefore, be conduits for teaching the values that help people resist prejudicial and exclusionary thinking.

> Schools need to become caring institutions—institutions in which students, teachers, bus drivers, principals, and all others receive positive affirmation for kindness, empathy, and concern. Participants need opportunities to work and have fun together, develop intimacies, and share successes and pain. Students also need opportunities to consider broad universal principles that relate to justice and care in matters of public concern. Discussions should focus on the logic and values, implications and consequences of public actions, as well as the philosophical heritage that underlies these principles. In short, caring schools will acknowledge diversity on the road to moral concern. They will invoke emotion and intellect in service of responsibility and caring (Oliner and Oliner, 1988, pp. 258–259).

In his book, *Celebrations of Life*, René Dubos advocates people finding local solutions to global problems. His challenge that we should think globally but act locally has become a bumper sticker (Dubos, 1981). The meaning he conveys through that phrase, however, is profound. We need to be aware of and concerned about world problems, but the work needed to confront them usually must be done in our own homes, communities, and schools. Understanding and respect for human differences must grow from the "bottom up" rather than from the "top down." Homes and schools that educate children to be sensitive, just, and compassionate will promote a citizenry that is more inclusive in its attributes and actions. Teachers must "act locally" within their classrooms to teach children to understand each other in ways that will liberate society from the detrimental effects of prejudice.

DISCOURAGED LEARNERS

It sometimes seems that students who are part of a stereotyped group live up to that stereotype. Children from a "bad" part of town may, in fact, act "bad." Students expected to have a "chip" on their shoulders may dare you to knock that chip off. Students with the reputation for being "lazy" may certainly appear that way. This is the well-known concept of the self-fulfilling prophecy—people will meet our expectations of them, good or bad.

There is another important social phenomenon that teachers should consider when dealing with students from diverse backgrounds. This is the concept of *horizontal violence* as defined by Paulo Freire. In his book, *Pedagogy of the Oppressed* (1974), he describes what he believes may happen psychologically to people who are part of a group that has been defined as inferior by another (dominating) group. He refers to this psychological phenomenon as "horizontal violence." This is violence directed toward another member of one's own minority group. An example of this would be violence directed toward others within one's own group rather than toward an external oppressor. Another example would be using terms for one's own group that are negative and insulting. Freire discusses five other psychological traits that may develop when people's live are damaged by racial, ethnic, or socioeconomic prejudice:

- *An Attitude of Fatalism and Resignation*: People may feel that nothing can be done to improve their lives.
- *An Attitude of Self-Depreciation*: People may internalize the prejudices of others and come to believe that they are, in fact, inferior.
- *An Attitude of Self-Distrust*: People may come to doubt their own perceptions and thoughts about themselves and the world around them.
- *A Magical Belief in the Power of the Oppressor*: Oppressed people may come to believe that their oppressors have the power to know and do things that go beyond normal human capacities.
- *A Feeling of Being Property*: People who have been placed in inferior social positions may feel that they are less than human. They may come to believe that the attitudes and actions that regard them as property rather than people are deserved (Freire, 1974).

It is critical that teachers recognize that many students will come to their classrooms with the belief that the stereotypes about their ethnicity, gender, or some other distinguishing characteristic are true. It is also important that teachers understand that this belief can lead to the discouraged and resigned belief that nothing can be done about it. On the other hand, it is important for teachers to find ways of counteracting this discouragement.

FOODS, FAIRS, FESTIVALS, AND MORE

In recent years, the multicultural realities of our society have come to be more clearly displayed in the curricula and activities of schools in the United States. More and more schools involve themselves in what have been called the "foods, fairs and festivals" of multicultural education (Grant and Sachs, 1995, p. 100). These are also important to the development of pride in students from groups that have previously received little attention in our education system. The celebration of certain days, periods of special recognition, and an emphasis on the contributions of women and people of African-American heritage, for example, are extremely important. More important, however, is the need for students to learn about the concepts of interdependence and social responsibility in a complex and diverse society.

CARING FOR SELF AND OTHERS

It has long been recognized that the concept of *self* is based upon the interaction of the individual with others. Self-esteem and self-respect depend largely on the individual sense of belongingness and competence within a social group (Branden, 1969). What a person thinks of herself or himself is intertwined with the acceptance and support felt from others. A person's internal life cannot be separated from the external environment. Siccone (1995) has conceptualized the interaction between self and others along the following dimensions:

- *Independence*: This is the internal experience of self-worth. It involves the sense that one is an independent and unique person in the world. It includes the issues of who and what make me special.

- *Interdependence*: This is the recognition that I need others. It is a sense of the need to belong to a family, community, school, and society. It includes the needs of connectedness, affiliation, and friendship.
- *Personal Responsibility*: This is the recognition of the power to exercise control in one's life. It involves the sense of being capable of purposefulness, self-direction, and competence.
- *Social Responsibility*: Social responsibility is the ability to move beyond self-interest and to accept responsibility for the world around us. It is a belief not only in the importance of accepting responsibility for others, but also in the competence that I have to help others (Siccone, 1995).

Teachers can influence students in each of these dimensions by encouraging them to recognize the value of themselves and others. A classroom atmosphere that rewards cooperation, self-respect, and respect for others can promote independence, interdependence, personal responsibility, and social responsibility.

Trice and Beyer have proposed five types of rituals that can help promote group solidarity in an organization. Applied to classrooms, these are techniques that can help students feel a commonality that makes them a group even though each person has special differences. They refer to these rituals as rites:

- *Rites of Enhancement*: In a classroom setting, this can be accomplished by the teacher and the peers recognizing individual and group accomplishments (for example, encouraging students to praise each other for good work).
- *Rites of Conflict Reduction*: Finding ways of easing stress and tension by celebrations and play activities (for example, providing group activities that are enjoyable and encourage laughter).
- *Rites of Integration*: Activities that help students learn about the values they share (for example, discussions about issues that are important to this age group, role-playing, reading stories and asking students to discuss their meanings).
- *Rites of Renewal*: Providing help to students that will motivate them and help their morale (for example, one-to-one tutoring with difficult material, buddy systems for peer support).
- *Rites of Passage*: Group recognition of birthdays and other important life events (for example, birth of a sibling, accomplishments in Scouts) (Trice and Beyer, 1985).

In her book, *The Good High School: Portraits of Character and Culture,* Sara Lightfoot describes a principal who created a truly caring school. She shows how the leadership of a principal or teacher can promote an environment where each student knows that he or she is considered a "winner."

> Time and time again, I heard . . . [him] refer to his belief that "all our students are winners" and that "winning" has more to do with being a good, caring, and generous person than with visible and lofty achievement. It is an inclusive, rather than an exclusive, educational vision—one that does not focus superior or prideful attention on the narrow band of top achievers, or create a school image based on their great suc-

cesses. . . . Each year the principal offers the message of charity to the graduating seniors. He rehearses the words to me with great feeling, "I tell them, you need to leave this school with a sense of appreciation for other human beings. That is the primary lesson we teach at this school. I don't care if you are going to Columbia University pre-med, or if you have been tops in our Honors program. If you don't give a bit of yourself to someone else, you are a failure" (Lightfoot, 1983, p. 117).

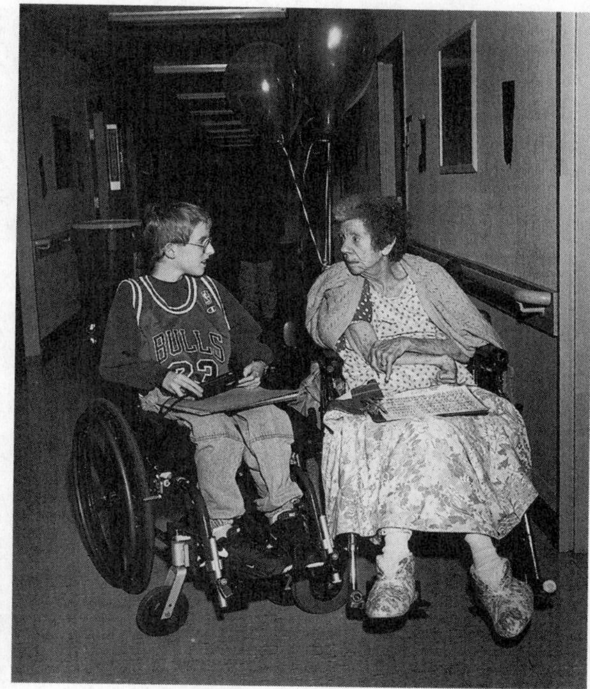

SHAFFER PHOTOGRAPHY

DIVERSITY: QUESTIONS FOR TEACHERS

There are a few questions that teachers can ask themselves that may help sensitize them to the extent to which they are attempting to make their classrooms more welcoming of the ethnic, gender, and other differences that students bring to them. On a regular basis, these questions may be helpful:

- To what extent have I avoided thinking about students in terms of stereotypes and acting toward them on the basis of these stereotypes?
- To what extent have I recognized that students may bring different learning styles and needs to my classroom because of their differences?
- Do I know the name that each student prefers and why he or she has that preference?
- Am I treating each student as an individual with unique needs, interests, history, and beliefs?
- Have I included the contribution of diverse groups of people as part of my teaching?
- Am I attempting to understand more about the history and perspectives of the diverse students in my class?
- Do I acknowledge to my students the value of the group identifications that are important to them? (McCormick, 1994)

These questions, however, are only reminders of a value that is critical to the creation of an inclusive classroom environment. That important value is the value of caring. Teachers must communicate and students must learn that care is a precious goal. Care for other individuals, care for themselves, and care for groups of people are the messages that nurture friendships, self-respect, and a sense of community.

Case Studies and Questions to Consider

STUDENT: FRANKIE DONN

SCHOOL: SANDY MIDDLE

CURRENT PLACEMENT: GENERAL SIXTH

AGE: 11 YEARS, 10 MONTHS

Family Structure and Home Environment

Frankie lives with his mother, Elsie Donn. Ms. Donn is fifty-four years old and is a full-time homemaker. Frankie's father is deceased, having died shortly before Frankie's birth. Ms. Donn is a graduate of Sandy High School. Frankie has a number of older brothers and sisters. Only two of his siblings, however, live at home with him and his mother. Leslie, a brother, is fifteen and is in the tenth grade. Johnny is twenty years old and is a high school graduate. He is currently unemployed.

Parental Perception of the Student's School Problem

Frankie has been experiencing a variety of difficulties that have interfered with his learning at school. His report indicates that he has poor self-control and is constantly rationalizing his actions. He is also described as being generally disruptive at school.

Ms. Donn feels that Frankie is an intelligent youngster and is capable of doing good work at school. She also believes that he has the capacity of exercising greater control over his behavior.

Frankie's mother believes that he lacks confidence in himself and that at least some of his problems result from his poor self-concept. She thinks that this may be linked to feelings about his father's death. She reports that Frankie is very sensitive and defensive about the fact that he has grown up without a father.

Ms. Donn thinks that two physical matters may be related. First is Frankie's bed-wetting. This continues to be a problem for him and one that causes him a great deal of concern and embarrassment. Second is the question of what one physician thought were irregular brain wave patterns that were possibly epileptic in nature. This physician prescribed an anticonvulsant for Frankie after he fell and seriously cut himself. Apparently, the physician felt that the fall was due to a seizure. Ms. Donn has strong negative feelings about the drug being prescribed. Because of her feelings and the side effects she thinks she has observed, she has stopped giving the medication to Frankie.

Additional Considerations

Ms. Donn feels that Frankie's personal and social behavior is within normal limits compared with other children his age. She feels, however, that his skills break down in school. Again, she attributes this to a lack of self-confidence. As a contrast, she points out that he has experienced a lot of success in his karate classes. This has been a boost to his self-concept and has improved the way he interacts at home and in the neighborhood. She does not think that he has found any comparable source of self-esteem at school.

Ms. Donn seems to be genuinely concerned for the welfare of her youngest child. She hopes that his behavior will improve in school so that he can be, as she says, "the kind of kid I know he is." She says that when he wants to be, he is a sweet and affectionate child.

Questions

1. Should Frankie be evaluated for special education services?
2. What questions need to be explored more fully with Ms. Donn?
3. What do Frankie's teachers need to know about him?

STUDENT: DANNY COLDWELL

SCHOOL: HERMITAGE HIGH SCHOOL

CURRENT PLACEMENT: NINTH

AGE: 16 YEARS, 2 MONTHS

Family Structure and Home Environment

Danny lives in a pleasant home with his parents, Archer and Phyllis Coldwell. Mr. Coldwell is a meat manager with a food store chain. Ms. Coldwell is a homemaker. Additionally, Ms. Coldwell oversees the care of her eighty-year-old father-in-law and the management of his home. Mr. Coldwell is forty-three years old, and Ms. Coldwell is forty.

Danny has a very close relationship with his elderly grandfather. The two have had a long-standing and consistent commitment to one another. His grandfather has just returned from the hospital, where he was being treated for congestive heart failure. Ms. Coldwell expresses concern that, even though she checks on him frequently, he insists on staying alone in his own home. She says she will feel more at ease this summer when Danny will stay with his grandfather. Ms. Coldwell explains that Danny is also very close to her mother, who lives fifty miles away. She says that he is very sensitive to the importance of frequent contacts with his grandmother.

Danny lives in a warm, orderly, and supportive home. A great deal of energy and concern have been invested in his development and well-being.

Parental Perception of the Student's School Program

Ms. Coldwell speaks positively of the help that Danny has received since his initial referral for special education services. She says that she has seen a "big difference" in him since his learning disabilities were identified and he started receiving help in overcoming them. She is concerned now, however, that he resents going to the resource room period that is part of his school schedule. She feels that Danny's overall attitude toward school is good, and she appreciates all of the help he is given. She emphasizes, however, that the resource room period has become problematic for Danny. Ms. Coldwell hopes that some alternative arrangement can be made.

Ms. Coldwell feels that Danny has problems with his self-concept and in his ability to relate effectively with other people his own age. She thinks that his large size has made him feel self-conscious and awkward in some situations. She also thinks that, correct or not, Danny believes that other students make fun of him because of his size. She doubts that he always feels good about himself, and she attributes this to his inordinate height and weight relative to his age.

Contrary to Danny's difficulties in dealing with some of his same-age peers, he seems to have some notable strengths in dealing with adults. Ms. Coldwell describes Danny as being close to both her and Mr. Coldwell. She says that she and Danny have always had particularly good and open communication. In addition to his grandparents, Danny also has strong emotional bonds with a number of elderly neighbors. To quote Ms. Coldwell: "I think that Danny is an unusual child. He is caring. He loves old people and will sit with and help those in our neighborhood."

Additional Comments

Danny is a regular participant in a church youth group. In addition, he is a junior volunteer at General Hospital. His mother says that this volunteer work is very important to Danny, and she feels that he will eventually make a career in some medical field. She adds, however, that she wants him to choose for himself what to do with his life. She says that she will be happy as long as he does constructive things with his time and energy.

Questions

1. Should Danny's parents be encouraged to remove him from resource room services? What would be your advice to them?
2. Based on the information available, should Danny receive any kind of special services at school?
3. What activities or services might be helpful in preparing Danny for adult life? How can his personal strengths be best utilized in this regard?

References

Altmann, L. K. "Children's AIDS Study Finds AZT Ineffective." *New York Times*, February 14, 1995: C13.

American Association of University Women and Wellesley College Center for Research on Women. *How Schools Shortchange Girls.* A study of major findings on girls and education. Available from AAUW, 1992: 124 pp.

Ayers, W. "Teaching Is an Act of Hope." *Teaching Tolerance*, *4*(2), 1995: 22–25.

Branden, N. *The Psychology of Self-Esteem: A New Concept of Man's Psychological Nature.* Los Angeles: Nash, 1969.

Centers for Disease Control. *HIV/AIDS Surveillance Report.* Washington, DC: U.S. Department of Health and Human Services, 1994.

Council for Exceptional Children. "Department of Education Challenges Schools on Number of Minority Students in Special Education." *CEC Today*, *2*(3), 1995: 7.

Diamond, J. "In Black and White." *Natural History*, October 1988: 8, 10, 12, 14.

Drew, C. J., M. L. Hardman, and D. R. Logan. *Mental Retardation: A Life Cycle Approach.* 6th ed. Columbus, OH: Merrill, 1996.

Dubos, R. *Celebrations of Life.* New York: McGraw-Hill, 1981.

Edelman, M. W. *The Measure of Our Success: A Letter to My Children and Yours.* Boston: Beacon Press, 1992.

Erikson, E. *Gandhi's Truth.* New York: Norton, 1969.

Freire, P. *Pedagogy of the Oppressed.* New York: Seabury Press, 1974.

Garmezy, N. "Resiliency and Vulnerability to Adverse Developmental Outcomes Associated with Poverty." *American Behavioral Scientist*, *34*(4), 1991: 416–430.

Grant, A. G., and J. M. Sachs. "Multicultural Education and Postmodernism: Movement Toward a Dialogue." In B. Kanpol and P. McLaren, Eds., *Critical Multiculturalism: Uncommon Voices in a Common Struggle.* Westport, CT: Bergin and Garvey, 1995: 89–103.

Herrnstein, R., and C. Murray. *The Bell Curve: Intelligence and Class Structure in American Life.* New York: Free Press, 1994.

Hodgkinson, H. *A Demographic Look at Tomorrow.* Washington, DC: Institute for Educational Leadership, 1992.

———. "American Education: The Good, the Bad, and the Task." *Phi Delta Kappan*, *74*(8), 1993: 619–623.

Janesick, V. J. "Our Multicultural Society." In E. Meyen and T. Skirtic, Eds., *Special Education and Student Disability: An Introduction.* 4th ed. Denver, CO: Love, 1995: 354–378.

Kaiser, M. "Young Patients Find Help Through Pediatric AIDS Program." *Small World*, Spring 1990: 4–8.

Kierstead, F. D., and P. A. Wagner. *The Ethical, Legal and Multicultural Foundations of Teaching.* Madison, WI: Brown and Benchmark, 1993.

Lesar, S., M. M. Gerber, and M. I. Semmel. "HIV Infection in Children: Family Stress, Social Support, and Adaptation." *Exceptional Children*, *62*(3), 1995: 224–236.

Lightfoot, S. L. *The Good High School: Portraits of Character and Culture.* New York: Basic Books, 1983.

McCormick, T. M. *Creating the Nonsexist Classroom: A Multicultural Approach.* New York: Teachers College Press, 1994.

Mudrick, N. R. "Disabled Women." *Society*, *20*(3), 1983: 51–55.

Office of Special Education Programs. *Sixteenth Annual Report to Congress on the Implementation of the Individuals with Disabilities Education Act.* Washington, DC: U.S. Department of Education, 1994.

Oliner, S., and P. Oliner. *The Altruistic Personality: Rescuers of Jews in Nazi Europe.* New York: Free Press, 1988.

Roberts, S. *Who We Are: A Portrait of America Based on the Latest U.S. Census.* New York: Times Books, 1995.

Sadker, M. *Failing at Fairness: How America's Schools Cheat Girls.* New York: Charles Scribner's Sons, 1994.

Sadker, M., D. Sadker, and S. Steindam. "Gender Equity and Educational Reform." *Educational Leadership, 46*(6), 1989: 44–47.

Sadker, M., D. Sadker, and L. Stulberg. "Fair and Square? Creating a Nonsexist Classroom." *Instructor, 102*(7), 1993: 44–46, 67–68.

Savage, S., P. Mayfield, and M. Cook. "Questions About Serving Children with HIV/AIDS." *Day Care and Early Education, 3,* 1993: 10–12.

Schvaneveldt, J. D., S. L. Lindaver, and M. H. Young. "Children's Understanding of AIDS: A Developmental Viewpoint." *Family Relations, 39,* 1990: 330–335.

Siccone, F. *Celebrating Diversity: Building Self-Esteem in Today's Multicultural Classrooms.* Boston: Allyn and Bacon, 1995.

Smith, J., B. Le Rose, and R. Clasen. "Underrepresentation of Minority Students in Gifted Programs. Yes! It Matters." *Gifted Child Quarterly, 35,* 1991: 81–83.

Stent, M., W. Hazard, and H. Rivlin. *Cultural Pluralism in Education: A Mandate for Change.* New York: Appleton-Century-Crofts, 1973.

Trice, H., and J. Beyer. "Using Six Organizational Rites to Change Culture." In R. H. Kilman, Ed., *Gaining Control of the Corporate Culture.* 1st ed. San Francisco: Jossey-Bass, 1985: 370–395.

Turnbull, H. R. "Free Appropriate Public Education: The Law and Children with Disabilities." Denver, CO: Love, 1993.

U.S. Department of Education. *To Assure the Free Appropriate Public Education of All Handicapped Children: Fourteenth Annual Report to Congress on the Implementation of the Education of the Handicapped Act.* Washington, DC: U.S. Department of Education, Office of Special Education and Rehabilitation Services, 1992.

Zangwill, I. *The Melting-Pot, Drama in Four Acts.* New York: Macmillan, 1909.

Chapter 12

Creating the Inclusive School: Strategies for Getting Started

Deborah Kallikak: It's the Book What Made Me Famous

The psychologist Henry Goddard founded his classic and influential research on heredity and mental retardation on the family background of a young woman to whom he gave the pseudonym Deborah Kallikak. Deborah was living at the Training School for Feeble-Minded Girls and Boys in Vineland, New Jersey, in 1912 when the study was published. Goddard was director of research there. The study and Goddard's interpretation of what he had found concerning Deborah, her relatives, and her ancestors was the substance of his book, *The Kallikak Family: A Study in the Heredity of Feeble-Mindedness.* Since Deborah was the starting point for his research, it is essential that Goddard's diagnosis of her as having mental retardation (being "feeble-minded") was accurate. A profile of Deborah, however, and scenes from her long life of institutionalization bring into question the validity of her classification as feeble-minded. They also bring into focus the tragedy of her life of confinement and exclusion.

Deborah's residence at Vineland and her diagnosis as feeble-minded was basic to Goddard's argument of the hereditary "bad seed." She was to serve as his central example of the continuing and inevitable influence of genetic defectiveness. She was also central to his argument for the need to institutionalize children and adults with even mild disabilities. Accordingly, he described Deborah in detail in order to present a convincing picture of her status as a *moron*, a Greek word that he applied to mild mental retardation.

A review of his description today, however, casts considerable doubt on her diagnosis and, certainly, on the necessity of her lifelong confinement in an institution. From the commitment information of November 1897, when Deborah was eight years old, the following excerpts are taken:

> Average size and weight. No peculiarity in form or size of head. . . . Washes and dresses herself, except for fastening clothes. . . . Knows all the colors. Not fond of music. . . . Can use a needle. . . . Careless in dress. . . . Obstinate and destructive. . . . Does not mind slapping and scolding (Goddard, 1912, p. 2).

When she was ten, the reports indicate that Deborah was able to do some reading, writing, and counting, but that her conduct was "quite bad—impudent and growing worse." By 1900, when Deborah was eleven years old, the reports contradicted the earlier description of her not enjoying music:

> Good in entertainment work. Memorizes quickly. Can always be relied upon for either speaking or singing. Marches well. . . . Knows different notes. Plays "Jesus, Lover of my Soul" nicely. Plays scale of C and F on cornet (Goddard, 1912, p. 3).

The reports of 1901 include the following comments:

> She plays by ear. She has not learned to read the notes . . . simply because she will not put her mind to it. She has played hymns in simple time, but the fingering [of the cornet valves] has had to be written for her. . . . Excellent worker in gardening class. Has just completed a very good diagram of our garden to show at Annual Meeting. . . . Has nearly finished outlining a pillow sham. . . . Is very good in number work, especially in addition. . . . Likes to be first in everything. . . . She could learn more in school if she would pay attention, but her mind seems away off from the subject in discussion (Goddard, 1912, pp. 3–4).

By the time she was fifteen, Deborah had become a quite adept seamstress, and she was making some of her own clothing. She continued to play the cornet, and she had learned to read music. Her behavior was evaluated as being "fair."

Four years later, the reports listed some deficits, primarily in academic skills, but indicated that her behavior had improved. She continued to be praised for her talent in crafts and artistic works.

> Drawing, painting, coloring, and any kind of hand work she does quite nicely. . . . This year she has made a carved book rest with mission ends and is now working on a shirtwaist box with mortise and tenon joints and lap joints. The top will be paneled (Goddard, 1912, p. 5).

At age twenty, reports indicated that she had

> made the suit which she had embroidered earlier in the year, using the machine in making it. Helped F. B. put her chair together and really acted as a teacher in showing her [F. B.] how to upholster it. Will be a helper in wood-carving class this summer (Goddard, 1912, p. 6).

In 1911, the year before Goddard's Kallikak book was published, twenty-two-year-old Deborah was described in the institutional notes as a skillful and hard worker but who lacked confidence in herself. She continued to excel in woodworking and dressmaking. Academics were, however, still problematic at times.

> Can write a well-worded story, but has to have more than half the words spelled for her (Goddard, 1912, p. 6).

The descriptions of Deborah's progress at the Training School from which these excerpts were taken are disturbingly similar to the kinds of diagnostic profiles that are found for children and adults with learning disabilities. An almost classic picture of language-related difficulties along with marked strength in nonverbal areas emerges. Psychologists and educational diagnosticians today would be more likely to view her difficulties from a learning disabilities perspective, rather than diagnosing her as having mental retardation.

It should also be noted that Deborah's early childhood was marked by poverty and abandonment. Every consideration would have to be given to possible emotional components in her learning problems and in her social difficulties. Following her birth in an almshouse (otherwise called a "poorhouse"), she had lived with her mother in conditions that, from Goddard's descriptions, were characterized by social, economic, and physical flux. Her mother married a man who insisted that she send away the children who were not his own, and so Deborah was sent to the Training School. Both early reports and later accounts of her life characterize Deborah as an easily disturbed and volatile person. The degree to which her difficulties were emotional rather than intellectual is certainly open to question.

Goddard's accounts of Deborah's ancestry, if viewed from an environmental perspective, portray a family that for generations had existed in poverty. There were apparently very few opportunities for formal education for her predecessors. There are indications that the family had always lived in exclusion from the culture that surrounded it. At the Training School, Deborah was evaluated according to standards and values that were alien to what her early life experience had taught her.

Still, the records indicate that Deborah was, in fact, learning and growing during those years at the Training School. Each year brought new developments in her life, particularly in nonacademic learning and in social skills. Goddard argued that her institutionalization was justified, that it was good for her—she was learning, becoming a more functional person, and achieving greater personal independence. Institutionalization, he contended, would allow her to live a more productive life.

Deborah, however, would never be a member of a social group other than that of an institution. She was destined to live a total of eighty-one years in two institutions. From the time she entered Vineland Training School until she died at the State School across the street, she would never know life free of institutional influence. At her death in 1978, she was buried in the institution's cemetery under a marker bearing only her name.

Descriptions of Deborah following the publication of the Kallikak study repeatedly refer to her beauty, charm, and attractive personality. In 1983, Eugene Doll, son of Edgar Doll (who worked with Goddard as an assistant from 1912 to 1917, and in 1925 became director of research at Vineland), wrote:

> There is no doubt that, whatever her mentality, she radiated that extra spark of personality which makes one stand out in a crowd and which not only attracts but holds friends. J. E. Wallace Wallin[1] wrote urbanely of his first encounter with Deborah—finding her in charge of the kindergarten at the Training School and mistaking her for the teacher. At lunchtime he was surprised to find the same attractive young woman waiting on his table.
>
> Time and again visitors in both the Training School and the Vineland State School to which Deborah was later transferred, commented on her seeming normality (Doll, 1983, p. 30).

Helen Reeves, executive social worker at the Vineland State School, commented on Deborah's transfer there from the Training School:

> For our part we knew we had acquired distinction in acquiring Deborah Kallikak, for by this time the story of her pedigree was becoming well known. And such a capable, well trained and good looking girl must be an asset. . . . Deborah at this time was a handsome young woman, twenty-five years old, with many accomplishments, though her academic progress had remained stationary just beyond second grade. She excelled in the manual arts of embroidery, woodcraft and basketry, played the cornet beautifully and took star roles in all entertainments as a matter of course. She was well trained in fine laundry work and dining room service, could use a power sewing machine and had given valuable assistance as a helper in cottages for low-grade children. Her manner toward her superior officers was one of dignified courtesy (Reeves, 1938, pp. 195–196).

Deborah was given special responsibilities during most of her institutional life. As an adolescent, she worked in the home of the superintendent of the Training School. In addition to housekeeping duties, she cared for the family's infant son. She later assumed child care responsibilities for the family of the assistant superintendent of the State School. Children from both of these families continued to visit and correspond with Deborah throughout her life. One of them acknowledged her affection and respect by naming her own daughter after Deborah (Doll, 1983).

In the early 1920s, during an epidemic in one of the buildings at the State School, Deborah served as a nurse's aide. It was reported that she "mastered the details of routine treatment and was devoted to her charges." During this period, a patient bit Deborah's hand as she was feeding her. One of her fingers was so badly injured that it later had to be amputated. According to Helen Reeves, Deborah wore "this disfigurement as a badge of honor" (Reeves, 1938, p. 196).

---

[1]Wallin was a psychologist and educator who had worked at the Training School early in his career and often returned for visits. He was a pioneer in the development of public school programs for children with mental retardation.

On occasion, Deborah traveled with the families for whom she worked to the New Jersey shore for holidays. Her own preference for vacations, however, seems to have been a series of yearly excursions that she and social worker Reeves took together. According to Reeves' recollection of their 1939 autumn trip to Washington, D.C.:

> As we rolled along southward I did not realize—though I should have—that I was establishing a precedent and that the succeeding five years would find me doing exactly the same sort of thing at this season of the year. Nineteen-forty would see us at the World's Fair in New York City; Luray Caverns would be visited in 1941 and Niagara Falls the year following; New York City again in 1943, and then—gasoline being scarce and traffic facilities constricted—1944 would find us in Philadelphia for those three precious days (Reeves, 1945, p. 3).

One of the photographs of Deborah in Goddard's book shows her sitting with a cat on her lap. She raised a long line of Persians and particularly relished the kittenhood of her charges, constructing a pink and blue bassinet to shelter the new arrivals. Her kittens were popular in the institution, and she sold them to a select clientele of Training School employees at bargain prices. Her cat family grew faster than the market for them, however; and she was eventually forced to keep only one, her favorite. She called him Henry. "He is named for a dear, wonderful friend who wrote a book. It's the book what made me famous" (Reeves, 1938, p. 194).

Deborah had a deep love of nature that she expressed in many ways. Eugene Doll writes:

> Her published photographs show her with stray animals she had befriended; unpublished ones show her peeking coyly through the apertures of a rose garden. In the spring she loved to walk among the daffodils and flowering shrubs. "She had a child's appreciation for the daisies and the dandelions or a bouquet of colorful leaves." She was fond of church and religious festivals, alternately exulting and suffering on Christmas and Good Friday. She reveled in the rhythm of poetry (Doll, 1983, pp. 31–32).

While on her excursions with Helen Reeves, Deborah kept bits of toast from breakfast in her handbag on the chance that they might encounter a bird or squirrel. She loved visiting Central Park, the Museum of Natural History, and the Bronx and Philadelphia Zoos. According to Reeves, Deborah considered her devotion to animals her greatest virtue (Reeves, 1945, pp. 6–7).

Deborah's beauty is evident from her photographs in Goddard's book. Her charm and appealing appearance are frequently mentioned by those who knew her. Doll quotes one acquaintance as saying, "Hers was a body which moved with full knowledge of the impact of its movements on the opposite sex." He also cites the impression of an employee who had accompanied a group of the institution's girls on a boardwalk stroll: "Every time we passed a man or group of men, they would stop, turn, look after Deborah, and occasionally start to follow us. I do not know what signals Deborah was sending out, but it seemed that one glance from her eyes could summon a following. I was uneasy until we got home, though Deborah had done nothing really fresh or out of order" (Doll, 1983, p. 32).

While Deborah was serving as a nurse's aide during the epidemic, she stayed in a room near her patients. While there, she was not under the same close supervision as in her usual living area. It appears that her woodworking skill enabled her to alter her window screen for easy exit and entry. She had fallen in love with an employee of the State School (a maintenance worker), and it seems that they enjoyed the moonlit grounds, and each other, in romantic interludes. Upon being discovered, however, the young man was "kindly dismissed by a lenient justice-of-the-peace," and regulations were tightened for Deborah (Reeves, 1938, p. 196). After a similar experience sometime later, she mourned,

"It isn't as if I'd done anything really wrong. It was only nature!" (Reeves 1938, p. 197). Years afterward, she would again fall in love. Helen Reeves gives us an additional insight into the attitude within the institution concerning Deborah's feelings of love and her right to romantic involvement.

> In the early fall of 1939 I returned to Vineland after a month's leave to find Deborah's spirits and morale at low ebb. She had worked hard during the summer, trying to do justice to a housework job for one of the official family, keeping on meanwhile with her responsibilities as custodian of the gymnasium and costume room. She had also managed to fall in love while I was away, which romance had been discovered and quietly nipped in full bloom without her knowledge (Reeves, 1945, pp. 2–3).

How can it be, then, that a woman of considerable talent in several areas of her life, a woman of beauty and charm, a woman lacking in academic skills but able to perform productive work, should be institutionalized for eighty-one of the eighty-nine years of her life? When so much of the information that is available indicates that Deborah had the potential for living successfully in society instead of being separated from it, what factors contributed to her lifetime of segregation?

Repeatedly in accounts of Deborah's life, references are made to her appearance of normality. Visitors and new employees expressed disbelief that she had mental retardation. Time and again, this skepticism about the accuracy of classifying Deborah as being feeble-minded, as being a "moron," was countered with the results of standardized intelligence tests. Throughout the reports, her performance on tests of academic or abstract ability was held to be of far greater importance than all of the obvious strengths that she demonstrated in her daily life. Subsequent descriptions all seem to echo to some degree Goddard's summation of Deborah's abilities:

> This is a typical illustration of the mentality of a high-grade feeble-minded person, the moron, the delinquent, the kind of girl or woman that fills our reformatories. They are wayward, they get into all sorts of trouble and difficulties, sexually and otherwise, and yet we have become accustomed to account for their defects on the basis of viciousness, environment, or ignorance.
>
> It is also the history of the same type of girl in the public school. Rather good-looking, bright in appearance, with many attractive ways, the teacher clings to the hope, indeed insists that such a girl will come out all right. Our work with Deborah convinces us that such hopes are delusions.
>
> Here is a child who has been most carefully guarded. She has been persistently trained since she was eight years old, and yet nothing has been accomplished in the direction of higher intelligence or general education. Today if this young woman were to leave the Institution, she would at once become prey to the designs of evil men or evil women and would lead a life that would be vicious, immoral, and criminal, though because of her mentality she herself would not be responsible. There is nothing that she might not be led into, because she has no power of control, and all her instincts and appetites are in the direction that would lead to vice (Goddard, 1912, pp. 11–12).

Goddard later tempered his thinking somewhat concerning the unmodifiable nature of feeble-mindedness, the incurability of the moron. Deborah, however, would be constrained by this assumption for the rest of her life. Perhaps the greatest tragedy, Deborah came to believe that life in an institution was the only one possible for her. In 1938, she told Helen Reeves, "I guess after all I'm where I belong, I don't like this feeble-minded part but anyhow I'm not idiotic like some of the poor things you see around here" (Reeves, 1938, p. 199). In 1945, Reeves reported that "Deborah, in spite of her conscious superiority, does not feel secure away from the institution. . . . 'The world is a dangerous place,' she will tell you . . ." (Reeves, 1945, p. 2).

Deborah was in a wheelchair during her final years. She was often in intense pain because of severe arthritis. She was unable to continue with the crafts that she had loved so much throughout her life. In these last years, she was offered the opportunity of leaving the institution to live in the community from which she had been segregated for almost all of her life. She declined; she knew that she needed constant medical attention (Schultz, 1979). Surely the outside world must have appeared to be an even more dangerous place to her then; the institution was the only community she understood and trusted. "As long as she was able she sent her friends photographs and dictated letters (she could no longer write) of the meaningful events of her life. Not only did she pride herself on her fame, she made a profound impression on all who knew her, and had a queen's knack for inspiring devotion" (Doll, 1983, p. 32).

In his book, Goddard described the custom at the Training School of children writing letters to Santa Claus for their Christmas wishes. He listed Deborah's requests from age ten through twenty-two. Although his reasons for including these in the book are not clear, the list offers both a poignant close to a view of her life and an illustration of her development during those years.

1899 Book and harmonica

1900 Book, comb, paints, and doll

1901 Book, mittens, toy piano, handkerchief, slate pencil

1902 Wax doll, ribbon, music box

1903 Post cards, colored ribbons, gloves, and shears

1904 Trunk, music box, Fairy Tales, games, ribbons, big doll

1905 Ribbons of different colors, games, handkerchiefs, music box, Fairy Tales

1906 Pair of stockings, ribbons, rubbers

1907 Watch, red ribbon, brush and comb, paper

1908 Three yards of lawn (light cotton fabric), rubbers

1909 Nice shoes, pink, dark blue, and white ribbons

1910 Money for dentist bill

1911 Rubbers, three skirts, blue scarf, three yards linen, two yards lawn for fancy work (Goddard, 1912, pp. 8–9).

The life of Deborah Kallikak is a sad testament to the philosophy of exclusion. It serves as a compelling reminder of the mistaken belief that people with differences are unsuited for life in society. It serves also as a reminder of the importance of caring and inclusive schools and classrooms.

Creating a Sense of Leadership and Support for Greater Inclusion

AS DISCUSSED EARLIER IN THIS BOOK, debates about inclusive classrooms have been going on for decades. Whether under the title of *mainstreaming*, the *regular education initiative*, or some other term, controversies about and experiments in the integration of children with disabilities in general classrooms have not yet resulted in more inclusive classrooms in many communities.

What is done in the name of inclusion, of course, varies greatly. In some schools, the brief physical presence of a child with a disability in a classroom may be considered sufficiently inclusive. In other schools, genuine efforts are made to create a program for each student with a disability that truly integrates and welcomes those students into the total community of the school.

The legal mandates discussed in Chapter 1 make it clear that general classroom placements for students with disabilities must be the first consideration before any special placement is assessed as an option. Placement outside of the general classroom of students for even brief periods must be justified on the basis of the needs and best interests of those students.

Perhaps even more important than the legal basis for inclusion, however, are the moral issues that it involves. In 1968 Lloyd Dunn argued that the segregation of students with disabilities created a moral dilemma for education. He said that the practice had a negative effect on teachers as well as students. Dunn stated that "by removing students with disabilities from regular classes we contribute to the delinquency of regular education. We reduce the need for regular teachers to deal with individual differences. It is morally and educationally wrong" (Dunn, 1968, p. 20).

RESPONSIBLE INCLUSION

More recently, Thomas Lombardi in his discussion of "responsible inclusion" has examined the moral issues inherent in the question of inclusive education.

> Students with disabilities have a right to be educated with their peers in integrated settings. To deny them this right is a form of discrimination. Students who are educated in separate classes often feel unmotivated, inferior, and helpless.
>
> Recently I heard someone talk about a "tolerance theory" of inclusion. The implications were that some regular teachers have a greater tolerance range than others toward accepting students with disabilities in their classroom. This no doubt is true. However, the education of students with disabilities is too important to be left to teachers' choices of whom they will or will not accept in their classes. Needing assistance, training, materials, and guidance is understandable; arbitrary refusal to accept students with disabilities is not.
>
> One of the criticisms of inclusion is that it could have a detrimental effect on the learning progress of students who are not disabled. Actually, the opposite is more likely. As teachers begin to individualize instruction to accommodate the student with special needs, other students, particularly those considered at risk, also will benefit from accompanying support systems. . . .
>
> Segregated settings do not prepare students to live in an integrated society. Re-

sponsible inclusion does. Conversely, responsible inclusion does not leave students in regular programs and classes without the necessary support systems to meet their needs (Lombardi, 1994, pp. 12–13).

INCLUSION AS A VALUES ISSUE

Norman Kunc has also explored inclusive education as a values issue. He argues that the fundamental principle of inclusion is the valuing of diversity in the human community. Kunc believes:

> When inclusive education is fully embraced, we abandon the idea that children have to become "normal" in order to contribute to the world. Instead, we search for and nourish the gifts that are inherent in all people. We begin to look beyond typical ways of becoming valued members of the community, and in doing so, begin to realize the achievable goal of providing all children with an authentic sense of belonging.
>
> As a collective commitment to educate *all* children takes hold and "typical" students realize that "those kids" do belong in their schools and classes, typical students will benefit by learning that their own membership in the class and society is something that has to do with human rights rather than academic or physical ability. In this way, it is conceivable that the students of inclusive schools will be liberated from the tyranny of earning the right to belong (Kunc, 1992, pp. 38–39).

The positive lessons that students without disabilities may learn in inclusive classrooms are actually many and varied. Almost two decades ago, an outstanding teacher with a disability spoke about the movement that was then referred to as *mainstreaming*. Joe Campbell emphasized that many people grow up with misinformation and generalizations about people with disabilities because they have been artificially separated from the realities of disabilities. Commenting on Mr. Campbell's perceptions of the importance of mainstreaming both students and teachers with disabilities, Bogdan and Sokoloff observe:

> Typical students and teachers learn lessons, too—that people with disabilities function well in society and can fill positions of responsibility. The able person need not be fearful; they can overcome any discomfort they might have in being around disabled people.
>
> Too often affirmative action programs are approached with the spirit of doing the minority a favor. Joe Campbell points out the benefits to both children and the schools when disabled adults are part of the mainstreaming plan. As he exemplifies, their limitations offer advantages. From him, too, we can understand we have yet to learn the more profound meaning of mainstreaming (Bogdan and Sokoloff, 1982, p. 114).

INCLUSION IMPLEMENTATION: STRATEGIC STEPS

While inclusion can have many positive effects for teachers, parents, and all children, it must be done properly. If it is to reach its promise and if it is to be implemented in a truly responsible manner, planning and preparation are required. This preparation must include all members of the educational community. It has been pointed out that this training

> must include knowledge of disabilities, encouragement of appropriate attitudes, legal and ethical issues, collaboration and

methods of friendship development. Specific preparation and training is also necessary for teachers and administrators in assessment, advanced collaboration skills, effective practices for direct instruction and service delivery, transition, and the evaluation of education outcomes. The responsibility for this training rests directly with individual schools and the professionals within those schools, along with local and state/provincial educational agencies (Smith and Hilton, 1996, p. 1).

There are strategic steps that may be helpful in implementing a plan for creating more inclusive schools and classrooms. Each step must, of course, be modified to meet the particular needs of individual school communities. Wisniewski and Alper have offered the following guidelines:

Elizabeth Crews/Stock Boston

- *Develop a Network*: Teachers, parents, and other community members must develop a network that works collaboratively to provide leadership and support for creating more inclusive school environments. A major initial function of this network is to assess school, parental, and community attitudes toward inclusion. When negative attitudes exist, it is the work of this network to help others to overcome these attitudinal barriers by highlighting the positive effects of inclusive classrooms.
- *Assess School and Community Resources*: In this step, network members assess the school resources that are available for providing the services mandated to students under the provisions of IDEA. Members also examine local educational policies and practices regarding students with special needs. An examination is also made of the particular administrative rules that have an impact on the services provided to students with special needs.
- *Conduct an Inclusion Strategy Review*: In this step, network members look at the options that may lead to successfully implementing more inclusive schools and classrooms. These options may include new ways of grouping students for instruction, the utilization of peer tutors, collaborative teaching, the use of volunteers, the promotion of friendships between students with and without disabilities, and the use of instructional technology.

- *Implement Inclusion Strategies*: During this step, network members install those inclusion strategies that have been deemed most appropriate and likely to be effective. This is accomplished by first increasing the awareness of all parties involved of the reasons for the adoption of these strategies. This is followed by providing teachers, students, and parents with the resources to successfully implement these strategies.
- *Develop a Feedback and Renewal System*: This step is achieved as network members collect data and evaluate how well the inclusion strategies are working. Based on this continuing evaluation, changes and innovations become a part of a dynamic program of greater inclusion (Wisniewski and Alper, 1994).

Many of the techniques and concepts mentioned in these steps toward inclusion have long been used by educators. There is nothing new, for example, about cooperative and collaborative learning or peer tutoring. What is relatively new, however, is the creative application of these methodologies in ways that will facilitate learning by students with disabilities in general classrooms. When these concepts and techniques are utilized accordingly, an inclusive classroom with the following characteristics may be created:

- Teaching is a shared, active, and creative process.
- Students are placed in groups for the sake of diversity for some activities and because they have similar needs for other activities.
- Instead of students leaving the classroom for special services, support and resources are brought into the classroom for students who have special needs.
- Students are placed at grade levels appropriate to their ages and provided with instruction according to their needs.
- The curriculum of every student (both those with and those without disabilities) is individualized.
- Special education personnel and special resources are used to assist any student who has a need that can be met by these services.
- All student progress is assessed according to individualized goals and standards.

Preparing and Encouraging Teachers

READINESS FOR INCLUSION

The readiness of a school for more inclusive classrooms may be the key to whether or not the greater integration of students with disabilities will be truly successful for all the parties concerned. Schultz (1994) has identified ten key categories of readiness that are prerequisites for a more welcoming and inclusive school. He believes that each of these characteristics must be largely evident if a school is to have a high likelihood of becoming a truly inclusive learning environment.

- *Attitudes*: Teachers and administrators must believe that greater inclusion will result in improved teaching and learning for all.
- *Relationships*: Friendships and cooperation between students with and without disabilities must be viewed as a desirable norm.

- *Support for Students*: There must be available the personnel and other resources needed to provide the services required for the successful learning of diverse students in inclusive classrooms.
- *Support for Teachers*: Teachers must have the opportunities for training that will equip them to work with a more diverse student population.
- *Administrative Leadership*: The principal and other administrators must be enthusiastic in their support and leadership for a more inclusive school.
- *Curriculum*: The curriculum must be flexible enough so that each student is challenged to achieve her or his best.
- *Assessment*: Achievement and goal attainment must be assessed in ways that give an accurate picture of each student's accomplishments.
- *Program and Staff Evaluation*: A system must be in place for evaluating the school's overall success in providing a welcoming and inclusive environment for each student.
- *Parental Involvement*: Parents of students with and without disabilities must understand the plan for creating a more inclusive school and must be involved in its implementation.
- *Community Involvement*: Through school publications and the media, the community must be informed of and involved in the effort to promote the full citizenship of students with disabilities in the life of the school. Citizens must be encouraged to extend this acceptance into the community itself (Schultz, 1994).

There are also questions that teachers should ask themselves as they face the challenges of becoming more inclusive in their teaching. It is important for a teacher to ask, for example, about her or his preparedness to work with students with various kinds of disabilities and levels of severity of those disabilities. If there are types or severities of disabilities that a teacher does not feel prepared to work with, appropriate information and training may create more openness and confidence in that teacher. Communication is a key feature of creating more inclusive classrooms, and teachers should be encouraged from the outset to voice their doubts and apprehensions.

MODIFICATIONS IN METHODS AND MATERIALS

Teachers may also be unsure of how to make modifications to their materials, methods, and expectations so that they can provide appropriate instruction to students with diverse needs. Lombardi (1994) has described several instructional models that may help promote success in inclusive classrooms. These models include:

- *Direct Instruction*: An emphasis is made on highly structured and scheduled use of classroom time, efficient use of all teacher resources (both general and special education) in the general classroom, and careful monitoring of progress;
- *Strategy Intervention*: An emphasis is made on teaching skills like listening, note taking, self-questioning, test taking, and error monitoring;
- *Teacher-Assistance Teams*: Teachers (general and special education) work as teams. They meet frequently to solve

problems and provide help to one another. Teacher-assistance teams most often provide help to their members on managing student behavior and with questions about academic problems;

- *Consulting Teacher Model*: Special teachers trained as consultants provide consultation and assistance to teachers in general classes. They also help train paraprofessionals assigned to general classrooms to help with students with disabilities. In addition, they do team teaching along with general classroom teachers of students who have special needs regardless of whether or not they have been identified as having disabilities (Lombardi, 1994).

Lombardi points out, however, that the teaching methods that general classroom teachers have found to be most effective with their students without disabilities can also be effective with students with disabilities. Good teaching is, in many respects, good teaching regardless of the specific characteristics of the learners. He also recognizes, however, that some instructional modifications have proven to be particularly effective for students with disabilities in general classrooms.

> Good teaching methods have no boundaries. Although an inclusive classroom does focus on the individual, there are some generalized instructional modifications that are especially suited to students with learning problems. These include using advanced organizers, preteaching key vocabulary, providing repetition of instruction, previewing major concepts, making time adjustments, using manipulatives, and providing corrective feedback. Cooperative groups, peer tutoring, whole-language instruction, unit teaching, and behavior modification procedures all have received support in the literature (Lombardi, 1994, p. 31).

Another question that teachers must ask themselves as they prepare to become more involved in inclusive educational practices is the extent to which they expect all students to meet the same standards. Acceptance of individual progress toward personalized goals is critical to working with students with special needs. Being able to praise and value the progress of these students is also important. Rigid standards for success and recognizing only the achievement of these standards may be detrimental to the education of all students.

TEACHER NEEDS

A survey of elementary school teachers' perceptions of their needs related to the inclusion of children with disabilities revealed that a high percentage of them reported a need for training about students with special needs. A low percentage, however, reported that they had actually received that training (Wolery et al., 1995). In addition to training, teachers have been found to need other basic types of support in order to provide the kinds of inclusive classroom environments that will benefit all students. Among these are:

- The number of students in the general classroom must be small enough so that the teacher can know and work with each student.
- A well-trained paraprofessional should be present who can offer individualized instruction and other assistance to students with and without disabilities (Cipani, 1995).

Another survey found that teachers have a positive opinion of inclusion when they are provided with appropriate instructional materials and adequate time to carry out the requirements of individualized education programs and other support services (LRP Publications, 1995a).

THE SUPPORT OF THE PRINCIPAL

Without the backing of administrators, the effort to create more inclusive classrooms is not likely to succeed. Teachers need to be given the unqualified commitment by the administrators of the school that they and their students will be given the support they need for this effort. It has also been pointed out that, along with this wholehearted administrative commitment to inclusion, there is another key to administrative support—an understanding of the challenges faced by teachers and students involved in more inclusive educational practices (LRP Publications, 1995b).

The principal is usually the most important administrator and leader in any school. Principals in schools where students are becoming more integrated into the total school program need to have a good working knowledge of special education policies and procedures. A number of other characteristics of principals who successfully facilitate inclusive schools and classrooms have been observed:

- The principal takes a clear position in support of the beliefs and values underlying the inclusion of students with disabilities.
- The principal is visible, is proactive, and shows a commitment to these values.
- The principal's expectations of teachers and students are clear.
- The principal is a good communicator.
- The principal provides teachers with adequate preparation and planning time.
- The principal encourages parental involvement (Burello and Wright, 1992).

Preparing and Encouraging Parents

PARENTS OF STUDENTS WITH DISABILITIES may experience anxieties about having their children educated in inclusive classrooms. When these parents compare the class size and resources of a special class to those of a general classroom, they may feel that placing their children in an inclusive classroom is risky (Woelfel, 1994).

On the other hand, many parents actively seek inclusive placements and are skeptical of even limited removal of their children from these placements for special services. A key issue for many of these parents is the social impact of segregated educational settings on their children. As one parent explained:

> To me as a parent, the most important issue of inclusion is self-esteem. We must realize that many of the social problems our society faces today are the result of poor self-esteem in individuals who never had the environment or the opportunities to develop a healthy appreciation of themselves. . . .
>
> With inclusion, we are placing children with special needs in the regular classroom, giving them the opportunities they deserve and allowing peer modeling of appropriate behavior. We are subconsciously letting them know that they are equal to any other human being and capable of meeting our expectations (Oberti, 1993, p. 19).

This same parent speaks directly to teachers about the importance of attitudes that are inclusive of students with disabilities.

Believe in your students. Believe in the fact that every child has a gift that is very individual. Believe that everybody can learn. Believe in cooperation and sharing among your students. Then you will have the power to liberate their human potential to the best of their ability. Set our children free (Oberti, 1993, p. 21).

INCLUDING PARENTS

Parents must be encouraged to be partners in the inclusive education of their children. They must be involved in the decisions and planning that lead to a student's placement in an inclusive classroom. Following the placement, however, they should be encouraged to be involved in a continuing dialogue with the teacher. Some questions that may encourage the involvement of parents and that may provide valuable information to the teacher are:

- How is your child reacting to her/his new class placement?
- How is your child doing academically in her/his new class?
- Have you noticed any changes in your child since he/she has been in this class?
- Are you satisfied with the opportunities you have had to be involved with your child's educational programs?
- Do you have any suggestions for facilitating your child's adjustment to this class?
- What inclusion policies/practices in this school do you like? What would you like to see changed? (Salend, 1983)

Once parents have been welcomed as partners in an inclusive classroom, there are other means of communication that may help to strengthen and broaden these partnerships. These means include:

- *Informal Exchanges*: Important information may be exchanged when parents pick up and deliver their children. It may be very helpful if teachers can plan to have a few minutes for brief conversations with parents during these times.
- *Parental Observations*: Parents should be made to feel welcome to visit the classroom at any time. Watching their children work and interact with other students can provide them with important information about how they can help with their child's educational experience.
- *Telephone Calls*: Parents should be encouraged to call teachers with questions or comments. Providing a telephone number and a good time for calling may be a powerful incentive for keeping communication open.
- *Written Notes*: Frequent notes sent home can be very helpful and reinforcing for parents. Particular attention should be given to sending home notes about positive accomplishments.
- *Two-Way Journal*: An elaboration of written notes is a two-way journal that travels back and forth from teacher to parent. This may encourage more frequent written communication and provides a lasting record of that communication.
- *Audiotapes and Videotapes*: Audiotapes may be a more effective means for communicating with some parents. Even a two-way journal may be established by means of tape rather than in writing. Videotapes may be provided to parents who have difficulty visiting the classroom for observations.
- *Newsletter*: A class newsletter may be a nice way of communicating with parents.

Through the newsletter, parents may learn more about their children's classmates. They can also be kept informed of recent activities and upcoming events in this way (Allen and Schwartz, 1996).

Preparing and Encouraging Students

In 1993 Anastasia Somoza, a nine-year-old, was a student in an inclusive classroom in New York. Anastasia has cerebral palsy and uses a wheelchair for mobility. She also uses a walker, stander, and braces for some activities. She uses special computer software and hardware to help with her schoolwork.

Anastasia had previously attended a special school for students with disabilities. In comparing these two educational settings, she said:

> I like being in a regular class because I now have lots of friends. As my friends live nearby, they come over to my house for play dates and even sleepovers. At my old school, my friends lived too far away and they never came for play dates. We could not go to their house either because we do not have a car. All of the kids at my old school were disabled and it was hard for their parents to bring them to my house.
>
> My best friend at school is called Natalie. She is not disabled. She helps me with lots of things, and she plays with me at recess time. I am the only one in my class who cannot walk but that's okay. My friends push me around (Somoza, 1993, p. 17).

Anastasia made an appeal on national television to the President to help her sister Alba to be included in a general classroom.

> I have a twin sister who goes to the same school, but she is in a special class. She uses a computer to talk, and a different computer to do her studies. She also uses a wheelchair and stander. She is very smart and I hope she can soon be in a regular class just like me. Thank you (Somoza, 1993, p. 17).

Anastasia and Alba are now both in general public education classes.

The full impact of inclusive classrooms on stereotypes and negative attitudes toward students with disabilities continues to be a question for further study (Sale and Carey, 1995). It is clear, however, that the way students are grouped in schools teaches powerful lessons to the students in those schools. When students with disabilities are segregated from other students, this separation may teach students with special needs negative lessons about themselves. It may teach other students that there is not a place in their world for other people who are different in certain ways. On the contrary, Davern and Schnorr (1991) emphasize that the education of people to be welcoming of people with disabilities requires interaction with these people. Students learn to understand and value people with learning, physical, or emotional differences through shared experiences.

In an important study of the impact of inclusion on teachers and students, Giangreco et al. (1993) found that a transformation occurs in classrooms that move from a segregated to a more inclusive model. In this study, it was found that teachers who were reluctant, cautious, or even negative about inclusion experienced an increasing willingness, as they learned more about these students, to:

1. Interact with the students with disabilities;

2. Learn additional skills that would benefit students with disabilities; and
3. Accept the students as valuable members of the class.

The study found that the students with disabilities became more responsive to their teachers, their fellow students, and other school personnel as the school year progressed. These students also learned new social, communication, and academic skills that enhanced their lives at home and in the community, as well as in school.

A third important finding of the study concerned students without disabilities in these classes. These students reported that they had a greater awareness of people with disabilities because of the inclusion programs in their classrooms. These students were also more accepting and comfortable with their peers with disabilities as the inclusion program progressed (Giangreco et al., 1993).

The most important implication of these findings may be that inclusion is a process and that it takes time for that process to work. Although planning and preparation are essential to the implementation of inclusive classrooms, it is the actual experience of inclusion that yields positive results for students and their teachers. In this sense, the best preparation of students for inclusive classrooms is their actual immersion in these classrooms. Involving students with and without disabilities in work and play together, along with sensitive support and encouragement, may be the most powerful technique for the achievement of greater understanding and cooperation.

The inclusion of students with disabilities in general classrooms is increasing. A growing number of students are receiving the majority of their instruction in classrooms with their nondisabled peers. While the goal of inclusion is being pursued more vigorously, however, important issues must be raised concerning how it is being pursued.

The creation of inclusive schools is first and foremost an issue of preparation and training. Inclusion is, in this sense particularly, an educational issue. It is an issue of education for teachers and administrators about the meanings of disabilities and about the children who have them. It is an issue of education for students who do not have disabilities but who need to understand and welcome their peers with disabilities into their classrooms. It is an issue of preparing children with disabilities who have previously been in more segregated educational environments for greater involvement in the mainstream of schools. It is an issue, foremost, of helping schools come to view themselves as inclusive communities that must find ways of better understanding and serving all of their members. It is an issue of education for the integration and acceptance of all children, and the best provision of services to all children.

Inclusion is, more than anything else, an issue of educating school communities in ways that will allow them to change their understanding of, and attitudes and behavior toward, students who have traditionally been viewed as so atypical that they required segregated education. McLaughlin and Warren, in a most insightful manner, have articulated the need for creating the supports necessary for staff development and renewal. These observations, while directed at the need for staff development, also apply to the needs of parents and students.

> Ultimately, the success of any change in the way regular education and/or special education is defined or designed will depend on the support and capabilities of the staff who must implement the programs. It is

> people who change systems. Clearly, the task that everyone acknowledges as critical to restructuring is to ensure that all staff learn new skills and the new ways of approaching their roles. The importance of professional staff development and support is such that a resource commitment to this endeavor should precede even the development of a mission statement. All staff, instructors, and administrators must have ongoing support and assistance through the often long, hard task of restructuring. Such intensive development requires human and fiscal resources and top-level commitment to provide such resources for the long term. . . .
>
> As professionals begin to explore more collaborative ways of providing special education within the context of regular education, all educators in the schools need to gain new understandings about students with and without disabilities, as well as how to accept a broader, more communal responsibility for the learning outcomes of those students. Staff development that responds to such broad responsibility needs to be designed by the individual recipients and should provide long-term support, not episodic topical workshops or seminars (McLaughlin and Warren, 1992, pp. 67–68).

McLaughlin and Warren have also suggested that there are basic strategies that must be employed at the level of the individual school in order to create the atmosphere and expertise needed for more inclusive environments.

- Organize staff development activities around the shared goal of creating a more inclusive school.
- Involve the whole school staff in the planning of this staff development program, which is specifically designed to meet the need for greater understanding of children with disabilities and their need for greater inclusion in their school.
- Include parents in this staff development process.
- When the school staff deems it appropriate, it should contract for the services of consultants with expertise in special education and inclusion to assist the school in the planning and training needed to create a more inclusive environment.
- Use peer-coaching and peer-mentoring between members of the school staff to help with this staff development. Special education staff members should be released from some teaching duties to provide training for other teachers.
- Establish school guidelines and procedures for preparing children with disabilities for placement in more inclusive educational settings within this particular school.
- Develop guidelines and procedures for preparing children without disabilities for the placement of children with disabilities in their classrooms.
- Use the technologies available to them in the delivery of the staff development and other activities described above.
- Demonstrate support for these efforts by the total involvement of the principal and other school leaders (McLaughlin and Warren, 1992).

If students, parents, teachers, and schools are to thrive in an environment of greater fairness, greater sensitivity, and a renewed sense of mission, it is necessary that an atmosphere of increased trust and cooperation be created. All of the people involved in the challenge of preparing students with disabilities for life in a more open society must be in communication with one another. To this end, education for these students must be truly an individually designed effort that takes into account the need for inclusion, the need for special services, and the need for supportive environments that students require for educational success.

Case Studies and Questions to Consider

PUPIL: ANDY MARTIN

SCHOOL: SANDY MIDDLE SCHOOL

CURRENT PLACEMENT: GENERAL SEVENTH

AGE: 13 YEARS, 2 MONTHS

Family Structure and Home Environment

Andy lives with his mother and father, Jan and Joseph Martin, and his sister, Sherry. His mother is forty-one years old and is a dietary supervisor at Community Hospital. She has a second job cleaning homes in the evenings several days each week. Andy's father is forty-two years old and has two jobs also. He is employed as a bus driver and works at the Waffle House at night. Sherry is fifteen years old and is in the tenth grade. Andy's father earned a GED certificate, and his mother finished eleventh grade.

Andy has an older sister, Phyllis, who recently graduated from college. Phyllis is now living in Pennsylvania with her aunt and is seeking employment there. Ms. Martin says that Phyllis moved to Pennsylvania because of the disturbances that Andy's behavior has created in their home. She expresses fear that Andy's other sister, Sherry, may also leave if he continues to disrupt their family life.

Parental Perception of the Student's School Problem

Mr. and Ms. Martin believe that their son has a serious problem. Ms. Martin comments that Andy was in special classes in the second, third, and fourth grades because of his inability to control his behavior. She adds, "He wouldn't take that now." When asked to explain, she says that Andy has threatened to kill himself if he is put in special classes again. She says that she thinks that Andy is "just out of control" and that she does not know what to do.

Additional Considerations

Mr. and Ms. Martin feel that maintaining a positive self-image has been a struggle for Andy. They feel that their son has often taken to heart the comments of the other students concerning his receiving special services in school, and that he has felt that it was a badge of personal deficiency. Recently, for example, Andy was experiencing a low period emotionally and was referring to himself as being mentally retarded. It took the reassurance of his pediatrician to convince him that this is not true.

Mr. and Ms. Martin have worked devotedly with Andy to convince him that he is a worthy and capable human being. They feel that his teachers have also been important to him in this regard as well as in promoting his academic skills. Mr. and Ms. Martin feel that Andy has made considerable progress in academic skills in recent years. They report that he still has some difficulties with reading and other basic skills but that he has come a long way in overcoming his learning problems. They also believe he has benefited greatly from receiving special services for his emotional disabilities. It is their hope that Andy will develop even stronger academic and social skills. They feel, however, that this help will have to come to him in a way that is not stigmatizing to him.

Questions

1. From the information provided, do you think Andy's parents should ask that he be evaluated for special services?
2. What could you suggest to the Martins that might help Andy learn to control his behavior and that could bolster his self-confidence?
3. What could be done in Andy's classroom to help him with his struggle for a more positive self-concept?

PUPIL: MARIA NICOLE

SCHOOL: HERMITAGE MIDDLE SCHOOL

CURRENT PLACEMENT: GENERAL EIGHTH

AGE: 13 YEARS, 11 MONTHS

Family Structure and Home Environment

Maria lives with her mother, Ms. Ramona Nicole. Ms. Nicole is a twenty-nine-year-old single parent. At present, she is not employed outside of her home. Ms. Nicole did not graduate from high school, but she did earn a GED certificate. Maria also lives with her brother, Riccardo, who is eight; a sister, Tiffany, who is five; and a sister, Monique, who is three.

Ms. Nicole does not feel that Maria has any serious deficits in her capabilities for academic performance. She thinks that all of her daughter's basic skills in reading, writing, and mathematics are adequate to allow her to perform appropriately for her grade level.

Ms. Nicole acknowledges that Maria has not done well in some subjects, but she attributes this to factors other than her daughter's academic ability. She believes that Maria's difficulties are social and emotional in origin.

Parental Perception of the School Problem

Maria is experiencing difficulties in her classes due to behaviors considered peculiar by others. She is reported to engage in excessive fantasy and is described as overly active. She also has difficulty in interpersonal relations.

Ms. Nicole is aware of Maria's difficulties in relating to other students at school. She is also aware that, at times, her daughter has not had strongly positive relationships with some of her teachers. Ms. Nicole feels, however, that during the last year there has been an important and disturbing influence in her daughter's life.

Maria and Ms. Nicole have been seeing a counselor at the Mental Health Clinic who is helping them deal with a recently disclosed trauma. During the last year, Maria was sexually molested by an adult neighbor and friend of the family. Ms. Nicole felt that something had been wrong with Maria for some time but had no idea how serious it was until Maria was able to confide in her. They are both currently working with a lawyer, and the case should be heard in court soon.

This year Maria seemed to withdraw dramatically from her schoolwork. Ms. Nicole says that Maria has done practically no homework since the beginning of the academic year. She feels that because of the emotional stress her daughter has been feeling, she simply quit trying to concentrate on school matters.

Additional Considerations

Ms. Nicole hopes that things can be better for Maria at school. She feels that some form of special services would be helpful to her daughter. Maria is apprehensive about the idea. She fears that she would be stigmatized by receiving special services.

Ms. Nicole has high hopes for Maria. She would like to see her become a teacher or librarian. Maria has expressed the same hope.

Ms. Nicole wants to see her daughter feel better about herself. She says she wants Maria to know that she is "somebody."

Questions

1. Should Maria be evaluated for special education services?
2. What other school/community resources might be helpful to Maria and Ms. Nicole?
3. What can be done in her classroom that might be helpful to Maria?

References

Allen, K. E., and I. Schwartz. *The Exceptional Child: Inclusion in Early Childhood Education.* 3d ed. Albany, NY: Delmar, 1996.

Bogdan, R., and M. Sokoloff. "The Advantages of Limitations: A Teacher with a Disability Speaks About Mainstreaming." *NASSP Bulletin,* 66(456), 1982: 109–114.

Burello, L. C., and P. T. Wright. *The Principal Letters: Practices for Inclusive Schools.* Bloomington, IN: National Academy/CASE, 1992.

Cipani, E. "Inclusive Education: What Do We Know and What Do We Still Have to Learn?" *Exceptional Children, 61*(5), 1995: 498–500.

Davern, L., and R. Schnorr. "Public Schools Welcome Students with Disabilities as Full Members." *Children Today, 20,* 1991: 21–25.

Doll, E. E. "Deborah Kallikak: 1889–1978, A Memorial." *Mental Retardation, 21,* 1983: 30–32.

Dunn, L. M. "Special Education for the Mildly Retarded: Is Much of It Justifiable?" *Exceptional Children, 35,* 1968: 5–22.

Giangreco, M. F., R. Dennis, C. Cloninger, S. Edelman, and R. Schattman. "I've Counted Jan: Transformational Experiences of Teachers Educating Students with Disabilities." *Exceptional Children, 59,* 1993: 359–372.

Goddard, H. H. *The Kallikak Family: A Study in the Heredity of Feeble-Mindedness.* New York: Macmillan, 1912.

Kunc, N. "The Need to Belong: Rediscovering Maslow's Hierarchy of Needs." In R. Villa, J. Thousand, W. Stainback, and S. Stainback, Eds., *Restructuring for Caring and Effective Education: An Administrative Guide to Creating Heterogeneous Schools.* Baltimore, MD: Brooks, 1992: 25–39.

Lombardi, T. P. *Responsible Inclusion of Students with Disabilities.* Bloomington, IN: Phi Delta Kappa Educational Foundation, 1994.

LRP Publications. "Pennsylvania Teacher Poll Shows Inclusion on the Rise, Supports Lacking." *Inclusive Education Programs, 3*(1), 1995a: 7–8.

———. "Principal Interest: Can Your Staff Bank on the Building's Leadership?" *Inclusive Education Programs, 3*(2), 1995b: 1, 10–11.

McLaughlin, M., and S. Warren. *Issues and Options in Restructuring Schools and Special Education Programs.* College Park, MD: Center for Policy Options in Special Education, University of Maryland, 1992.

Oberti, C. "Inclusion: A Parent's Perspective." *Exceptional Parent, 23*(7), 1993: 18–21.

Reeves, H. T. "The Later Years of a Noted Mental Defective." *Journal of Psycho-Asthenics, 43,* 1938: 194–200.

———. 1945. "Travels with a Celebrity." *Training School Bulletin, 42:* 119.

Sale, P., and D. M. Carey. "The Sociometric Status of Students with Disabilities in a Full-Inclusion School." *Exceptional Children, 62*(1), 1995: 6–19.

Salend, S. "Mainstreaming: Sharpening Up Follow-Up." *Academic Therapy, 18*(3), 1983: 299–304.

Schultz, H., Director, Vineland State School. Personal communication, April 5, 1979. Cited in R. D. Scheerenberger, *A History of Mental Retardation.* Baltimore, MD: Paul H. Brookes, 1983: 151.

Schultz, J. J. "Inclusion: The Debate Continues." *Instructor, 104*(4), 1994: 55–56.

Smith, J. D., and A. Hilton. "Position Statement on the Need for Adequate Preparation and Training of the Educational Community for the Inclusion of Students with Developmental Disabilities." *MRDD Express, 6*(2), 1996: 1.

Somoza, A. "Inclusion: A Child's Perspective." *Exceptional Parent, 23*(7), 1993: 17.

Wisniewski, L., and S. Alper. "Including Students with Severe Disabilities in General Education Settings: Guidelines for Change." *Remedial and Special Education, 15*(1), 1994: 4–13.

Woelfel, K. "Inclusion, Exclusion, Confusion, and Infusion." *Principal, 73*(4), 1994: 48, 50.

Wolery, M., M. G. Werts, N. K. Caldwell, E. D. Snyder, and L. Lisowski. "Experienced Teachers' Perceptions of Resources and Supports for Inclusion: Education and Training." *Mental Retardation and Developmental Disabilities, 30*(1), 1995: 15–26.

Creating a More Caring Community

Uncle, Brownie, and the Sausage Biscuit: Recapturing a Spirit

An uncle may be a very special person to a child. At times he may be nurturing and protective in a way that supplements or, in some cases, substitutes for the love of a father. He may also be a close friend or big brother to a boy or girl who needs one. An uncle might also be a man who allows a child to see the world through the eyes of another male; he may broaden the vision of life's possibilities that a good father has already provided.

My Uncle Ganiel was the kind of man who made the world more interesting and exciting for me as a boy growing up in Virginia in the 1950s. He was a big man with a bold voice. He walked and talked with bravado, and he made me laugh. He kidded me in a way that I always knew expressed affection. Over the years he joked with me about girls, about remembering me as a toddler who used to have accidents in his pants, and about being too tall and skinny as an adolescent. He had rusty hair and freckles on his arms. He appeared to be strong against the world's stings, but I often saw his eyes puddle with tears when he spoke of children in need. More than once I was aware that he bought groceries for a family in trouble. He had them delivered anonymously.

From the time of my earliest recollections, I called him Uncle, just Uncle. I continued to call him Uncle until he died. I think he enjoyed being called by that name. Maybe it reminded him of the earlier days of our relationship when I was a child and he was a young man. I miss Uncle greatly. It is hard to accept death when it comes to one so full of life.

Uncle liked to hunt. One of my early memories is of a deer head mounted on the wall of Uncle's living room. The antlers were shiny with shellac, and the fur was stiff. But it was the brown glass eyes that were a source of amazement and intimidation to a four-year-old. They seemed to follow me wherever I walked in the room. I remember being afraid of staying alone in the room with the head. If Uncle was in the room, however, I felt safe.

Uncle owned a small hunting cabin. It was actually a house trailer that he had covered with a zinc roof and to which he had added a porch. It was located on a few acres of land in a very secluded forest area. A beautiful mountain creek ran by it. Every fall Uncle went to his cabin during deer season for a few days. He would meet there with some of his friends and sometimes with his son, my cousin Orbie. One of his best friends had a cabin on an adjoining lot. It was a time for renewing and strengthening friendships, but I am not sure how much hunting was actually done. In fact, I am not sure how many deer Uncle ever killed or wanted to kill. The only one I have evidence of was the trophy with glass eyes in his living room.

In addition to being with his friends, hunting was important to Uncle for another reason. It was a good excuse for having a dog. Over the years, Uncle had a series of dogs that started out as working animals or strays and ended up as beloved friends to him. Each seemed to come to him by appearing out of a storm or being abandoned along an isolated road. In every case, however, Uncle found a special feature of the dog that was worthy of repeated praise. His dog was always the smartest dog he had ever known, or the fastest dog he had ever seen, or the sweetest animal that he had ever seen around children. The first of Uncle's dogs that I remember was Brownie. I have a vivid image of Brownie lying on the wide wooden porch that wrapped around the house that Uncle shared with my Aunt Catherine, Orbie, and my younger cousin Lisa. Brownie seemed to always be there sleeping in the sun while, as Uncle assured me, he was also doing his work of protecting the house. Actually, I don't think I ever heard Brownie bark at anyone or anything. Uncle once explained that Brownie was getting old and had already done his share of the world's work. He had been, according to

Uncle, the best hunting dog he had ever seen. I'm not sure if that was true, but I always believed that Brownie had been the dog that flushed the deer on Uncle's wall out of the woods. I'm inclined to believe today that it was the only deer that either of them ever needed. I think of the deer on the wall as a symbol of the bond between Uncle and Brownie that was complete in itself; no further evidence of their shared hunting adventures was required.

I have wonderful memories of visits to Uncle's house as a child and teenager. Aunt Catherine always went out of her way to make me feel at home, Lisa was full of fun, and Orbie was inevitably involved in a project that fascinated me. He is a few years older, and he taught me much about history, art, and philosophy through the model ships and planes that he constructed, the music he listened to, and the books that he talked about. Uncle consistently told me at the table that I didn't eat "enough to keep a bird alive," but he also let me know that I didn't have to eat anything that I didn't want. Uncle himself had interesting dietary preferences. I don't remember a single time that pinto beans were not served at lunch and dinner by Aunt Catherine. She once told me that Uncle had asked for pintos on their wedding day, and since that first day of married life, she had always kept a pot of beans on the stove. She explained that he had grown up in a large family where pintos were the staple that enabled the family to be fed adequately day in and day out. Aunt Catherine also usually had mashed potatoes on the table at every noon and evening meal. Fresh corn bread or slices of "white bread" were common, and during the summer, sliced tomatoes and green beans rounded out the meals that I now think of with great pleasure.

I do not remember ever seeing Uncle eat meat at lunch or dinner. Again, Aunt Catherine explained to me that it was because meat had been so expensive and scarce in his family while he was growing up in rural poverty. Indeed, I remember once when Uncle came to our house one afternoon to pick up Aunt Catherine. She had been visiting with us for the morning. He had not had anything to eat since breakfast, yet he declined my mother's offers of leftover fried chicken or anything else in our kitchen he might want. He made his own inventory of the contents of the refrigerator. He then proceeded to fix a sandwich of cold mashed potatoes on the heel slices from a loaf of bread. The experience of watching Uncle eating a cold mashed potato sandwich made quite an impression on me!

Uncle was not a vegetarian. The first time I remember seeing Uncle eat meat, however, was on an early morning ride I took with him. It was in the pickup truck that he used in his work for a hardware company. The night before, he, Aunt Catherine, Orbie, Lisa, and I had squeezed into the truck cab for a ride to buy ice cream cones. In the process of getting in and trying to get settled, however, I left my hand in the hinge as the door was slammed shut. The pain was awful. I cried and felt panic. Immediately, my fingernails turned purple. Soon we were back in the house. Aunt Catherine carefully soaked and bandaged my fingers. Uncle paced and cussed at fate, at the truck, and perhaps even at himself. I knew, however, it was not directed at me.

The next morning Uncle offered to give me another ride in his truck. I don't remember where Aunt Catherine, Orbie, and Lisa were, but I do remember that Uncle, Brownie, and I went for a ride. By this time Brownie was both blind and arthritic. Uncle had to help him into the truck. Soon Brownie was curled up on the floorboard. As we drove through the quiet streets of Roanoke, Virginia, Uncle asked me if my fingers still hurt. He told me to be sure to keep soaking them regularly until the swelling, which was now very obvious, went down.

Uncle pulled the pickup into the parking lot of a diner that was a local legend. It was one of those places that during the 1950s and 1960s sold hamburgers that were about the size of half dollars. They were sold for about fifteen cents each. For fifty cents you could buy four. In the mornings, the same deal was offered for "sausageburgers" of the same size. Uncle parked the truck, went into the diner, and soon returned with a bag. He insisted that I have two of the sandwiches. He only had one. The fourth sausage sandwich was served to Brownie on the floor of the truck's cab. Although it took him a moment to catch on, the burger was greatly appreciated once Brownie recognized the bun and meat for what it was. Almost apologizing for giving the sandwich to a dog, Uncle told me that he thought it was important to remember that "an old dog like Brownie deserves to have a friend."

Uncle and Catherine lived modestly. They were not people who wasted things or indulged themselves, let alone a pet. Uncle wanted me to know that the sausageburger for Brownie was special. Brownie finished the sausage but left some of the bread. Uncle drove us back to the house in silence; I will always remember that brief ride. By taking me on this special trip, he had shown me in a simple way that he cared about me, and he had allowed me to see him caring about Brownie. I also gained some other new insights into the beauty and depth of his character.

Uncle's last dog was named Benji. The two of them rode everywhere together in Uncle's car and were pretty much inseparable friends in most other respects. Among their rituals was an early morning ride and visit to the drive-through at a local fast-food franchise. The days of the old diner and sausageburgers had, of course, given way to sausage biscuits at Hardee's. Because of his health problems, he could no longer eat sausage or the rich biscuits that the patties were served on. His trip to the drive-through was just for Benji. Apparently, the workers at the Hardee's window looked forward each morning to seeing the dog sitting up with what they thought looked like a grin on his face in anticipation of his breakfast.

I once asked Uncle about Benji and his breakfast trips. He told me that it meant more to him to see his dog enjoying those sausage biscuits than if he were still able to eat them himself. He said that it was the same kind of feeling that he got when he saw something good happening for one of his grandchildren; it felt better than if it were happening for him. He said that "after a certain point in life, you have had enough of almost everything for yourself, and then the best times for you are when you see children and young people made happy by the little things you can do for them. And it's the same with Benji and his biscuits too." He added, "Of course, there has never been another dog quite like Benji."

I was a pallbearer at Uncle's funeral. I left for the funeral early and stopped for coffee at the Hardee's where Uncle and Benji had made their morning visits. I sat and thought of the years I had known Uncle and the good things that he had done for me. He had made me feel important by giving his attention to me, even through his joking and kidding. He had taught me some important lessons about life by letting me see some of the sensitive and tender parts of his character. I knew that he was always glad to see me. I miss him, but he lives on in my heart through my many warm memories of him. I'm glad and proud that he was my Uncle.

An eminent developmental psychologist, the late Erik Erikson, has described four overarching tasks of adult life. He felt that for an adult to have lived out the best potentials and possibilities, it is necessary that the life span of that person include: the development of an independent sense of identity, the achievement of the capacity to be truly intimate and committed in relationships, and the ability to be wise and insightful about the temporary nature of one's own life and the achievement of peace concerning death. A fourth task of life that he thought is critical to adult development is the capacity for what he calls generativity. He used the term in part to describe the nurturing of a new generation as it is done by parents, and through which they discover new ways of caring for others. Through the experience of nurturing children, we may gain a new sense of the joy of giving and the meaningfulness of making sacrifices for them. Erikson felt, however, that we become generative not only with our own children but in the many ways that as adults we may care for extended families, neighbors, communities, churches, and even other people's children.

My memories of Uncle serve as an example for me of what it means to be generative. His model of finding simple joy in the nurturance of others, even greater joy than in finding rewards for himself, is encouraging to me. I believe that this is the essence of being "grown up." Maturity means being more engaged in the growth and benefit of others who need your help than you are involved in your own gain. Erikson, in fact, described the opposite of generativity as self-absorption or stagnation. He felt that the adult who is unable to become generative becomes so self-focused that he or she is incapable of the joy of maturity. This is a person who spends time and energy in a continuing attempt to seek gratification for self and to ease the pain of a lonely existence through self-absorption.

Uncle's happiness in seeing the joy of others has also caused me to reflect upon our society as a whole. I have come to believe that we as a nation must recapture a sense of the generativity that earlier characterized our ideals. We as a nation must "grow up" enough again to look outward for the gratification of helping others to learn, to be healthier, to be more secure, to have better living conditions. The most fortunate among us have sought wealth, power, independence, and pleasure for ourselves and have found it. It is incumbent upon us now, if we are to be a truly generative nation, that we face the poverty, homelessness, discouragement, and hopelessness in those all around us and find true gratification in helping others find nourishment, shelter, opportunities for growth, and belief in themselves. It is critical to our health as a culture that we become a more caring and inclusive community.

Inclusion: Benefits for Students

The U.S. Department of Education reports that general classroom placements of students with disabilities continue to increase. At the same time, the use of special education resource rooms has decreased. These overall figures for the United States, however, have been disproportionately influenced by large increases in the numbers of students with disabilities placed in general classes in a relatively small number of states. Some of these increases may, in fact, be the result of improved data collection and reporting procedures rather than actual changes in placement practices (Office of Special Education Programs, 1995).

The figures, however, are encouraging. During the 1992–93 school year, 39.8 percent of students with disabilities were served in general classrooms. An additional 31.7 percent were served in resource rooms, and 23.5 percent were served in separate classes that were housed in regular school buildings. Only 5 percent of students with disabilities were served in separate schools, residential facilities, or homebound hospital settings (Office of Special Education Programs, 1995).

The placement patterns for students with disabilities continue to vary greatly according to age. Students with disabilities in elementary schools are the most likely to be in general classrooms. Almost 50 percent are in inclusive settings. Students with disabilities ages 12 through 17 are much less likely to be in inclusive classrooms. Only 30 percent are in these settings. Only 23 percent of students with disabilities ages 18 through 21 are in inclusive environments (Office of Special Education Programs, 1995).

Inclusive placements also vary according to types of disabilities. Students with speech and language impairments were served in 1992–93 almost exclusively in general classrooms, with a small percentage in resource rooms. A large percentage of students with learning disabilities were served in inclusive settings (43.9 percent). Far fewer students with mental retardation, serious emotional disturbance, and several other categories of disability were served in general classrooms. The smallest percentages of inclusion were found for students with autism and deaf-blindness. Separate classes and separate schools were the most common placements for these students (Office of Special Education Programs, 1995).

The fact that inclusion is more likely to be a reality in the lives of students with some disabilities and not in the lives of students with other disabilities is dramatically portrayed in a statement by the Association for Retarded Citizens (ARC). In its *1995 Report Card on Inclusion in Education of Students with Mental Retardation*, the ARC states:

> On the eve of the 20th anniversary of the Individuals with Disabilities Education Act, the ARC is extremely disappointed to issue this report verifying that for children with mental retardation, placement in segregated educational environments continues to be the rule of the land. Tragically, only 7.1 percent of children with mental retardation were receiving their education in regular classrooms in the school year 1992–93, the most recent year reported. . . . When the ARC issued its first report on inclusion in education based on 1989–90 data, 6.7 percent of children with mental retardation were being educated in regular classes. Some critics said the data was too old, and that looking at it a few years

later would document much progress in terms of placing children with mental retardation in inclusive settings. This report, however, reveals that with an improvement of less than one half of one percentage point (.47%), there has been virtually no progress (Abeson, 1995, p. i).

The zeal that the ARC invests in advocating for inclusive classrooms for students with mental retardation is based upon its belief in several basic principles. These principles include:

- Preparation for life in the community best occurs when all students of different backgrounds and abilities learn and socialize together in classrooms and other school settings where all have a chance to achieve and receive instruction designed to develop and enhance successful living within the community.
- Each student with a disability belongs in an age-appropriate classroom with peers who are not disabled.
- Each student has the right to receive individualized education that provides choices, meets the student's needs, and offers the necessary support.
- All students should receive instruction that facilitates an understanding and acceptance of human differences.
- Each student should have the opportunity to follow the same daily schedule as followed by all students in their neighborhood schools.
- Each student should have the opportunity to participate in recreation and extracurricular activities, with appropriate support and supervision by school personnel.
- Each student should be encouraged and supported toward developing meaningful social interaction and friendships with other students (Davis, 1995, p. 2).

The ARC also summarizes the results of a number of studies that document the benefits of inclusion:

- Students with significant disabilities had greater success in achieving IEP goals than did matched students in traditional programs (Ferguson et al., 1992).
- Special needs students educated in general classes do better academically and socially than comparable students in noninclusive settings (Baker, Wang, and Walberg, 1994).
- For students with disabilities, gains occurred in self-esteem (Burello and Wright, 1993), acceptance by classmates (Christmas, 1992; Marwell, 1990), and social skills (McDonnell, McDonnell, Harriman, and McCone, 1991).
- The academic progress of nondisabled students was not slowed down by having students with disabilities in their classrooms (Staub and Peck, 1994).
- Nondisabled students benefited from inclusion as follows: 1) reduced fear of human differences accompanied by increased comfort and awareness, 2) growth in social cognition, 3) improvement in self-concept, 4) development of personal principles, and 5) warm and caring friendships (Staub and Peck, 1994).
- Parents confirmed improved outcomes for their children who did not have disabilities when children with severe disabilities were included in the classroom (Giangreco, Edelman, Cloniger, and Dennis, 1992).

BOX 13.1

Inclusion and Positive Results: Academic Skills

- IEPs for students with disabilities in general classrooms are higher in quality than those for students with disabilities in special classes (Hunt, Farron-Davis, Beckstead, Curtis, and Goetz, 1994).
- Students with disabilities show greater levels of time engaged in learning in general classrooms compared to students with disabilities in special settings (Hunt, Farron-Davis, Beckstead, Curtis, and Goetz, 1994).
- In classrooms that include students with disabilities, the levels of time engaged in learning are increased for students without disabilities and for those with milder disabilities (Hollowood, Salisbury, Rainforth, and Palombaro, 1994).
- Students with disabilities in a general classroom do not cause disruptions to classroom learning time (Hollowood, Salisbury, Rainforth, and Palombaro, 1994).
- Students with disabilities in general classrooms do learn targeted skills (Hunt, Staub, Alwell, and Goetz, 1994; Wolery, Werts, Caldwell, and Snyder, 1994).
- The inclusion of students with disabilities is not associated with a decline in the academic or behavioral performance of students without disabilities on standardized tests or report cards (Sharpe, York, and Knight, 1994).

Source: Office of Special Education Programs. *Seventeenth Annual Report to Congress on the Implementation of the Individuals with Disabilities Act.* Washington, DC: U.S. Department of Education, 1995, p. 20.

- Teachers and administrators perceived integrated students with moderate disabilities to have increased independence and improved functional skills. Social benefits to integrated students with disabilities included acquiring age-appropriate behaviors and tastes, developing friendships, and increased self-esteem. Students without disabilities were perceived to have grown in their self-esteem and in their acceptance of individual differences (Janney, Snell, Beers, and Raynes, 1995). (Davis, 1995, pp. 3–4)

POSTSECONDARY EDUCATION

Students with disabilities are, in general, less likely than other students to enroll in postsecondary education and training programs (Marder, 1992). Those students with disabilities who do become participants in postsecondary programs, however, are likely to have been involved in inclusive classrooms while in public schools. Seventy percent of these students spent more than 75 percent of their high school time in general classrooms. Only 7 percent of the students who spent less than 25 percent of their high school time in general classrooms went on to postsecondary programs (Office of Special Education Programs, 1995).

EMPLOYMENT

Students with disabilities who spend a large percentage of their high school time in general classrooms also fare better in terms of employment after leaving school. Students who spend 75 percent or more of their high school program in inclusive classrooms are more than five times more likely to be employed after leaving school than students who spend 25 percent or less of their high school time in these classrooms. These students also earn salaries that are much lower than those of students with disabilities who have more inclusive high school programs (Office of Special Education Programs, 1995).

INDEPENDENT LIVING

Independent living is one marker of the transition to adulthood for many people. Living alone, with a spouse or roommate, or in college or military housing may be an important step toward psychological and sociological maturity. This step becomes problematic for many young people who simply cannot garner the economic resources necessary for living independently.

Young people with disabilities may have greater difficulty finding the resources necessary for independent living than their peers without disabilities (Marder, 1992). Educational experiences in inclusive classrooms, however, may better prepare these students for independent living. Two-thirds of these students who were found to be living independently after high school had been involved in general classes at least 75 percent of their time during high school. Those students with disabilities who were found not to be living independently had spent 25 percent or less of their high school time in inclusive classrooms (Office of Special Education Programs, 1995).

A number of other studies showing the academic and social benefits of inclusive classrooms have been summarized by the Office of Special Education Programs (1995). These benefits are presented in Boxes 13.1 and 13.2.

Several reasons have been formulated for the positive results of inclusive classrooms for students with disabilities. Inclusive school experiences may benefit students with disabilities because:

- Inclusive environments may be more stimulating, varied, and responsive than segregated environments.
- Inclusive environments may be more likely to provide a developmental curriculum rather than a deficit model curriculum.
- Inclusive environments may provide greater opportunities for students with disabilities to interact with other students who have acquired higher-level motor, social, language, and cognitive skills and to emulate these skills.
- Inclusive environments may provide more opportunities for students with disabilities to learn academic skills from other students. Some academic skills may actually be learned more easily from peers than from teachers (Allen and Schwartz, 1996).

Another contributing factor to the positive results experienced by students with disabilities in inclusive classrooms may be the influence of increased motivation. Students

BOX 13.2

Inclusion and Positive Results: Social Skills

- High school students report that their relationships with students with disabilities resulted in more positive attitudes, increased responses to the needs of others, and increased appreciation for diversity (Helmstetter, Peck, and Giangreco, 1994).
- Students with disabilities in general education settings are alone less often and show more social contact than students in special classes (Hunt, Farron-Davis, Beckstead, Curtis, and Goetz, 1994; Kennedy and Itkonen, 1994; Romer and Haring, 1994).
- Students with disabilities in inclusive settings demonstrated more social gains than those in segregated settings (Cole and Meyer, 1991).
- Students with disabilities in general classroom settings experienced greater social acceptance and more opportunities for interactions not associated with their level of functioning (Evans, Salisbury, Palombaro, Berryman, and Hollowood, 1992).
- Participation in general classrooms by students with disabilities helps establish and maintain social networks for them (Kennedy and Itkonen, 1994).

Source: Office of Special Education Programs. *Seventeenth Annual Report to Congress on the Implementation of the Individuals with Disabilities Act.* Washington, DC: U.S. Department of Education, 1995, p. 20.

may be stimulated to work harder in these environments, particularly if it is an environment that is both challenging and supportive. In the area of behavior, for example, Peterson has observed that an environment that is more challenging to a student with disabilities may "push the child ahead to develop more appropriate behavior repertoires" (Peterson, 1987, p. 359).

INCLUSION: THE BENEFITS FOR ALL STUDENTS

In her essay about her classmate, who has a disability, a fourth grader explained why she liked having Mike in her class. Megan, aged ten, commented:

> Mike has really changed my life. But in a good way! I like Mike a lot. He's a lot of fun to be with. He has ways of talking too, he smiles for yes and drops his head for no. I was scared of Mike before because I've never been around a handicapped person before (Zeph et al., 1992, p. 11).

The benefits of inclusive classrooms for those students who do not have disabilities have already been noted in this chapter and in earlier chapters. This is an important issue, however, that deserves additional emphasis. Odom and McEvoy (1988) report that they found no evidence of negative effects on other students of the integration of children with disabilities into early childhood programs. Sharpe, York, and Knight (1994) also found that there was no negative effect on the performance of students in inclusive environments on academic and behavioral measures.

Perhaps the most compelling evidence for the positive effects of inclusion for students who do not have disabilities, however, is to be found in the comments of those students themselves. Vaughn asked students in her inclusive classroom what they had learned from the students with disabilities who had been integrated into their classroom. She describes their responses:

> Here is what I found out from them. Overall, the regular education students indicated that learning in the same room with the special needs students was "fine," "good," "okay," and "not bad at all." Many expressed that "most of the time they are good workers just like me." Most felt that the special needs students learned differently so "school must be harder for them." One believed, "they don't read like me but I don't read like some other kids in my class either." A sophisticated awareness was revealed by several who wrote, "they're different about how they show what they know." While one child thought "they are different because they are more special than me," another felt "they are not really different because they can do stuff just like me" (Vaughn, 1994, p. 69).

Vaughn provides other quotes from her students that illustrate how they became more insightful as a result of coming to know their peers with disabilities:

- "Sometimes they do better work and act better than me."
- "I think they are smart in their own way like math and art and playing on the playground."
- "They hug me and make me laugh. I enjoy them."
- "Sometimes quiet, sometimes loud. But they are a lot better now. I know because they were in kindergarten and first grade with me."
- "I understand how kids are not alike" (Vaughn, 1994, p. 69).

Vaughn closes her observations about the benefits of inclusion for all students with a quotation from another source. She uses this quotation to emphasize that students are powerful teachers of each other. This understanding is at the core of the values involved in the creation of inclusive classrooms.

> More than 100 years ago, Ralph Waldo Emerson said, "I pay the schoolmaster but 'tis the schoolboys that educate my son." It is still true today, even if the schoolboys (and girls) are a mix of special needs and regular students in the same classroom. In my particular situation, I found that when administrators, teachers, and students totally support one another, students do successfully learn in an integrated setting (Vaughn, 1994, p. 69).

ELIZABETH CREWS/STOCK BOSTON

Inclusion: Benefits for Educators

RESEARCH HAS INDICATED FOR A number of years that many teachers have negative attitudes toward the concept of inclusion. Classroom teachers, particularly those with little training or experience in working with students with disabilities, are often resistant to the idea of having students with special needs in their classes. Some educators, in fact, question whether students with serious disabilities can actually benefit from schooling (Alexander and Strain, 1978).

In recent years, a number of professional educational organizations that represent the interests of students and teachers have expressed concerns about the movement toward greater inclusion. These concerns range from: 1) support for the concept of inclusion but fear that the continuum of special services may be jeopardized, to 2) concern that the needs of students with disabilities may not be adequately met in general classrooms, to 3) concerns about the additional burdens that inclusion may impose on teachers in general classrooms (Vaughn et al., 1994).

The intensity of the feelings about inclusion that some teachers have can be illustrated by a comment that one teacher made about the reaction of some of her colleagues: "If you try to cram it down their throat, most of our faculty would just say 'No way, not on your life! I would rather pump gas'" (Vaughn, 1994, p. 13).

When teachers are given the support and encouragement they need to make their classrooms more inclusive, however, they report a number of benefits from this change (Rainforth, 1992). Among these benefits are:

- *Teaching and Learning About Disabilities*: Teachers report learning a great deal about disabilities because they have students with these disabilities in their classrooms. They also report that they learn a great deal about treating people with disabilities with respect and openness by watching the way their students interact. They remark that the children start teaching adults in inclusive settings. An example:

> Second-grade teacher: "The children seem so natural, especially by the time they're in second grade. They have developed relationships from kindergarten and first grade. And I think that the first year that the teacher has children with these kinds of needs in the room, that adult is coming with a certain amount of baggage, so to speak, and I think it's wonderful to watch the children, because it's so natural for them. . . . If you just kind of stand back and let it flow, you start getting rid of some of that baggage" (Rainforth, 1992, p. 10).

- *Curriculum and Materials*: Teachers in inclusive classrooms report that they tend to move from an emphasis on paper and pencil tasks to the use of more manipulatives and more creative methods. Many report that because they had students with disabilities in their classrooms, they made changes in their curriculum that benefited all of their students.
- *Success for All*: Teachers report that having students with disabilities in their classrooms strengthened and deepened their commitment to helping every child succeed. This benefited many children who were not classified as having special needs but who regularly experienced failure.
- *Collaborative Problem Solving*: Teachers in inclusive classrooms reported using more collaboration between students and teachers, and between students and students in solving problems. They expressed enthusiasm for having students devise strategies for a more inclusive environment, both because the students devised quality solutions to problems and because of the learning that occurred in the process.
- *Expectation of Inclusion*: Teachers and students in inclusive classrooms came to expect that all children with disabilities would be participants in general classroom activities. The factors that seemed to promote this expectation were a growing sense of the class as a family, the availability of supports to make inclusion successful, and greater confidence in the ability to implement an inclusive environment.
- *Teams*: Teachers in inclusive classrooms report greater utilization of a team approach. Teams often included the teacher; a support (special education) teacher; and speech, occupational, and physical therapists. Teachers report that the benefits of the team approach extended to all children in their classrooms, not just those students with disabilities.
- *Student Assessment and IEPs*: Teachers in inclusive classrooms reported that they were active participants in the assessment procedures and the development of IEPs for students with disabilities in their classrooms. They report that this involvement facilitates their understanding of those students and how to better help them reach their goals. They feel that this promotes a greater feeling of "ownership" for their students with special needs.
- *Flexibility*: Teachers in inclusive classrooms report that they become more flexible in their teaching. They feel that having students with disabilities in their

classrooms gave them "permission" to be more flexible in teaching style, in classroom structure and design, and in creating activities that promote success for all children.

- *Let It Go*: Teachers in inclusive classroom environments report that this experience leads them to consider carefully the relative importance of expectations they have of students and the demands they make on them. They also report that they are more likely to stand back and let students work out things for themselves. "Letting go" is illustrated by the following teacher comment:

  > Over the last five years, since we've had children with special needs in the building, one thing that we've absolutely learned is that kids are kids are kids. And where some of these behaviors are a lot more exaggerated than they are in typical kids, *nobody* likes to come in off the playground. . . . And with Jeff, and John, and Randy, and with hearing impaired children, and emotionally disturbed children, I really wanted to see growth at the same rate. I wanted these disruptive behaviors to stop immediately and they don't. But then I had a couple other kids who are really as much or more of a problem last year who aren't classified. They were typical kids who weren't typical. And so I think one advantage we've had in the last five years is that we've begun to look at children as individuals. And when something is more exaggerated with a classified child, it has to be dealt with, and then sometimes when we have children who aren't classified who have some of these exaggerated behaviors, we have to problem solve that individually also (Rainforth, 1992, p. 10).

- *Stress*: Teachers in inclusive classrooms report that they experienced increased stress when they first embarked on the experience of serving children with disabilities in their classrooms. This stress subsided, however, as they became more confident and comfortable with this classroom change. Speaking of stress, one teacher said, "But I think in time, that really eases up. I don't really think it's a big deal anymore. Plus, if you have a really good support system, you get the help you need" (Rainforth, 1992, p. 44).

- *Accountability*: Teachers in inclusive classrooms report a growing commitment to the ethics of continued growth and continuous accountability in their teaching. The influence of having students with disabilities in their classes seems to have stimulated an increase in reflective practice that brought benefits to all of their students and colleagues (Rainforth, 1992).

Warger and Pugach have referred to the benefits of inclusion for teachers as a "shift in thinking" (Warger and Pugach, 1996, p. 65). This kind of shift in the thinking of teachers who work with students with special needs may lead to an increased recognition that unique learning needs are the norm rather than the exception. This may also lead to a different perspective on the relationship between students, teachers, and curricula. In this sense, inclusive classrooms hold great promise for helping to create more positive and compassionate environments for teaching and learning.

Inclusion: Benefits for All

An excellent example of how the creation of inclusive schools and classrooms can benefit all members of school communities is the school reform program that has been created in Vermont. The State of Vermont is a leader in the movement to include students with disabilities in general classrooms. The Vermont Act 230 was passed in 1990. It established a requirement that all school districts in the state must devise a system for promoting the success of students with disabilities in general education classrooms. It further required that the system must be created through collaboration efforts with parents (Vermont Department of Education, 1993).

In order to facilitate implementation of the mandated inclusion effort, 1 percent of the state's special education budget was committed to training educators for inclusive classrooms. An emphasis was placed on creating collaborative teams of educators for each school. These teams were to have as their goals the diminishment of referrals of students for segregated special education services and the increase of support for teachers of students with special needs in general classrooms.

The results of Vermont's effort to create more inclusive school environments are impressive. They include:

- The number of students in Vermont schools referred and identified as eligible for special education services decreased by 18.4 percent between 1990 and 1995.
- The increase in the number of students with special needs in general classrooms did not diminish overall student performance.
- Every school in Vermont has an Instructional Support Team. These teams have been found to be effective in helping teachers find ways of teaching students with special needs in their classrooms and decreasing the likelihood that they will refer students for segregated special education services.
- Many Vermont schools have chosen to merge special education and general education. This allows students who are not eligible for special education to benefit from these services. As a result, 22,000 students who are not eligible for special education but are at risk for school failure have been given access to special education services in their classrooms.
- All of Vermont's schools continue to use state funds to train educators in collaboration techniques, in the use of educational technology, in classroom management, in crisis prevention, and in other techniques for successful classroom inte-

Lydia Gans/Impact Visuals

gration (Vermont Department of Education, 1993, 1994, 1995).

Thomas Lovitt has argued that there are two disparate forces in education. These he describes as the forces of the outsiders and those of the insiders (Lovitt, 1993). In fact, it is only the insiders of education who have had the force of power and influence with them. The outsiders of education have traditionally lacked power and influence. They have lived on the margins not only in schools but in all of society's institutions.

In its best and most important sense, inclusion is an effort to eliminate insider and outsider thinking in schools and classrooms. It is a movement that aims for the goal of helping the outsiders become insiders.

When all students become insiders, society benefits. Children growing up with inclusive attitudes toward all people are more likely to be positive and contributing members of their communities. Workplaces that are characterized by greater cooperation among people are likely to be more productive.

Inclusive classrooms are a goal toward which teachers, students, parents, and communities must strive with even greater commitment. In a future filled with human challenges, no child can be left outside the care and nurturance that these classrooms can provide.

Case Studies and Questions to Consider

PUPIL: TAMMY CAPER
SCHOOL: HAVEN ELEMENTARY
CURRENT PLACEMENT: GENERAL FIRST
AGE: 6 YEARS, 10 MONTHS

Family Structure and Home Environment

Tammy is described by her teacher as having trouble with spatial concepts (for example, matching objects according to size or shape.) She repeated kindergarten last year and was reported as still not making adequate progress while repeating. She continues to experience difficulty with number and letter recognition.

Tammy lives with her mother, Ms. Evette Caper. Ms. Caper is a thirty-nine-year-old single parent. She works at Light and Bright Cleaners as a folder. Ms. Caper completed the eighth grade.Tammy also lives with her older sister, Sandy, who is eighteen. Sandy has a daughter, Lynn, who is four years old and who also lives with the family. Ms. Caper has three older children who live away from home.

The Caper family lives in a small rented house. Their home is very modest but is obviously cared for and well maintained.

Parental Perception of the Student's School Problem

When asked whether Tammy has a school problem, Ms. Caper responds, "I don't know. It's hard to say." She has difficulty with the idea that there is a problem with Tammy's ability to learn. She thinks her daughter is "just as smart" as other children her age. Ms. Caper also believes that Tammy likes school and works hard at it. She says that her daughter loves to read and count. Ms. Caper is at a loss for explaining her daughter's school problems. She wants Tammy to have special help if she needs it, but she is concerned that people will think there is something "wrong" with her child.

Ms. Caper also feels that Tammy's social and emotional development is typical for a girl her age. She says she has had no problems with her.

Ms. Caper's primary goal for Tammy is that she grow up to be a woman who can work and take care of herself. There is no major facet of Tammy's personality or behavior that she would want to change. She is pleased that her daughter is a happy child. She is troubled, however, over her daughter's lack of progress in school.

Additional Considerations

Ms. Caper is open to suggestions on ways her daughter's school performance might be improved. Her major concerns for Tammy at this time, however, focus on some very basic needs. Ms. Caper says that since she has been working, and not receiving public assistance, she has been unable to provide dental care for Tammy. She is also afraid of what would happen in a medical emergency. She hopes to hear from social services soon, so that she will receive some help with these matters.

Questions

1. Should Tammy be evaluated for special education services? Why or why not?
2. What advice would you give Tammy's mother about home tutoring?
3. Are there other ways that your school could help Tammy and the rest of the Caper family?

PUPIL: BILLY MACK

SCHOOL: HOPEFUL HIGH SCHOOL

CURRENT PLACEMENT: SPECIAL EDUCATION

AGE: 17 YEARS, 10 MONTHS

Family Structure and Home Environment

Billy lives at the Helping Harbor, a facility that provides foster care to children and adolescents from broken or troubled homes. Mr. Goodman, the director, explains that Billy came to the Helping Harbor five years ago through the auspices of Castle County Social Services. Billy and his three older sisters were removed from their parents' home due to the inability of their mother and father to care for them adequately.

Billy returns to Castle County frequently on weekends. Mr. Goodman reports that Billy visits with his maternal grandmother on these trips and sometimes sees his mother while there.

Although Billy still carries the emotional scars of his unstable family life, Mr. Goodman says he has done remarkably well in establishing a new life and a positive personal identity. He describes Billy as a "likable boy who is easy to be around."

Parental Perception of the School Problem

Mr. Goodman feels that Billy has responded well to the special education curriculum he has been provided at school. Billy has been in a full-time class for students diagnosed as having mild mental retardation. Mr. Goodman thinks that this placement was very appropriate and that Billy has benefited significantly from the instruction he has been given. Mr. Goodman feels at this point, however, that consideration should be given to moving Billy more into the mainstream of the school next year. He will be classified as a junior at that time. He feels confident that Billy is socially capable of such a move. He is less certain of Billy's academic ability to function outside a special class, but he feels consideration should be given to this possibility.

Additional Comments

Mr. Goodman feels that, in general, Billy's personal and social skills fall within normal limits for a young man of his age. He reports that Billy's interests approximate those of other teenage boys. He recently passed the required tests and was issued a driver's license. Billy talks constantly, and probably dreams, about cars.

Mr. Goodman feels that Billy has all the potential for becoming an independent, productive, and happy adult. He thinks that Billy is optimistic, that he likes other people, and others like being around him.

Questions

1. What suggestions would you make about moving Billy more into the mainstream of school next year?
2. What suggestions would you make for a transition plan for Billy from school to the adult world?
3. How could you encourage peers in the mainstream to interact with Billy and become friends with him?

References

Abeson, A. *Prologue Commentary on the ARC's 1995 Report Card on Inclusion in Education.* Arlington, TX: ARC, 1995.

Alexander, C., and P. S. Strain. "A Review of Educators' Attitudes Towards Handicapped Children and the Concept of Mainstreaming." *Psychology in the Schools, 15,* 1978: 390–396.

Allen, K. E., and J. S. Schwartz. *The Exceptional Child: Inclusion in Early Childhood Education.* Albany, NY: Delmar, 1996.

Baker, E. T., M. C. Wang, and H. J. Walberg. "The Effects of Inclusion on Teaming." *Educational Leadership, 52*(4), 1994: 33–35.

Burello, L. C., and P. T. Wright, Eds. "Strategies for Inclusion of Behaviorally Challenged Students." *Principal Letters,* Winter 1993: 10.

Christmas, O. L. *The 1992 Michigan Non-Mandated Aide Pilot Project.* Lansing, MI: Michigan State Department of Education, 1992.

Cole, F. A., and L. H. Meyer. "Social Integration and Severe Disabilities: A Longitudinal Analysis of Child Outcomes." *Journal of Special Education, 25*(3), 1991: 340–351.

Davis, S. *1995 Report Card on Inclusion in Education of Students with Mental Retardation.* Arlington, TX: ARC, 1995.

Evans, I. M., C. L. Salisbury, M. M. Palombaro, J. Berryman, and T. M. Hollowood. "Peer Interactions and Social Acceptance of Elementary Age Children with Severe Disabilities in an Inclusive School." *Journal of the Association for Persons with Severe Handicaps, 17*(4), 1992: 305–312.

Ferguson, D. L., G. Meyer, L. Jeanchild, L. Juniper, and J. Zingo. "Figuring Out What to Do with the Grownups: How Teachers Make Inclusion 'Work' for Students with Disabilities." *Journal of the Association for Persons with Severe Handicaps, 17*(4), 1992: 218–226.

Giangreco, M. F., S. Edelman, C. Cloniger, and R. Dennis. "My Child Has a Classmate with Severe Disabilities: What Parents of Nondisabled Children Think About Full Inclusion." *Developmental Disabilities Bulletin, 20*(2), 1992: 1–12.

Helmstetter, E., C. A. Peck, and M. F. Giangreco. "Outcomes of Interactions with Peers with Moderate or Severe Disabilities: A Statewide Survey of High School Students." *Journal of the Association for Persons with Severe Handicaps, 19*(4), 1994: 263–276.

Hollowood, T. M., C. L. Salisbury, B. Rainforth, and M. M. Palombaro. "Use of Instructional Time in Classrooms Serving Students with and Without Severe Disabilities." *Exceptional Children, 61*(3), 1994: 242–253.

Hunt, P., F. Farron-Davis, S. Beckstead, D. Curtis, and L. Goetz. "Evaluating the Effects of Placement of Students with Severe Disabilities in General Education Versus Special Class." *Journal of the Association for Persons with Severe Handicaps, 19*(3), 1994: 200–214.

Hunt, P., D. Staub, M. Alwell, and L. Goetz. "Achievement by All Students Within the Context of Cooperative Learning Groups." *Journal of the Association for Persons with Severe Handicaps, 19*(4), 1994: 290–301.

Janney, R. E., M. E. Snell, M. K. Beers, and M. Raynes. "Integrating Students with Moderate and Severe Disabilities into General Education Classes." *Exceptional Children, 61*(5), 1995: 425–439.

Kennedy, C. H., and T. Itkonen. "Some Effects of Regular Class Participation on the Social Contacts and Social Networks of High School Students with Severe Disabilities." *Journal of the Association for Persons with Severe Handicaps, 19*(1), 1994: 1–10.

Lovitt, L. C. "Retrospect and Prospect." In J. Goodlad and J. Lovitt, Eds., *Integrating General and Special Education.* New York: Macmillan, 1993: 253–274.

Marder, C. *How Well Are Youth with Disabilities Really Doing? A Comparison of Youth with Disabilities and Youth in General. A Report from the National Longitudinal Transition Study of Special Education Students.* Menlo Park, CA: SRI International, 1992.

Marwell, B. E. *Integration of Students with Mental Retardation.* Madison, WI: Madison Public Schools, 1990.

McDonnell, A., J. McDonnell, M. Harriman, and G. McCone. "Educating Students with Severe Disabilities in Their Neighborhood School: The Utah Elementary Model." *Remedial and Special Education, 12*(6), 1991: 34–45.

Odom, S. L., and M. A. McEvoy. "Integration of Young Children with Handicaps and Normally Developing Children." In I. S. L. Odom and M. B. Karnes, Eds., *Early Intervention for Infants and Children with Handicaps.* Baltimore, MD: Brookes, 1988: 131–153.

Office of Special Education Programs. *Seventeenth Annual Report to Congress on the Implementation of the Individuals with Disabilities Act.* Washington, DC: U.S. Department of Education, 1995.

Peterson, N. L. *Early Intervention for Handicapped and At Risk Children.* Denver, CO: Love, 1987.

Rainforth, B. *The Effects of Full Inclusion on Regular Education Teachers: Final Report.* San Francisco, CA: California Research Institute, San Francisco State University, 1992.

Romer, L. T., and N. C. Haring. "The Social Participation of Students with Deaf Blindness in Educational Settings." *Education and Training in Mental Retardation and Developmental Disabilities, 29*(2), 1994: 134–144.

Sharpe, M. N., J. L. York, and J. Knight. "Effects of Inclusion on the Academic Performance of Classmates Without Disabilities." *Remedial and Special Education, 15*(5), 1994: 281–287.

Staub, D., and C. A. Peck. "What Are the Outcomes for Nondisabled Students?" *Educational Leadership, 52*(4), 1994: 36–40.

Vaughn, S., et al. "Teachers' Views of Inclusion: 'I'd Rather Pump Gas.'" Paper presented at the Annual Meeting of the American Educational Research Association, New Orleans, LA, April 4–8, 1994. ERIC ED 370 928.

Vaughn, T. "Inclusion Can Succeed." *Equity and Excellence in Education, 27*(1), 1994: 68–69.

Vermont Department of Education. *Vermont's Act 230 Three Years Later: A Report on the Impact of Act 230.* Montpelier, VT: Vermont Department of Education, 1993.

———. *Act 230 Evaluation: 1993–1994 Preliminary Results.* Montpelier, VT: Vermont Department of Education, 1994.

———. *Vermont's Act 230 and Special Education Funding and Cost Study.* Montpelier, VT: Vermont Department of Education, 1995.

Wagner, M., Ed. *The Secondary School Programs of Students with Disabilities: A Report from the National Longitudinal Transition Study of Special Education Students.* Menlo Park, CA: SRI International, 1993.

Warger, C. L., and M. C. Pugach. "Forming Partnerships Around Curriculum." *Educational Leadership, 53*(5), 1996: 62–65.

Wolery, M., M. G. Werts, N. K. Caldwell, and E. D. Snyder. "Efficacy of Constant Time Delay Implemented by Peer Tutors in General Education Classrooms." *Journal of Behavioral Education, 4*(4), 1994: 415–436.

Zeph, L., D. Gilmer, D. Brewer-Allen, and J. Moulton. "Kids Talk About Inclusive Classrooms." *Creating Inclusive Educational Communities, 3,* Washington, DC: U.S. Department of Education, 1992.

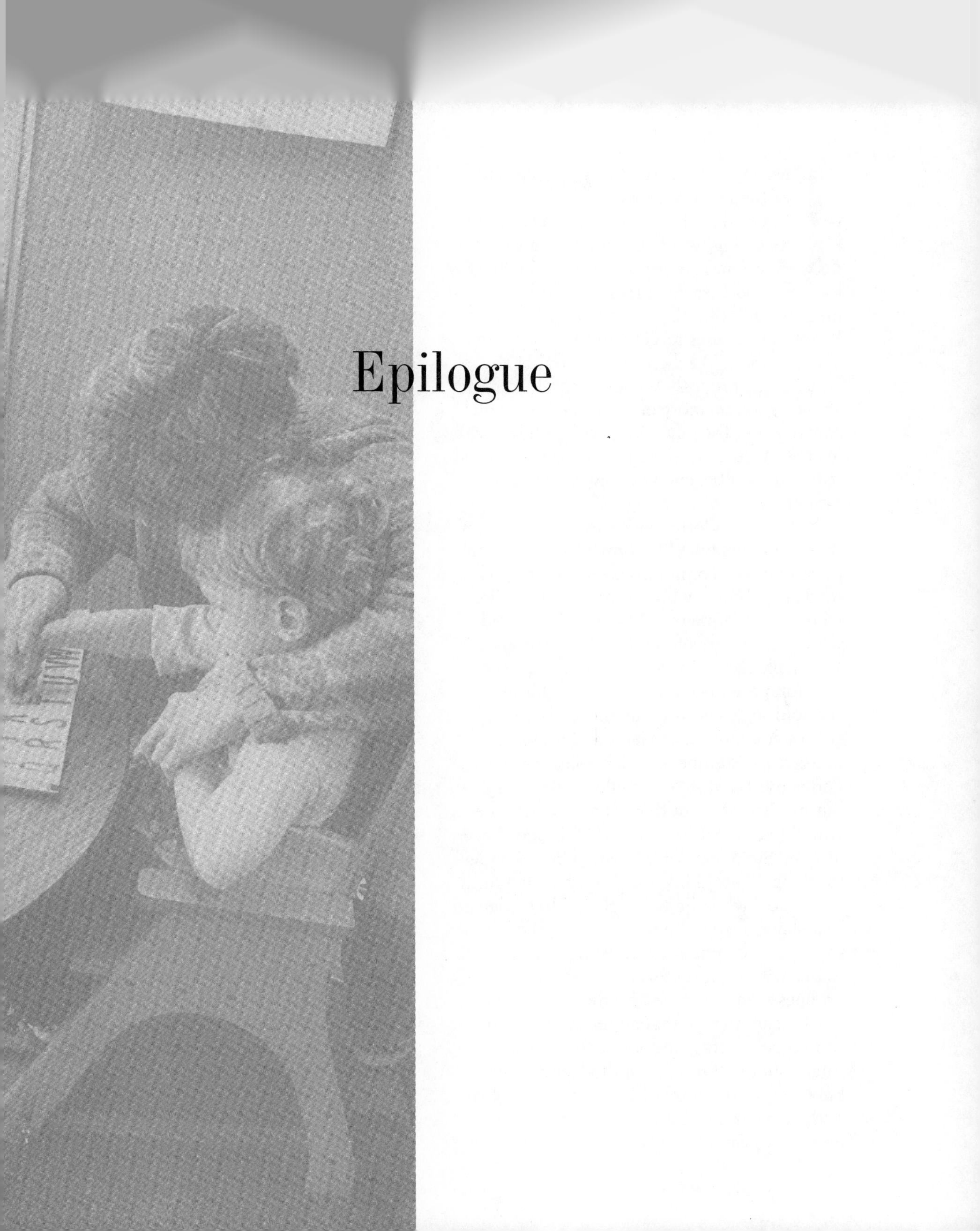

Epilogue

I BELIEVE THAT A LOVING TEACHER IS ONE of the most powerful and positive forces that there can be in any society. Teaching, at its best, is a journey of the heart, and an opportunity to touch lives forever. Good teaching is an unselfish investment in the potential and dignity of students. People sometimes forget a most basic truth about schools: Teachers are the soul of the educational process. Ask anyone, ask yourself, about a good memory of a teacher. Soon your conversation (or reflection) will be filled with images of a teacher who loved teaching, loved students, and believed deeply in the profession of teaching.

I have wonderful and warm memories of those teachers who lifted my vision from the poverty of the commonplace to the beauty of ideas, teachers who set my curiosity afire, who launched me on a life of learning, and who touched my life with both nurturance and challenges. I am reminded of a remark that John Steinbeck once made to his eleven-year-old son, who was lamenting having to go to school for what seemed like so many more years. Steinbeck told his son that he understood that school could be drudgery, but he also told him that if he was lucky he would find a real "teacher." If he found that teacher, Steinbeck said, it would be a wonderful thing. He told his son about having found a "teacher" when he was a child. He explained that she so inspired her students and created so much excitement for learning that they ran to her with their discoveries as if these new findings were "captured fireflies."

I make no case that all teachers are, or should be, saints going about their work in total nobility of intent, method, and result. I know about the teacher whose heart is filled with anger and selfishness, the one who can no longer give. I know about the teacher who cannot find the energy to lead and inspire. I know about the teacher who is putting in time rather than devotion. I know about the teacher whose carelessness amounts to educational malpractice. But rightly done, the way so many educators do it, teaching is precious work. Indeed, it can be the work of liberation.

I noticed recently that the Scholastic Network, an on-line computer service, had conducted a poll of students and teachers about the women they most admired. Ranked among the top ten was Helen Keller. I was delighted with this result. As you know from the preceding chapters of this book, Helen Keller has long been one of my heroes. The story of the way that she became a voice for others in spite of the darkness and silence imposed upon her by her disabilities is truly inspiring.

Another of my heroes, one who is also discussed in this book, was not listed in the Scholastic poll results. She has, in fact, often been overshadowed by the public memory of Helen Keller. That hero is, of course, Annie Sullivan, Helen Keller's teacher. Most people know the story of the breakthrough that came for Helen when she finally understood that letters spelled into her hand represented the water that she felt. We sometimes forget, however, the long days of labor that Annie Sullivan put into making that moment possible. A few years ago I found a letter, written by Helen Keller, in the Manuscripts Division of the Library of Congress. In the letter, dated 1918, Helen describes the moment when she understood what her teacher had been trying to convey to her—that the finger spelling and signing in her hand had meaning. In looking back on that revelation and the dedication of her teacher, she said that she felt that at that moment Annie Sullivan "thought me into being."

Educators are often challenged to "think their students into being." We are called upon to be advocates for students and families that sometimes have no other advocates. We are challenged to find hope in students whom others have deemed as having no hopeful future. When I think of these challenges, I recall Helen's words about the woman whose name she asked to be spelled into her hand soon after the epiphany of the word *water.* Responding to Helen's query about what she was called, Annie identified herself to her student simply as "Teacher." That is the name that Helen would forever use for the woman who "thought her into being."

The play and movie entitled *The Miracle Worker* derives its title from the miraculous accomplishments of Helen that were founded on Annie's teaching. The true miracle, however, was not the extraordinary progress that Helen made once she had a basis for communicating. Nor was the miracle the worldwide fame she achieved as a person who was both blind and deaf. The true miracle occurred when young Annie Sullivan, herself having a visual impairment, got on a train in Boston and embarked on a journey to Tuscumbia, Alabama, to work with a little girl who could not see, hear, or speak and who was described as unmanageable. The true miracle was her willingness to try to make some difference, however small, in the life of a girl whom others viewed as hopeless.

In the rush and complexity of our work, we can easily forget the values that originally motivated us to become educators. Occasionally, however, it is important that we pause and recall that we started on this journey believing in the worth of and the possibilities in the lives of the students we teach. We need to recognize that our belief in the promise and potential of all people continues to be what is truly miraculous about our profession.

Name Index

Subject Index

- N. Fulton Elem. – Alpharetta Elementary
- Holcomb Bridge Middle